W9-BCM-516

Public Policy in Action

cy in Action

THE POLICY PROCESS

Victor Bekkers

Menno Fenger

Peter Scholten

Erasmus University Rotterdam, the Netherlands

Edward Elgar
PUBLISHING

Cheltenham, UK • Northampton, MA, USA

© Victor Bekkers, Menno Fenger and Peter Scholten 2017

All rights reserved. No part of this publication may be reproduced, stored in a retrieval system or tra
in any form or by any means, electronic, mechanical or photocopying, recording, or otherwise withou
prior permission of the publisher.

Published by
Edward Elgar Publishing Limited
The Lypiatts
15 Lansdown Road
Cheltenham
Glos GL50 2JA
UK

Edward Elgar Publishing, Inc.
William Pratt House
9 Dewey Court
Northampton
Massachusetts 01060
USA

A catalogue record for this book
is available from the British Library

Library of Congress Control Number: 2017936569

Printed on 30% PCR Stock
ISBN 978 1 78100 452 4 (cased)
ISBN 978 1 78100 460 9 (paperback)
ISBN 978 1 78100 453 1 (eBook)
Printed and bound by Thomson-Shore, Inc.

Typeset by Servis Filmsetting Ltd, Stockport, Cheshire.

Contents in brief

Full contents

Figures

Tables

Boxes

1

Politics and policies in a changing world

💡 **LEARNING OBJECTIVES**

After reading this chapter you should be able to:

- Define what is meant by *politics*, *policies* and by *governance*.

- Define and recognize the different phases of the policy process, the so-called "*policy cycle*".

- Understand how societal transformations (such as the network society, liquid society, the risk society and the empty state) impact the policy process.

1.1   Introduction

Water is one of the most vital resources in a society. We need water to keep us alive. We also need water to support the production of goods and services, in agriculture as well as in industry. Moreover, sanitation services depend on the availability of clean and thus safe water. The absence of clean water and the absence of sanitation facilities has enormous consequences for human health, for safety, for the environment and for our socio-economic development. This especially applies for cities where thousands of people live together, while at the same time the number of people who actually live and work in cities is still increasing. This implies that water management and urban management are closely related issues. However, there is also another face to be shown. The abundance as well as the lack of water also represents a rather dark side, if we look at the pain that water-related disasters like floods and droughts bring. A striking example that was breaking news was the tsunami that led to the meltdown of a nuclear plant facility at the Japanese city of Fukushima in 2011. Six years before (2005) a hurricane – called Katrina – devastated large parts of the city of New Orleans,

USA. Eighty percent of the city was flooded, 1863 people were killed and the damage was about 81 billion dollars. In both cases not only thousands of casualties were counted, but also the complete social and economic infrastructure of these areas was destroyed. This implies that in many countries water protection is an issue which is high on the political agenda, especially in countries, in cities and regions that are below sea level. At the same time many of these countries, regions and cities are especially vulnerable because the water levels in rivers, seas and oceans are increasing as a result of global warming and climate change. It may even cause some islands to disappear under the sea. Climate change also means that some countries are confronted with droughts, which puts the availability of safe water under pressure, not only in, for instance, Africa but also in Australia.

As we can see from this example of the management of water supply, water protection as well as all kinds of water-related sanitation services raises all kinds of interesting questions. For instance, what is the price that people want to pay for water protection, if the chance that a flooding takes place will statistically only happen once in a hundred years? If a city wants to grow and it needs space to build new houses for an increasing population and wants to plan industrial areas for their economic developments, does this also imply that these houses and industrial plants can be built in the forelands of rivers and seas? And, what about a city council that has to choose between the necessity to replace a more than one hundred-year-old sewerage system that is leaking and that is not able to deal with the increasing amount of water that falls from the sky on the one hand, and the necessity to deal with increasing feelings of unsafety among the inhabitants of rather deprived neighborhoods. How does the council choose between a new sewerage system which is put under the ground and the call for more police officers that are visible in the streets? What choice will this city council make? Water management issues not only raise a series of interesting choices to be made and dilemmas to be solved. Water management issues also stimulate large numbers of people, groups and organizations that have different viewpoints to raise their voice. It mobilizes many stakeholders: not only local and regional governments but in many cases also national or even international governments, while at the same time it touches upon the interest of companies and citizens. For instance the sand fill by hydraulicking of the sea beaches or the embankment of dikes requires a national and integrated approach as well as heavy investments. In other cases even water boards, which have a specific responsibility for the supply of water or the protection against water, have to be included in the decision-making process. In some countries water services have been liberalized and the water supply and water sanitation services are carried out by private firms.

These examples show in a nutshell the essence of politics and policy making. Politics and policy making are closely related to the ways in which societies deal with challenges and problems which these societies as a political community are wrestling; challenges that not only involve different interests but also mobilize a large number of different people, groups of people or even organizations that try to influence the definition of these challenges as well as how to deal with these challenges (Stone, 2001). This question also raises another, closely related question: how should governments intervene and what are the capacities and capabilities in order to intervene effectively? This intervention question can be seen as a governance challenge (Scharpf, 1997a; Rhodes, 1997). In the next section (1.2) we will describe politics, policies and governance as three closely related concepts. Societal challenges are often the offspring for the development and implementation of all kinds of policy programs. However, these programs differ in nature (1.3). Hence, we will present a typology of public policies in order to get a better understanding of the nature, and thus complexity, of these programs. At the same time, it is important to notice that the development of these programs does not take place in a vacuum. Policy making takes place in a changing world, which does not generate new problems to be addressed, like the rising of the sea level due to global warming. In this changing world also the role of politics is being challenged. In section 1.4 we will introduce a number of concepts that help us to understand, on a more fundamental level, the changing context in which politics takes place and policies are formulated. In section 1.5 the outlook of this book will be sketched.

1.2   Politics, policies and governance

What is politics? And, how can the political realm of a society be related to the world of policies and policy making? When dealing with these issues, we will also introduce another concept, namely governance. As such politics, policies and governance can be viewed as the three sides of a triangle which are closely related to each other, because they tell us something about how societies deal with challenges that address the functioning or well-being of the society (Stone, 2001).

Politics

Politics has always been an inseparable element in the history of mankind, in the way in which we organize our lives. It refers to the way in which a community of people tries to deal with a number of questions and challenges with which the community is wrestling (Stone, 2001:18). Very often it is necessary that specific actions are taken. When confronted with the rising water level in our seas and rivers, it is important that the inhabitants of a society are protected. When a sewerage system is leaking because it is too old, it is important that a society takes measures so that the leaking sewerage water does not contribute to the emergence of all kinds of diseases which affect public health. However, the planning of these actions implies that decisions have to be made. Given these challenges all kinds of values and interests have to be balanced against each other. For instance, when discussing the issue of whether houses or plants can be built in the forelands of seas and rivers, the value of economic growth has to be balanced against the value of safety. When discussing the issue, if money has to be spent on the replacement of the sewerage system or on the enlargement of the police force, safety in two different domains has to be balanced against each other. This balancing act requires a system that makes it possible to organize collective decision-making. In many cases this decision-making system deals with challenges that can be called *"wicked problems"* (Rittel and Webber, 1973), also described as "intractable policy controversies" (Schön and Rein, 1994). Typical for this type of problem is that there is no consensus among the involved parties as to what relevant causes and effects of the societal problem are to be handled. They also dispute the relevance of the measures to be taken. Moreover, there is no consensus about the values and norms that should be taken into consideration in order to judge what measures are effective or appropriate. An example is the discussion about the causes and effects of global warming and the measures that have to be taken in order to deal with this.

In western societies this collective decision-making process is embedded in constitutional democracy. *Constitutional democracy* refers to specific institutions, rules, procedures and routines that have been developed to facilitate the process of collective decision-making. They structure the process of decision-making. These institutions, rules, procedures and routines have been given additional weight because they are based on the Rule of Law. Rights and obligations as well as tasks, competences and responsibilities have been allocated among different actors. They have a legal basis. For instance, citizens have been given the right to vote, while parliament has been given the right to decide by majority. Hence, we see that in most western countries the system of representative democracy as well as the Rule of Law generate a set of rules to be followed, which not only adds to the democratic and legal nature of the decisions that are made and implemented but also adds to their legitimacy (Morris, 1998; Beetham, 1991).

It is not only formal rules which specify the conditions under which this process of collective decision-making takes place; more informal rules, which refer to the grown decision-making practices in a country, can specify how this process should take place (March and Olsen, 1989a). Collective decision-making processes take place in a specific political culture which also influences the content and course of this process. For instance, in the Netherlands collective decision-making is rooted in a culture in which consensus, compromise and collaboration is embraced. This practice has emerged from the Dutch fight against the water: in order to survive, in order to acquire land for farming and housing, it was necessary that people collaborate with each other in order to establish a number of vital collective provisions, like dikes. Hence, a decision-making practice emerged that is also known as the "Dutch Polder Model".

Democracy offers the possibility to organize a collective decision-making process in such a way that is considered by the members of the political community as being legitimate, without causing substantial disorder. According to Bernard Crick (1992:33) politics should be considered as "a way of ruling divided societies without undue violence – and most societies are divided, though some think that is the very trouble." If this collective decision-making process follows specific formal and informal rules, the decisions made are being considered as binding for society as a whole; they are considered as being legitimate (Luhmann, 1969). They have authority (Easton, 1965:278). That is why Easton (1965:107) defines "politics as the binding allocation of values for society as a whole." Or to put it more bluntly, we could also refer to Lasswell (1958) who defines politics as: who gets what how and when?

Answering this question becomes even more difficult if we add another complication. Who gets, what how and when implies that not every wish can be satisfied. Scarcity is the context in which this question has to be answered: the amount of means (especially money) to fulfill all demands and wishes is too limited (Easton, 1965). Should a city council spend the limited amount of money that they have at their disposal on the replacement of the sewerage system or on putting more police officers on the street? Should the whole coastline of a country be reinforced in order to deal with the increasing level of seawater, or should only the most vulnerable spots be addressed? This implies that priorities have to be formulated, which also complicates the collective decision-making process. Priorities and values have to be balanced in order to establish an order of importance. The tragedy is, however, that this balance is not an optimal one; it is an appropriate balance which fits the specific political, social, and economic circumstances of that moment. In doing so a satisfying solution is achieved (Simon, 1961). Hence, a political decision can be seen as a codification of the balance between specific values that can be considered to be, as much as possible, an appropriate way of dealing with a specific societal challenge (March and Olsen, 1989b:160).

As a result of the complicated balancing act, politics also refers to struggle, to competition, to persuasion. It also starts up processes of bargaining, negotiation and compromise in which the involved stakeholders try to push forward their interests and views. Cities and regions that are repeatedly confronted with flooding will try to get political attention so that, for instance, the national parliament will address the issue and that funds will be made available to address the weakest spots. They will try to organize themselves so that they talk with one voice, they will try to persuade members of parliament but also influential civil servants that something should be done. In doing so, they develop and implement different types of strategies, thereby mobilizing resources in order to build up and exercise power in such a way that it serves their interests and needs (Lindblom, 1977).

Coordination arrangements

We have defined politics as *the way in which societies deal with the balancing and allocation of values that is necessary to deal with challenges that a society as a political community is confronted with*. However, it is not the state that has the monopoly on the allocation of these values. A society can also opt to handle these specific challenges by making use of other institutions. For instance, in many countries the provision and distribution of clean drinking water is seen as a task of local or regional government, due to the fact that clean drinking water is guarded as a necessary condition to improve public health. However, in other countries the provision and distribution of clean drinking water is taken up by private companies that compete with each other. They compete with each other to get a license from government to provide and distribute drinking water in a specific area. However, households may also have the opportunity to choose their own drinking water provider, although these providers may share the same distribution network. In these cases a market is created in order to deal with the challenge of how to give the people of a city access to clean drinking water. In other cases, it is the community itself, without interference from the state or from private companies, that organizes the production and distribution of clean drinking water. For instance, in rural Africa the inhabitants of a village beat their own well in order to have access to drinking water.

In general, a distinction is made between three allocation arrangements: the state, the market and the community (Lindblom, 1977). These arrangements differ in the way they offer a society the possibilities to deal with collective challenges. Moreover, each arrangement favors another coordination mechanism. When the allocation of values, like clean drinking water, takes place through the *state*, then the coordination is based on the (legal) authority that resides in the state. The state has the authority to develop rules and regulations and to develop plans that prescribe what clean drinking water is, how it will be produced, and how and under what conditions the inhabitants of a state, a region or a city have access to clean drinking water. Moreover, the state unilaterally determines how much these inhabitants have to pay (for example, by imposing water taxes) for making use of these clean water facilities. In doing so the state has the monopoly on the provision and distribution of drinking water. When the allocation of clean drinking water is organized by the *market*, the coordination is based on the price mechanism. The price to be paid is the outcome of the degree in which the supply of drinking water is able to satisfy the demand for clean water. Markets emerge when demand and supply are able to meet each other and companies can compete with each other to provide specific goods or services that differ in price and quality. In a market situation there is no monopoly, because in essence there are many clean water providers and many customers. When the allocation of drinking water is organized by a (local) *community*, then the coordination that is necessary to beat a well is based on the trust that the members of this community have in each other. Trust is necessary to share resources to beat the well or to create a shared understanding regarding the need to have a well (Putnam, 1995; Pierre and Peters, 2000). The trust that the members of a community have in each other often reflects the social capital that resides in this community (Schuller, Baron and Field, 2000). Social capital refers to the strength of social networks in a community (for example, do people know each other, do they communicate with each other), the reciprocities that the members of a community have (for example, the need to have clean drinking water) and the way in which they value these reciprocities (for example, accepting that clean drinking water can only be established when they collaborate) (Schuller, Baron and Field, 2000:1).

At the same time, we see that in literature several reasons are given to opt for a specific way of allocating values, thereby making use of a specific coordination mechanism. In the economic literature allocation by making use of the state is legitimized by referring to the inherent weaknesses of the market. For instance, a market is not really capable of providing collective or semi-collective goods, like the provision of dikes or a sewerage system. A market is very good at satisfying individual needs, but fails when it has to satisfy collective needs and provide goods or services which are available for everybody: nobody can be excluded. Another reason for state intervention is the existence of market failure, due to the misuse of power. If there is only one provider on the market or just a small number of collaborating providers, there might be a chance that price arrangements occur. In doing so free competition cannot be achieved, which often leads to high prices and lack of quality or services that do not meet the needs of citizens. This might happen if there is just one company which completely controls the market for the provision and distribution of clean water in a state. A third reason is the existence of external effects that could either harm a society or that would help society. These are goods and services that in principle could be provided by private companies that operate in a specific market. However, this might imply that negative effects would emerge for society as a whole or for specific groups in society. For instance, the health of the inhabitants of a city or region could be damaged if the drinking water that is provided does not meet the highest quality standards. In such a case, state provision is being legitimized, by stating that a specific price and water quality have to be guaranteed and that it is necessary that all citizens have access to the same water quality, thereby preventing citizens from being forced to make use of lower quality drinking water. The external effects argument not only focuses on the prevention of harmful effects that are caused by sheer market production. State intervention can also be defended by the production of positive external effects. In doing so state intervention is focused on the creation of merit goods and services. These are, again, services and goods that can be provided by the market. However, the incentive for private companies to do so is not so strong. That is why the state is doing this. For instance, for a private company it would be too costly to add fluoride to the drinking water to strengthen the teeth of especially younger children. However, adding fluoride may have positive effects for public health. In order to achieve these positive external effects, a government might decide to provide these services themselves.

The choice for a specific institution to allocate values is not only an economic one. Ideological reasons may also play a role in the way in which specific allocation arrangements and coordination mechanisms are preferred. For instance, the embrace of liberal ideas regarding the functioning and organization of the state in the 1990s, starting with the political victory of Ronald Reagan (USA) and Margaret Thatcher (UK) set in motion a more than twenty-year process of privatization and liberalization of government services. Public management reform ideologies like New Public Management also embraced the blessings of the market in improving the functioning of the public sector (Hood,1991; Pollitt and Bouckaert, 2004). In New Zealand this led to the privatization of water companies. However, the financial crisis that started in 2007 with the collapse of the Lehman Brothers bank and merged into public expenditure and monetary crisis at the beginning of 2010, has led to a rediscovery of the community as a basic organization principle of public goods and services. The idea of the so-called "Big Society" as launched by the former British Prime Minister David Cameron, tries to stimulate local, bottom-up initiatives that try to satisfy the needs of citizens in a community.

A final remark. These three allocation arrangements can also be mixed. In public sector practice we see that these arrangements are combined, in order to make use of the strengths of each arrangement. For instance, water quality can be safeguarded by the authority of the state which legally prescribes what the minimum quality should be that has to be provided by water supply companies. Moreover, it is the state that controls whether these private water companies are able to do so.

Policies and policy processes

The provision of clean drinking water presupposes that specific values have to be balanced, such as the quality of the water in order to contribute to the public health of a society, the costs that are involved with the production and distribution of the water and the equality of the citizens in making use of these provisions. This requires a collective decision-making process. Collective decision-making processes are mostly focused on more or less concrete ideas or plans that are being developed, that are the subject of decision-making or that are being implemented. That is where policies and policy processes come in. *Policies can be described as a more or less structured set of means and resources that are used to influence specific societal developments and to solve problems in a desired or planned way* (see also Dunn, 1991).

Political decision-making is, on the one hand, focused on the formulation of policies which give direction on how to achieve specific, but interrelated, *goals*. For instance, in the Netherlands all kinds of measures have been taken to achieve a specific goal: to give water more space so that rivers and other water channels are able to transfer the increasing amount of (rain) water as quickly and as smoothly as possible to the sea. In order to do so the capacity of rivers and other water channels but also sewerage systems have been enlarged. These goals can be seen as the expression of a political consensus in which different values are being balanced against each other. Values that have been translated in goals and conditions that should be taken into consideration. Hence, policies refer to a course of action that is the manifestation of considered judgments which also relates to a specific field of activities that is in essence value laden (Parsons, 1995:14; Hogwood and Gunn, 1984:13-19; Goodin, Rein and Moran, 2006:5).

On the other hand, political decision-making is also focused on the selection of *means and instruments*, the formulation of specific *measures* and the utilization of specific financial and other *resources* that are needed to achieve these goals. In the Dutch example, the policy program "give space to the river" not only addresses a whole set of specific measures to be taken at

30 locations. It also deals with the allocation of funds that are necessary to develop and implement the projects that are necessary. In this decision-making process attention is also paid to the question of how to use these instruments and resources in a systematic way. In doing so policy resembles to some extent a plan or a program in order to organize and implement a set of specific actions that, politically speaking, are considered as being appropriate (Parsons, 1995:14; Hogwood and Gunn, 1984:13-19; Goodin, Rein and Moran, 2006:6). Hence, a policy program specifies what the goals to be achieved are and how they can be achieved, although the degree of concreteness might vary. As such we can state that public policies result from the decisions made by politics, while at the same time the decision to do nothing can be guarded as policy (Howlett, Ramesh and Perl, 1995:4).

Moreover, in many cases we see that there is not one single political actor within government that has the authority to take these decisions (Howlett, Ramesh and Perl, 1995:6). Policies are the result of multiple decisions taken by *sets of actors* rather than a sole actor, often scattered throughout complex government organizations, who have all kinds of links with other organizations that have specific interests in the policies to be developed. Hence, they also try to influence this course of action, knowing that in many circumstances these decision-makers are also dependent on the support and the resources that are controlled by other actors. The relations between them can be understood in terms of policy networks (for example, Rhodes, 1985; Kickert, Klijn and Koppenjan, 1997; Koppenjan and Klijn, 2004) or policy communities (Sabatier and Jenkins-Smith, 1993). For instance, the enlargement of river beds implies that dikes have to be altered, that they have to be moved. Private property, for example, farmland, has to be acquired or disowned, while municipalities have to give up their building plans in order to create additional housing. Sometimes this reconstruction process is also combined with improving the natural quality of the surroundings, for instance to give nature a chance. As a result this reconstruction process mobilizes not only all kinds of different municipalities, regional and national governments, but also within these governments different units and agencies (water management, urban and rural planning, environmental protection) have to be involved. Also citizens, housing companies, urban and regional development companies as well as interest groups (for example, of citizens, of farmers, of environmentalists) will try to influence the shaping of this reconstruction project.

Furthermore, it can be argued that, in some cases, politics actually sets off the goals, thereby having the deliberate intention to influence specific societal challenges. This can be called "intended policy making". However, in other cases, politics is not in the lead. Policy programs emerge from the complex interactions between a number of relevant stakeholders; interactions which lead to outcomes in which a specific pattern can be distinguished. This is called "emergent policy making" (Mintzberg, 1994). The role of politics is twofold in this case. First, politics is just one of the relevant stakeholders, besides other public and private stakeholders, although they have special competences, responsibilities and resources. Second, politics tries to codify the emerging consensus regarding the appropriateness of a specific set of actions in a policy program (Koppenjan and Klijn, 2004).

Now that we have defined policies and have shown that policies are grounded in politics, it is important to acknowledge that policies are closely related to specific policy processes. The policy realm not only refers to the development of policy programs and the formulation of specific actions to be taken. Policy programs do not stand on their own; they generate different processes. These process can be seen as the policy cycle. This cycle consists of a number of phases that in principle build upon each other. Each phase deals with another but sequential sub-process. As we will argue later, in Chapter 2, this idea is a contested idea, because it is closely related to a specific approach of policy and policy making. However, for the sake of the argument, the following policy processes can be distinguished. In Table 1.1 we describe these stages.

Table 1.1 Phases in the policy process

	Definition
Agenda setting	The identification and selection of those problems, among many, that need to receive the serious attention of public officials; considering that action is needed
Policy development	Development of a proposed course of action for dealing with a public problem; considering what kind of alternative actions/options are possible; assessing possible effects of the options
Policy decision-making	Deciding politics on the possible courses of actions that are suitable by accepting the most appropriate proposal so that it becomes pertinent
Policy implementation	Application of the policy by one or more government organizations, thereby applying the measures and instruments that are set out in order to deal with the problem
Policy evaluation	To determine if the efforts that were made by the government in order to deal with the problem were effective, and why and why not (did the policy work?)

Source: Adapted from Anderson, 2003:28; Parsons, 1995:77.

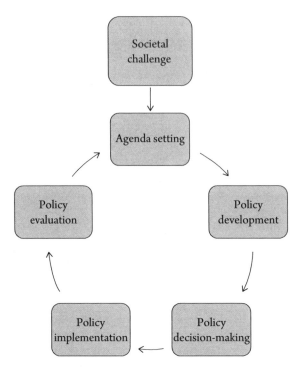

Figure 1.1 The policy cycle

If we visualize these phases the following scheme can be presented (Figure 1.1). We explain it with an example. If a specific region is confronted with flooding of rivers that has resulted in damage and casualties, questions will be raised. What is the quality of the water protection measures that have been taken in the past? Have the dikes been properly maintained? What is the capacity of the rivers and other water channels to stow and transport water? If an issue draws enough political attention, it is said that it has become an issue on the political agenda. This may be an incentive for the responsible politicians and policy makers to look into the issue. What has caused the repeated flooding? What was the damage? Why did the original measures not prevent this from happening? What is the quality of the dikes? What additional measures have to be taken in order to reduce the chance of future flooding? What costs are involved? These are questions that are addressed when plans are developed to deal with flooding. This takes place in the policy development phase. In these plans several options may be put forward, options which generate specific costs and benefits. The question of which option to choose is addressed in the decision-making phase. The next step is that the selected options will be further developed in terms of concreteness in order to be implemented. Concrete actions are taken up to implement the actions that are being formulated. For instance, the actual height of dikes will be enlarged or water channels will be broadened and deepened in order to increase their storage and transport capacity. This is the implementation phase. After a while, it is necessary know whether the measures that have been taken were successful. Hence, the effects of these measures need to be studied. Were these enlarged rivers capable of handling the increased amount of water in a proper way? What is the quality of the heightened and strengthened dikes after several years? Should additional measures be developed? Are the original goals of the policy program capable of addressing new water management challenges? These questions are raised during the evaluation phase. The outcomes of these evaluation studies may be an incentive to put the water management issue again on the political agenda.

Governance

The development and implementation of a specific policy program can only be successful if government is able to mobilize relevant resources in such a way that the policy goals that have been determined and the actions that have been selected can be accomplished. A policy program can be seen as a specific structured way in which government tries to intervene in society. This intervention can be seen as a steering act, in which a government tries to influence specific societal challenges in a desired way. The ability to intervene is based on the problem solving capacity of government which depends on the ability to mobilize and combine relevant resources to achieve political goals that are laid down in a policy program (Bekkers, 1994; Scharpf, 1997a). These resources may refer to the legal tasks, responsibility and competencies (and thus the authority) that a specific government actor has, to the specific knowledge and expertise that is necessary to deal with a specific issue, to financial resources that are needed to implement specific measures, or to the political and public support that government encounters. At the same time, this problem solving capacity and the resources that are needed are dispersed among many actors. An effective intervention implies that it is important that these resources have to be exchanged and shared among the involved actors. For instance, as argued before, effective water protection, which involves large changes in the water infrastructure, implies that within government all kinds of organizations or agencies have to work together, that different layers of government are involved but also that all kinds of private organizations are involved. In the latter case we can think of engineering agencies that bring the necessary knowledge to develop highly sophisticated plans as well as construction companies that have the people, the means and machines and operational knowledge to dredge a river, to change the bedding of a river, to build a dike or to renew a sewerage system. Moreover, it may also involve the participation and support of citizens and citizen groups, like farmers that have to be compensated for the loss of their farmland.

In literature this challenge is called the governance challenge (Kickert, Klijn and Koppenjan, 1997). It draws attention to the shift from state-centric "*government*" in which state actors have a central role in societal steering, to more complex forms of "*governance*" which involves problem solving strategies in multi-actor networks (including but not limited to government institutions) and in multiple ways (including but not limited to "policy") (Kjaer, 2004). Some scholars (such as Colebatch, 2009) even argue that forms of "government" have always coexisted with "governance", whereas others contend that especially the increase of societal complexity triggers a shift from "government" to "governance" (Pierre and Peters, 2000). Key assumptions behind the governance concept are:

- Government is not an entity but a conglomerate of actors.
- Government is not the only actor which tries to influence societal problems.
- Government interventions generate continuing interactions between all kinds of public, semi-public and private actors within several societal domains and at different levels that try to influence the shaping of policy processes.
- The governance capacity of each actor refers to the problem solving capacity of each actor, which depends on his ability to mobilize and combine relevant resources in a structured way to achieve specific policy goals or to address specific societal challenges (Rhodes, 1997; Scharpf, 1997b).

Given these assumptions and when addressing a specific societal challenge, policy makers have to ask themselves: Do I have the capacity and the capabilities to address this issue on my own, or do I need the support of other actors? The answer to this question also depends on the specific nature of the policy program that is being developed or implemented.

1.3   A variety of policy programs

The complexity of many policy processes also depends on the specific nature of the problems and challenges that are being addressed and the complexity of the measures that are being proposed or implemented. For instance, in many western countries the quality of surface water is under control. All kinds of measures have been taken to prevent and detect water pollution. Sewage treatment has been developed in rather sophisticated ways so that this type of water can be purified in such a way that it can be used to drink, to wash or to prepare food. The policy programs that are directed to sewage treatment are mostly focused on monitoring the existing water quality. However, when we talk about water management policies that are directed toward the negative effects of global warming, such as drought or flooding, then the complexity increases enormously. For instance, the Dutch policy program "give space to the river" implied a paradigm shift. For instance, for decades the general idea was that water flows have to be controlled: the idea was to get abundant water as fast as possible to the sea. The new policy program implied that it was impossible to transport increasing amounts of water as fast as possible to the sea. The idea was to create natural or artificial reservoirs that could be used to store water for a longer time and it could be absorbed more easily by its natural surroundings. In doing so the general assumptions behind a long tradition of more strategic policy plans were replaced by other assumptions that did not fit with the heroic past of many water management organizations. In contrast to the previous sewerage treatment policy program this new program was a strategic policy program or a transformative program, while many sewerage treatment programs have an operational nature.

In order to understand the variety of policy programs, the following types of public policies can be distinguished (Lowi, 1972; Parsons, 1995):

- *Distributive policies* which aim at the distribution or allocation of new resources among actors. Re-distributive policies aim at changing the existing distribution or allocation among actors. Resources may refer to the allocation of, for instance, budgets and tasks, competences and responsibilities.
- *Constitutional policies* refer to setting up new or reorganizing existing institutional arrangements or establishing new organizations with special tasks. For instance, the liberalization of the water supply and sanitation services in some countries, like Australia, can be seen as an example of constitutional policies. Another example, which is in line with the previous one, is the establishment of a Water Authority, as a supervisory agency that controls if these private water companies comply with specific water quality and service delivery norms.
- *Regulatory policies* deal with the regulation and control of specific activities through the establishment of specific (very often operational) norms that should be taken into account; norms which also deal with specific rights and obligations that should be taken into consideration. Examples of regulatory policies are the hygienic norms that water supply companies have to take into consideration in order to provide safe water. Regulatory policies might also address the rights and obligations and the

conditions that have to be fulfilled in order to ensure that citizens have access to water and make use of these facilities.

- *Provisional policies* refer to policies that are focused on the creation of specific facilities, like dikes or the establishment of specific (service) infrastructure like the establishment of a sewerage system.
- *Stimulating policies* which aim at the creation of incentives that motivate actors to take specific decisions which are in line with the goals that policy makers had in mind. In doing so they try to stimulate a type of behavior that is considered as being desired without imposing it. An example is the use of subsidies to industrial firms so that they can take measures in order to improve the quality of their waste water or recycle their waste water. Also policies can be focused on presenting information in order to change the behavior of actors. For instance, information can be given to farmers so that they know how much water specific crops need in order to prevent water scarcity.

This categorization helps us (to some extent) to understand the variety of specific policies, by looking at the functions that specific policy programs might target. At the same time it is a rather simplified way of understanding the variety of policies, and in practice these functions often overlap (Parsons, 1995:132).

1.4 Policy making in a changing world

Now that we have introduced the central concepts in this book, the next step is to understand the context in which policy processes take place. This context can be described and understood in terms of all kinds of changes. On the one hand these changes are closely related to a specific policy field or policy sector. Each field or sector can be understood in terms of its own developments, changes and challenges; sometimes they overlap but sometimes they are different. This implies that each sector has its own complexity and dynamics. However, despite these differences, it is possible to sketch a number of macro-sociological changes and developments in our society that fundamentally challenge the content, course and outcomes of politics and policy making. These challenges will be sketched in terms of four images that represent the transformation of the world in which we live. Moreover, the importance of sketching these changes is based on our conviction that policies are not only grounded in politics but are also grounded in society. This implies that, in order to develop and implement effective and legitimate policies, it is important to opt for an outside-in approach to policy process, thereby taking into account the changes that take place in different societal sectors: in the political, economic, social, cultural and technological realms;

changes will often co-evolve with each other. This outside-in perspective helps us to be more aware of the needs, wishes and preferences that exist among citizens, companies, societal organizations and other actors. In doing so more guarantees can be built in to create a more responsive government. This is important, because one of the reasons why some policies fail is that they are primarily being developed and implemented from an inside-out perspective: policy making that is based on and derived from historically grown and well established practices. These practices provide the main frame of reference that policy makers use when developing and implementing policies. As a result only those policies that fit with these established practices are being selected and adopted.

Four images will be presented. First, we will start with the introduction of the "network society" (Castells, 1996). This concept helps us to understand the roles that interdependency, globalization and information technology play in modern societies. The second image is the image of a "liquid society" (Bauman, 2000). In this society different social and cultural changes that have come together during the last centuries have created a life that has been conceptualized as being fluid. The third image refers to the "risk society" (Beck, 1999) which helps us to understand the role that a modern, global and interdependent society creates with all kinds of risks that we have to address but often disregard. The last image is called the "hollow state" (Rhodes, 1997), which refers to the idea that the central state as an important political governing principle has lost its significance.

The network society

The network society is a concept coined by Manuell Castells (1996, 1997, 1998), a Spanish sociologist, which tries to understand a number of fundamental changes in our world that are rooted in a paradigm shift in the production technology of modern societies.

Information technology as a revolutionary force

The core of this revolution refers to the vital role that information and communication play in modern society and the pervasiveness of the technologies that support the processing of information processing and communication (Castells, 1996:31). These technologies have penetrated in all domains of human activity. They are no longer an exogenous source of impact but they are the fabric of our modern society; all our activities have been interwoven with these technologies. An example of this penetration is the creation of permanent monitoring systems which enable water authorities to follow the development of water levels in real-time. Another example is the development of "intelligent dikes". Sensor technology helps water managers to have a better understanding about the quality of the dike. This is important because when a dike gets older, the protection quality diminishes.

The penetration of information and communication technologies in our society also stimulated another development which has been observed since the Second World War: a development which refers to the vital importance that information and knowledge play in our economic life. Information and knowledge have become a vital resource in the production and distribution of goods and services. This does not imply that traditional, more physical goods and services have lost their significance. It refers to the fact that those economic activities that are based on and make use of the production, collection, combination, upgrading, refinement, and exchange of knowledge and information have become a major and more influential economic sector. For example: in society nowadays containers with all kinds of goods are still shipped from China to London, New York or Berlin. These containers make use of all kinds of transport infrastructures (water, rail, road, air). However, this requires a rather complex logistics planning process, especially if the shipping process has to be just-in-time in order to reduce costs. This can only be accomplished when information is being shared and refined. What we see is that the economic value of these information and knowledge-based logistical planning activities creates more economic value than the sheer shipping of these containers. As a result complete information and knowledge-driven industries emerge. Another example is the financial world. Physical bonds and stock are no longer exchanged on the stock market. The productions that are being exchanged are information-based productions. They are virtual products which have an imaginary relationship with material stocks and bonds. Other virtual products are futures and warrants. At the same time, in order to grasp the complexity of the new products and markets, new information and knowledge-based services and companies emerge: stock market analysts.

Information and communication technologies support this process and add new possibilities to it, because their power is based on another revolutionary development, namely digitalization (Negroponte, 1995). Digital products are based on the ability to transform text, speech, images and communications or other symbols like numbers into bits and bytes (into a code consisting of all kinds of infinite combinations of 0 and 1). Information and knowledge as well as communication is primarily based on text, speech, image, symbols and it can, thus, be digitized very easily. The advantage of digitalization is that digital products can be easily transported. The Internet shows the possibility to transport information and knowledge in a speedy way and on a global level. As a result, it is rather easy to change information: all kinds of geographical, organizational or time-related borders are no longer an obstruction to exchange information and to effectively communicate with each other. Another advantage is that digital products are flexible, which opens the possibility to re-use, to refine but also to manipulate digital products rather easily. A digital photo of a person can, for instance, be photoshopped in such a way that the presented photo looks even better than the actual image of that person: different eyes, another hair colour, and so on. Another advantage of digitalization is that it represents the capacity to integrate information and knowledge-based products, and the devices and infrastructures that are used to produce and exchange them. An example is the possibility of adding music to the video that you produced yourself when making use of the camera function of your smartphone. At the same time this phone, and your laptop, personal computer or even tablet offers all kinds of possibilities to integrate sounds, images, text, graphics and so on, and exchange them with your television or upload them to the Internet. Multimedia can be seen as the icon of the integration potential. That is why Castells (2009) in his more recent work emphasizes the importance of the shift from information technologies toward communication and multimedia technologies and the power that these new technologies represent. Examples refer to, for instance, the deep penetration of social media in our society and the growing importance of visualization and visual technologies like YouTube.

For governments this process of digitalization is even more vital because policy processes are heavily information and knowledge-based:

> Government is information. Its employees are nearly all information workers, its raw material is information inputs, its products is those inputs transformed into policies, which are simply an authoritative form of information. So in a narrow sense, to consider government information policy is not far from considering the essence of government itself. (Cleveland, 1986:605)

Flows, nodes and timeless time: real-time connectivity on a global scale

The capacity that information and communication technology offers to create, transport and store information, knowledge and communications becomes even more important if we look at another development, namely the globalization of production and consumption patterns. On a global scale we see a process of specialization in the production of goods and services. Goods and services are mostly produced or assembled in locations where the production costs are the cheapest. This is important, given the fierce worldwide competition between companies. It is also no longer necessary to produce goods and services that are located near to the market place. The production and assembly of goods and services takes place in locations that produce a specific type of quality against the lowest possible costs. As a result of these scattered production and processes all kinds of flows emerge: flows of goods, of components, of people, of information and knowledge. An example is, for instance, all kinds of vegetables or flowers that are produced in Africa, where labor is cheap, and then, by making use of airplanes, they are shipped to the supermarkets in London, Rome, Berlin or Paris. One day after the vegetables are harvested or these flowers are picked, they can be bought thousands of miles further away. Another striking example is the use that companies in the USA or Europe make of call centers or administrative support organizations that are located in India. For a client who calls from London, he does not have the faintest idea that the person he is talking to is sitting in India.

This process of globalization specialization has radicalized the already existing process of structural differentiation, which can be witnessed since the beginning of the Industrial Revolution in the eighteenth century. Five results can be witnessed.

First, we see that specialization has led to an increasing degree of interdependency which can be understood in terms of a network. For instance, not only are supermarkets dependent on production in other countries and the effective logistical planning in order to get cheap vegetables just in time to the supermarket. Interdependency can also be seen in another way. The intensive agricultural production in Africa sometimes contributes to exhaustion of the water supply that is necessary to produce these goods. Dealing with this problem in Africa would also imply a change in the consumption behavior of people in Europe.

The second consequence is that this degree of specialization has become institutionalized, because we make use of highly specialized organizations. On the one hand these organizations are rather autonomous, while on the other hand they are dependent on other organizations (Pfeffer and Salancik, 1978). As a result, the complexity that we mentioned earlier has grown into "organized complexity" (Willke, 1991; Mayntz, 1987).

The third consequence is that, due to the complexity which emerges from these interdependencies, it is rather difficult to intellectually grasp this complexity. Knowledge and information is locked up in these rather autonomous highly specialized organizations. Moreover, a large variety of highly task-specific and organization-specific perspectives prevail without grasping the whole picture, thereby seeing and acknowledging these interdependencies. Hence, we are trapped in situations of bounded rationality (Luhmann, 1984a).

The fourth consequence is that as result of this interdependency, exchange relationships exist. These exchange but also coordination relationships are defined by Castells (1996:42) in terms of flows, which are described as "the material organization of time sharing practices that works through flows." For instance, when looking at the functioning of a harbor, you see that this harbor can be seen as a network of organizations which are connected through flows, supported by information and communication technology, in which information and knowledge is being shared, regarding the time that a ship will enter the harbor and the nature of the cargo that is being transported. This sharing of information generates a whole variety of different but related activities in a wide variety of organizations that have a role when a ship approaches a harbor, when it wants to anchor and when it is fit to be released. For instance, pilots have to come on board, the customs officer and the coast guard (for example, when the ship has a dangerous load like chemicals) has to be warned, as do shipping agents, forwarding agencies and so on. The harbor authorities also have to be informed. The entering of a ship into a harbor can be seen as a social practice that works through information and communication flows. Another example is the capital market which consists of stock markets and stock brokers, banks, private equity firms, insurance companies and so on who buy and sell all kinds of financial products (which are in essence information-based products); in many cases this buying and selling is done by computers that automatically buy and sell shares, bonds, warrants, futures and other products. Moreover, this idea of time sharing social processes means that increasingly activities that are being fulfilled have a real-time nature. Castells (1996:464) calls this "timeless time", which is the "compression of occurrence of phenomena, aiming at instantaneity or else by introducing randomness (. . .) become undifferentiated." An example is the international tsunami warning system that is used to detect tsunamis in advance and issue warnings to prevent loss of life and damage. It consists of a network of sensors to detect tsunamis and a communications infrastructure to issue timely alerts to permit evacuation of coastal areas. When a warning is given, it is instantaneously sent to a wide variety of involved organizations in different countries – like Thailand, Malaysia, and Indonesia – so that they can take the necessary precautions.

The last consequence is that these flows come together in specific nodes. Typical for those nodes is that in these nodes the necessary resources that are vital for the operation of these flows are located. Mostly it refers to the concentration of sophisticated knowledge and expertise that is necessary to operate and coordinate these flows. For instance, London and New York are nodes in the financial world and in these nodes all kinds of specialized and highly professionalized service providers can be found that are necessary for the functioning of the stock market as well as all kinds of specialized providers (like banks, brokers) that control all kinds of supporting services (like lawyers, market analysts and ICT specialists). Other examples of nodes are the harbors of Shanghai, Rotterdam, Hamburg or Antwerp. They all function as nodes in complex networks of flows (flows of vessels, flows of goods and people that move and flows of information) in which a wide variety of different organizations fulfill different roles in coordinating the traffic on the water but also exchange of traffic and cargo-related information. Sometimes these nodes can be virtual. On the Internet and on social media, networks like Facebook, websites or blogs can be found that act as a platform for discussion and the exchange of information regarding all kinds of topics. Water management is one of these topics.

Between these nodes specialization occurs, which also leads to a kind of hierarchical order in terms of more or less importance. However, in most cases these nodes need to have a physical space in which they can come together. The spaces are mostly cities. Cities not only provide the necessary economic and technological infrastructure that is necessary to support these flows; they also provide the housing, cultural, educational and leisure facilities that are necessary to attract the people that are needed to make a node function. In the words of Castells, cities but also regions, such as Silicon Valley, can be seen as "spaces of flows" (1996:376).

BOX 1.1

"IF MAYORS RULED THE WORLD" (BARBER, 2013)

The book *If Mayors Ruled the World* by the political theorist Benjamin Barber highlights the growing importance of cities in today's network society. According to Barber, cities are key to responding to various global governance challenges at a time when nation-states seem increasingly unable to do so. This includes challenges such as global climate change, migration, poverty and the growing impact of new forms of communication on our lives. Barber sees the development of various city-to-city networks all over the world as a sign that cities are also increasingly taking on this leading role in global governance. He even advocates the establishment of a world parliament of Mayors.

In- and exclusion

The network society has winners and losers (Castells, 1996). There are people who can benefit from the chances and possibilities that the network society offers (like the need for knowledge workers), but also people who are excluded from these possibilities. Two types of exclusion can be discerned. First, there are regions or countries which are not connected to this global network society, such as North Korea and many African countries. As a result of this social and economic deprivation flows of people emerge: flows of immigrants who want to improve their life by trying to find work, and improve their life in general. Sometimes they find work, sometimes they do not have a chance. As a result new spaces are created in which these "have nots" live, such as the modern ghettos that many suburbs of Paris and London constitute. This implies, second, that in the core of the network society itself, in highly developed cities, spaces exist that are not connected to the possibilities that the network society offers. This is the second type of exclusion that can be discerned.

The diminishing role of politics

The organization and functioning of the network society has important implications for the role of politics and for our policy processes. The network society shows us that the leading role that we attach to politics to govern our society, to deal with a number of societal challenges in an effective way, is limited. Politics is primarily organized in relation to a specific political community that is rooted in a geographical area. Politics is primarily location-based and geographically demarcated, given the borders of a state, the borders of a region or a municipality. The globalization of our economic but also our social and cultural life has created flows that cross the borders. In doing so, these flows challenge the governance capacity of governments as well as the capacity of politics to deal with these issues. For instance, if the Netherlands wants to improve the quality of the water in the Rhine, it makes no sense that the Dutch government deploys all kinds of measures on its own. It requires that norms have to be developed at an international level, based on co-operation between the Netherlands, Germany and Switzerland. This is also the case if we talk about the shipment of highly contagious cargo by ships that make use of the Rhine or make use of the seas. It is important that vital information is being exchanged by the responsible authorities in order to act in an effective and speedy way, when something goes wrong.

Politics is not only challenged by the flows in the network society that cross borders and thus cross the jurisdiction of governments. It is also challenged by nodes in this network society. Although many nodes can be located physically in a specific area, like a harbor, these nodes not only have a local function (in terms of for instance creating jobs); they also have a global functioning. Disturbances in this node may have worldwide effects, and may affect the functioning of other nodes. For instance, the flooding of farming lands or the extreme droughts in specific areas will not only have local effects for the population but will also influence the availability of raw materials (like coffee and cereals) that are necessary to produce specific goods or services. Or, the increase of living standards in the fast-growing metropolitan areas in China and India, especially in relation to the emergence of a fast expanding middle class, generates new demand for more luxurious foods, which leads to a heavier use of water in those areas where the raw materials and consumables are produced. In some cases this leads to water depletion. The consumption changes in one area generate water problems in another part of the world, for instance in Africa. This limits the power of local politics to deal with this issue. Moreover, the economic and social development of this area also depends on the ability to meet these increasing consumption needs and the needs of industries which lay behind these needs.

The liquid society

It is not only the social and economic structure of our world which is changing, but also our culture. These cultural changes also challenge the role of politics and the way in which we develop and implement all kinds of politics. The cultural changes can be framed in terms of "liquid life" (Bauman, 2000). Bauman defines the state of western mankind as "being light and liquid" (Bauman, 2000:1-2). Behind this concept several institutional transformations and cultural developments can be identified. At the same time liquid life also generates a number of effects that influence politics and policy making.

Institutional loss

The emergence of liquid life can be seen as the outcome of a number of closely related societal developments. Essential is that in our modern society a melting process takes place, which accelerates the melting pot which society in essence is (Bauman, 2000:6). As a result life becomes fluid. This raises the question: what is melting? The answer is that our institutions on which we have relied for centuries are losing their functions. Institutions create order and stability by stressing specific values that we think are important. Examples of relevant institutions are the family, the church, the school, the army, the police, the labor union and also politics (Dahlgren, 2009:28). As such these institutions play an important role in the socialization of people: they prescribe how to deal with certain circumstances, given specific values that this institution wants to put forward as being essential for the ways we want to live or want to behave. However, the authority of the institutions and the values that they try to protect are being questioned. The code of behavior that these institutions expect from you is increasingly being questioned. During the last decades people have liberated themselves from the socializing influence of these institutions, which has led to another type of relationship between people and the representatives of these institutions. For instance, your father and mother are no longer persons whom you obey but they are your friends. In terms of authority a horizontal relationship has emerged that challenges or replaces the previous more vertical or hierarchical ones. In the world of politics, citizens consider themselves as no longer a subject of government who has to comply with all kinds of regulations but they consider themselves as a client. These clients have specific rights based on the regulations to which government has to comply and which defines government as the producer of specific services, just like a company is. The diminished socializing influence of these institutions creates space, and gives people the freedom to take their lives into their own hands.

Liberalization and emancipation

This diminishing role of institutions has a number of important consequences. First, people have been forced or have been inspired to develop their own life courses, to find their own style. They have the chance to change these courses and styles. Second, personal autonomy has also increased through the successful training and education of the mass population. They possess the capacities and competences to gather knowledge and information as well as to assess information, if this is needed. And third, this freedom of choice has also become possible because – especially in the western world and rising economies in Asia – people saw their income substantially increase during the last 40 years, which enables them to satisfy their own needs in more compelling ways. As a result of this emancipation and liberalization process people not only acquired more objective freedom (given the formal rights to choose and having the resources to choose). They have obtained more subjective freedom: they also actually experience more freedom, they feel their freedom (Bauman, 2000:17). In doing so they are more able to act as an individual instead of a member of a specific societal group and its specific traditions. They do not act according to the traditions and the norms and values of being a Catholic, a Protestant or a liberal, being a blue-collar, a white-collar worker or a farmer. The ability to choose your own, individual life, has also led to a variety of all kinds of different lifestyles; lifestyles which are also very flexible and dynamic (Dahlgren, 2009:27). Moreover, this liberalization and emancipation process has also increased the mobility in society. Not only in a physical way, because people have nowadays the ability to travel much more easily, to meet new people in places that, 40 years ago, could not be travelled to very easily. But also in a socio-economic way, upward mobility has increased enormously due to improved education that people have received and the funds that are available to receive education (Bauman, 2010:91, 130).

However, there are also a number of shady sides to mention, which influence politics and policy making. First, the ability of people to form their own life, according to their own needs and interests, leads to a situation in which people have increasing expectations regarding the role of government and the way in which government and politics should facilitate this liquid and light life. Second, these increased possibilities and chances also create uncertainty and anxiety. Hence, we see that citizens expect that the life that they live is a life that should be free of any risk. Only in a safe environment are citizens able to enjoy this light and liquid life, free of risk. So they expect that governments develop policies that are focused on reducing the chance that uncertainty and anxiety may disturb their life: this also adds to these rising expectations (Boutelier, 2004). The third consequence is that in this world of unbridled but also anonymous opportunities and chances, there is a risk that people get lost. That is why Castells (1998:346) argues that in the liquid and networked society identity is very important. Moreover, this identity is also difficult to find, due to the diminishing role that institutions play in society. That is why there is a tendency to re-establish an identity by returning to specific roots that can be found by being a member of a specific region, belonging to a specific regional culture, tradition or religion or belonging to a specific population group. Moreover, it is also possible to create a specific identity or to have more identities, by making use of the Internet, for instance in terms of being a member of a specific discussion group. The last reason is that people as voters will no longer vote according to the values, norms and traditions of the societal group to which they and their parents belong.

The experience economy

Liquid life has two other important consequences which we have addressed by introducing relevant concepts which show what the influence of this process of de-institutionalization, liberalization and emancipation is. First, we see that in the economic realm the so-called "experience economy" anticipates the socio-economic consequences. Given the possibility that people have more money to spend and have more autonomy in their choices, they have to be seduced, by appealing to their freedom, to their ability to live a liquid and light life. Through the creation of unique experiences, marketing experts try to anticipate this process of individualization and construct possible new consumer groups in order to influence the process of choosing. This idea has been labeled as "the experience economy" (Pine and Gilmore, 1999). The idea of an experience economy refers to a development that commodities, goods and services as such have a limited value. Experiences have become important too, especially if they can be linked to buying a specific product or to a specific process of service delivery. This enhances the economic value of commodities, goods and services. Experiences are memorable and personal. Because they are created within the customer, customers have the idea that they are buying a unique product or service (Pine and Gilmore, 1999:6-13). According to some authors this has led to unbridled consumerism (Castells, 1996; Bauman, 2000; Deuze, 2007).

The drama democracy

The second consequence of this liquid life relates to the world of politics. The diminishing role that ideology plays in political life – due to the fall of communism as well as the emancipation of citizens – has led to a development in which the visual aspect of politics has become more and more important. Image and image-building has penetrated the world of politics and policy making and has influenced the substance of politics and policy making. People have liberated themselves from the socio-economic and cultural background and the ideological frames of reference that were pushed forward by the institutions that told people how to behave politically. As such the citizen as a voter has increasingly become a drifting voter, who is seduced by the personal image that politicians and policy makers want to push forward as being attractive and convincing, thereby appealing to our emotions. Due to the increased role that images play in politics, mass media and especially television have become very important in political life in order to gain attention and to acquire public support. Politics and democracy have become mediated politics and mediated democracy (Bennett and Entman, 2000:5). As a result of the growing influence of the mass media, we see that media logic plays a vital role in the way politics is being represented and portrayed by the media and how politicians make use of the media logic in terms of trying to strategically influence the image that they want to communicate (Bennett, 2007). First, the media are more likely to report on surprising and unexpected occurrences than they are to pay attention to non-surprising or expected occurrences. The larger and more unusual an occurrence is, the sooner it will be reported. Second, the complexity and ambiguity of these occurrences can be reduced to simple, clear and consistent, almost binary occurrences (good versus bad, David versus Goliath), which tend to become personalized and dramatized. Third, the selective imaging created by the aforementioned mechanisms, increased by the tendency of the media to refer to each other in their coverage, creates a repetitive effect (Bennett, 2007). As a result politics is being perceived as an object of political marketing or political public relations, while at the same time spin doctoring has become normal practice in politics and policy making (Louw, 2005). The Belgian philosopher Elchardus (2003:49) has described the growing influence of media logic and strategic communication in the political process as the emergence of the so-called "drama democracy". Politics is being portrayed as a theater and politicians seem to be the actors on stage, while citizens are defined as the watching, rather passive audience that needs to be entertained. Entertainment is being created by presenting policy issues in terms of drama, in terms of a game that tries to stimulate our emotions. In order to stimulate our emotions framing is very important, in such a way that the frames that are put forward have to be appealing ones.

The risk society

Another concept that helps us to understand some fundamental challenges in our present society is the concept of the risk society, which has been developed by Ulrich Beck (1999). This concept refers to the changing nature of the risks that society is confronted with. Flooding and drought are examples of disasters that are as old as the history of mankind (Beck, 1999:50). Even in the Bible dramatic stories are told about the devastating effects of these disasters. Fire, war and famine are examples of classical risks that societies might face. Before the Industrial Revolution these disasters and other calamities were perceived as risks or dangers that go beyond the sphere of influence of mankind. They just happen, they are inevitable and express the will of God. However, since the Industrial Revolution and since the Enlightenment, disasters have been increasingly related to the intended or unintended outcomes that go back to a number of deliberate or non-deliberate decisions that people, organizations or even societies make. Risks that very often are related to the process of modernization and rationalization that people, organizations or societies aim for. An example is Fukushima. In order to meet the increasing demands for energy, policy makers and civil engineers and nuclear physicists designed a nuclear plant that was able to absorb earthquakes, however they did not seriously look at the risk that a tsunami would strike the nuclear installations in such a way that a meltdown could occur.

The risk calculus

Beck argues that the modernization of society has created new risks, risks that are made deliberate, because calculations have shown that the chance that such an event will occur is acceptable. This type of risk calculation is justified by referring to the efficiency and efficacy gains that can be achieved when choosing a specific solution, choosing a specific way of producing or consuming. For instance, cities in order to support their economic growth, although they are located near a river, deliberately opt to build houses or create a commercial area near the river, thereby making use of the river foreland. They justify this decision by pointing out that the statistical calculations show that the chance the new area will be flooded will only be once in say 100 years. Beck (1999:51) argues that the modernization of society has been based on the calculus of risk, which has undermined the political nature of risk definition processes. The idea is that, due to the use of advanced calculation models, risks can be forecast. When risks can be calculated, they can also be controlled. In doing so an illusion of control is being fostered. In the slipstream of this illusion a complete new emergency and risk management industry has emerged. Representatives of these industries and the companies and governments that make use of them, cherish the idea that risk management can be seen as a form and process of social engineering (Beck, 1999:51-52). As a result citizens have such high expectations regarding the effectiveness of the policies that they ask government to make, while governments suggest that by taking these measures these risks are under control. As such we create a safety utopia or a safety illusion (Boutelier, 2004). The creation of all kinds of safety regulations and all kinds of supervisory bodies add to this utopia. Every time new and more advanced norms, techniques and other measures as well as more refined regulations are put in place, this illusion is being reproduced.

This process of thinking in terms of calculated risks leads to a situation in which no real and open political and ethical debate exists regarding one central question: what risks do we want to accept as a society, and which risks do we do not want to accept, what risks do we really face and what do we know about these risks (Douglas and Wildavsky, 1983). What risks do we really face, when looking at the rising water levels in the sea as a result of the melting of the ice at the North and South poles? Beck (1999:73) argues that societies find it rather difficult to be engaged in a process of self-confrontation in which these risks are addressed in an open and critical way. One reason for this lacking debate is that we live in "a truncated democracy", due to political influence of all kinds of vested interests that economically benefit from the way in which risks are being defined (Beck, 1999:70). That is why, Beck argues, it is important to democratize the process of risk definition in societies, a process of democratization which opens up the rather narrow-minded discussion that takes place in the formal institutions of democracy (like parliament and all kinds of parliamentary committees). It is important that a public space is created in which alternative perspectives and alternative knowledge and information can be exchanged and shared (Beck, 1999:70-71).

New risks

What are the types of risks that Beck wants to be discussed in these public spaces? Let's take the example of the flooding of the Fukushima nuclear plant disaster. On the one hand, earthquakes and tsunamis are examples of classic risks that have always existed. On the other hand, building a nuclear plant in an area that is vulnerable to earthquakes and tsunamis is an example of a new, calculated risk that has deliberately been taken because it was economically defendable to build this plant in this area, given the number of additional risk prevention measures that have been taken. Modernization has created new risks that can be characterized as follows. First, the effects of the crisis that emerge from these new risks are no longer restricted in time and place. The meltdown of the Fukushima nuclear facilities did not only threaten the municipality of Ōkuma in the district of Futaba, but the fall out of nuclear material also threatened areas and cities which are located much further away. In the worst case Tokyo could be threatened. Moreover, the effects of the fall not only led to the immediate evacuation of the nearest areas during March 2011: the fall out will have long-lasting effects. In the area that is most close to the nuclear plant, no living and no farming will take place for a long time, or even forever. Second, the effects of the earthquake set in motion a whole chain of other effects that has exponentially increased the chaos and disorder that took place: "it became an event with a beginning and no end; an open festival of creeping, galloping and overlapping waves of destruction" (Beck, 1999:54, 77). If you look at the history of Fukushima, you see the following chain reaction: it started with an earthquake in Sendai, which created a tsunami. Automatically the three nuclear reactors of the plant were shut down, but although they were shut down it was important that these reactors were cooled by making use of cooling water. The electricity that was necessary to feed the water pumps was also closed, which implied that the emergency power units had to take over the electricity provision. However, the tragedy was that these emergency generators were flooded by the water that entered the nuclear facilities. As a result the nuclear reactor could not be cooled sufficiently, so these units got overheated. This led to a fire which also set in motion a set of blue water gas explosions and fires which were not restricted to just one reactor but also damaged other reactors. But there were also some unexpected side effects. For instance, the Nikkei index went down by 1200 points (12 percent) when the Japanese government warned that the radiation levels were threatening the Japanese population. All kinds of spillo-ver effects were created which also penetrated other domains of human life. The third implication of these new risks is that it is quite difficult to answer the question of who is responsible for what. In this chain reaction so many decisions were made, that it is quite difficult to reduce the emergence of all these effects to just one decision-maker. Very often a whole network of deci-sion-makers is involved, decision-makers who all have specific tasks, com-petences and responsibilities that only deal with one specific aspect of the crisis. Due to this diffuse network of responsibilities, there is often no over-view when dealing with a crisis. Also in the Fukushima disaster it became clear that the coordination and communication between responsible deci-sion-makers was not organized effectively and efficiently. The fourth effect is that it is quite impossible to compensate for involved costs. For instance, it was estimated that the disaster with the Fukushima nuclear plant cost at least 100 billion American dollars.

The hollow state

A final more fundamental change in our society is that the state as the domi-nant institution that primarily deals with challenges with which we as a modern society are wrestling, has lost is significance. It is no longer the exclu-sive right of the state to provide the platforms on which the authoritative allocation of values for society as a whole takes place. What we can witness is a shift from "government" toward "governance". The state can no longer be viewed as having the monopoly, the expertise or the resources that are necessary to govern. When government wants to govern, it must rely on the plurality of interdependent organizations and other actors drawn from within and beyond government (Newman, 2001:11-12). In the traditional government perspective, government was put at the center of attention, gov-ernment was the focal point when addressing all kinds of challenges and problems. Governments were supposed to be able to intervene effectively in societal developments, like the struggle against the rising water levels in the sea and the rivers, and to solve these problems from a centralized and hierarchical position, detached from society and according to the goals that were laid down in a policy program. Ineffective government interventions were primarily seen as flaws in the "machinery of government" (Bekkers and Fenger, 2007:16). Since the 1990s this idea has been met with a lot of criticism.

Shifts in government

The criticism regarding the central role that is attached to government in governing society focuses on showing that the capacity to govern has shifted toward other societal and other governmental domains. What are relevant shifts in governance that have taken place and that challenge the governing monopoly of the state (van Kersbergen and van Waarden, 2004)?

- A vertical upward shift in which competences of the state have been transferred to international governing bodies. An example is the transfer of competences of the European national states to the European Union. For instance, water quality standards are increasingly formulated at the European level and implemented at the national level. Another example is the transfer to intergovernmental organizations like the United Nations or the World Trade Organization.
- A vertical downward shift, in which competences of the state have been transferred to lower local and regional authorities, due to a process of decentralization. For instance, in the Netherlands the urban and rural planning competences of the Ministry of Planning that also affect the balance between water management and nature preservation in a specific area have become decentralized in favor of the municipalities and the provinces.
- A horizontal shift in favor of the judiciary. In some countries one can see that the judiciary system has become increasingly important in deciding how specific values have to be allocated toward society or toward societal groups. In doing so the jurisprudence of the judiciary increasingly influences the content of public policy. Also, citizens and interest groups increasingly go to court when they are confronted with policies and policy decisions that do not match their interests.
- A horizontal shift in which specific policy implementation, public service delivery and policy enforcement activities (and the competences and responsibilities that are related to these activities) are being transferred to specific agencies that operate at a distance from policy making units. This process is also known as agentification, which leads to a strengthening of all kinds of forms of functional government. An example is the Next Steps Program in the United Kingdom which in the beginning of the 1990s led to the establishment of a whole range of rather independent agencies that were located away from Westminster and Downing Street and acquired a lot of autonomy when dealing with specific tasks.
- A horizontal shift toward companies that took over the production and distribution of services that in essence have a public nature but are organized in a private way. An example is the privatization of drinking

water and clean water production and distribution facilities as well as the privatization of water purification.

- A horizontal shift toward society and societal organizations, thereby trying to mobilize the self-organization capacity that is present in society and in societal groups. For instance, in the United States there is a strong tradition in which grass roots organizations play an important role in providing welfare services to specific groups of citizens, like elderly people, socially and economically deprived people or young adults. It is the community itself that provides assistance and support and not the state. As mentioned before, the big cut back operations in especially European countries forced many governments to stop offering state-funded and public-organized help and support activities on the one hand. On the other hand governments stimulated new forms of social innovation which built upon community driven services.
- A horizontal shift toward the citizen as a co-producer of government policies or government services. Governments increasingly call upon citizens to help them or ask them to participate in the development and implementation of public services and public policies. For instance, farmers are being asked to fulfill specific tasks when monitoring the water levels in the little rivers that cross their farmland, or they are asked to fulfill a number of tasks in the maintenance of the dikes of the rivers that cross their land.

From these shifts we can derive four conclusions. First, what we see is that central government has lost its significance, due to the upward, downward and horizontal shifts in governance that favor international government, local and regional government and functional government. Second, we see a shift from the public toward the private sector: companies, societal organizations and citizens. As a result of this process collective decision-making has been privatized, while at the same time private decision-making has increasingly become more public (Lindblom, 1977). For instance, the decisions that private water cleaning companies make can affect public health, while they try to reduce costs and aim for lower quality. Third, not only have the amount of involved organizations or actors increased, but also interdependency between these organizations and actors has increased, which adds to the complexity of governing. Fourth, and as a result of these shifts "the state is being hollowed out" (Rhodes, 1997:17). Last but not least, this hollowing out of the state is also compensated for by the emergence of all kinds of new organizational but hybrid arrangements in which public and private organizations and actors collaborate. This implies that hybridity is another essential aspect of the governing challenge of modern societies. Given these conclusions we can say that not only has power in society shifted from the center to other places, but also that this power has even, more than before, been split up.

Politics and policies in changing society

In this section we describe a number of vital transformations in society nowadays that not only challenge the effectiveness and efficiency but also the legitimacy of the way in which collective decision-making processes take place; collective decision-making processes that deal with all kinds of societal challenges. In doing so decision-makers have to balance different values against each other, like the balance between efficiency and security, freedom and equality, efficacy versus support. Our overview has shown that the idea that societies can be governed from one super-ordinated governing center – which are state institutions – has to be put into perspective. Government is just one of many actors, while at the same time government is not an entity but is also a variety of all kinds of organizations which act at different levels. We have observed that we live in a complex society which is organized around a variety of all kinds of highly specialized organizations that are rather autonomous on the one hand. On the other hand they are rather dependent or interdependent on each other. At the same time we see that these organizations operate at different levels, while the decisions that are taken at the local level may have effects at the national or even international level and vice versa. Dependency and interdependency not only affects organizations but also the levels at which these organizations act: they are also interdependent and closely interconnected. An important force that deepens the nature of these interdependencies is the pervasiveness of information and communication technologies that support the processing of information, knowledge and communications. As a result our present society can be seen as a collection of flows and nodes that operate at a local and global level.

This complexity has not only a structural nature but also a cultural one. Due to the fact that our institutions have lost their significance and the diminished role of ideology, we see that people have become freer to make their own choices: as a consumer but also as a citizen or as a voter. The result is a process of cultural differentiation in which a variety of different and fluid lifestyles (and flexible combinations of them) is being embraced. This process of cultural differentiation also influences the way in which people attach added value to the role that politics plays in modern society. Moreover, this process of cultural differentiation is also being strengthened by the fact that in a highly organized and specialized world, each organization and their representatives have – in this multitude of organizations – rather narrow perspectives on how to handle challenges, given the specificity of their task and competences. This also colors the way in which they look at societal challenges and the role of politics.

The increased levels of structural and cultural complexity influence the governing capacity of government and the central role of politics in dealing with societal challenges. At the same time, we see that citizens and all kinds of societal groups have rather high expectations regarding the governing or problem solving capacity of politics and government, also in relation to the management of all kinds of risks. Citizens expect to live in a world free of risks, so that they can enjoy life, so that they can develop themselves. As a result we live in a society in which there is not a real political and public debate about the risks that our modern life inevitably has.

1.5 Outlook of this book

Water management has been the central topic of this first chapter. By making use of a number of examples in this field we showed what the essence of politics, policy making and governance is. We also showed that, if we want to understand the challenges with which policy makers are confronted, it is important to take into account a number of social, economic and political transformations that take place. Given this starting point, the next step is to go deeper into the nature of the policy processes that are closely related to the political challenges that modern societies are facing. We will make this next step along three lines.

The first line, starting in the next chapter, argues that policy processes refer to different meanings that are important in politics and society, when dealing with societal challenges. These meanings also refer to different bodies of knowledge that have been acquired as well as to different research traditions and puzzles in policy studies. When policy makers develop and implement plans, information and knowledge is important in order to get a better understanding about the causes and effects of the rising of water levels in the sea or in rivers. Given this knowledge and information they are able to take measures in a planned and deliberate manner as well as to monitor the effect of these measures. Rationality is therefore an important characteristic of policy processes. However, the actions that are taken also affect the interests and positions of a variety of stakeholders. As said before, the creation of flooding areas so that river water can be stored will affect the interests of farmers if they have to give up their farmland. Given these different interests, all kinds of actors try to influence the content and course of the policy process by making use of their power. This illustrates that the nature of policy making is also political. However, behind these interests we see that values play an important role, also given the idea that politics has to deal with the binding allocation of values. This implies that policies and policy processes are in essence normative processes. In doing so, substantive values play a role, such as efficiency, effectiveness, security, equity or freedom. For instance, how to achieve a balance between water safety on the one hand and efficiency on the other hand, when discussing the costs and benefits of the heightening of river and channel dikes. Procedural values also play a role. The values refer to the way in which decisions have to be taken, how this process has to be organized in order to have binding policies, for instance when looking at the support for the measures to be taken, the transparency of the decision-making process or the degree in which all interests have been able to participate (Moore, 1995). Last but not least policy making is also about meaning and sense-making. In doing so they are culturally or even institutionally embedded. Policy making is also about how to make sense of the challenges that the rising level of the sea represents as well as how to convince people that the actions that are proposed make sense. In this sense-making process, framing, by making use of language and images, plays an important role. Policy making is about creating a common grammar among different actors so that they are able to create a shared understanding about what is happening and how to proceed. For instance, the title of the Dutch water management plan (as mentioned earlier) "give space to the river" is a way of sense-making by showing that it is important to frame the water management policies in a completely different way. At the same time it is important to understand that this sense-making process does not take place in a vacuum, but that it is influenced by all kinds of well established, grown practices that come forward in vested habits, ways of thinking, roles, procedures, routines and all kinds of systems. Hence, in the next chapter (Chapter 2) we show that, if we really want to understand the complexity of policy processes, we need to break up these policy processes, by acknowledging that in these processes different meanings simultaneously play a role: it is about being rational, being political in terms of serving specific interests, it is about values and it is about sense-making.

The second line that is being developed in this book follows the different phases of the policy circle. In Chapter 3 we pay attention to the agenda setting process and in Chapter 4 we address the development of public policies and the decision-making process. Chapter 5 focuses on the implementation of public policies while Chapter 6 draws our attention to the evaluation of public policies. In each chapter we will show what relevant insights are from a rational, political, normative and cultural perspective. For instance, when talking about the evaluation of public policies we show how the evaluation process can be filled in from a rational, political, normative and cultural perspective. We show the relevant issues that are addressed by these different perspectives.

The third line of reasoning is that, when looking at the policy process and going through all the phases of the cycle, policy processes are all about learning and change. The development and implementation of policy programs aims at changing a situation. The evaluation of policy programs focuses on trying to understand whether the outcomes of the actions that have been taken actually brought a change in the way that policy makers had in mind. Hence, it is important to pay attention to a number of issues that tell us something about the learning capacity of policy processes and policy sectors. This learning capacity is an indication of the way in which policy processes and policy sectors are able to adapt themselves to changing conditions, to all kinds of societal, economic and political developments and even transformations. The ability to do so also influences the legitimacy of politics and policy processes. In Chapter 7 we address the issue of policy learning and policy change, while in Chapter 8 we end our book with an exposé regarding the legitimacy of policy making and the challenges that it evokes for policy sciences.

2

Four perspectives on the policy process

💡 LEARNING OBJECTIVES

After reading this chapter you should be able to:

- Understand the *multiplicity* of factors that shape the policy process, including rationality, power, institutions and images.

- Understand and apply four theoretical perspectives on the policy process; the *rational perspective*, the *political perspective*, the *cultural perspective*, and the *institutionalist perspective*.

- Compare these four perspectives in terms of *different aspects of the policy process*, including explanatory mechanisms, human behavior, policy instruments, evaluation criteria, the role of knowledge, the structure of the policy process and the role of politics.

2.1 Introduction

Shortage of donor organs is a policy issue in almost all countries of the world. Increasing the number of people that decide to donate their organs after they have died might save the lives of many people or might contribute significantly to the quality of life of others. At first sight, this policy issue may present itself as a simple, technical issue: a problem that needs to be solved for which policy instruments need to be developed and implemented. For instance, people could be forced, by law, to donate their organs. However, every government that tries to do so will get confronted with the multiple faces of public policy. Soon, it will discover that people have strong feelings about the integrity of their bodies after death, be it from religious, ideological or private reasons. And willingly or unwillingly, government will become a participant in a network of actors that all feel they have a say in the process of organ donations: religious groups, medical specialists, representatives of patients, political parties and loads of others. Actors represent different interests and in order to protect these interests they try to influence the discussion about how to proceed. They also frame their arguments in a specific way, for instance in terms of the number of people that could be saved if more people were willing to donate their organs. The power and resources of these actors influence the interactions in these networks. Finally, a government will also see itself confronted with all kinds of formal and informal rules that limit the possibilities to implement creative and innovative solutions. Rules that, for instance, refer to legal norms and constitutional values that safeguard someone's free will.

This short example illustrates the multiple faces of public policy. In this chapter, we introduce four alternative approaches to public policy: a rational, political, cultural and institutional approach. In the practice of public policy, these approaches are often intermingled. However, distinguishing the multiple perspectives of public policies may contribute to the abilities of policy makers, students and scholars to adequately describe, analyse and explain the complexity of public policy processes. Policy problems are often multi-faced problems, because they are socially constructed problems (Morgan, 1986; Stone, 2001). All kinds of actors give different meanings to the problems at hand as well as to the approaches that are being looked for. Very often these meanings refer to different bodies of knowledge, to different theories that try to describe and explain the course, content and outcomes of public policy processes; bodies of knowledge and theories that try to catch the essence of what the nature of public policy is. However, behind these bodies of knowledge lie – implicitly or explicitly – different views and assumptions about how society and politics functions, and how groups and people operate when dealing with societal challenges that touch upon a society as being a political community (Burrell and Morgan, 1979; Stone, 2001). That is why we try to catch these different meanings (and assumptions that lie behind them) by making use of four analytical perspectives. The use of these perspectives enables us to analytically unravel the complexity of the different meanings that actors attach to public policy. One advantage of making use of this multi-perspective approach is that it may offer participants in processes of public policy new concepts, new tools and frames of reference to understand and use the multiple faces of public policy. In doing so they might increase their professional capacities to participate in these processes. Policy makers are often stuck in one specific approach. For instance, because they adhere to a more rational approach, they are not willing or able to see how the interests and power but also grown practices shape the content, course and outcomes of specific policy processes. As we will discuss later (in the chapter on policy design and in the last chapter, when discussing the characteristics of the reflective policy analyst) contemporary policy making can be seen as playing chess at different tables. Each table represents a different set of meaning (thereby referring to different bodies of knowledge as brought together in the four perspectives). The challenge for contemporary policy makers is that they possess an open mindset in order to deal with these different meanings and that they are aware of the paradoxes that these different meanings generate.

In this chapter, we introduce four different approaches to public policy that guide our explorations of the different elements of the policy process in the chapters that will follow. In section 2.2 we introduce the analytical framework through which we compare the four approaches. After that, we elaborate on each of the approaches more in-depth. Section 2.3 deals with the rational approach, section 2.4 with the political approach, section 2.5 with the cultural approach and section 2.6 with the institutional approach. In section 2.7 we offer a brief overview of the differences between these approaches and try to sketch a way to integrate them.

2.2 Comparing policy perspectives: an analytical framework

In this book, we distinguish four different approaches to the policy process. Of course, we are not the first to advocate a multiple-perspective approach to public and political issues. Ground-breaking has been the work of Graham Allison (see Allison and Zelikow, 1971, 1999) who used three different perspectives to analyse and explain the decision-making that took place during the Cuban Missile Crisis, one of the most shocking events in international relations. Also in organizational sciences the work of Gareth Morgan (1986) can be seen as an illustration of this approach, because he tries to understand the complexity of modern organizations by making use of different metaphors. Each metaphor represents a different image of an organization, while at the same time the complexity of the organization cannot be reduced by just one image. However, we will turn to the complexity of public policy processes. Building upon Allison and Zelikow (1999) and inspired by many other authors (see for instance Abma and In 't Veld, 2001; Bobrow and Dryzek, 1987; Stone, 2001; Fischer, 2005) in this book we distinguish the following four perspectives on public policy:

- The *rational perspective*. This perspective can be considered as a "primer" for the other approaches. It considers public policy as a means to solve societal problems. The scientific quest is to identify factors that contribute to effective and efficient problem solving. When these factors have been identified, policy makers can look for instruments and actions that help to tackle the problem. Information and knowledge play an important role in trying to understand what the problem at hand is and what kind of action would probably work. Practically, the application of scientific information and rational methods of decision-making are considered as a means for effective and efficient policies. This perspective is also described in the literature as the objectivist or the positivist perspective, as it involves a positive approach in terms of societal engineering based on sound knowledge and information.

- The *political perspective*. This perspective focuses on the power struggles between (inter) dependent stakeholders in a policy domain; struggles that are focused on protecting interests or developing common interests. In doing so stakeholders make use of different resources and develop all kinds of strategies. Support from these stakeholders is a necessary condition for effective policies. In scholarly terms, this approach tries to explain the conditions that contribute to support from stakeholders. From a practical perspective, this approach articulates the importance of political and strategic skills.

- The *cultural perspective*. The cultural perspective acknowledges that our perspective on the world is biased by our past experiences, beliefs, values and positions. Interaction processes are about sense-making: creating a shared understanding of the world in which we live by looking at the (different or convergent) frames that actors develop. This implies that in the cultural perspective public policy is an endeavor to bridge the diverging ideas about policy issues and integrate them into a shared understanding. For policy scholars, the cultural approach highlights the importance of language, symbols, visuals and interactions in policy processes in framing issues. For practitioners it offers insights in the backgrounds of diverging ideas in policy processes and may be helpful in developing framing strategies to deal with these diverging ideas in an open and equal dialogue. This perspective is also sometimes described in the literature as the social-constructivist perspective.

- The *institutional perspective*. Institutions can be defined as the formal and informal rules that affect or even guide actors' behavior, for instance if we look at the routines, procedures but also grown habits that have to be followed. These rules are often formulated to protect specific values that we consider important. Policy processes are socially and historically embedded processes. They are embedded in different and linked institutions, like the welfare state or the "Rechtstaat". Public policies can be considered as elements in the evolution and confirmation of these rules. Policy defines appropriate and inappropriate behavior and therefore affects the effectiveness and efficiency of policies. Many scholars are interested in the relation between different sets of rules (which can also be seen as institutions) and policy performance. For practitioners in the policy process the institutional perspective helps to identify and perhaps even overcome the limits these informal and formal rules represent, when implementing new policies or adjusting existing policies.

To be able to systematically compare these four approaches, this book distinguishes seven characteristics that will be used to highlight the distinct features of each of these approaches. These characteristics are:

- Dominant *explanatory mechanism*. This concerns the basic explanations that are usually provided by the approach for the way policy processes evolve.
- Perspective on *human behavior*. The basic explanation in the previous characteristic usually is based on a more abstract picture of what people are and why they behave like they do. Revealing this picture is helpful for characterizing each of these approaches.
- *Policy instruments*. Different perspectives on the policy process and human behavior also lead to different tools for interventions. Each of "our" perspectives offer guidance on tools that may be successful in specific settings and on the way these tools need to be implemented.
- *Evaluation*. The perspectives also differ in their perceptions of what successful policies are. They do this on the basis of different criteria. We will discuss the different criteria for each of the approaches.
- The role of *knowledge* and *information*. In each of the perspectives, scientific and policy-relevant information is an important asset. However, its meaning varies between the different perspectives.
- The *course of the policy process*. The perspective of the policy process varies between our four approaches. Is policy development to be considered as a linear, sequential process of different stages or is it much more complex and random?
- The role of *politics*. Finally, the perception of the role of politics and politicians varies between the four perspectives. This is closely connected to the issue of the primacy of politics in democratic regimes.

The next sections discuss in detail the four approaches of public policy according to the characteristics that have been defined above. We would like to highlight that the approaches that are presented are ideal-typical approaches. Accordingly, we discuss the approaches as such. This implies that our descriptions are aimed at discussing and explaining the differences between the approaches, rather than presenting all the ins and outs of the approaches.

BOX 2.1

KNOWLEDGE "OF" THE POLICY PROCESSES VERSUS KNOWLEDGE "IN" THE POLICY PROCESS (LASSWELL, 1951)

Harold Lasswell was one of the founding fathers of the policy sciences. He drew a distinction between "knowledge of the policy process" and "knowledge for or in the policy process" (Lasswell, 1951). The modern policy sciences have their roots in a strong policy-orientation, or emphasis on "knowledge for" public policy. However, as Lasswell but also DeLeon (1997) and Radin (2000) show, the policy sciences evolved in a more academic research field for knowledge of public policy. Initially, this involved a primarily rationalist or "positivist" orientation (Dunn 1994). This is why notions such as the policy cycle but also strict ideas on how to define means–ends relations and how to evaluate policy effectiveness, have been so important to the genesis of this research field.

Especially since the 1990s (for instance Fischer and Forester 1993, Pierson 1994, Baumgartner and Jones 2002, Sabatier 1998), the academic development of "knowledge of the policy process" generated more varied perspectives on public policy. The four perspectives presented in this book (rationalism, institutionalism, political perspective and culturalism) provide a current overview of this development.

However, besides being an indication of academic maturity of the policy sciences as a research field, these four perspectives or "traditions" are also important for two other reasons. First, the growing complexity of societal developments (see Chapter 1, the risk society, network society, hollow society, liquid society) also requires a more complex theoretical toolkit for understanding these developments. After having become aware that the rationalist account cannot explain policy processes fully, the development of political/institutionalist/culturalist perspectives has helped to grasp some of the complexities of policy making in current society. Thus, the multi-perspective orientation on public policy that is presented in this book is key to "knowledge of policy".

Second, this complexity also has implications for "knowledge for policy", as policy practitioners are also faced with this growing complexity of societal developments. Being able to look at policy and governance dilemmas from various perspectives can help resolve problems and promote reflexivity and innovation. In Chapter 8 we will look in more detail at how working with the four perspectives can help the reflective policy practitioner.

2.3 The rational perspective on public policy

In many handbooks of the policy process the rational model serves as a straw man, often depicted as a caricature. This straw man serves as a means to justify the superiority of alternative approaches by pointing at the weakness of the rational model. However, as we will show in this book, the rational model may offer useful insights in specific situations, while in other situations it might suffer from shortcomings. Therefore, we need to assess this model by its merits rather than writing it off as naïve and outdated. To be able to assess its merits, we will discuss its basic assumptions.

Dominant explanatory mechanism

In this perspective, policy and policy processes are connected to the realization of goals. Cochran and Malone's (1995:5-6) definition of public policy reflects this: "Public policy consists of political decisions from implementing programs to achieve societal goals." Other scholars also depart from this perspective in their definition of public policy. For instance, Hoogerwerf (1989:20) defined policy as "the realization of goals through the application of means according to specific time choices." Supporters of this model focus on the final assumptions in public policies: goals and means are the ground structure of public policies. Politically determined goals refer to a number of societal challenges with which political communities are wrestling (Stone, 2001). The fulfillment of goals is the reason why policy makers do what they do. Goal rationality can therefore be considered as the dominant explanatory mechanism in this approach. Goals constitute the starting point of policy processes. Once these goals are formulated the next step is to explore how these goals can be accomplished, in terms of what actions have to be selected to contribute to the achievement of a goal. For instance, in order to reduce the shortage of donor organs to prevent people from dying at an earlier stage when suffering kidney or liver diseases, then a goal could be to increase the numbers of people that are willing to donate their organs after their death by 10 percent.

Perspective on human behavior

With goal rationality being the guiding explanatory mechanism in the rational model of public policy, it is no surprise that human beings are considered as rational actors in this perspective. Their actions are based on rational calculations of the costs and benefits of alternatives that contribute to the realization of their goals. Weber (1922/1928) has labeled this form of rationality as "Zweckrationalität" or instrumental rationality (see Campbell, 1981). In the rational perspective on public policy, the policy process consists of actors that behave as rational actors according to the model of the *homo economicus*. Building upon Allison and Zelikow (1999:18) the following elements are characteristic for decision-making by the homo economicus:

- The agent has a pay-off function which ranks all possible sets of consequences in terms of his or her values and objectives.
- The agent must choose among a set of alternatives displayed before him or her in a particular situation.
- To each alternative is attached a set of consequences or outcomes that will ensure that that particular alternative is chosen.
- Rational choice consists simply of selecting that alternative whose consequences rank highest in the decision-maker's pay-off function.

The *homo economicus* thus departs from the goals he or she wishes to realize. In the example of the donor organ case, a rational policy maker will scan and select possible alternatives to raise the number of donations. For instance, he will see if he can persuade people to sign a declaration in which he/she states that after his/her death organs can be given to somebody else who is in need of them. This is called the opting in system: people are not obliged to give their organs but they do so on a voluntary basis. An information campaign can be designed to inform or convince people to do so and sign the declaration. Or, a policy maker can choose to make use of an opting out system: in general people are obliged to give their organ for medical purposes, but they are given the opportunity in advance to say no. A policy maker will try to assess what the benefits and costs of both systems are in order to increase the number of organs to be donated. He or she will choose that alternative which contributes to the achievement of defined goals as much as possible against the lowest costs.

However, hardly ever are the assumptions of full rationality met in real life decision-making. Rather than therefore abandoning the model of rationality, Herbert Simon (1961) introduced the concept of bounded rationality. He claimed that there were several limitations to making rational decisions. Limits to the amount of information, to the amount of time and to the information-processing capacity prevent the making of fully rational decisions. These limits refrain people, organizations, policy makers and politicians from knowing all the alternatives, from being able to assess all the costs and benefits of all alternatives and to select the best alternative to reach their goals. Rather, people tend to formulate a set of minimal conditions that an alternative has to meet, and once an alternative has met all these conditions, it is selected. Simon (1961) presents his "satisficing" mode of bounded rational decision-making as an alternative to full rationality while preserving the basic assumption of goal-oriented behavior that underlies rational approaches. People tend to behave as rationally as possible when taking into account the limits for full rationality. Therefore, Simon's work should be considered as an amendment to the rational model, rather than as a critic to it (see Birkland, 2001).

The idea of the *homo economicus* also presupposes a single, unitary actor that defines goals, assesses and selects policy alternatives and implements these. In doing so, government is seen as a whole, functioning as an organic body. Governments are perceived as actors that steer societal processes on the basis of the goals that have been formulated. The rational model expresses the idea of the "makeable" society and the capacity to control and manage societal processes and developments (van Gunsteren, 1976; Scott, 1998). These developments and processes are controlled by a sovereign, unitary central actor that formulates policies. This actor has a reliable system of means and tools at its disposal to communicate the policies to other public and private organizations, citizens and other stakeholders. Not only is it possible to communicate these measures in a clear and understandable way. The people that need to implement these measures are loyal and their acts conform to the message that is given. The same is true for society and all kinds of societal groups that are involved: they follow the instructions. If they fail to do so, government is able to enforce the rules, because it makes use of adequate systems of monitoring and control.

Policy instruments

Goal rationality as a guiding principle affects the way policy instruments are perceived in this perspective. This can be observed in at least three ways. First, goal rationality implies that the actions that have to be taken have to be programmed and planned. In order to achieve specific goals, it is important to specify what has to be done by whom and in what order (Dunsire, 1978). In doing so, rather broad goals are translated into more concrete and operational sub-goals and actions that have to be performed. That is why planning and programming are important activities in the rational approach (van Gunsteren, 1976). For instance, in our example of the organ donation case, the option to implement an opting out system, in which everybody in principle is viewed as a donor unless he or she clearly states that he or she will not, sets a whole set of actions and instruments in motion in order to achieve this. For instance, it requires that a law is drafted to regulate the system. Furthermore, citizens have to be informed about the consequences of this opting out system, so an information campaign has to be organized. In order to give people a chance to play no part in the system, their wish needs to be registered. Hence, a registration system has to be implemented.

Second, the actions that have to be performed in this approach imply that policy makers have to devote their attention to the design and selection of policy instruments that they want to use. Effective policy will be reached through the application of well-designed policy instruments, and, oppositely, failing policy may be explained by inadequate policy instruments. The selection of policy instruments may be considered from an engineering perspective, in which the policy makers possess a set of instruments from a "toolbox" (Hood, 1983). Policy instruments are considered as the neutral tools of the policy makers that can be applied to realize the formulated goals. While choosing a tool, policy makers take into account the strengths and weaknesses of tools that are available, given the goal to be accomplished and the context in which it has to be applied.

Third, within the rational model, three main types of policy instruments are usually distinguished: regulative, economic and communicative instruments, sometimes illustratively labeled as sticks, carrots and sermons (Bemelmans-Videc, Rist and Vedung, 1998). Regulative instruments may be defined as "measures taken by governmental units to influence people by means of formulated rules and directives which mandate receivers to act in accordance with what is ordered in these rules and directives" (Bemelmans-Videc, Rist and Vedung, 2003:10). Economic instruments involve the handing out or the taking away of resources while the subjects of the instruments are not obligated to perform the actions at which the instrument is directed (Bemelmans-Videc, Rist and Vedung, 2003:11). The third type of policy instrument attempts to influence people through the transfer of knowledge, the communication of reasoned argument, and persuasion (Bemelmans-Videc, Rist and Vedung, 2003:11).

Policy evaluation

The importance of goal rationality implies that the assessment of policies particularly is based on the extent to which the policy goals have been reached. Many authors acknowledge that effectiveness and efficiency are the basic criteria for evaluating public policy, specifically from a rational perspective (see for example, Nagel, 1986). Some authors add a third element, for instance consistency (Ringeling, 1993) or equity (Nagel, 1986). As we will meet many of the other criteria in the other perspectives in this chapter, here we focus on effectiveness and efficiency as the two most important evaluation criteria in the rational perspective.

According to Nagel (1986:99), effectiveness of public policies can be defined as the extent to which the policies are achieving the benefits they are supposed to achieve plus any unanticipated side benefits. This presupposes that the goals of a policy are clear and are formulated in such a way that evaluators are able to assess to what extent these goals are actually fulfilled. However, indicators that are used for measuring the success of a policy often are the product of various, intertwined and complicated causal chains. This makes it difficult to assess the contribution of a policy to that indicator.

In general, two forms of efficiency may be distinguished: transformational and distributional efficiency. Transformational efficiency refers to the relation between costs and benefits of a policy intervention. In this meaning, efficiency is a measure of how economically resources (funds, expertise, time and so on) are converted into results. The term "results" refers to the output, outcome or impact of a policy intervention (OECD DAC, 2002; see also Nagel, 1986). Distributional efficiency refers to the impact of a policy program on society as a whole (see Posner, 2007). A program is considered efficient if it makes at least one individual in society better off without making anyone worse off (Pareto-efficient) or if the individuals who are better off can satisfactorily compensate those who are worse off (Kaldor–Hicks efficient). Both interpretations may be used within the rational perspective although the first is more common in policy evaluations.

Role of knowledge and information

Because rationality is a key concept, in the rational perspective much significance is given to the role of knowledge – preferably scientific knowledge – and information as well to the role of information and communication technologies. Building upon the ideas of the Enlightenment of progress and control of society, knowledge and information are considered as the fundamentals for effective policy making (Wilensky, 1967; van Gunsteren, 1976). This becomes especially manifest in the stages of policy formulation and policy implementation.

In the stage of policy formulation, knowledge and information serve two goals. First, it is required to process-trace the causal mechanisms that lead to the occurrence of a societal problem and to identify factors that may be receptive to policy interventions (Pawson, 2006). The more insight in these causal processes policy makers have, the better they will be able to intervene effectively in these processes. Second, knowledge is useful to predict adequately the impact of different interventions. Evidence-based knowledge ensures the selection of "proven practices"; policy instruments that have proven to be successful after thorough scientific analysis.

In the stage of policy implementation, knowledge and information are important to monitor the policies' progress. The behavior of citizens and officials that have a role in the implementation process need to be observed and, if necessary, the policy needs to be adjusted to enhance its performance. In the stage of policy implementation, governments act as information processors (Zincke, 1990:192). This perspective embraces the notion that knowledge in the policy process presents the power to produce new outcomes that were not previously attainable. Dutton and Danziger (1982:13) in this regard speak of "managerial rationalism". Through the application of large-scale and sophisticated IT-systems, governments can process ever-larger amounts of information and thus overcome the limited cognitive capacities of individuals and organizations. This enables better informed, more rational and therefore more effective policies. From this perspective, knowledge and information are seen as neutral and objective tools that increase the performance of public policies.

The course of the policy process

In the rational perspective, policy making is considered as a linear and cyclical process that consists of several sequential stages or phases. Sabatier (2007:6) speaks of the "stages heuristic". To solve policy problems, the policy process moves through the stages of agenda-setting, policy design, decision-making, policy implementation, enforcement and policy evaluation. For effective and efficient policies, each of these stages should be followed sequentially. A lot of research has searched for the factors and actors that play a role in each of these stages. Moreover, the rational perspective seeks conditions that contribute to an optimal performance in each of these stages, resulting in optimally efficient and effective policies.

The general idea is that once a societal challenge gets enough political attention, it becomes an issue on the political agenda. Issues that are part of the political agenda may lead to the development of a policy program which has to be decided upon in order to give it political authority. Once this program has been sanctioned, it will be implemented and it will be enforced. In order to see if the program is effective and efficient, it will be evaluated, when looking at its outcomes. Given the assessment of these outcomes, the program can again be an issue on the political agenda, for instance, because it has to be terminated or because it has to be changed in order to enhance its effectivity. It is this cycle that gives order to the different policy processes, thereby showing how the quality of each stage adds to the quality of the next stage. For instance, vague goals that have been formulated in the policy design phase and decision-making goals, because of the controversy of a specific issue, may lead to vague measures and actions that have to be implemented.

The role of politics

The goal rationality also has implications for the role of politics in the rational model. The rational perspective departs from the idea of the primacy of politics. There is a sharp division between "politics" and "administration" (Wilson, 1887). Politicians are the principles that guide the bureaucratic process and that follow from ideological goals. The stage of decision-making involves the political acceptance of ideas and alternatives that may have been prepared by civil servants, but that do not hold any power as long as democratically elected political officials have not formally accepted them. It is politics and the political nature of the decision-making process, which involves democratically elected officials that are given a mandate to choose, that renders authority to a policy program.

Within the rational perspective on public policy, constitutional as well as democratic arguments require a distinction between politics and administration. Constitutional, because the separation of powers is an important building block for the so-called "Rechtsstaat". The legislative power (giving political authority to a policy program) is separated from the executive power (developing and implementing a policy program) to prevent the abuse of power. Democratic, because setting policy goals involves the allocation of values within society. This can only be legitimate if the officials that have a mandate from the population allocate these values.

2.4 The political perspective on public policy

As we have stated in the introduction of this chapter, public policy is not only a matter of rationality. It is also about balancing different, often competing values and the different interests that often lay behind a specific interpretation of these values. A decision might be rational from a specific set of values; that is, the right of self-determination in the case of organ donation is rational from a value set in which liberty plays an important role. Contrastingly, from a perspective of solidarity or justice, a system of "donation unless stated otherwise" might be considered as rational. The political perspective acknowledges the fact that governmental decisions inevitably are value-loaded. Therefore, power – rather than ratio – is used to protect interests and positions and to advocate specific values in the way policy problems and solutions are defined. These ideas take a central place in the political perspective on public policy.

The dominant explanatory mechanism

An important fundamental of the political approach is that policy processes are characterized by a continuous struggle between different, competing values (Lindblom, 1965). Conflicts of interests characterize the policy process, rather than harmonious problem solving. The power conflicts and political strategies of the stakeholders therefore much more determine the development, decision-making and implementation of policy processes than the rational process of inquiry and deliberating. To influence public policies, stakeholders need power: the capacity to realize desired behavior. Power always is a relational concept: one actor is able to influence other actors' behaviors (Dahl, 1961).

The earliest versions of a political perspective on public policy depart from the idea that the power struggles primarily are between different political elites. This idea has been introduced by Dahl (1961) and radically challenged the idea that the governance of society was in the hands of a single, homogenous politically and economically powerful group: "*the*" elite. In addition, the idea of neo-corporatism as it has been introduced by Schmitter and Lehmbruch (1979) might be said to specify the origins of the different elites. Employers and their organized interests, employees and their trade unions, and governments together are involved in a continuous struggle between socio-economic interests, between labor and capital, between political "left" and "right", and so on. Characteristic of the neo-corporatist approach is that public policy is developed in institutionalized arenas for negotiations between the triangle of employees, employers and government. Negotiation and exchange are used as peaceful means to bridge conflicts of interests that may seem unbridgeable. The government's role in this process may be considered as process supervisor and guardian of the formal and informal rules of conduct that guide this process.

With this, the uni-centric perspective that characterizes the rational approach is traded for a multi-actor perspective or a poly-centric perspective (Teisman, 2000). Not only are policy processes determined by the political strategies of the actors involved, the poly-centric perspective also highlights the presence of multiple, often competitive, venues that all may involve the same policy issue (Baumgartner and Jones, 1993). As a result, policy processes take place in an arena or in different and often linked arenas (Lasswell, 1958; Lowi, 1964; Allison and Zelikow, 1971; Crozier and Friedberg, 1980). In such an arena all kinds of power-driven interactions (like negotiation, coercion, persuasion, compromise) take place between different stakeholders. They deploy all kinds of strategies to safeguard or advocate their interests.

Building upon this perspective, since the 1990s the concept of policy networks has gained popularity in public administration and policy sciences. A policy network may be defined as a social system in which mutually dependent actors develop processes of interaction and communication that show some sense of sustainability and that are aimed at policy programs or policy issues (see Marsh and Rhodes, 1992; Kickert, Klijn and Koppenjan, 1997; Klijn and Koppenjan, 2012). In the policy network approach, the division of power and interests varies among a policy domain or policy issue. Within a specific policy domain and around a specific issue, a network may be observed that consists of a wide variety of actors. The nature of the dependencies between them generate all kinds of strategic interactions of actors in the network. These interactions – as well as the formal and informal rules that guide the interaction processes – influence the content, course and outcomes of the policy process. The dominant explanatory mechanisms in this perspective may be labeled as "power", "dependency" and "interests".

For instance, in an Australian report regarding organ and tissue donation, the following stakeholders were identified. The process of donating and transplanting organs in Australia is complex and involves a large number of people and organizations that carry out different roles (Thomas and Klapdor, 2008). Apart from individual donors and recipients and their families themselves as well as all kinds of political parties, there is a large organ transplantation sector and many mechanisms in place to allow for transplantation to occur, like:

- Regulatory bodies, such as the Therapeutic Goods Administration (TGA), are responsible for regulation and licensing, and the National Health and Medical Research Council (NHMRC) provides advice on ethical issues.
- Professional colleges and societies are involved in developing clinical guidelines and representing health workers. Professional education programs are developed through agencies such as the Australasian Donor Awareness Program (ADAPT).
- Eye and tissue banks, which are usually state-based, coordinate the retrieval of eyes, bones, skin, heart valves and musculoskeletal tissue.
- State-based organ donation agencies are responsible for promoting and coordinating organ donation within their jurisdictions.
- Transplant centers within hospitals are specialized locations where transplantation of certain organs can occur.
- Organ donation-related data collection is primarily undertaken through the Australia and New Zealand Organ Donation Registry (ANZOD).

ANZOD draws together information collected through organ-specific registries.

- The Australian Organ Donor Register (AODR) and the NSW Roads and Traffic Authority act as registers of consent for the donation of organs following death.
- Community organizations, including peak bodies and foundations, develop awareness campaigns, while other disease-specific groups such as Kidney Health Australia are also involved in promoting organ donation (National Clinical Taskforce on Organ and Tissue Donation, Final Report, 2008).

However, given the shortages of donors, we can also enlarge the policy network by looking at all kinds of organizations that play a role in the international trade of organs, like international health and police organizations.

In the network perspective on policy processes a horizontal perspective prevails, because the idea is that due to the interdependency relations between the involved actors, there is no central actor that is able to impose its will. However, this assumption can be questioned. Government is just one of many actors, but its position still differs from other non-state actors. It can still use specific resources (authority, knowledge, information or money) to intervene in a rather hierarchical way. Government has still the authority to draft and impose laws and regulations in order to intervene so that they can for instance control the access to or distribution of resources across the network. That is why several scholars talk about "networked governance in the shadow of hierarchy" (Scharpf, 1994; Börzel and Risse, 2010; Durant and Warber, 2001).

Perspective on human behavior

In the political perspective, human behavior is guided by self-interest. Actors' strategies therefore are aimed at protecting and advancing their own interests. Because of the unequal access to and distribution of resources, actors rely on other actors to reach their goals. This creates dependency between actors. Pfeffer and Salancik (1978) argued that dependency emerges because some actors can control the access, availability and allocation of scarce resources that are vital for other actors to pursue their goals. Resources may be financial resources, but also capital goods, information and authority. The unequal distribution of scarce resources leads to strategic processes of interaction. Conflict, persuasion, coercion, negotiation, exchange, compromise and coalition behavior are patterns of interaction that may be observed from this perspective, rather than collective problem solving.

The public policy process is about balancing actors' self-interests and the general interest. However, from a political perspective it is always unclear what the general interest is and how it is to be pursued. Following Stone (2003), this requires the careful design of democratically legitimized processes of deliberation in which the balancing of interests and values can take place. Power and influence determine the outcome of this process. The public interest in this vision may be regarded as the outcome of a process that is considered as legitimate by the stakeholders that are involved in the process (Luhmann, 1969).

Policy instruments

In the political perspective, policy instruments are not considered as the neutral and objective tools of government as the rational perspective suggests. Policy instruments are considered as sources of power and therefore may be the inputs as well as the outcomes of processes of strategic interactions (Hood, 1983). The design of a policy instrument may strengthen the power position of some actors while weakening that of others, because they also change the nature of dependency in an arena or policy network. As actors usually have a significant amount of freedom in the implementation of policy instruments, their capacity to apply the instrument in a specific situation or not, can be viewed a source of power in itself.

It is important to note that from this perspective not only the application of the policy instrument as such, but also the consecutive shifts in power relations may be an explicit or implicit goal of the policy instrument. Therefore, the design and implementation of policy instruments from a political perspective affects the interaction processes and performance of policy networks. Strategies of network management – the design of the formal and informal rules and relations in policy networks – therefore are considered as important policy instruments in the political perspective (Kickert, Klijn and Koppenjan, 1997). Klijn, Steijn and Edelenbos (2010; Klijn and Koppenjan, 2004) distinguish four types of network management strategies:

- *Connecting strategies.* These strategies are aimed at initiating connections and interactions between stakeholders that are involved in a specific policy issue. This may involve the creation of incentives for co-operation or the removal of barriers for co-operation or mediation.
- *Arranging strategies.* Once the interactions between stakeholders have been initiated, a formal or informal set of arrangements needs to be defined to shape the interactions between stakeholders. This involves the

development of organizational arrangement like project organizations, boards or temporary committees.

- *Content exploration strategies.* Within policy networks, stakeholders should be challenged to discover common ground to bypass their self-interest. Strategies that may be used for this are idea competitions, scenario studies or collecting research and information.
- *Process strategies.* These strategies are aimed at governing the relations between actors. Examples are entry and exit rules and decision-making rules.

Policy evaluation

From the perspective of a single actor, policy will primarily be judged on the extent to which it advances that actor's interests (Allison and Zelikow, 1971; Crozier and Friedberg, 1980). From that perspective an actor will also assess his/her own role: to what extent did the political strategies that he/she applied safeguard or increase his/her interests, his/her power position and the access to vital resources? However, specific interests are also linked to other interests because they are connected to each other in an interdependent network. That is why we can also take into account the perspective of the network itself. From the perspective of the overall network, criteria for successful policies are not so much concerned with the content of the policies, but much more with the process through which they have been designed and implemented. Support, acceptance and legitimacy then become important success criteria for the successful development and implementation of policies within the overall network. More specifically, Koppenjan and Klijn (2004) have defined three types of evaluation criteria for policy process with multiple stakeholders and multiple interests. First, content criteria, which are aimed at the extent to which the actors in the network have managed to build a shared image of the policy issue and to intertwine their individual goals. Second, process criteria, which are aimed at the progress of the process, the absence of blockaders and stagnation in the process, and the openness, transparency and legitimation of the process for third parties. Finally, network criteria, which are aimed at the extent to which the network relations between actors have become durable and embedded in organizational arrangements.

The role of knowledge and information

In the political perspective on public policy, knowledge and information are perceived in terms of "resource politics": knowledge, information and information and communication technologies represent power (Kraemer and King, 1986:492; Homburg, 2000). Knowledge and information are reservoirs of powers that may be used to advocate specific positions and interests in the policy network. Information and knowledge is used to substantiate and legitimize specific claims. The result is that in relation to many policy problems, uncontested knowledge is absent. As there are no final scientific answers to the causes and solutions for many policy problems, the political and strategic use of knowledge and information becomes even more prominent. In the absence of shared conceptions of the causes and solutions, knowledge strategies are aimed at advocating one's own position and challenging that of others. In the political perspective knowledge production and research are politicized as well, so actors have to anticipate on strategic games about the research question, appropriate methods and conclusions (Wildavsky, 1979). However, at the same time it can also be argued, that collaborative knowledge production may contribute to the bridging of conflicts of interests, because a pooled or shared knowledge base is created (Bekkers, 1998).

Perspective on the policy process

In contrast with the idea of a sequential, predictable policy cycle, the political perspective provides a much more dynamic and iterative perspective on the policy process. Three reasons can be given for this.

First, building upon Lindblom's (1959; see also Lindblom and Woodhouse, 1993) seminal work, we may characterize public administration as "the science of muddling through". Lindblom introduced the concept of *incrementalism* to characterize the pace of policy processes from his perspective. Characteristic of incrementalism is that decisions in the public domain hardly ever involve major shifts, based upon a rational analysis of the nature of the problem and a rational estimation of costs and benefits. Usually, small steps forward are taken, steps that follow from previous steps and therefore involve only gradual adjustments of the status quo. In that regard, incrementalism is closely related to Simon's (1961) ideas of bounded rationality: as policy makers – like all decision-makers – are only boundedly rational, they are unable to oversee the full consequences of major decisions and therefore stick to gradual steps forward. Moreover, Lindblom argues that issues of public policy are not only complex because of the causal processes that shape them, but also because of the divergent normative principals from the actors that are involved in them. Balancing the different normative viewpoints of different actors can only take place through careful processes of exchange and interaction, with empathy for winners as well as losers. Characteristic of democratic societies is that there are institutions and rules of behavior that safeguard a peaceful allocation of values. As a consequence, "the intelligence of democracy" (Lindblom, 1965) creates incremental processes of "muddling through" as the preferences, demands and wishes of actors are continuously adjusted to each other.

Second, many studies have shown that the stages of policy design, decision-making, implementation and evaluation as they have been introduced in the previous section, are not sequential at all. In their classical study "Implementation", Pressman and Wildavsky (1973/1984) have shown that the implementation of a politically approved plan is not self-evident at all. Policy implementation takes place in a fragmented and complex network of actors with different interests and perspectives. The interactions of these actors may lead to significant deviations of the intended plan. Policy implementation therefore may be considered as "delayed policy design": a stage in which resources and power may be used to compensate for losses from an earlier stage. It is a new round in the policy process, which offers new chances: policy development in the context of policy implementation.

Finally, the non-linear and even chaotic character of policy processes may be illustrated by the work of Cohen, March and Olsen (1972) who introduced the so-called "garbage can model" of organizational decision-making. Rather than well-defined perceptions of organization problems and solutions that build upon that, organizations may be perceived as a garbage can in which definitions of problems and definitions of solutions freely float around. Internal and external events may create a window of opportunity, in which a specific "fix" between a problem and a solution takes place (see also Kingdon, 1984). These fixes may occur rather randomly rather than through a rational process, for instance, because earlier defined solutions are linked to newly defined problems. This, again, obstructs the idea of sequential stages.

Role of politics

In contrast with the rational perspective, in the political perspective politics and administration are not separate items, but closely intertwined. Political choices are made by all actors in the fragmented, complex policy systems and cannot be retraced to a single, democratically-legitimized authority. Political decisions do not always have an official character; they may also take place in an informal way. In the rational approach, "politics" is located by the formally elected or representative institutions of government: the president, the mayor, the Senate, and so on. In the political approach, these institutions are considered as one of many actors in a policy process. Perhaps they have specific authorities, and therefore they occupy specific power positions, but nonetheless they are just one of many actors (Dahl, 1965; Crenson, 1971). However, given the unequal distribution of scarce resources, these political actors depend on other actors for the realization of their goals. This implies that creating, deciding and implementing public policies is much more an item of collaboration and coproduction of public, private and not-for-profit actors, rather than the singular task of elected politicians and their bureaucratic institutions (Rhodes, 1997; van Kersbergen and van Waarden, 2004). Moreover, these actors, just as any other actor, are presumed to pursue their own self-interests, rather than being an abstract "personification" of the general interest.

Furthermore, in the political perspective the sharp distinction between the political role of politics and the neutral role of bureaucracy (see the dichotomy between politics versus administration as formulated by Wilson, 1887) is also questioned. Within a bureaucracy, based on the expertise that civil servants have and fueled by the internal organizational interests that are at stake (for example, the budget that a department has), civil servants and the units they represent are able and willing to play a vital political role behind the scenes of formal power (Allison and Zelikow, 1971; Svara, 1998).

2.5   The cultural perspective on public policy

The cultural perspective builds upon the assumption that our view of the world, the challenges that we perceive, is essentially socially constructed. The ideas of social constructionism have gained wide popularity in a wide variety of disciplines including sociology, political science and organization science through the work of Berger and Luckmann (1966). Social constructionism rejects the idea of an objective, knowable social reality. Instead, people create social reality through interactions, language, symbols and other means of communication. To be able to meaningfully talk about what is happening and to develop meaningful actions, people develop a shared understanding through processes of sense-making (Weick, 1969, 1995). Sense-making is a collaborative process of creating shared awareness and understanding out of different individuals' perspectives and varied interests. According to Weick, "in an equivocal, postmodern world, infused with the politics of interpretation and conflicting interests and inhabited by people with multiple shifting identities, an obsession with accuracy seems fruitless, and not of much practical help, either" (Weick, 1995:61). The cultural approach focuses on a voluntarist approach to sense-making or the ability to give meaning. Actors themselves explore and discover their shared views on policy issues and policy approaches, based on their free will. In processes of communication and interaction they try to achieve a certain level of shared understanding. However, as we will learn later in the fourth (the institutional) perspective, all kinds of formal and informal rules as well as grown practices also play an important role in this sense-making process. In doing so they limit the degree in which this free will can be exercised. Furthermore, in these sense-making processes goal rationality and power can still play a role, because they can give sense or meaning to the behavior of people, groups and organizations. However, in the cultural perspective itself the emphasis lies on the process of sense-making and the communication processes that constitute this sense-making process. It is the process that seems to matter, not its content.

The dominant explanatory mechanism

In the cultural approach, policy is considered as a socially constructed perspective on reality which results from continuous processes of interaction between participants in policy processes (Stone, 2001). In these interaction processes, the role of language, symbols and metaphors is important. Through communication, actors try to construct shared perceptions of reality. The inputs that they offer in these communication processes are their own perceptions of reality. Through language actors are able to share their individual perceptions (Stone, 1989, 2003; Hajer and Wagenaar, 2003). Language has the ability to define issues in such a way that a shared understanding emerges. Processes of framing and re-framing may be important in creating shared understandings and interpretations. Framing refers to the creation of an interpretative context in which information, knowledge, beliefs and experiences get a specific meaning. The ultimate goal is to develop a shared frame of reference that can be seen as the ability to develop "a consensually validated grammar for reducing equivocality by means of interlocked behaviours" (Weick, 1969:3). For instance, the frames of "global warming" or "the Great Recession" give a specific meaning to information, observations and experiences of individual actors by linking them together in a meaningful way. When these are shared in the context of such a frame, it may become easier to reach a common understanding of these observations than when they are presented as isolated facts, observations or experiences. For instance, in the discussion of organ and tissue donation one frame seems to be very dominant. That is the frame that organ and tissue donation should be viewed as a "gift of life" in which an altruistic individual, on a voluntary basis, donates blood, an organ or organs to an anonymous recipient or recipients without expectation of financial or other reward (Thomas and Klapdor, 2008).

> [T]there is no formal contract, no legal bond, no situation of power, domination, constraint or compulsion, no sense of shame or guilt, no gratitude imperative, no need for penitence, no money and no explicit guarantee of or wish for a reward or return gift. They are acts of free will; of the exercise of choice; of conscience without shame. (Titmuss, 1970:102)

However, this gift-frame may be contrasted with another frame, the commodity frame that refers to the buying and selling of blood or organs, wherein blood and/or organs are treated as a commodity to be bought and sold in the marketplace (Thomas and Klapdor, 2008).

In addition to the role of language, the cultural approach also shows the importance of other means of communication like images, symbols or metaphors. The idiom "a picture is worth a thousand words" also holds true in policy processes (Bekkers and Moody, 2015). Images, symbols and metaphors may create strong incentives to give direction to processes of communication and interaction, given their persuasive power. Numerous examples illustrate this. For example, following the dramatic shootings in the headquarters of the satiric *Charlie Hebdo* magazine in Paris, France, people united behind the phrase "Je suis Charlie" (I am Charlie). This phrase came to represent the freedom of speech and guided the policy responses in the aftermath of these attacks; including higher-than-ever popularity for the magazine. When talking about the roles of visuals, we can refer to the shot in Al Gore's movie *The Inconvenient Truth* of a lonely polar bear, sitting on a drifting ice floe. As such this picture tells us a rather complex story in one shot about the effects of global warming (Bekkers and Moody, 2015). Castells (1997) already argued that images play an important role in the network society, due to the penetration of information and communication technologies and media technologies (traditional and new media) in the fabric of society, and thus of democracy. This has led to an increased proliferation of images (photos, videos, films but also graphics) as ways of sense-making in political and public policy debates (Bennett and Entman, 2001).

Perspective on human behavior

As we have discussed above, in the cultural perspective the abilities to interact and communicate are central features of human beings. Through interaction, individuals create a shared perspective on the world, society and each other. Of course, interaction and communication are also a central element in politics and policy. Basically, both are created through language. There is no objective reality waiting to be discovered and defined; the characteristics of policy and politics are created through processes of interaction and communication. Policy gets meaning through words, signs, symbols and images, in processes of social interaction.

Society may be viewed as an infinite reservoir of potential meanings and processes of sense-making (Silverman, 1971; Meyer and Rowan, 1991). Economic, cultural, technological and scientific progress depends on human beings interacting with each other and collectively creating a shared understanding of the world and the policy challenges that are related to them. In policy processes, the dominant driver of human behavior is the urge (or desire) of human beings to develop and share their interpretations of the world in order to contribute to a common understanding of that world and what is happening in it. Or, put simply, sense-making interaction is what drives actors in policy processes. Not only do these actors make use of frames to give meaning to their own behavior. They also want to persuade other actors of the rightfulness of their frames in such a way that they are able to influence the behavior and frames of references of these other actors. However, an interesting question is what will become the dominant frame of reference that is being accepted by the actors involved. This presupposes a process of inclusion and exclusion (of elements) of other frames, which according to Stone (2003) is in essence a political process, because if refers to processes in which power is being exercised. The latter implies that it is important to link the cultural perspective on policy processes to the political perspective.

Policy instruments

In the cultural perspective, two views on policy instruments may be distinguished. Both of them follow from the central premise that interaction and communication determine policy and politics. The first view builds upon Habermas' (1981) idea of the *Herrschaftsfreie Kommunikation* (power-free communication). To solve societal problems, policy makers should enable open processes of communication between stakeholders. According to Habermas (1981), the only power that should count is the power of argumentation. Policy instruments should be aimed at providing the means for this open dialogue. The starting point in this dialogue is not the diverging interests and motives of stakeholders, but the content of the policy problem and the interdependencies that follow from it (Koppenjan and Klijn, 2004). There are three ways in which this open dialogue can be facilitated. The first is by creating platforms where stakeholders can meet to interact openly. By creating more or less institutionalized arenas, policy makers create meeting points for stakeholders in which processes of interaction can take place. Second, once stakeholders start to interact, policy makers may define the rules of communication, safeguarding the conditions for a power-free dialogue based on arguments. Third, policy makers can appoint process managers that guide or supervise the interaction process not based on results or outcomes, but based on the conditions for a successful, open and again power-free dialogue. The ultimate goal of this process is that stakeholders discover a common frame of reference or a shared paradigm (Termeer, 1993).

Rather than dismissing the role of power, the second view on how to use policy instruments in the cultural perspective treats power as an inevitable necessity. All actors are continuously defining the world according to the beliefs and interests, and try to *frame* and *reframe* policy issues in order to convince others of their views. Policy makers are part of this process, whether they like it or not. In this perspective, language, images and symbols are important discursive tools that may be used by all actors, including policy makers, in processes of policy and politics. A consensus or a shared understanding may not be the outcome of an open, power-free dialogue, but of the discursive and visualization strategies of participants in the process. Discursive and visualization strategies are focused on developing and disseminating persuasive frames and messages in which cues are inserted that – according to a specific storyline – try to convince other actors (not only other policy makers but also the wider public or target groups) of the claims that are being pursued (Bekkers and Moody, 2015). This approach to policy instruments is closely related to the role of power in the political perspective. There is, however, one big difference: the means that actors use are increasingly discursive and visualization means.

Evaluation

It may be clear that in a social world that does not have an "objective reality", criteria of efficiency and effectiveness are not of much use for evaluating the success of policy processes. In the cultural perspective, two criteria are important for determining the success of public policy. The first criterion focuses on the outcome of policy processes. It refers to the extent to which actors that play a role in a policy issue have managed to create a common frame of reference about the issue, its causes and solutions. If this common frame of reference has emerged from the interaction process, actors will be able to implement a sustainable solution themselves.

The second criterion focuses on the quality of the interaction process. It assesses to what extent the interaction really has been open, power-free and accessible for all actors, to what extent diverging and competitive viewpoints have been able to enter the arena and have been subjected to serious consideration and it assesses the quality of the argumentations that have been issued by the stakeholders (see also Habermas, 1981).

The role of knowledge and information

The social-constructivist roots of the cultural approach challenge the idea of objective knowledge and information about a "knowable" social reality

(Berger and Luckmann, 1966). Therefore, the role of knowledge and information in policy processes differs substantially from that of the earlier two approaches. In the most radical interpretation of social constructivism, scientific knowledge does not differ from the personal experiences and observations of actors in the policy process. They are building blocks in the process of collective sense-making. Some of these sources are easily accessible for all actors in the process because of their form and the way they have been produced. Examples are scientific publications, background studies, policy research, evaluation reports, benchmarks, or monitoring information. Other sources of information build much more on the lived experiences and tacit and informal knowledge that actors hold. Tacit knowledge refers to the personal experiences of, for instance policy makers or groups of policy makers, being based on the personal and collective experiences that they have gathered while being involved in specific policy fields (Nonaka, 1994). These are by their nature much harder to share.

Much more important than the way knowledge and information has been produced, is the way they fit in the common story that is constructed by the participants in a policy process. As such this story can be seen as the embodiment of knowledge and information that makes sense. These stories may be considered as ways of structuring the different diverging interpretations of reality into a coherent, shared frame of reference (Stone, 2001). A frame (of reference) can be seen as "an account of ordering that makes sense in the domain of policy and that describes the move from diffuse worries to actionable beliefs" (Hajer and Laws, 2006:257). The frame that organ and tissue donation can be seen as "a gift of life" tries to link diffuse beliefs, claims, norms and values, and interpretations in such a way that a more coherent story evolves in which it justifies why it is noble for people (who have died) to give their own organs and tissues to other people who are desperately in need of these organs. A story is convincing because of its internal coherence, the quality of its argumentation and its connection to the worlds of those affected by it, not because of the rigorous scientific methods that have been applied in its construction (Hajer and Laws, 2006). Hence, knowledge, information, rhetoric and visuals (like photos, videos and films but also graphics) can be used to produce such a story or a storyline that consists of different but linked frames that are inserted in a policy program. This also implies that knowledge and information that are introduced into a policy process, serve primarily as pieces of information that create a social reality that asks to be understood. They are part of the raw material out of which and with which the sense-making process should take place (Feldman and March, 1981). Moreover, the gathering of knowledge and data in itself, also by making use of ICT, may be considered as part of the sense-making process. For instance, the strong reliance in public administration on gathering and analysing information, by making use of monitoring systems and performance and benchmark systems, fits within a story of control and rational management (van Gunsteren, 1976, Zincke, 1990).

The policy process

As interaction is the driving force in the cultural perspective, the course of the policy process is also defined by processes of continuous interaction in which meaning is given to specific policy challenges. In these interactions a specific narrative or storyline is being produced and reproduced (Hajer, 1993; see also Fischer and Forester, 1993). In these interactions so-called *discourse coalitions* play an important role, because frames and stories are being created in discourses that are developed in a specific coalition of relevant stakeholders that share more or less the same beliefs. That is why the content, course and outcomes of policy processes can be understood in terms of looking at the interaction that takes place within and between different discourse coalitions. "A discourse coalition is thus the ensemble of a set of story lines, the actors that utter these story lines, and the practices that conform these story lines, all organized around a discourse" (Hajer, 1993:47). For instance, in relation to the discussion about organ and tissue donation around the necessity to enhance the number of donations, different discourse coalitions can be found. One coalition underlines the importance of the free will of people to donate their organs, because donation should be seen as a "gift of life". As such this is seen as a moral action. They state that "donation of organs and tissues is an act of altruism and human solidarity that potentially benefits those in medical need and society as a whole" (Thomas and Klapdor, 2008:27). However, other coalitions question the morality that lies behind this heroic altruism. People do not always or entirely donate their organs for selfless or altruistic reasons. They advocate an approach in which donors and would-be donors would need to be understood and treated in neutral terms when it comes to their motivation and behavior. The frame that they advocate is to consider donors as rational and autonomous decision-makers, that with the provision of factual information can be persuaded to give their organs (Thomas and Klapdor, 2008:30-31). In this alternative frame potential donors have a calculated self-interest to donate their organs, because they hope that if other people also do so, they have a greater chance of getting an organ if they need one.

The shaping of policy programs can therefore be understood in terms of the stories about how to interpret the nature of the problem, the need to intervene as well as how to intervene, that are constructed in different discourse coalitions; coalitions that produce different claims about how to proceed. In the stories to be produced normative as well as analytical convictions are being pushed forward (Hajer, 1993:47). At the same time, it is interesting to look at the question of whether there is a dominant discourse coalition around a specific policy issue. The dominance, or the lack of dominance, also influences the content, course and outcomes of specific policy processes. This also relates to the degree to which a discourse coalition has been institutionalized, which also generates a specific bias of how to look at specific issues (Hajer, 1993:48). At the same time, especially in relation to highly disputed issues, there might not be a dominant discourse coalition present which is able to impose a specific frame.

Hence, policy processes should be understood as continuous processes in which interpretations of the social reality are produced, adjusted and reproduced by making use of narratives. Each new stage in the policy process challenges the current interpretation by introducing new observations, experiences or beliefs. The implementation stage may show new, unexpected problems and therefore introduce new ideas. But also external events like disasters or – less dramatic – elections may challenge the common frame of reference and re-open the interaction processes in which specific frames are pushed forward (see also Kingdon, 1984; Sabatier, 1987; Jenkins-Smith and Sabatier, 1993). At the same time, within policy processes actors continuously adjust their positions, interpretations and ideas through interaction. Therefore, policy processes may be considered as continuous processes of policy adaptation and learning in which frames are being produced, contested and institutionalized (Sabatier, 1987; Sabatier and Jenkins-Smith, 1993). The latter also points in the direction of the fourth, institutional perspective on policy processes.

The role of politics

Finally, we discuss the role of politics and politicians in the cultural approach. We have already encountered one crucial task for politics and politicians. In our modern, highly complex and fragmented network societies, politics should be the arena that closely resembles the idea of the power-free interaction. In ideal political settings, everyone is free to speak openly and without barriers. Politics in this perspective is not a power game of winners and losers, but it's a collective endeavor of sense-making. Politics may take place in traditional, formal and institutionalized arenas like parliament, the municipal council or the United Nations. But there are also numerous other less institutionalized arenas in which groups of people deliberate about binding collective decisions (Hajer, 2003; Fischer, 2003a). In this perspective politics is about deliberation and argumentation, while at the same time an important task for politicians is to create and safeguard public spaces in which a deliberative democracy can flourish.

A second task for politics and politicians is in articulating inspiring views on social reality that have the potential to bind people in shared stories. Even in a power-free dialogue, some politicians may take a special position because of their ability to bind people through their use of argumentation, persuasion and ideology. Inspiring politicians can bridge differences between people, create energy, engagement and support (cf. March and Olsen, 1989a). Martin Luther King's "I had a dream", or Al Gore's "Inconvenient Truth" may be considered as examples of how politicians can use symbols, rhetoric and language as tools for sense-making in the cultural approach (Edelman, 1967, 1977).

2.6 The institutional perspective on public policy

The institutional approach highlights the rather deterministic character of the social context in which policy processes take place. Practical approaches that have been translated in all kinds of operating procedures, routines and systems have evolved over time into institutions, into grown habits that have a logic of their own, with their own formal and informal rules (March and Olsen, 1989a:22). The concept of institutions is probably one of the most contested concepts in social sciences. At this stage, we build upon Turner's inclusive definition of institutions as "a complex of positions, roles, norms and values lodged in particular types of social structures and organizing relatively stable patterns of human activity with respect to fundamental problems in producing life-sustaining resources, in reproducing individuals, and in sustaining viable societal structures within a given environment" (Turner, 1997:6). These institutions constrain actors' freedom to interpret and understand the world: the institutions transmit a shared view of the world and therefore strongly affect actors' ability and freedom to shape policies. The institutions determine the course and the content of policy processes to a large extent. In the remainder of this section we will elaborate on the various elements of the institutional perspective.

Explanatory mechanism

In the institutional perspective, public policies and the processes through which they are created are not the product of the design of rational actors, nor the outcomes of political negotiation processes. The systems of rules through which policies are created constrain the options that are available to these actors and therefore significantly predetermine the outcomes of policy processes. Following March and Olsen (1989a:22), institutional rules in the political realm can be defined as *"the routines, procedures, conventions, roles, strategies, organizational forms and technologies around which political activity is constructed."* From a functional sociological perspective, institutions define the role and place of individuals and organization actors in society in such a way that a basic level of cohesion is reached that enables a society to sustain itself. To reach these goals, a basic level of predictability and stability is required in the behavior of individuals, organizational actors and governments. The stabilizing character of institutional rules for instance may be seen in the role of a constitution. A constitution may be considered as the most essential set of legal rules at the national level. In most countries, the procedure to change the constitution is complicated and often requires a double approval from the population. Initiated to protect citizens and other actors from volatile government policies, these constitutions – once established – constrain the policy options for politicians and policy makers. Constitutions reflect the norms, values and opinions from the time they were established and in this way they lay the path for future decisions. Therefore, the concept of *path-dependency* is an important explanatory mechanism in the institutional perspective. Following Pierson (2000), we use Levi's (1997) description of path-dependency. She states that "path dependency has to mean (. . .) that once a country or a region has started down a track, the costs of reversal are very high. There will be other choice points, but the entrenchments of certain institutional arrangements obstruct an easy reversal of the initial choice." Following Arthur (1994), Pierson (2000:253) describes how processes of increasing returns shape path-dependency. Processes of increasing returns have the following four characteristics:

1. *Unpredictability.* Because early events have a large effect and are partly random, many outcomes may be possible. We cannot predict ahead of time which of these possible end-states will be reached.
2. *Inflexibility.* The farther into the process we are, the harder it becomes to shift from one path to another. (. . .) Sufficient movement down a particular path may eventually lock in one solution.
3. *Non-ergodicity.* Accidental events early in a sequence do not cancel out. They cannot be treated (. . .) as "noise" because they feed back into future choices. Small events are remembered.
4. *Potential path efficiency.* In the long-run, the outcome that becomes locked in may generate lower pay-offs that a forgone alternative would have.

When applied to our organ donation case, we could say that in many countries there is a discussion about a change-over from an opting-in to an opting-out system of organ donation. In many countries organ donation is organized around the opting-in system, in which people on a voluntary basis give their consent to donate their organs. This is the dominant system which is translated in all kinds of routines and procedures that have to be followed, when somebody wants to be a donor. This is the path that has been created. The change-over to another system implies that another path is going to be followed. This implies that existing routines, procedures and conventions have to be changed in order to install another system with a complete other logic, based on other assumptions and giving donors another role: from a (in principle) voluntary set-up to a compulsory system. The opting-out system in which everybody is a donor, unless he or she does not give his consent in advance is a different set-up with different procedures to be followed. This will lead to all kinds of change costs. The question is if actors are willing and able to take these costs; and if they want to improve the existing system, will they seek adjustments by improving the opting-in system because that is the path that has been created, or are they really willing to consider another path?

Perspective on human behavior

In this perspective, human behavior is guided by institutional rules that try to stress the importance of specific values or value-sets that societies or groups in society consider important. Interaction between humans is guided by sets of formal and informal rules that also determine our perspective on reality. The autonomy and free will of individuals and organizations is therefore restricted. Within the public sector, this primarily is about the rules that guide the functioning of democracy, bureaucracy and the rule of law. For instance, bureaucracy can be seen as a set of operating rules (created through a process of specialization, standardization and formalization) that are organized around a number of values that societies consider important when governing a society. These values refer to the idea that decisions have to be based on the non-arbitrary exercise of power in which each person is equal before the law (Weber, 1922/1928). Institutions reflect a specific set of norms and values and structure the ways in which policies are formulated and implemented. In many other spheres of public, private and social life, individuals and organizations are constrained by formal and informal rules. With this regard, and put rather negatively, an institution may be considered as an "iron cage" that reduces the free will (DiMaggio and Powell, 1983).

Institutions are remarkable phenomena. On the one hand, they are created and confirmed by individuals, while simultaneously guiding and directing the behavior of individuals. In other words, institutions contain elements of "structure" and "agency" (Sewell, 1992). Structure refers to the recurrent patterned arrangements which influence or limit individuals' choices and opportunities, whereas agency refers to individuals' capacity to act independently and to make their own free choices. Giddens (1979) has introduced the concept of duality to refer to the two-sided character of institutions. While institutions enable and constrain the behavioral options of individuals, the individuals also have the power to create, adjust or abolish these institutions.

Until now, our explanation of the institutional perspective has strongly focused on individual behavior. However, a lot of research in the institutional perspective has highlighted the important role of policy communities, which may create an iron triangle of established stakeholders, in constraining and enabling the options to be followed in specific policy domains (Heclo, 1978). Scott (1995:56) describes a policy sector as "a community of organizations that partakes of a common meaning system and whose participants interact more frequently and fatefully with one another than with actors outside of the field." A policy sector can be regarded as a regulative, normative and cognitive infrastructure which conditions as well as facilitates the behavior and performance of individual organizations within the sector. The regulative pillar refers to the explicit regulatory process, that is, "the capacity to establish rules, inspect others' conformity to them, and, as necessary, manipulate sanctions – rewards or punishments – in an attempt to influence future behavior" (Scott, 2014:59). The normative pillar refers to the moral norms and values that are dominant within the sector. The cognitive pillar refers to the collective self-image of the sector, to the information and knowledge that the sector needs and to the image that outsiders have of the sector (according to the stakeholders within the sector).

These three pillars prescribe the roles that participants should play in the sector and the level of freedom they have when interpreting these roles (March and Olsen, 1989a). Human behavior in the institutional perspective therefore is role-guided behavior. The content of these roles follow from a diverse set of rules at the macro level (a country, a supranational institution) and the meso level (a policy domain).

Policy instruments

As in the other perspectives that we have discussed, the ultimate goal of policy instruments in the policy process is to promote desired behavior or to discourage undesired behavior. In this perspective, institutions determine behavior, so changing behavior requires changing sets of formal and informal rules. However, we have also seen that these rules may be path-dependent and persistent. This affects the use of policy instruments in two ways. First, the use of policy instruments itself is institutionally determined (Howlett,

1991). This implies that previous choices affect the choice and application of policy instruments in a specific situation. On the one hand, this is closely related to the authorities and tools that policy makers already use in the specific context. For example, extending or amending existing authorities or instruments is more obvious than creating new ones. Increasing fines for speeding, extending the secret service's authorities to tap communication channels or increasing taxes on cigarettes are clear examples of this. On the other hand, policy sectors often may have a cultural or normative tradition in the application of specific policy instruments. In some policy sectors there is consensus that citizens should have a free choice to conform to policy instruments which makes the use of economic instruments more obvious. Other sectors have a tradition of legally binding instruments (Howlett, 1991).

Second, in the institutional perspective the creation and design of policy instruments can be considered as a process of institutional design (Goodin, 1998). Following Klijn and Koppenjan (2006) we may distinguish two important ways in which institutional design strategies may be implemented. First, through interventions that are directly aimed at changing rules. This is the case with, for example, legislation or with other attempts to change formal and informal rules so that the rules of the game are changing in which actors have to operate. For instance, in relation to the organ donation case the introduction of an opting out system does change the rules of the game, because citizens are given another role in contrast to the opting-in system. Second, through interventions that indirectly influence the perceptions or interaction patterns of actors:

> If we assume that rules may also be changed as a result of actors changing their strategies, interpreting rules differently or no longer following rules, institutional design strategies may also be aimed at bringing about sustainable changes to actors' perceptions and strategies and by that achieving changes in the rules in the longer run. (Klijn and Koppenjan, 2006:152)

For example in relation to the organ donation case, by continuously questioning the effectivity of the opting-in system, while pointing at organ shortages, the perceptions of people might change about the necessity to donate their organs and tissues.

Role of knowledge and information

The importance of rules in the institutional perspective can also be retraced in the role knowledge and information play in the policy process. Three elements need to be highlighted here. First, institutional rules to a large extent determine which knowledge is available for policy makers in the policy process. They influence the gathering, processing and use of information and knowledge in policy processes. The organization of the scientific research infrastructure, the policy research industry, the advisory sector and the available management information all depend on institutional rules that are the outcomes of previous processes, preferences and ideas. In doing so they are biased. This institutional setting determines which information becomes available and which information does not become available. Following Baumgartner and Jones (1993), this might imply that the available knowledge and information primarily reproduce the existing information. This is specifically the case in policy domains that are characterized by strong policy monopolies. However, it should also be noticed that institutional settings may exist which embrace the introduction and exchange of new ideas (Bonoli and Trein, 2015).

Second, the institutional approach also highlights the role that information plays in structuring the policy process. Throughout the policy process, actors are required to report monitoring and accountability information in information systems. These information systems in turn embody earlier choices and ideas about which issues are important and which issues are not important (Kraemer and King, 1986). Moreover, these choices guide the access to this information and define the relation and integration of information from different sources. This also affects the extent to which integrated information about all aspects of the policy process is available for actors in the process.

Third (and with reference to the earlier mentioned cognitive pillar of institutions), institutions themselves can be seen as a reservoir of knowledge and expertise. Grown practices can be seen as the embodiment of experiences that have been built up during a long period (March and Olsen, 1989a; Scott; 1995).

Policy evaluation

To understand how the institutional perspective considers the success or failure of public policies, it is necessary to make a distinction between the logic of consequence and the logic of appropriateness. This distinction has been made popular mainly in the field of organizational studies by March and Olsen (1989b) and March and Simon (1993), introduced by March and Olsen (1989b:23-24). In the logic of consequence, people make decisions on the basis of a subjective consideration of alternatives, assessment of their outcomes and preference-driven choices (March and Simon, 1993; see also Schulz, 2014). In other words: they make rational decisions based on the model of the *homo economicus* that we encountered in the rational model. Typical criteria for assessing the success or failure of public policies in the logic of consequence are also derived from the rational model: efficiency and effectiveness. Alternatively, in the logic of appropriateness decisions are considered as fixed, standardized responses to defined situations. "Actors recognize a situation and connect it to an appropriate action consistent with relevant rules (often anchored in the identities of the actors)" (Schulz, 2014:3; see also March and Olsen, 2004). March and Olsen (2004:9) state that "fitting a rule to a situation is an exercise in establishing appropriateness, where rules and situations are related by criteria of similarity or difference by reasoning through analogy or metaphor." This implies that assessing public policies in the institutional perspective is focused on analysing whether the appropriate actions have been taken. In terms of evaluation criteria, this requires a deconstruction of the process of determining "what is appropriate" in a specific context and an assessment of whether an actor did the right thing in this specific context.

In addition, evaluation in the logic of appropriateness may also be aimed at the decision-making context itself. It is not always obvious which rule(s) apply in a specific context, or how to select specific rules within a context of multiple competing rules. Again following March and Olsen (2004:9-10), we can state that "the problem is to apply criteria of similarity in order to use the most appropriate rule or account. (. . .) Rules and identities collide routinely (Orren and Skowronek, 1994), making prescriptions less obvious. Actors sometimes disobey and challenge some rules because they adhere to other rules." The ability to select the "appropriate" rule not only depends on the individual's capacities, but also on the precision of the rule, its distinctive capacity from other rules, and the available knowledge and information about the rule. Moreover, sometimes actors may know what to do but not be able to do it because prescriptive rules and capabilities are incompatible. "Actors are limited by (. . .) the distribution and regulation of resources, competencies, and organizing capacities" (March and Olsen, 2004:10). So a final set of criteria refers to the institutional capacities to act appropriately. For instance, in relation to the organ and tissue donation case, the evaluation of the success and failure of the opting-in or opting-out system, not only relates to the number of organs that per year have been donated and the costs that are involved, but also relates to the degree in which both systems fit within the context in which they are implemented. In countries in which the idea of having a free choice is an essential part of the dominant political and legal systems, the choice for an opting-out system, may perhaps be considered as less appropriate, given the obligatory character of the system. Because of this lack of appropriateness it might lead to resistance or a rather low degree of acceptance.

The policy process

Formal and informal rules play an important role in the institutional perspective. These rules not only structure the content of policies or the behavior of stakeholders, but also affect the course of the policy process. We have concluded that institutions prescribe roles to organizations and individuals. Following Ostrom, Gardner and Walker (1994) we can state that rules shape the arena in which decisions are taken and therefore shape the course of the policy process. Although Ostrom's work often builds upon formalized models of decision-making processes, the way she describes the rules that shape the decision-making process or policy process is useful for understanding the institutional perspective on the policy process. According to Ostrom, Gardner and Walker (1994), seven classes of rules can be identified (see also Blom-Hansen, 1997):

1. Position rules which specify a set of positions in the policy process (that is, initiator, co-producer, participant).
2. Boundary rules which specify how participants are chosen to hold these positions and how participants leave these positions.
3. Scope rules which specify the set of outcomes that may be affected and the external inducements and/or costs assigned to each of these outcomes.
4. Authority rules which specify the set of actions assigned to a position and a step in the process.
5. Aggregation rules which specify the decision function to be used at a particular step to map actions into intermediate or final outcomes.
6. Information rules which authorize channels of communication among participants in positions and specify the language and form in which communication will take place.
7. Pay-off rules, which prescribe how benefits and costs are to be distributed to participants in positions.

From the institutional perspective, the routines, procedures and instructions that have been developed within policy sectors determine the course of the policy process. Depending on the institutional characteristics of the policy sector, in some sectors this may resemble the policy cycle that we have encountered in the rational approach, but in other sectors other practices may have evolved. Anyway, the routines, procedures and instructions that have evolved also structure the outcome of the process. For instance, in many countries there are specific, detailed, standard approaches for preparing and deciding about large infrastructural projects like railways, highways or dams. Often, the number of alternatives that should be developed is prescribed, as well as the way the population should be involved in the design stage and the decision-making stage and the criteria by which the different alternatives should be assessed.

So, from the institutional perspective, the level of freedom for actors within the policy process to shape the process according to their own ideas or preferences is limited by the routines, procedures and instructions that have been developed earlier (Allison and Zelikow, 1971).

The role of politics

The duality that characterizes the institutional perspective is obvious in the role of politics. On the one hand, the task of politics is to shape the basic rules in society, given the primacy of politics in representative democracy; on the other hand politics itself is governed by a variety of rules with regard to what politicians can and should do and how they should do it. Concerning the first task of politics, we have now presented how formal and informal rules shape the behavior of actors in society. Concerning the institutional embeddedness of politics, the constitution and all the legislation that has been derived from it outlines the channels, procedures and rules through which politics does what it should do: authoritatively allocate values for society as a whole. In complex issues with diverging values, the system of parliamentary democracy and the rule of law does not give solutions but it prescribes the path through which a solution should be reached. This path provides stability to the decision-making processes which makes it predictable and transparent. It also gives legitimacy to the decisions to be made (Luhmann, 1969). This also implies that in the institutional perspective there is no doubt about the primacy of politics in the policy process. It's the task of politics – in the interest of the state and in the general interest – to integrate and balance diverging interests and thus guarantee society's stability (Willke, 1991; Luhmann, 1984a, 1984b).

In the institutional perspective politics is also an institution which functions according to specific rules that stress specific values that are related to the embeddedness of politics in a specific democracy model, like representative democracy (see, for example, Barber, 1984). However, the rules that structure the functioning of politics as an institution may also be ambiguous, contested or unfamiliar to some actors so that they are being challenged, for instance, because questions are raised regarding the quality of representation of those people who are elected to govern. Politics in the institutional perspective is also concerned with the continuous assessment and reassessment of the basic rules that guide the behavior of actors in society. When these rules are unclear or contested, politics is also about addressing the question, how to ensure the vitality of politics as an institution, which relates to the question of whether the rules (as well as the roles of politics in society and identities of politicians as representatives of the political institutions) are still appropriate, given all kinds of sociocultural, economic and technological changes (March and Olsen, 1989b:161).

2.7 CHAPTER SUMMARY

In this chapter, we have introduced the four perspectives on the policy process that guide our discussion of the different elements of policy processes in the remainder of this book. As discussed in the introduction of this chapter, these perspectives may be considered as "ideal types". In the discussion of these perspectives, we have highlighted their differences. However, practically as well as theoretically there is overlap between the perspectives.

Practically, the application of these perspectives to the policy process will show that each of these perspectives may be true. They are not mutually exclusive, nor are they meant to be so. Application of a different perspective will highlight different factors, variables or elements. By using such a perspective, a specific conceptual lens is being embraced. This lens helps students and policy makers to give meaning to the complexity which is often typical for policy processes. This is not to say that "anything goes" in the application of the perspectives. In some cases, some perspectives will be better equipped to understand the specificities of a concrete policy process than others. In some cases, the policy process may be dominated by one perspective, whereas in other cases elements of all perspectives may be intertwined. These perspectives are meant to be included in the analytical toolkit of policy analysts. Depending on the explanatory question the policy analyst has, he or she may decide which perspective(s) to apply. The professional training, as well as the following chapters in this book, may be helpful in determining which perspective(s) to apply in which situations. For participants in policy processes the application of these perspectives may be useful to better understand their own and others' behavior in policy processes.

Theoretically, there is some overlap between the political and rational perspectives on the one hand, and the cultural and institutional perspectives on the other. In the rational model and the political model, actors have goals which they want to reach and act upon. This may be either to the use of ratio (rational perspective) or the use of power (political perspective). Actors act intentionally, and have the capacity to do so. We could briefly summarize that these two models assume that actors in policy processes have *agency*. Because they have agency, they are able to maximize their utility. If this maximization is power-driven or based on something different, it is hard to distinguish conceptually, theoretically, and also practically. Also in the cultural perspective actors have agency, because they give meaning to a specific policy challenge and how to act. In trying to give meaning, they can follow more rational or more interest and power driven goals (or a combination of both). The institutional perspective highlights the role of the context in which these actors operate. It is this context, defined as informal and formal rules that have to be followed because they refer to grown or established practices that limit the actor's agency, that gives meaning to actors in terms of how to interpret all kinds of developments and challenges. In other words these rules and practices structure the actions to be pursued. Actions within a specific context not only have to be effective but they also have to fit within this context, in terms of being appropriate. Furthermore, in the political and rational perspectives some elements of this institutional perspective can be found. When we try to understand the actions of actors in an arena, we see that these actors are bounded because they often take place in already established (and historically grown) dependency and power relations. We often see that these existing relations reproduce the actions of specific actors (given the power that they hold or lack). Very often the main challenge is to break through these power relations in order to develop new policy problem definitions and solutions. Also, in the rational perspective traces of the institutional perspective can be found. What we very often see is that actors, when constructing reality, refer to all kinds of myths that give meaning to specific policy challenges. These myths, like the will to know or the primacy of politics or the neutrality of bureaucracy, can be seen as institutionalized frames of reference that people use to give meaning in a more rational way. Furthermore, these myths are not only found in the rational perspective; in a political perspective myths can also play a role (Meyer and Rowan, 1991).

When we follow the line of reasoning above, we can also see how in practice these perspectives mutually constitute each other. In practice they are often intertwined and converging. Actors who are involved in all kinds of policy processes try to frame the specific societal challenges that manifest themselves as policy problems on the political agenda in a specific way as well as what possible approaches are in order to deal with these challenges. In doing so they (re-)construct social reality in terms of policies and policy processes by making use of all kinds of frames that they seek to get adopted by other actors. However, in this construction of reality they make use, in a rational way, of the knowledge and information that is available, while at the same time they also try to protect their specific interests while defining all kinds of goals they want to achieve. Goal rationality and the use of power can often be seen as communicating vessels. However, given the fact that policy processes take place in a specific arena, the interaction that takes place in this arena – focusing on trying to create a negotiated or imposed definition of reality regarding what the challenge is, and/or how to deal with this challenge – does not take place in a vacuum. It is shaped by all kinds of formal and informal rules that guide the communication, negotiation, exchange as well as the application of power that takes place between the involved stakeholders that differ in terms of degree of (inter)dependency. Hence, context really matters. Furthermore, in many cases policy programs and policy processes have a history which leads to all kinds of path-dependencies that have to be followed.

In Table 2.1 we briefly summarize the main characteristics of each of these perspectives:

Table 2.1 Four perspectives on the policy process

	Rational perspective	Political perspective	Cultural perspective	Institutional perspective
Explanatory mechanism	Goal rationality	Power, dependency and interests	Sense-making and interaction	Grown practices and established formal and informal rules as well as path-dependency around values
Human behavior	Homo economics in which people look for (sub) optimal choices between costs and benefits	Humans as political actors, aimed at defending positions and interests that operate in an arena	Humans as communicative beings that (re-)construct social reality through frames and story telling	Humans caught in the iron cage of formal and informal rules that prescribe how to behave
Policy instruments	Rational selection of tools from the toolkit of government Programming and planning	Policy tools as sources of power Network management as an important policy tool	Constructing and facilitating open, power-free dialogue Persuasive rhetorical and visual strategies for framing	Directly and indirectly rules that structure decisions by actors in the policy process
Evaluation criteria	Effectiveness, efficiency and coherence	Support, satisfaction by actors	Quality of argumentation and discourse	Logic of consequences Logic of appropriateness
Role of knowledge and information	More knowledge and information leads to better policies	Knowledge and information are sources of power to be used to protect interests	Knowledge is socially and culturally constructed by making use of frames Interpretative knowledge	Institutional setting (thus rules) determines type of use of knowledge and information
Structure of the policy process	Policy process looks like a cycle in which different stages logically follow each other	Capricious, non-linear Incrementalism Garbage can: Random order of different stages	Interaction of ideas, information, knowledge, experiences and observations, produced in discourse coalitions	Informal and formal rules define policy processes
Role of politics	Primacy of politics, division between politics and administration	Politics as part of the policy game Politics as struggle for power	Politics as sense-making Politics facilitating discursive space for argumentation and debate	Politics is an institution that functions according to specific formal and informal rules which are reproduced and contested

3

Policy problems and agenda setting

LEARNING OBJECTIVES

After reading this chapter you should be able to:

- Appreciate the diversity in *types of problems* that policies face and define different types of problems.

- Appreciate the implications that problem constructions may have for different groups, and define different types of *target group constructions*.

- Understand the complexity of *agenda setting*, and apply the four theoretical perspectives (rationalism, institutionalism, culturalism and the political perspective) to agenda setting.

3.1   Introduction

In 2015 a "refugee crisis" captured the attention of Europe and many other parts of the world. Via Greece but also via Italy and various alternative routes (the Strait of Gibraltar and even Northern-Norway), refugees from Syria but also from Afghanistan, Libya, Eritrea and Somalia made their way into Europe. Many met their deaths while trying to get into Europe on overcrowded boats, delivered in the hands of criminal human smugglers. Through various European countries, trajectories emerged which the refugees followed on their journey toward North-West European countries, in particular Germany and Sweden.

However, before the refugee situation finally captured the world's attention in 2015, immigration from the politically, socially and economically very unstable Middle East had already increased since 2011. Instability in Libya, political and economic unrest after the Arab Spring, the conflict in Afghanistan and especially the civil war that ravaged Syria since 2011, were important "push-factors" for migration toward Europe. In 2013 the world's attention was captured for a brief moment by overcrowded boats that perished on their way toward the Italian island of Lampedusa. But regardless of objective figures on increasing immigration into Europe, the idea of a migration crisis did not immediately emerge on the political agendas of Europe and EU member states such as Germany. In fact, for a considerable time they held on to a firm belief that current immigration policies were sufficient to bring refugee migration to a halt and that the instability in Europe's surrounding areas was temporary and that hence refugee migration would be temporary as well. Clearly, there was not a direct relationship between the increase of refugee migration and the rise of this topic on the agenda.

The migration crisis did emerge on Europe's political agenda in 2015 in response to various factors. On the one hand, one could say that the migration figures in 2015 passed a certain threshold. Indeed, figures in 2015 were higher than in 2014, but what then determines this threshold? Other factors came into play in 2015 as well (Geddes and Scholten, 2016). The media images of drowned refugees captured the imagination, particularly the famous picture of the Kurdish boy Aylan Kurdi washed up on the shores of Turkey. Suddenly, Europe became much more tangibly aware of what was happening in the Mediterranean.

Furthermore, the refugee situation signaled that something was going wrong, beyond the scope of the mass refugee deaths in themselves. Europe was seemingly unable to bring this immigration to a halt, or even to manage it in a proper manner. Some countries, including Germany, started violating European law by reinstating border controls. Others even started building fences at their borders. Clearly Europe's institutional and policy responses were failing. Furthermore, the refugee situation became an object of political conflict in Europe. In many European countries, fierce political struggle emerged on how to respond to the crisis. Think of the criticism that Germany's State Chancellor Merkel received for her statement "we are able to handle this" ("Wir Schaffen Das"), which was read by many of her opponents as an open invitation to refugees to come to Germany.

This example shows some of the complexities of agenda setting. An agenda, be it a political agenda, a media agenda or a policy agenda, does not offer a representative overview of all topics relevant at any given point in time. Rather, agendas tend to be highly selective. Their carrying capacity is rather limited (Hilgartner and Bosk, 1988). Some topics will be off the agenda, with specific actors seeing it as in their interest to keep a topic off the agenda, whereas other actors might push for a specific topic to emerge on the agenda. There will also be competition between topics for the limited amount of attention that can be allocated on a (political/policy/media) agenda. For instance, only one item can be the lead item in the evening news on TV or on the front page of a newspaper.

Furthermore, actors' definitions and interpretations of the problem to emerge (or not to emerge) on the agenda, can differ significantly. This is very clear also in the case of the refugee crisis, where some actors perceive a lack of openness of Europe toward war refugees whereas others see refugees as a potential security threat and a liability to Europe's welfare states. Agenda setting is inherently connected to problem definition, as it is often in this stage that prevailing problem definitions are challenged and a potentially new problem definition arises. If successful, the agenda setting of a specific policy problem will have consequences not only in terms of a redefinition of the policy issue, but also for the quest for solutions and for decision-making in subsequent stages, and even for how current and past policies are evaluated.

This chapter will focus in-depth on problem definition and the first stage of the policy cycle heuristic; agenda setting. First, we will discuss how problems are defined, and what makes a problem a "policy problem" (section 3.2). This includes a discussion of why policy problems are social and political constructions. We will look into several dogmas concerning agenda setting, from the four theoretical perspectives of this book. We will draw a few conclusions in the final section.

3.2 Types of policy problems

When browsing through a random newspaper, one will see different issues calling for a government's attention to come up with a solution. How should a European country respond to the ongoing euro-crisis? By installing even more reforms, and if so, which ones? Climate-researchers emphasizing the risk of the North Pole being completely ice-free within just a few decades; how the United States can install carbon taxation without risking major firms moving to other countries; the ongoing issue in Germany about what needs to happen with nuclear power plants in the country, especially after the situation with the Fukushima plant in Japan; all examples of national and international policy issues calling for the attention of a government.

What is a policy problem? For a long time there was no attention for problematizing policy problems within the rational approach to policy

(Hoppe, 2011). In this regard, a policy problem is defined as "the discrepancy between a benchmark (a principle, norm or goal) and the conception of the existing or the expected situation" (Hoogerwerf, 1989:26). However, the question is whether or not this benchmark is objective. Different parties can have different conceptions of the desired or expected situation. We can illustrate this by the example of subjective and objective safety. The police can show that data on criminality in a neighborhood (for example, robberies, theft, threats) does not indicate a problem. Perhaps it is even far below the national or regional average. But citizens feel unsafe or threatened. Street gangs, poorly lit streets and squares, limited social cohesiveness in neighborhoods or a predominantly aged population (elderly people usually feel threatened more often than youth does) increase feelings of insecurity or being unsafe. Additionally, citizens might be less inclined to report a crime, because they feel it does not make a difference. Consequently, registered crime does not match with factual crime or factually experienced nuisance. Hence, there is a discrepancy between the factual and the perceived safety in the neighborhood. The benchmark used by citizens is different from that of the police, while both have different perceptions of the existing and desired situation. Therefore, an "objective" definition of the safety issue in this neighborhood is not given. This conclusion counts for many of the policy issues brought to the attention of the government.

Oftentimes, the concerned parties in a certain policy issue are in disagreement about the underlying causes of a problem. Armed with certain knowledge, the police will say that the data on criminality shows there is no real problem. Citizens question whether this knowledge is adequate, or reliable. Data does not always indicate how citizens feel in a neighborhood, or how they experience it. What certainty do we have about the knowledge that is brought in to the equation? For example, the police force, the central statistical office and the local municipality may produce different information about the safety of the same neighborhood based on different sources. The police force bases its information on reported crimes, the statistical office on a public survey of crime victims. These sources both refer to the *objective* safety. The municipality bases its information on a survey of citizens' feelings: the *subjective* safety. If these three sources of information diverge, then which policy are policy makers to design for the neighborhood? Whether or not we can be certain about the knowledge required to understand a policy problem also determines the nature of the problems that a government is confronted with. Sometimes, these problems are too complicated, our knowledge is insufficient and there is a difference in opinions about how a problem is built up. There is a lack of consensus about what knowledge is required in order to be able to understand a certain problem.

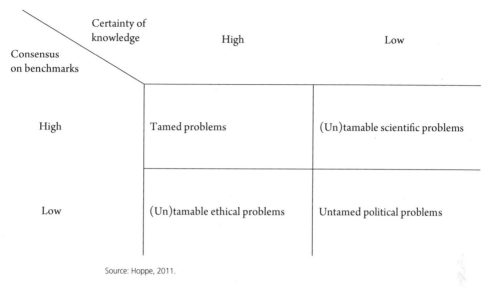

Source: Hoppe, 2011.

Figure 3.1 Types of policy problems

Additionally, we see that it is possible that the parties involved also use different benchmarks to legitimize certain demands. Returning to the example used above, citizens in the neighborhood will want to see more police in the streets, while the police will not see any "objective" reason for this. They, on the other hand, are confronted with neighborhoods in which the presence of more police is really necessary. As such, the lack of consensus about the benchmarks to be used also says something about how a policy problem is built up (Hoppe, 2011).

Based on these two approaches (certainty of knowledge and consensus on benchmarks), Hoppe (2011) arrives at the following typology of policy problems (see Figure 3.1).

Tamed problems are problems of which we know how they are built up (van de Graaf and Hoppe, 1989:11). To a certain extent, a policy theory is available based on insight into the cause–effect and goal–medium relationships. One example of this is water pollution. We are aware of the minimum chemical and biological conditions necessary for a river to be sufficiently viable for fish. Measurements and calculative models make this clear; they decide what level of water purification is desired. Policy makers then know what demands they need to record in the provision of permits for making it possible to discharge on the water surface, and how important it is to actually maintain these permits. The rational approach of policy is very suitable to tackle tamed problems.

In the case of *(un)tamable scientific problems*, there is a discussion about the quality of the knowledge that is brought in. Parties agree about the benchmarks that need to be set and the desirable degree of government interference, even though the knowledge necessary to determine what measures to use is insufficient (Hoppe, 1989:11). Additional research can fill this knowledge gap. It is also possible to choose several different measures, all based on divergent insights and theories, but all expected to improve the situation. Practice shall teach which measures work best. Based on this knowledge, the policy program is further developed. In that case, one can speak of "evidence-based policy": policy that is shaped based on knowledge of the question of which approaches have proven to work, and which have not (Pawson, 2006). The tackling of youth criminality can be seen as an example of a currently untamed scientific problem. Successful youth criminality policies are most commonly considered policies focusing on prevention; on that most people agree. However, the question is which measures are most effective. Is it better to punish existing offenses more quickly, clearly and strictly, so that the offender immediately gets confronted with the hard consequences of their deeds? Because a tough approach has a deterrent effect and prevents future criminal behavior. Or should we find those factors in the direct environment that cause youth to get involved in wrong activities, and improve those, for example by offering some sort of family support? The problem in this case is that there are many different treatments that are being developed, but a systematic insight into what does and does not work is not always available. In this case, we see that a rational approach to policy can offer a helping hand. Because of that, there is an increasing need voiced from within the preventive youth criminality policy making process for a systematic evaluation of the many intervention strategies that are being tested. Nevertheless, advocates and opponents of certain "theories" can clash, leading to a battle between paradigms. The battle between believers and non-believers will then play an important role in the development of policies and the political approach will prevail in the implementation of policy.

Furthermore, there are *(un)tamable ethical problems* (Hoppe, 1989:12). Parties share common knowledge about a problem and accept this knowledge as valid and trustworthy. But they differ in their opinion on what values need to be taken into account when a government decides to (not) intervene. A common example is the ongoing discussion about euthanasia in cases of unbearable suffering, in cases where people are not physically ill, but are mentally at the end of their tether (for example from Alzheimer's). A different example: scientifically, we know what consequences an advanced stage of cancer has in terms of pain and failure of vital bodily functions. We also know how we can end this unbearable suffering in a reliable and safe way. But, do we want this? Is it acceptable and if so, under what circumstances? How can we make sure that there is no abuse, but that everybody is careful – the patient, their family and the responsible physicians? The lack of consensus on benchmarks can lead to "politically sensitive" issues. Because the matter concerns the values we want to pursue in society, the implementation of policy is more likely to happen through a political approach.

Lastly, there are the *untamed political problems*, also known as *wicked problems* (Rittel and Webber, 1973; Hoppe, 1989:12-13). In such cases there is a lack of unambiguous moral benchmarks. Second, our knowledge of possible causes, possible interventions and possible effects underlying these problems leads to fundamental gaps. Many problems faced by the government are untamed political problems. The legitimacy of a government is partly due to such problems, because it is the *"intelligence of democracy"* – quoting Lindblom (1965) – to tackle such problems in a peaceful, but timely and satisfying manner.

When solving such problems, parties often propose diverse measures and all parties are convinced of the validity of their own proposals and deliver proof to confirm this. However, parties often question the effects of certain measures proposed by others and they are in disagreement on which measure is most suitable to handle the issue. Arguments brought in to the conflict are often based on different perceptions of (and stories about) the nature of the problem and possible solutions. Perceptions that may result from certain historically formed positions, practices and interests. As such, the policy process is mostly a battle in these cases, and the political approach can provide more handles to understand this process.

It is important to note that the status of a policy problem can change, due to an expansion of relevant knowledge or because of a political or societal consensus on certain problems is reached. For example, the AIDS problem was mostly characterized by uncertainty in the 1980s. There was no clarity about the causes of the issue, but there was also no answer to the question of what the effects could be to society – taking into account the uncertainty about the size and spread of the risk of infection. What did this mean for the importance and place of public health in society? This was an untamable political problem. However, throughout the years, we have significantly expanded our knowledge of the nature of the virus, the possible causes of infection, the nature of the risks associated with the behavior of certain groups within society and the effects of possible treatments. As such, the problem turned into being more like a tamed problem, even though there is still no clearly effective treatment against infection. There are, however, treatments that slow down or stop the virus from working, and the knowledge that the size of certain groups with increased risks is limited also ensures less risk for public health.

Elements in the construction of policy problems

Based on the typologies discussed above, we can deduce that the definition of the nature and size of policy problems can cause a heated atmosphere when there is a lack of consensus. Definitions compete for priority. This means that it is important to consider policy problems as social and political constructions. With this, we mean that they are defined from the perspective of the interests of the actors involved. They are perceived problems that, by definition, are based on a selective and subjective view of reality. This also has consequences for the way in which we solve these problems. Our perception of the nature and size of a problem therefore partially decides the way in which we select certain strategies or measures. A certain problem definition can lead to the preference for different strategies or measures, so we can speak of a pre-filtered approach.

The social and political constructivist character, and with that the subjective way of looking at a policy problem and the measures we select because of this, are determined by the following factors. Various factors have been derived mostly from the political, cultural and institutional approaches to policy. First, the political approach to policy teaches us that actors try to direct the way policy problems are defined by prioritizing their own *interests* and position. Also, they will use any sources of *power* available to them to directly influence the problem definition. In discussing how to deal with the euro crisis, countries such as Germany and France completely disagreed with one another in 2012. German chancellor Merkel mostly pointed at the poor management of government finances by some countries as a cause of the crisis, calling for extreme measures of budget cuts to get the economy back to where it was. French president Hollande, on the other side, was looking for solutions to stimulate the economy and wanted to remediate the debts of member states by introducing so-called Eurobonds. With this, the problematized countries would be able to lend money at low interest rates to cover their shortages. Due to its strong economical position, Germany was able to decide the problem definition and define how the problem should be tackled, thereby overtaking France. Additionally, Germany asked for support from countries that had their finances in order, such as the Netherlands and Finland.

Second, the cultural and institutional approach teaches us that in the definition of policy problems, the *referential framework* or *conceptual framework* of the involved actor plays an important role. Public service organizations will approach problems concerning the liveability of cities by trying to improve the quality of the physical environment, while the police consider it to be a safety problem that can be solved with increased police patrolling the streets. Hence, the task that is being carried out by an organization partially decides what aspects of a policy problem are (not) taken into account. Additionally, the professional background of an actor can play a role in this. A lawyer will have a different view on certain problems than, for example, a sociologist or political scientist. For a lawyer, power is based in the competences assigned to municipalities through laws and regulations. A sociologist or political scientist, on the other hand, will also review other sources of power, for example because a municipality has access to a wealth of information.

An important aspect of this referential framework is the concept actors have of man and world, an idea that is proposed mostly by the cultural and institutional approach of policy. This also decides the way in which parties define certain desired or undesired risks. Because of that, Douglas and Wildavsky (1983) ask themselves the question: based on which considerations, assumptions and rules do actors define policy problems as relevant and as potentially risky for our society, and neglect other problems? Each community has a selective view on the way in which a society functions (especially in relation to its natural environment) and thereby accepts certain risks. Douglas (1992; also Hendriks, 1996:51 and further) has made an attempt to classify the assumptions regarding the way in which we take or avoid risks by establishing certain concepts of man and world. From an individualistic concept of man and world, it is difficult to approach societal problems, because humans are incorrigibly selfish. Political institutions can correct undesirable and risky behavior to a certain extent, but that never happens easily. People and organizations will always tend to withdraw themselves from the influence of these institutions. Their co-operation can only be obtained if there is some sort of compensation. Policy making and implementation therefore means giving and taking, and can be characterized by battle, negotiation and trade. In an egalitarian concept of man and world, the most important value is equality among human beings. The assumption underlying many policy problems is that, to a certain extent, the problem concerns all people and organizations, which is why political institutions need to ensure equality. Because people and organizations are guided by this equality ideal, they will be more willing to co-operate. Moreover, they will also be more likely to accept the institutions making this possible. In a hierarchical concept of man and world, the expectation is that policy problems should mainly be the concern of one central governing actor (being the government) that should use (friendly) force to get people and organizations in the ranks. People also expect this from, for example, a government. There needs to be a clear description of what can be expected of people and organizations. This also means that there is an assumption that compliance to such norms and guidelines needs to be guarded effectively. In a fatalistic concept of man and world, every form of government intervention is destined to fail, because the behavior of people and organizations is capricious and unpredictable, while societal developments cannot be influenced, let alone controlled. Hence, policy by definition cannot improve the situation.

Third, inspired primarily by the institutional approach, we know that diverse *rules and institutions* within which actors need to function also decide the problem perception. For example, from the perspective of the city council, processes of interactive policy implementation – where citizens play an active role in the development of plans and decision-making regarding these plans (for example through advisory referendums) – are considered suspicious. How do certain practices relate to the primacy of the council? Devotion to the rules, therefore, partly decides the way in which an interactive approach of reconstructing a mall or another public area is assessed.

Fourth, the *language* we use to formulate the nature and size of a policy problem also influences the way the problem is defined. The cultural approach shows us that metaphors, slogans and symbols play an important role in this. They tell and visualize the story being told about the question of why government intervention is (not) desired by creating an image of the severity of the issue. The slogans used in election campaigns make an interesting example. In 2008, Barack Obama used "Yes we can" and "Change we can believe in" during his first run for presidency, while his Republican opponent John McCain used "Reform, prosperity and peace" and "Country first" – using words that already indicate the direction the candidate would take during presidency. Similarly, during the presidential elections of 2012, Obama's opponent Mitt Romney used the slogan "Obama isn't working" as a spin-off from the British "Labour isn't working." This phrase was used by the Conservative party in the elections of 1979, which were won by groundbreaking politician Margaret Thatcher and which announced a time of major changes in the field of policy making.

Stone (2001:163 and further) points out that not only words and stories are important for the way in which policy problems are formulated. *Numbers* might also be used to tell a story about the nature and size of a problem. For example, both Obama and Romney used statistics about the increasing unemployment rate in the United States during the presidential elections of 2012. However, numbers and statistics are not always objective indicators, because they steer our view on reality in a certain direction. The question of what is being measured and how it is being measured is essential to assess reliability. For example by limiting the definition of unemployment by omitting certain indicators such as disability, one can create a different reflection of reality. The demarcation of the definition decides if a problem increased or decreased, and indicates the direction that needs to be taken.

Causes can also be considered as a language used to steer the formulation of problem definitions in a desirable direction. There are several different "causal stories" told about many policy problems (Stone, 2001:188 and further). In those stories, the nature of the problem sets the tone and therefore leads to the formulation of certain solutions. For example, there are two stories that can be told about the utility and necessity of offering free day care to increase women's participation in the labor market. One story says that the costs for day care are too high, while the quality levels of the offered facilities are too low, which is why women decide to stay at home. Free day care could break this pattern, but then quality does need to be improved. A different story might say that a specific culture has a tradition entrenched in society of children being raised by their mothers. This culture cannot be changed. As such, free day care would only solve the problem partially. Successful policy should thus be focused on breaking certain patterns regarding roles and historical norms about "good motherhood".

Another language that can shape the way problems are defined is that of *responsibilities* (Stone, 2001:210 and further). The way in which we define a problem largely decides who the owner of the problem is. With that, an appeal is made to the involved actor who has certain responsibilities to come up with a solution. By defining the liveability of neighborhoods as a safety problem, it almost immediately becomes a problem that needs to be solved by the police. At the same time, it can be argued that citizens have an individual responsibility for what happens in their neighborhood. In the discussion about the gap between citizens and public service organizations, citizens are being held accountable for their responsibility as administrators of the public space. Because of this turn in problem-ownership, and with that the related responsibility, a different definition and solution of the problem arise.

A fifth element in the construction of problems, speaking to the political perspective in particular, involves the development of coalitions. Certain coalitions can come into existence regarding certain definitions of and approaches to policy problems that will take every opportunity to bring specific problem definitions or approaches to the forefront. In these cases, Sabatier (1987) speaks of so-called *advocacy coalitions*. One can see such advocacy coalitions coming into existence in the case of the new waterway that will be built through Nicaragua by the Chinese businessman Wang Jing. Within the country, as well as in the region and worldwide, this project has stimulated many discussions even before the build has started. Questions are being asked about the legitimacy of the deal and the transparency concerning the extremely short process of passing the bill through public debate in the Nicaraguan congress. The concern is that Nicaragua's political sovereignty has been put in the hands of the waterway's owner. Moreover, it will be a direct competitor to the Panama Canal, leading to economic concerns in Panama. As such, this project has caused several opposing coalitions to come into existence. However, the project might improve Nicaragua's poor economic position in the long run, and several international giants such as McKinsey support and co-operate with it. Consequently, there are also several coalitions that assess the project positively.

A final element in the construction of problems involves *communication*. Definitions of reality and thus of a certain policy problem are also realized through communication. They are not always imposed. Because of that, the cultural approach to policy values the formulation of policy as a process of common perceptions of the nature and size of a problem, as well as the question of how it should be dealt with. Within and through communication, parties are able to learn from each other and definitions of reality are adjusted and matched. For example, in the context of improving the situation in a neighborhood, citizens, associations and governments can try to formulate common goals that aim to develop a neighborhood, determine what facilities need to be established and how the neighborhood needs to be maintained.

3.3 Social classification of target groups

The construction of policy problems almost always also involves a construction of the groups that will benefit from the policy; the target groups. As such, there is a process of classification (Stone, 2001). Such social constructions of target groups can have an important effect on agenda setting in various ways. When a group is defined as deserving and in need of help and protection, this will provide an incentive to actors (including but not limited to politicians) to provide help. Everybody wants to be seen as supporting groups that are weak and deserving. Think for instance about the agenda setting of help to disabled people, or to single mothers.

Classification means there is a process of in- and exclusion of groups taking place: those who are within certain boundaries – within classifications – and those who are not. That is how rights and obligations are divided between demarcated groups, which is a political choice made in advance (Stone, 2001). Citizens in a threatened neighborhood may have more right to get police deployed in their neighborhood than citizens in a less threatened neighborhood. We can see this political character of the process of "drawing boundaries" back in the New Disability Act of the Dutch government, aiming to tackle the amount of people not being able to participate in the labor force because of sickness or disability and thereby decreasing expenditure on social security. In this New Disability Act, the central idea is that "for people with health problems or a disability the focus is no longer on what these people cannot do, but on what they still can do" (OECD, 2007:6). Through requalification, new boundaries were drawn between those citizens that are considered fully unable to work, and those who were considered less disabled and therefore able to work to a certain extent. Because of this, the number of people classified as fully disabled decreased, thereby changing the definition of the nature of the problem. For example, the new policy was considered successful in the eyes of the Dutch Minister of Social Affairs and Employment, because the problem reduced in size. By drawing new boundaries and classifying citizens differently, the status of the disabled changed. As a consequence, the division of related rights and obligations changed as well. Rights and obligations that were assigned based on a certain consideration of values – offering security and safety for those who are unable to participate in the labor force – and the stimulation of people to find suitable work after all, thereby actively participating in society. This kept the system affordable and intact.

Policy is usually directed to a specific group of citizens. For example, it can focus on the integration of immigrants, preventing alcohol abuse among youth, or better care for the elderly in residential homes. This means that the way in which we define policy problems also has consequences for the construction of the target group on which a certain policy program is directed. It is the target group that carries the problem definition and with that it legitimizes a certain approach. The way in which a target group is demarcated can work to the advantage of certain actors that have interests in the demarcation. This demarcation can be the cause for more resources and attention (positive as well as negative). Schneider and Ingram (1997:109-111) show that there are four ideal types of target group constructions (see Figure 3.2):

- *The advantaged.* Policy directed at the advantaged often wants to put a positive light on a group that meets certain standards, excels in something, or is relatively powerful. For example, policy that focuses on the hardworking, taxpaying middle class. Or policy directed at providing extra support for excellent scientists.

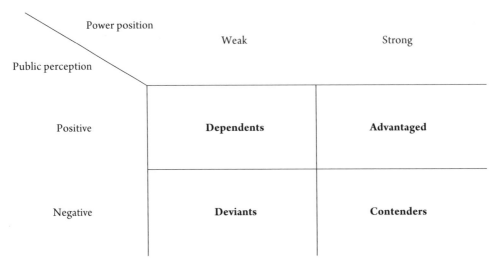

Figure 3.2 Four target group constructions

- *The challengers.* Policy directed at groups that might have a lot of power, but who challenge existing practices and therefore have a negative image. An example of this is policy directed at bonuses or high salaries for top executives of companies and societal organizations, such as hospitals, universities and housing corporations.
- *The dependents.* Policy directed at the support of groups who are in a difficult position causing them to be dependent on help and support of others, like the government. An example of this is policy directed at helping sick or disabled youth by offering them chances of a job or education so they can remove themselves from the difficult position they are in. Oftentimes these policies concern groups that are not organized strongly in a political sense, but that do have a positive image.
- *The deviants.* Policy directed at groups that deviate from existing norms and therefore have a negative image. This concerns for example criminal or anti-social behavior, behavior that is unhealthy or societally deviant. This behavior is often associated with certain stigmas. An example of this is the approach of the German governments in installing minimum wages to protect native Germans from the alleged threat of the growing number of Eastern European workers in the country.

Once again, it is important to be aware of the dynamic nature of target group constructions. Think of changes that have taken place in the social construction of "single mothers", from deviants that did not fit into institutionalized patterns of behavior of traditional society to dependents who are seen as definitely deserving of support. The homeless is also another category whose social construction not only tends to vary over time, but also between different social settings; in some cases they are perceived as a nuisance and in others as weak persons in need of help. Such changes will also have implications for policies toward these groups.

Important in Schneider and Ingram's work is the impact that target group constructions have on the policy process. If a group is seen as weak and deserving, this will provide incentives to actors to provide public support to these groups. In contrast, there are strong political incentives to publicly distance oneself or even provide "punishment" to groups that are seen as weak and negative (such as criminals or terrorists). So, in terms of agenda setting, there are positive incentives to put measures in support of dependents and advantaged openly on the public agenda, as well as to put negative measures toward deviants on the agenda. Importantly, the target group construct of "contenders" seems to discourage agenda setting. On the one hand, there are incentives against negative measures toward these groups, as contenders are classified as "powerful". For instance, if Germany adopts measures against its car industries (seen as contenders), this can have negative consequences for the German economy. On the other hand, helping contenders could be politically unwise as it involves a group that is perceived in negative terms. So Germany might want to help its car industries, but do so in a more depoliticized way, for instance via technical measures in the tax system that are often so complex that they are difficult to frame on the public agenda.

BOX 3.1

DEGENERATIVE POLICY DESIGNS

How groups are socially constructed has implications for politics toward these groups, as Schneider and Ingram (1993, 1997) argue. However, it also has consequences for the political system as a whole. Target group constructs provide incentives to treat groups differently, or in political science terms, to treat groups not in accordance with the one-man-one-vote rule of modern democracies. Groups that are seen as weak and deserving will obtain more support when compared to groups that are seen in a more negative perspective. This can, as Schneider and Ingram argue, have a potentially undermining or "degenerative" effect on democracy. It will lead to the exclusion of some groups, especially those seen as negative and weak. They risk turning their backs on democracy, and organizing their influence in different ways (such as crime). On the other hand, especially those defined as (positive and) deserving will obtain much more influence on democracy then their numerical position would warrant, for instance, home owners are a particularly influential group in modern democracies that manage to obtain far more benefits than a one-man-one-vote system would legitimize.

3.4　Types of agendas

An agenda is a collection of problem perceptions, views on possible causes, symbols, and views on possible solutions that draw the attention of different politicians, policy makers, *opinion leaders*, and administrators (Birkland, 2001:106). An agenda can consist of a list of law proposals under discussion in parliaments, or the decisions that are up for submission in a municipal council. An agenda can also concern certain viewpoints on the question of why a government – whether or not in co-operation with other parties, such as corporate organizations – has to get involved, taking into consideration the gravity and size of a certain issue. Agendas exist throughout all levels of government. Each policy directorate has its own agenda that is brought up in, for example, cabinet formations. Social organizations – such as employers and employees, environmental and consumer organizations – and corporate organizations have their own agendas depending on the societal issues that are at stake. All actors attempt to ask attention for their agenda. This happens in different ways, varying from setting up a lobby to a public appeal or open letters to ministers.

The most abstract type of agenda that can be distinguished is the so-called *agenda universe* (Cobb and Elder, 1972:85). This concerns all subjects that are considered to be significant for political discussion and deliberation by different parties. Some subjects in this universe of potential subjects are considered not negotiable, for example because they are in conflict with constitutions, international agreements like the United Nations' International Covenant on Civil and Political Rights or other covenants. For example, in most democracies it is not allowed, or even considered as a crime, to call into question the occurrence of the Holocaust (Birkland, 2001:106).

Those subjects that are acceptable are referred to as the *societal agenda*. This agenda concerns all subjects that members of a political community (for example, a municipality, a neighborhood, a country) collectively consider to be possibly politically relevant and refer to the competences and responsibilities of certain public bodies (Cobb and Elder, 1972:85). The *societal or public agenda* consists of those subjects of which members of a community think are negotiable (van de Graaf and Hoppe, 1989:183).

Additionally, there is the *political agenda*. This agenda concerns a selection of subjects derived from the public agenda and which – after filtering – are considered to be subjects needing explicit and careful political attention by politicians and public administrators (Cobb and Elder, 1972:85-86). These subjects are often mentioned in, for example, coalition agreements.

Next, there is the *decision-making agenda* (Cobb and Elder, 1972:86). This is the collection of subjects of which politicians, administrators and policy makers believe they need to be converted into actual policy programs or specific laws and regulations. When we look at the agendas of municipal councils, it offers us a relatively reliable insight into the decision-making agenda of a municipality, but this does not always have to lead to the development of a certain policy program. Not all responsible public officials are aware of the purpose and necessity of translating decisions into policies, which can lead to putting a decision on hold (van de Graaf and Hoppe, 1989:182). As such, it is important that a subject gets a spot on the *policy agenda*, which is considered as the final agenda in the agenda-setting process.

The question is: when can a subject change agendas? What is the reason that a subject jumps from one agenda to the other? According to Cobb and Elder (1972:82), *triggers* play an important role in this. This can be, for example, a disaster. After the explosion of the Fukushima power plant in Japan, the German federal government decided that nuclear energy was no longer the best source and caused it to turn to alternative energy sources. Similarly, the collapse of a cotton factory in Bangladesh unleashed an international discussion on the responsibilities of international firms in enabling unsafe working environments and the appropriate response of governments.

The relationship between these different agendas is visualized in Figure 3.3. This concerns concentric circles in which one agenda is a subset of a larger collection.

3.5   Rational perspective: the "discovery" of problems

What drives agenda setting? What causes one topic to emerge prominently on the political and policy agenda while other topics are ignored? Why do some actors try to put an issue on the agenda while at the same time and for the same issue other actors often seemingly try to hold off any new attention? To understand the logic of agenda setting, we will discuss the four central theoretical perspectives from this book: rationalism, constructivism, political perspective and institutionalism.

From a "pure" rationalist perspective the stage of agenda setting is not highly valued. Problems are not "set" on the agenda by particular actors, they by definition emerge on the agenda when objective indicators show that there is a problem. Problems are not "put" on the agenda by actors but are "discovered" by the actors based on sound evidence and information. And indeed, objective indicators often do play a key role in agenda setting.

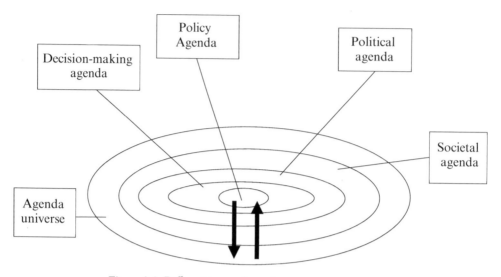

Figure 3.3 Different types of agendas

Think of monitors or evaluation studies that are meant to check whether a problem develops or a policy is not sufficiently effective. For instance, the OECD (Organisation for Economic Co-operation and Development) is an organization that publishes monitors and evaluates on various social and economic areas with the purposes of promoting policy developments in OECD states. This mission of OECD is based firmly on the belief that a rational and objective input into the policy process will actually trigger better policies.

The rationalist perspective also assumes that people not only have full access to and are able to understand information, but also that they will actually respond to knowledge and information. However, as discussed in Chapter 2, actors (all actors, not just politicians and policy makers) are boundedly rational. This means that rather than perfect information and processing capacities, the capacities of actors to assess objective knowledge and information will be limited. They may not have access or be aware of monitors or evaluations that might indicate a specific problem. Or they may not be able to understand or may even be ignorant of the meaning and implications of specific objective indicators. Or, as we will see in the political perspective, some may even choose to selectively pick-and-choose or rather ignore objective indicators even when they are able to understand them.

BOX 3.2

TRUST IN NUMBERS (PORTER, 1997)

In his article *Trust in Numbers* the social scientist Ted Porter showed how deep is the belief that people tend to put in the objectivity of "numbers". He shows that when problems or issues can be captured and phrased in "numbers", they tend to be much more convincing to a broader public. Numbers tend to endow a certain objectivity to problems. As a consequence, as Porter shows, the construction of numbers is an integral part of the policy making process, and even of politics as such. In an effort to be as convincing as possible and to gain broader support and legitimacy, actors will attempt to prove their "objectivity" by capturing their policy claims in numbers. And when captured in numbers, a policy claim is no longer just a claim but is considered a "fact".

Bounded rationality means that not all problems can emerge on the agenda if objective indicators state so, but that attention can be allocated only to a limited number of topics at any given moment. Hilgartner and Bosk (1988) describe this is as the carrying capacity of agendas, which is inherently limited and selective. This has led to various (more modestly) rationalist studies of how and why specific problems do make it onto agendas with limited carrying capacity. Perhaps the most famous application of such theories is the *barrier model* (Cobb and Elder, 1971). This model argues that problems need to overcome various objective barriers before they can emerge on the policy agenda. First, a topic must rise on the public agenda, capturing broad public attention. Issue attention is here taken as a proxy for issue salience. Second, issues with broad public attention will rise on the political agenda as well. Politicians all want to speak about the current topics of the day. Think of how many parliamentary questions are raised the day after a topic is highlighted in the evening news. Finally, once on the political agenda, an issue can make its way onto the policy agenda. Once politicians have discussed the topic it can be selected for consideration of policy alternatives.

A key element of the barrier model is the amount of public attention (especially media attention) a topic generates in order to make it onto the policy agenda. The barrier model pays a lot of attention to the process of *issue-articulation* and *issue-expansion*, because of which a yet-undefined issue, that is visible locally and experienced as problematic by certain people, grows out to be a subject that attracts the attention of a larger audience. They pay more attention to the first part of the agenda setting process, in which unstructured issues are translated into well-described desires. In the process of issue-articulation and issue-expansion, the following factors play an important role (Parsons, 1995:129):

- *The specific character of a subject.* The more ambiguous a subject is, the sooner it will get the attention of a larger audience. Small, specific subjects that only affect a small group will have a smaller chance of getting the attention of a larger audience.
- *The public meaning of a subject.* The more public meaning a subject has, the bigger the chance that a larger audience feels affected.
- *The temporality of a subject.* The more a subject has a long-term meaning to society, the bigger the chance that it will be taken up by a larger audience.
- *The technical character of a subject.* The more technical a subject is, and therefore the more knowledge is necessary to understand it, the smaller the chance that it will draw the attention from a larger audience.
- *The unique character of a subject.* The more unique a subject is, meaning that it is not a mere variation on a familiar theme (does not build on precedents), the bigger the chance that a larger audience will be interested.

Additionally, Cobb and Elder draw special attention to the language that is being used in the articulation and spreading of the subject. They emphasize the importance of powerful symbols, appealing metaphors, and rhetoric to be able to tell an appealing and inspiring story that is visual and/or speaks to one's imagination. It facilitates the process of identification. Stone (1989:295) stresses this as well. Symbols and statistics are, in their words, powerful instruments to tell an appealing story about causes and consequences, and with that steer the image of reality, making it easier for a problem to get on to the political agenda.

The *mass media* play, as said, an intermediary role in this as well. Especially the expansion of a subject to the larger audience that leads to politicians being more receptive to certain subjects, making it easier for that subject to gain access to the government and consequently get decision-making attention. When the mass media are capable of showing how conflicts or controversies arise regarding certain subjects and related desires, this can work to their advantage. It establishes the attention, but also generates new attention that is not only beneficial for the parties that want to get an issue on to a certain agenda, but also for the mass media itself (Parsons, 1995:129-130). The meaning that Cobb and Elder assign to this intermediary role of the mass media is, however, based on an image that is rooted in the 1970s. Since then, especially the mass media have gone through significant developments that influence their role in contemporary society. Nowadays, mass media – and not only television but also the Internet and social media – play an important role in independently creating issues. Especially the unifying character of social media like Twitter, Facebook and sites like Tumblr, enables individual or small groups of citizens to organize themselves as a powerful movement

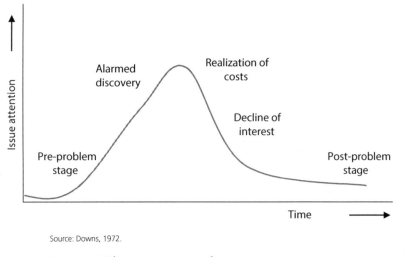

Source: Downs, 1972.

Figure 3.4 The issue attention cycle

incredibly quickly and at a rather large scale, usually outside of the horizon of policy makers. Additionally, we can see that there are several *cross-overs* between these new media and traditional media, making certain viewpoints even more powerful because they strengthen each other. It is not for nothing that people talk about the increasing sensitivity of politics for *hypes* created consciously by the media, with an emphasis on enlarging incidents that suddenly receive political attention and potentially lead to political decisions, but also evaporate just as quickly. An important challenge for policy makers is therefore how to deal with these issues, that often come up as strategic surprises; surprises that mostly turn out to be painful when there is a gap between the official goals of the policy and reality, putting the legitimacy of the government response up for discussion. As such, there is increasingly more attention for what we call *strategic issue management* (Bekkers et al., 2011a).

The barrier model suggests a rather linear perception of issue articulation, expansion and agenda setting. This linear view has been contested by various scholars. Downs (1972) suggests a more cyclical view in the form of the so-called *issue attention cycle* (Figure 3.4). This cycle shows how problems, after periods of being ignored, will often quite suddenly go through a moment of "alarmed discovery." This is what Cobb and Elder referred to as issue articulation and expansion. However, this is usually followed by a period where realism kicks in and awareness of cost and other limitations initiates a decline of public attention and interest. Most often, policy making will then have to take place in the post-problem stage in terms of attention, when a problem is on the policy agenda but no longer on the public agenda.

Furthermore, the linearity of the barrier model also comes forth in the preference it has for one-way traffic: through the public agenda the subjects move on to the political and policy agenda. However, the other direction is also possible: via the policy agenda to the political and public agenda. In contrast to the barrier model, which is an *outside initiation* model, there is also an *inside initiation* model (Howlett, Ramesh and Perl, 1995:113-114). In the latter, public officials increase the pressure on politicians – for example because interest groups suggest certain things, or form a coalition with influential opinion leaders and experts – so that administrators and politicians are forced to take these into account. Subsequently, these administrators and politicians influence the public opinion by raising certain issues (Cobb, Ross and Ross, 1976:136). These convictions show that broad public support is not necessary for gaining a place on the political agenda.

Finally, another criticism of the barrier model concerns the role of the media. The role of the mass media becomes more nuanced when we look at their role in channeling and guiding certain desires, thereby drawing the attention of politicians and policy makers. Three positions can be distinguished. First, issues are put in different perspectives. Politicians and administrators also use different information sources, like the information that is provided by lobby groups or research agencies (van de Graaf and Hoppe, 1989:194). Second, the independent role that mass media have in formulating certain subjects can be identified over the merely facilitating role. They have an interest in establishing attention, not because and for others, but also for themselves (Parsons, 1995:129). As such, some also talk about the so-called media agenda. With that, they determine the political agenda to a certain extent. This is strengthened by the contemporary dominance of the "image culture" and the related need for appealing symbols. The media are pre-eminently capable of creating these images and telling a "political" story, for example by personalizing, magnifying or dramatizing cases. Politicians increasingly perceive these images as "true"; they accept them. As such, some also talk about "drama democracy" in this context (Elchardus, 2003).

Third, the phenomenon of the mass media is put in a different perspective when it is associated with new media. The rise of the Internet and the rapid societal penetration of social media challenges the dominant role of established mass media in the formulation of subjects. The democratic character of the Internet, and especially social media like Twitter, Facebook and YouTube – in terms of accessibility and reach – means that every person or each (self-organized) group of like-minded people or stakeholders can start their own "channel", tell their own story. This can spread rapidly among large groups of followers (friends of friends who are connected through all sorts of networks and lists), and which is picked up on more and more often by traditional mass media (television, newspapers, magazines). We call this "*the micro-mobilization of bias*" (Tindall, 2004; Bekkers, Moody and Edwards, 2011b). Typical of micro-mobilization is that a single citizen or a small group of citizens can influence the public and political opinion relatively easily by seeking attention for a certain issue. The role of traditional intermediaries, like political parties, unions or interest groups that are mostly active on a sectoral level, is decreasing. One example of this is the influence that YouTube has had in the formulation of concern among American citizens about the course of events in the war with Iraq and Afghanistan. Because of videos posted by soldiers stationed in Iraq, a whole different image of the events taking place was spread that did not correspond with the official images released by the Pentagon. These images showed a realistic depiction of the dead and wounded, soldiers as well as citizens, which influenced the public opinion but also the reporting of the newspapers, television and magazines. Another example of this is the ongoing role that several social media platforms have played in igniting the Arab Spring and international awareness about developments in the region. As one Egyptian activist tweeted during the 2011 protests there: "We use Facebook to schedule the protests, Twitter to coordinate, and YouTube to tell the world." The extensive role that social media played in the organization of and reporting about the protests even led to a temporary nation-wide blockage of Internet access.

3.6 Political perspective: advocacy coalitions and multiple streams

From the political perspective, agenda setting needs to be seen through the perspective of Dahl's conclusion that power in any society is not in the hands of one elite, of one oligarchy, but that there are several different political elites with diverging powerbases that struggle for power in a community (Dahl, 1961). Policy is the outcome of a struggle between organized groups in a certain environment, such as a municipality or a country. However, there is a lot to choose from. What should the struggle between these elites focus on? What are suitable subjects? And that also counts for possible solutions that are being proposed; the political struggle can also focus on these. There is a high degree of variation between certain problems and directions for solutions that ask for attention. The freedom of these elites to choose between these therefore is an important source of power that mainly decides which subjects reach the political agenda (Schattschneider, 1960:69). What conflict are the elites prepared to tackle, and what conflict would they rather avoid?

There are certain beliefs underlying the choice that these elites make. These beliefs relate to the desirability of certain political conflicts on the one hand, and to the preparedness of an elite to actually tackle the conflict on the other hand. Because of this, Schattschneider (1960:72) describes agenda setting as *"the mobilization of bias."* "All forms of political organizations have a bias in favor of the exploitation of some conflicts and the suppression of others because organization is the mobilization of bias. Some issues are organized into politics and others are organized out" (Schattschneider, 1960:71). The choice for a certain subject, and with that also the choice for a certain struggle, therefore reflects a bias or conviction.

Bachrach and Baratz (1963, 1970) further developed the notion of agenda setting as a process of the mobilization of bias. They considered the struggle between certain (party) political elites as a way in which these elites can bring their views on the nature of societal problems to the forefront. When an elite is able to use its power – for example because they were helped to get a majority in elections – this power can be used to secure a definition of a problem, based on which a certain policy program can prevail. But, as Bachrach and Baratz (1963:632) state, this does not always have to lead to a political decision or to the draft of a policy program.

On the other hand, *non-decision-making* can take place, in which case certain subjects or interpretations are not taken into consideration. A process of filtering takes place. Certain subjects get the status of a taboo and are then botched. "Non decision is a means by which demands for change in the existing allocation of benefits and privileges in the community can be suffocated before they are even voiced; or kept overt; or killed to gain access to the relevant decision-making arena; or failing all these things, maimed and destroyed in the decision-making stage of the policy process" (Bachrach and Baratz, 1970:7).

Politically sensitive subjects, such as tax increases or softening immigration policies in times of economic crisis, are sometimes turned into taboos because of the crux they cause in politics. In the now classic example of the tackling of air pollution in the American city of Gary, Crenson (1971) shows that it is not only the struggle between political elites that causes certain subjects – in this case the problem of air pollution in this city – can lead to the omission of issues on the political agenda. Elites are also guided by the informal power of parties that are outside of the political spectrum. It is the unspoken but present informal power of US Steel on which Gary is economically dependent that causes political elites to be hesitant to take on the subject. In short, the powerful reputation of an actor outside of the formal political arena blocked the process of agenda setting. Because air pollution was not an issue within US Steel (taking into account the entailing costs), it was not an issue in the broader political community of Gary of which US Steel was a part (Parsons, 1995:140).

The multiple streams approach

An alternative model that challenges the linearity of the barrier model is the so-called streams model as developed by Kingdon (1984; 1995). Kingdon's ideas were inspired by the so-called *garbage can model* as developed by Cohen, March and Olsen (1972). This garbage can model was used by these authors to understand the chaotic nature of restructuring in universities. In this model, professional organizations and government bureaucracies are considered as an "organized anarchy". Although organizations do have formal and rational arrangements of tasks, responsibilities and competences, they also have another side. This other side consists of loose, fluid collections of ideas that are decided upon on the basis of *trial and error* and rarely on the basis of rational considerations (see Parsons, 1995). Organizations can therefore also be seen as garbage cans of possible decisions, in which all parties dump ideas about their problem perceptions and possible solutions. In this perspective, decision-making may be considered as a completely random linking of problems to solutions, but also of solutions to problems. This anarchistic idea of decision-making was a major source of inspiration for Kingdon (1984) in developing his streams model. In the streams model, Kingdon considers agenda-setting as the more or less incidental coupling of three different streams: the problems stream, the policy stream and the politics stream (see Kingdon, 1984; 1995; Zahariadis, 2007). We will elaborate on each of these streams below.

The first stream is the stream of *problems*, which consists of conditions that policy makers consider to be problematic, i.e. the actual state of the world does not match the state of the world that the policy maker desires on the base of his values and beliefs (Kingdon, 1995; Travis and Zahariadis, 2002). Policy makers need to become aware of the existence of these types of conditions. According to Kingdon (1995) three mechanisms play a role in focusing the attention of policy makers on conditions that may be considered as problems:

First, indicators play a role in assessing the existence and magnitude of a condition. Statistical offices around the world routinely produce an abundance of statistics about, for example, economic growth, unemployment levels, road crash victims or domestic violence, which may point out worrisome trends. But also special studies may produce indicators like for instance the number of airline safety regulation violations or the state of endangered species. These one-off indicators often also are produced with the goal of attracting policy officials' attention, in other words to point out the problematic status of a condition.

Second, dramatic events or crises can highlight the problematic character of a condition. Obvious examples are the terrorist attacks in Paris on the Charlie Hebdo headquarters in January 2015 and the Bataclan Theatre in November 2015 or, the so-called Brexit referendum in which a majority of British voters voted in favor of Great-Britain leaving the European Union. But also less radical events like the resignation of a cabinet member or the publication of the Panama Papers, the leaked documents which belonged to the Panamanian law firm and corporate service provider Mossack Fonseca that provided detailed information on financial and attorney–client relations of a large number of offshore entities. Birkland (2001: 116) uses the term "focusing events" for this type of event.

Third, feedback from inside or outside the policy system may highlight potentially problematic conditions. Examples of internal feedback are the monitoring of the United Nations' Sustainable Development Goals or the Paris Climate Agreement, but also national or local policy evaluations. Examples of external feedback are letters from constituents, op-eds in newspapers or topics discussed in talkshows on national television. Increasingly, these are complemented by external feedback from social media, for instance in so called vlogs (video weblogs) that seek attention for specific conditions.

Policies constitute the second stream according to Kingdon. They include a wide variety of ideas floating around in the "policy primeval soup" (Kingdon, 1984: 116). Ideas are generated by specialists in policy networks that include bureaucrats, congressional staff members, academics, and researchers in think-tanks who share a common concern in a single policy area, such as health or environmental policy, and are communicated in various ways, such as hearings, papers, and conversations. Some ideas survive this initial period rather unchanged, others are combined into new proposals, and still others disappear, either temporarily or indefinitely (Travis and Zahariadis, 2002).

The *political* stream is the third stream that Kingdon distinguishes. Perceived problems and possible solutions on their own are not enough to transfer an issue into an item on the political agenda, the political realm plays a role in this as well. This stream is composed of such things as the national mood, pressure group campaigns, election results, partisan or ideological distributions in Congress, and changes of administration. According to Kingdon (1995), the following elements from the political realm are important in explaining processes of agenda-setting:

- *The national mood.* More specifically, Kingdon argues that elected officials' interpretations of the national mood, and, even more important, of their constituents guides their behaviour and thus serves to promote some items on their own agendas and to restrain others from rising to prominence. One example is the growing awareness of the impact of climate change in many countries of the world, which is reflected in the positions of many politicians in all parts of the world. According to Kingdon, elected politicians judge their constituents' mood from such communications as mail, town meetings, smaller gatherings, and delegations of people or even individuals coming to them during their office hours in the district, whereas non-elected officials tend to sense the national mood from what they hear from politicians.
- *Organized political forces.* This includes the manner in which the political system is organized and the dominant position of all kinds of formal and informal political organizations, such as the changing landscape of political parties, the role of trade unions and business associations, but also the power of interests groups or pressure groups. Changes in this landscape may give prominence to some issues while pushing back others.
- *Turnovers in the position of the public authorities.* Of course, one of the most prominent changes in the political stream relates to the outcome of elections. With a new president, a new governing coalition or a new administration, the way to the agenda is open for new problems and new policies. Also, the assignment of new powers or the change of existing powers of government agencies or jurisdictions can lead to the creation of political events that are significant for the agenda. This also applies to changing the institutional procedures related to policy making, for instance by reducing the role of interest groups in the consultation process of by changing the role of the European Parliament in the legislative process in the European Union, as the 2009 Lisbon Treaty did.

These three streams develop independently from each other. They may be unrelated, but when they couple a so-called *policy window* opens, which creates a possibility for agenda-setting. So, this policy window opens when simultaneously a problem is recognized, a solution is available, and the political climate is responsive. Figure 3.5 provides an illustration of this. In the multiple streams approach, timing is an important explanation of why some issues never make it to the decision agenda: if a problem does not meet

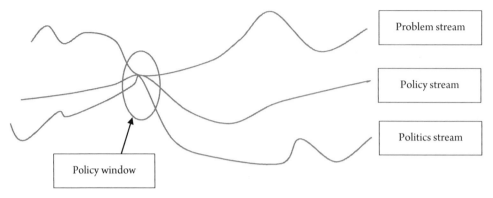

Source: based on Van de Graaf and Hoppe, 1989: 198

Figure 3.5 The multiple stream model

a proper solution in the right time nothing will happen. Policy windows mostly open occasionally, and do not stay open very long. Those wishing to have "their" item on the decision agenda therefore need to act rapidly or the opportunity might pass and they will have to wait until the next chance comes along (Kingdon, 1995, see also Guldbrandsson and Fossum, 2009).

An important role in the agenda-setting process in the multiple stream approach is attributed to the so-called *policy entrepreneurs*. Policy entrepreneurs are individuals willing to invest "time, energy, reputation, money to promote a position for anticipated future gain in the form of material, purposive or solidary benefits" (Kingdon, 1995, p. 179). Policy entrepreneurs may be part of the problems stream as well as the policy stream. Politicians, civil servants, lobbyists and academics may play a role as policy entrepreneurs, but in some cases also private persons do. While decision makers often shift their attention from one problem to another, policy entrepreneurs keep to their issue. The multiple stream model teaches us that it is not enough to have a problem, not even a pressing one, to get a subject on the decision agenda. A solution must be available within reach for the decision makers as well. Therefore, policy entrepreneurs may – and often do – play a role in problem recognition as well as in suggesting solutions (Guldbrandsson and Fossum, 2009; see also Mintrom, 1997; Béland and Howlett, 2016).

The multiple streams approach, with its central notion of policy windows, assumes that the agenda-setting stage of the policy process is much more chaotic than the rational model assumes. Timing and coincidence play an important role, as do policy entrepreneurs. In addition, the model shows that problems are not always the starting point for a process of agenda-setting: solutions or political events may as well be a starting-point.

We started this chapter with the example of the refugee crisis that the world, and more specifically Europe, experienced since 2016. In this case we can clearly distinguish multiple problem perceptions in the problems stream, and various indicators that show the development of the problem like the number of refugees or the number of people drowning in the Mediterranean. In the policy stream, various solutions can be distinguished within European countries, ranging from closing the borders by building a wall or a fence to creating a warm welcome for the refugees. The politics stream is amongst many other events characterized by various important elections in the UK, France, Germany and the Netherlands in 2017. Finally, the picture of the Kurdish boy Aylan Kurdi washed up on the shores of Turkey, which we already mentioned in the introduction, may have opened the policy window for finding a common European approach, resulting in the EU-Turkey Refugee Deal in 2016. Understanding why the implementation of this deal has been far from perfect will be the subject of Chapter 5.

The Advocacy Coalition Framework

The Advocacy Coalition Framework (ACF) is one of the most advanced political frameworks of the policy process. Although it says a lot about agenda setting, it does not take a specific stage of the policy cycle as a starting point, but rather adopts a heuristic perspective of the policy process as a whole. The ACF argues that the locus of the policy process is not so much the macropolitical level, but rather the level of *policy subsystems* (see Chapter 7). According to Sabatier, a policy subsystem consists of "actors from a variety of public and private organizations that are actively concerned with a policy problem or issue" (Sabatier 1998:99). This includes actors that are often formally involved in policy making, the so-called iron triangles of interest groups, bureaucracy and politicians, but can also include NGOs, experts, advisory bodies and think tanks, and even representatives of the media (Parsons 1995:196). For instance, in the policy subsystem for employment various actors are active, including government departments such as social affairs and economics, but also labor unions, employers' organizations and possibly expert organizations that provide data on the labor market situation or knowledge about policy alternatives. This focus on subsystems is an early reflection of what Beck (1999) has described as the growing manifestation of subpolitics as opposed to macropolitics; increasingly policy making (and political decision-making) has become fragmented over different policy domains, or in Sabatier's terms, policy subsystems, which have therefore become increasingly prominent as the unit of analysis for policy analysis.

Agenda setting can then be perceived as a process of putting issues that are usually dealt with by specific actors within a policy subsystem, on the broader (macro-) political agenda. The development of new and powerful advocacy coalitions is usually seen as an important factor in agenda setting. Within policy subsystems, there are usually several (often between two and four) advocacy coalitions. An *advocacy coalition* consists of "people of various governmental and private organizations that both 1) share a set of normative and causal beliefs and 2) engage in a nontrivial degree of coordinated activity over time" (Sabatier and Weible, 2007:198-223). This means that advocacy coalitions can be composed of a broad range of actors, including actors that are not formally or directly involved in the policy making process (such as media or experts). In fact, the broader an advocacy coalition is, the more complementary the resources will be that it can mobilize in the policy process (including material as well as immaterial resources). For instance, it can be very important for an advocacy coalition to have authoritative figures that can represent an advocacy coalition in the media to win over the public mood; the role that Al Gore played, with his movie *An Inconvenient Truth*, in setting climate change back on the public agenda is a clear example of this. Advocacy coalitions do not need to be coordinated in a formal way; there does not have to be a single representative body for an advocacy coalition. Often, advocacy coalitions are rather loose networks of actors that share beliefs and refer to and meet each other in diverse settings (conferences, media debates, and so on) and often coordinate their actions informally rather than formally.

3.7 Cultural perspective: the "framing" of problems

The emphasis on the role of media that we have stressed for the more modest versions of rationalism also provides a connection to more culturalist approaches to agenda setting. In the constructivism perspective problems are not "discovered" and do not make it through the "barriers" of issue attention because of their objectivity or because numbers indicate the urgency of a problem. Rather than knowledge, the cultural perspective emphasizes the role of ideas, images and stories or narratives in agenda setting. Think about the example at the beginning of this chapter, where the image of the Kurdish boy Aylan Kurdi washed up on the shores of Turkey seemed to have much more agenda-setting power than objective figures on the number of deaths amongst refugees attempting to cross the Mediterranean.

An important and much applied culturalist perspective is Rein and Schön's framework for frame analysis (1994). They define *policy frames* as "underlying structures of belief, perception and appreciation" (Rein and Schön, 1994:23). These play an important role in actual social practices: to provide a "way of selecting, organising, interpreting, and making sense of a complex reality to provide guide-posts for knowing, analysing, persuading and acting" (Rein and Schön, 1994:32). Frames are generally "tacit" or unknown to actors themselves. For actors themselves, a frame is not a selective interpretation of reality; rather it constitutes their reality.

When there are multiple frames of a specific issue, Rein and Schön (1994) speak of "*intractable policy controversies*" (see also "toward a typology of policy problems"). This means that there are various frames competing for attention and for influence on the policy making process. Because of the inherently subjective and selective nature of frames, intractable policy controversies cannot be resolved by simply collecting and studying "the facts" (as would be the case in the rationalist approach). Not only do actors often interpret "evidence" differently, they also tend to select different pieces of "evidence" based on their frames.

A key example of such controversies on framing involves migrant incorporation. There is a deep division between actors who frame migrant incorporation in a multiculturalist or an assimilationist way. For multiculturalists, incorporation is all about minority groups in need of protection and help in order to emancipate within the host society. For assimilationists, incorporation is all about migrants adapting to the host society's culture, values and norms. Both use very different words to describe the policy problem they address (emancipation versus adaptation), frame the involved groups differently (minorities in need of protection versus migrants needing to assimilate) and suggest very different courses of action (offering assistance versus setting criteria that migrants should meet).

Frames can be deduced or reconstructed based on the policy stories that actors tell about what they see as a problem, why, who is involved and what could and should be done about it (Scholten, 2011). The "*what*" question concerns the definition of the problem, including the language, rhetoric and symbols used to define a problem. Think about the different words being used by assimilationists and multiculturalists in the example above. The "*why*" question concerns a causal theory or "causal story" (Stone, 1988) that interprets a problem situation by attributing a plausible cause or source of the problem. The "*who*" question involves the definition and construction of involved target groups; who are the recipients of policy, are these defined positively or negatively, are they considered powerful or weak and dependent? Here a clear link is made with the social construction of target groups that we have discussed earlier (see section 3.3, Schneider and Ingram, 1993). Finally, the "*how*" question concerns a "leap from is to ought" by identifying possible programs or strategies for addressing the problem situation. A frame combines these four elements – problem definition, causal story, target group construction and normative prescription – in a consistent and convincing way. As such, a frame combines both a *diagnosis* of a problem situation as well as a *prognosis* for intervention (Snow and Benford, 1988).

Important in terms of agenda setting is that it is not the empirical validity of a frame that determines whether it leads to agenda setting, but rather the persuasiveness of a frame. As Emery Roe (1994) argues, policy claims often become convincing or persuasive by means of storylines or "*narratives.*" Just like regular "stories", such "policy narratives" involve plots with actors, events and a specific temporal sequence that provides order to the often unstructured complexity of policy problems. As such as their guideposts for sense-making; in other words, rather than being reflections of clear and distinct cognitive beliefs of persons (see the Advocacy Coalition Framework), the culturalist perspective argues that policy frames, stories or narratives help shape people's beliefs regarding specific problems.

3.8 Institutionalist perspective: negative and positive feedback

A key struggle of institutionalists that focus on path-dependency has been how to account for the fact that many studies show that policy areas indeed reveal path-dependency over relatively long periods of time, but also tend to be occasionally interrupted by major policy changes. Why does there seem to be incremental policy change during most of the time, and only sometimes non-incremental change? The punctuated equilibrium framework, developed by Baumgartner and Jones (1993, 2005) tries to account precisely for this pattern of "punctuated equilibrium." They account for both stability and change by studying the "politics of attention." Because of bounded rationality, but also because of constraints in information processing capacity, human beings as well as institutions can attend to only a limited number of issues at any given time. For instance, parliament does not attribute attention to all policy issues at the same time, but rather tends to deal with topics that rise up the political agenda in a serial manner, only taking several at a specific point in time. Similarly, the media also allocate attention to a limited number of issues at a given time; a newspaper only has one cover that can only bring two or three issues per day, and the 8 o'clock news also has only limited time to distribute amongst topics.

Therefore, issues have to "compete" for attention in institutional arenas such as the media and politics. Or in other words, entrepreneurs that try to raise a specific issue and advocate specific policy ideas, have to engage in the *"politics of attention."* The key for explaining stability as well as change lies, in this sense, in understanding how attention is allocated, so essential in agenda setting. Negative feedback is oriented at preventing an issue from catching attention. Baumgartner and Jones also define specific strategies for mobilizing negative feedback, and holding off challengers that do try to set an issue on the agenda. One such strategy is attention shifting, or trying to divert attention to another issue. Also, a widely used strategy of negative feedback is "ignoring" a challenge in the hope that the challenge will fade.

As long as there is no agenda setting, change is unlikely and the status quo is likely to be preserved. This means that a policy area will remain under

---

BOX 3.3

NON-CONTRADICTORY ARGUMENTATION AS A NEGATIVE FEEDBACK STRATEGY

Negative feedback can be an implicit consequence of institutional processes that inhibit change (institutional friction), but it can also be an explicit strategy by actors who wish to hold off challengers. Also in rhetorical or debating tactics, elements of negative feedback can be recognized.

Non-contradictory argumentation is such a rhetorical strategy for preventing your opponent from defining the rhetorical playing field. When challenged by a contender who tries to set a specific issue and frame on the agenda, non-contradictory argumentation means that you do not respond directly to the challenge nor define your position on the issue that is raised. Rather, you try to divert attention to another issue that you can frame yourself. This gives you the power to define the playing field for the debate, and prevents you from talking about an issue that you might not feel entirely safe with or where you feel your position might not trigger much support.

As an illustration, during election debates non-contradictory is a much used strategy. Oddly enough, if you do not pay attention to it, it is hardly noticed. Mind the use of sentences like "you may feel that . . .," "but what is really important is that. . . ." Or, it happens when one of the debaters asks questions to someone else, for instance "what I haven't heard you talking about at all, is what you think about. . . ." In terms of non-contradictory argumentation, the best defense is to attack. However, if there is a good debate leader, this strategy can backlash.

Also in policy debates, non-contradictory argumentation can be very present. Actors will try to shift attention to the issues that they wish to put on the agenda and frame in a specific way. When engaging in the politics of attention, this means that actors will often be more occupied with articulating their own views rather than responding to others.

control of what Baumgartner and Jones described as a *"policy monopoly."* A policy monopoly "has a definable institutional structure responsible for policy making in an issue area, and its responsibility is supported by some powerful idea or image. This image is generally connected to core political values and can be communicated simply and directly to the public" (True, Jones and Baumgartner, 1999:101; see also Baumgartner and Jones, 1993:7). In a clear combination of culturalism and institutionalism, Baumgartner and Jones thus define a policy monopoly as being constructed around a clear problem definition or "policy image" and specific institutional actors. These form "iron triangles" that have an interest in preserving the status quo in order to maintain their roles and positions within the policy monopoly and to keep off challenges. Actors from these policy monopolies are also the most likely sources of negative feedback strategies, such as attention-shifting.

However, the politics of attention that is central to the punctuated equilibrium framework can occasionally lead to non-incremental change, or *"policy punctuations."* A policy punctuation involves a major policy change, where usually not only the policy image on which a policy is based, but also the institutional structure of a policy field will change. As a consequence, policy punctuations also deconstruct policy monopolies. According to Baumgartner and Jones, once an issue manages to capture attention, and thus manages to break mechanisms of negative feedback, a process of *positive feedback* will emerge. This means that new actors, who had been "apathetic" during episodes of stability as a result of exclusion from a policy monopoly, will be "awaken" and will try to gain renewed influence in a policy area. Agenda setting thus opens a unique window of opportunity for actors to frame the policy issue and redefine the positions and roles of key actors in the policy field. This means that whereas during negative feedback challengers face "decreasing returns to scale" for their efforts, when positive feedback emerges they face "increasing returns to scale".

Several factors are distinguished as factors or strategies that are likely to contribute to positive feedback. *Image manipulation*, or "framing", is one strategy that could contribute to positive feedback. Here it is particularly important that a frame also needs to resonate with media or politics in order to capture attention. Dramatization or personalization of issues may be particularly helpful; sometimes it demands just a single dramatic case to bring down a policy monopoly. The media logic of focusing much attention on only a limited number of issues at a given time, "either feast or famine", tends to enhance the impact of dramatization and personalization on the policy process.

Second, if it may be less opportune to manipulate the policy image, it may be possible to search for alternative institutional venues (with alternative sorts of "agendas") that are more susceptible to the policy image. This strategy of *venue shopping* is very applicable when some venues are under control of a policy monopoly, but alternative venues may provide more opportunities for gaining momentum toward policy change. Taking an issue to the media can be a strategy of venue shopping for instance when a policy monopoly does not allow specific voices to be heard. Also, taking issues to court can be a strategy of venue shopping, for instance when actors believe that politicization or mediatization would do more harm than good to their policy ideas. An illustration of the latter are NGOs seeking to challenge the ban of headscarf wearing in public schools and public office in several European countries; given the political sensitivity of the issue, politicization would not be a fruitful strategy, but taking this issue to the courts was a strategy for getting around politics and getting authoritative legal rather than political statements as to what is permitted and what not.

Third, positive feedback may be fed by *mimicking*, or intelligent forms of copying, from other policy areas. Mimicking provides a strategy for making use of the momentum toward policy dynamics that has been created in one area, to promote change in other areas as well. It creates spin-offs between policy areas, which can lead to what DiMaggio and Powell (1991) have described as "mimetic isomorphism." This means that institutional structures of different policy fields become increasingly similar. An example of such mimicking involved the popularity and broad expansion of new public management strategies, but also the use of ICT in policy. A concept that often reveals that mimicking is taking place is "best practices."

Finally, *focusing events* can play an essential role in triggering positive feedback. Sudden events or incidents may provide strategic opportunities for redefining a policy issue and trigger broad media and political attention. Here it is important that actors recognize such events and attribute meaning to these events (hence Baumgartner and Jones speak of "attributed focus events"). This is also recognizable in the political strategy of "spinning." A key example of a focus event that became a motor of positive feedback involves the September 11 attacks. The idea of a focus event speaks closely to Mahoney's notion of critical junctures. A focus event tends to bring together ideas and institutional processes in a way that often cannot be predicted nor controlled by specific actors.

BOX 3.4

EUROPEANIZATION AS VERTICAL VENUE SHOPPING

European integration is often framed as a top-down process where European institutions gradually obtain more power over member states. In contrast, some scholars have framed Europeanization as a process of "multi-level governance", involving interaction between government levels, including top-down as well as bottom-up processes. In the context of the latter, member states often put issues on the agenda "in Brussels" because of their own national interest. This strategy has been framed as "vertical venue shopping" (Pralle, 2003; Guiraudon, 1999). This can take the shape of formally advocating specific policies in decision-making arenas at other levels, but also the shape of more informal processes of "lobbying", advocacy and mobilization.

Vertical venue shopping can have various purposes. One of them is to address a policy where the main competencies lie at another level. One example concerns the Europeanization of immigration policy. Most countries have to engage in vertical venue shopping to affect key migration regulations, such as on free movement within the EU, and on asylum migration and family migration from outside the EU. Another purpose is to make sure that a policy issue is addressed equally in other countries so that competitive disadvantages are avoided. For instance, if a country wishes to impose an eco-tax on polluting industries and services, vertical venue shopping is a key strategy for making sure that other countries will have to adopt this tax as well.

However, there can also be domestic reasons for engaging in vertical venue shopping. In some cases, adopting a law in the national political arena may be more difficult to achieve then advocating the passing of EU regulations. For example, with migration being fiercely politicized in many national political settings, a government coalition may wish to relocate migration policy making to the EU level in order to avoid a confrontation with the political opposition in the national arena. Another motivation may be that government coalitions wish to anchor policies into European legislation to make sure that it cannot easily be reverted once another coalition would come to power. In this sense, vertical venue shopping can be an important factor in the domestic political arena as well.

3.9 CHAPTER SUMMARY

In this chapter we have shown how the social and political constructivist characters of policy problems that differ in their nature of how tamable they are (and the target groups of policy that hide behind that), can be of influence on the way in which a certain problem is able to attract the attention of society, politicians and policy makers.

However, attracting attention is not a matter of course. Attention needs to be generated within different types of environments of actors; environments where each have their own agendas. Distinction was made between the social agenda, the political agenda, the decision-making agenda and the policy agenda. The path that needs to be taken by a social problem to reach maturity and be translated into an appropriately tailored policy program can be seen as the act of taking a large amount of hurdles. At the same time, it also needs to be recognized that the time is not always ripe for certain problem definitions or certain approaches. In that case, the *policy window* needs to be opened.

We continue on the route set out by us. The fact that a subject has been able to reach the political agenda and that politicians find it worthwhile enough to pay attention to it, means that a next step can be taken: developing a policy that is then subject of political decision-making, politically ratifying a policy program. Development and decision-making are also indicated as the phase of policy making of the implementation.

4

Policy formulation: development, steering, instruments and decision-making

💡 **LEARNING OBJECTIVES**

After reading this chapter you should be able to:

- Develop and interpret the rational, political, cultural and institutional perspectives of the development of policies, including their design logics.

- Recognize and define different perspectives on *steering*.

- Appreciate the diversity in *tools* that governments have, and recognize and define different types of (legal, economic, communicative) instruments.

- Apply the four theoretical perspectives (rationalism, institutionalism, culturalism and the political perspective) to *decision-making*.

4.1 Introduction

Once a specific issue has managed to draw the attention of politicians and policy makers, a possible next step deals with the question: what is an appropriate approach to deal with this issue? What kinds of plans and actions need to be drafted and implemented? What kind of instruments have to be used to achieve the goals that have been set out in the plan? Questions refer to the next phase in the policy cycle: the policy formulation phase. Once a plan or policy program has been drafted, it is important that this plan has a formal status, that it acquires the authority, that it is the right and legitimate way to go forward. In order to obtain this formal status, policy programs are subjected to all kinds of formal and informal decision-making processes. Not only the design or the development of a policy program but also the decision-making process to which the plan is subjected, is said to belong to the policy formulation phase.

When we look at the development of a policy program, the four perspectives that we used to understand policy processes can be found in the way policy makers and policy scientists think about the design of a policy program. Each perspective addresses a specific number of relevant themes and issues that is relevant when developing policy programs. Furthermore, in each perspective also specific design strategies are put forward. However, what we observe in the daily practice of policy making is that these four perspectives on how to design policy programs are combined. For policy makers it is important to think about goals and means, but always in relation to the existence of relevant stakeholders and the dependencies between them. However, they also take into their mind how existing routines, procedures and established rules influence their room to manoeuvre, while simultaneously they want to formulate programs and plans that are appealing. In doing so they develop convincing frames. In sections 4.2, 4.3, 4.4 and 4.5 we discuss how policy programs are drafted from a rational, political, cultural and institutional perspective and what the relevant design issues are per perspective. In section 4.6 we discuss the implications of using these different perspectives as a design logic.

However, the development of a policy program also touches upon the question of how to intervene. In sections 4.7 and 4.8 we explore this question. Thinking about interventions very often implies that policy makers have to develop a steering arrangement, which not only addresses the role and position of government vis-à-vis other governments, companies and citizens. Within such arrangements thoughts are also developed about how to apply the different policy instruments that policy makers have at their disposal. In section 4.8 we will look into this issue. And again, we will try to link these issues to the four perspectives on the policy process.

The drafting of policy programs does not take place in a vacuum. It is embedded in all kinds of informal and formal decision-making procedures and routines, in which the content of the plan is the subject of discussion, negotiation and power play. In order to understand the complexity of these decision-making processes, it is important to look at different models that try to grasp this complexity. In section 4.8 these models, which will also be linked to our four perspectives, will be sketched. This chapter ends with a conclusion (section 4.9).

4.2 The rational perspective on policy development: the evidence-based programming of goals and actions

Policies can be described as a more or less structured set of means and resources that are used to influence specific societal developments in a desired or planned way. In this approach a policy is defined as a relatively stable, purposeful course of action followed by an actor or set of actors in dealing with a problem or matter of concern (Anderson, 2003:2). Policies do not just happen and are not based on random occurrences. Actions and the course of actions are planned and are directed to the achievement of specific goals. Behind this idea lies a rational order, which stresses the need for systematic analysis and reasoning. This requires that policy makers collect and process relevant information and knowledge in order to understand what is happening and in order to make projections about what they have to pursue. Scholars who can be linked to the rational approach on policy development define policy making as an analytical endeavor (Dunn, 1994). In this rational endeavor a policy maker tries to structure his analysis by developing a number of assumptions, which will be used to draft a policy program; assumptions which also help to systematize and program the actions to be taken.

Three types of assumptions are relevant (Hoogerwerf, 2003). The first type refers to the causes and the effects of a specific issue that has acquired public and political attention and which has led to a call to act. What is the nature of the policy problem at hand? For instance, if policy makers are confronted with the question of how to improve the safety in a neighborhood, they first want to know, what is happening. How unsafe is the neighborhood, what has been the development of the crime rate, what kinds of crimes (for example, drug related) can be detected and how are these kinds related to specific groups (for example, like youngsters) or specific locations (for example, streets or even houses)? But they also want to know what the causes of these crime are. Are these causes related to poverty, to a tradition of gangs, to drug and alcohol abuse, to a bad socio-economic situation? But they also look at relevant effects. For instance, do these feelings of unsafety prevent older people from walking through the streets and instead stay in their houses? This question also shows that it is important to understand the specific context in which a policy problem like crime has developed. For instance, what is the history of a neighborhood? How successful were previous programs? Is it an area with an ageing population? In doing so, a policy maker tries to draft a causal model which helps him to understand the causal mechanism that lies behind a

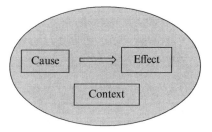

Figure 4.1 Causal model

specific policy challenge, in terms of possible causes and possible effects. In Figure 4.1 we have drafted such a model in its most essential form (Pawson, 2006).

The second set of assumptions that have to be addressed relate to the goals and means that constitute a policy program. Given specific causes and effects, what kind of interventions need be deployed? How can these interventions be linked to specific goals that have to be accomplished? And, if we know this, the next step is to see what these interventions will look like. What actions are going to be taken and what kind of instruments are going to be used? But also, it is important to understand what the strengths and weaknesses of these instruments are, and to understand under what conditions these instruments work. However, specific actions can also have side-effects. What do we know about these side-effects and how should we tackle them? And last but not least, what do these actions cost? Do these costs outweigh the reduction of crime? For instance, in order to improve the safety in a neighborhood, one action could be to increase the number of police on the street or to install CCTV cameras. The presence of more police in relation to a zero tolerance strategy could perhaps help to reduce the number of crimes, while CCTV cameras help to give citizens a feeling of safety because they know that streets are being watched. But more police in one neighborhood implies fewer police in another, given the limited number of police that are available. This could mean that crime will move to another neighborhood. Has this side-effect been taken into consideration? But also what are the long-term effects? For instance, would it not be better to give young people a perspective, for instance by improving their education and giving them a labor market perspective, in order to prevent them from getting involved in criminal activities? Hence, in order to understand the design of these possible interventions, a very basic intervention model can be drafted. In Figure 4.2 we show an example of such a model. If we know the causes and effects and we know what the context is, we have a series of possible intervention points that can be used as a way to structure the actions to be considered.

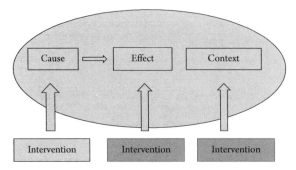

Figure 4.2 A simple intervention model

The third set of assumptions deals with a number of values that have to be addressed in the program. These values act as criteria that can be used to define what actions should be pursued, but they also help to prioritize these actions and help to formulate a hierarchy of goals to be achieved, in terms of which goals are super-ordinated to other goals. In the rational model of policy design this implies that this is the place where politics comes in. Based on political ideologies and preferences, but also in relation to electoral promises or political compromises that have been made, specific criteria can be deduced. Sometimes these criteria refer to a political assignment that has been given to the engaged policy makers. Given goals and criteria, policy makers try to formulate a plan to achieve these goals. For instance, the assignment is to substantially reduce the crime rate in a vicinity. Moreover, politicians can argue that it is important to accomplish immediate results, whatever it may cost, when dealing with this crime. This implies that effectiveness is more important than efficiency. This also entails that long-term, more "soft" programs will not be selected as relevant types of actions. As a result a hierarchy of goals to be pursued can be developed. Based on this hierarchy of goals and sub-goals, a goal-tree can be drawn to visualize the priorities that are laid down in a policy program, and to show how structured the policy program is (Figure 4.3; Hoogerwerf, 1987).

Based on these three clusters of assumptions policy makers and scholars that operate from a rational perspective try to design programs that are analytically convincing. According to Dunn (1994:62) this is to produce policy-relevant information that may be utilized to resolve problems in specific policy settings.

Most recently, the role of policy-relevant information has been put forward by scholars and policy makers that stress the importance of working as much as possible with "evidence-based policies" (Pawson, 2006). Policy-relevant

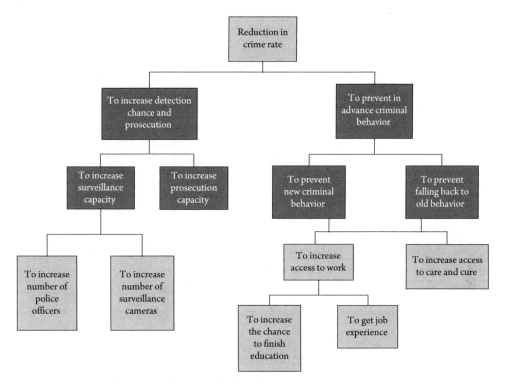

Figure 4.3 An example of a goal-tree

information not only refers to the role of facts, but in a broader sense, it deals with the use of validated descriptive, explanatory and prescriptive knowledge in policy making processes (Dunn, 1994). The knowledge that is needed not only refers to the description and explanation of how and why specific problematic situations occur, in terms of what are relevant empirical regularities and mechanisms (Dunn, 1994). It also refers to the prescriptive nature of policy making (Dunn, 1994). That is why advocates of evidence-based policy making especially want to know whether a specific approach or intervention will work, and how we know that it will work. In doing so it is important to make predictions of the future, based on valid information in order to justify the claims in terms of possible success that are put forward. What are relevant qualifiers and warrants, but also what are relevant disclaimers and how are they backed by relevant information and knowledge (Dunn, 1994)? Hence, a plea is made to assess the potential costs and benefits of specific actions and interventions in order to understand whether the sum of these costs and benefits helps to achieve the goals that have been formulated in the political assignment.

The term "evidence-based" has been borrowed from medicine (Pawson, 2006). As might be expected, in medicine drugs and treatments are tested all the time, their impact is closely monitored and in this manner, evidence is created about the question, does it work (Pawson, 2006; Head, 2008). There are several reasons why this term is embraced (Pawson, 2006; Head, 2008). First, evidence-based policy making expresses the idea that political ideologies have lost their significance in designing policy programs, while reform movements like New Public Management emphasized the importance of a more "business like" approach. A second reason refers to the idea that especially in times of austerity it is important to spend public money only on programs that really work. The third reason refers to the performance deficit of public administration (Salge and Vera, 2012). In order to achieve outcomes that really matter to citizens and companies, it is important, in advance, to know if the chance that a policy program would work, is a real one. Last but not least, the idea is that the more evidence-based a policy program is, the more it helps to improve the rationality of the political judgment that has to take place. In doing so, it can be seen as a way to discipline and structure the capricious nature of political decision-making processes.

At the same time an important reservation needs to be made. For many societal problems, it is quite difficult to draw causal models or to develop an intervention model, because most problems are not so simple that they can be caught in a linear and mechanistic cause–effect model. For instance, if we look at the viability of neighborhoods, we see that safety is just one issue, while the quality of physical environment (quality of buildings, streets, parks), the facilities in the neighborhood (for example, shops, schools) and the social infrastructure (do people know each other and trust each other) also seem to matter. And more, safety issues can be defined in terms of objective safety (for example, actual crime rates) and the subjective nature of safety (in terms of safety feelings). We refer here to the discussion about different types of policy problems that differ in terms of consensus about the knowledge that can be used as well as the values that are at stake. In many cases the knowledge as well as the value base is being disputed. Hence, multiple and interlinked causes and effects and all kinds of actions with all kinds of effects, side-effects and trade-offs can be discerned. They are also valued in a different way by different stakeholders, using different criteria, referring to different values but also using different knowledge and information (Rittel and Webber, 1973). This creates ambiguity and uncertainty, which implies that other issues and other logics may play a role in the development of a policy program; issues and logics that refer to other perspectives in the policy process. In the next section we address the development of a policy program from the political perspective.

4.3 The political perspective on policy design: managing interests, power and interdependency

In the political perspective, the development of a policy program is not seen as a rational and analytical endeavor; far from it. Policy design is in essence a political exercise, because it touches upon specific goals, interests and claims that are put forward by a variety of actors that have a specific relation to the problem that needs to be addressed and that have different powers (Lasswell, 1958; Dahl, 1961; Lowi, 1972). Each actor wants to influence the way in which a policy problem is influenced, the goals that are formulated and the actions that need to be taken, given his specific interests (Sabatier, 1988; Allison and Zelikow, 1971; Crozier and Friedberg, 1980). These interests also depend on the specific role and task that an actor has. The vital question, is: what actor or what coalition of actors has been able to formulate the problem at hand and the approaches to be followed (Koppenjan and Klijn, 2004). This implies that in the development of a policy program all kinds of definitions compete with each other (Stone, 2002). What definitions are included in the dominant definition and what definitions are disputed and excluded? As a result, the development of a policy program can be understood as a struggle between different stakeholders, with winners and losers. For instance, when dealing with the vitality of a neighborhood, a police department may define the problem at hand as a security and safety problem, which calls for more police officers or for an increase in budget. However, a public works department will address the vitality of a neighborhood primarily in terms of the quality of the public infrastructure (for example, roads), the quality of the buildings and physical environment (attractiveness of houses and shops). Hence, they would perhaps ask for a makeover of the neighborhood in terms of a refurbishment of old buildings or a replacement of these buildings by new houses, new shops and so on. A social welfare department would perhaps link the vitality of the neighborhood to the social fabric which could be very weak. Because people do not know each other, feelings of loneliness and anxiety could develop. Hence, an important challenge for a policy maker is to ensure that a dominant problem definition emerges. This also opens a new challenge: what are the relevant strategies to be used?

The most important challenge for policy makers is to develop a common problem definition and solutions or approaches, given these different views, interests and claims. In order to do so they have to be aware that the development of a policy program takes in an arena, with multiple actors that have different interests. When dealing with the vitality of a neighborhood, a municipality has to deal with the inhabitants, which are often organized in different groups, with local companies and shop owners, housing associations, with a national or regional police force, while at the same the municipality itself consists of different stakeholders: a local policy or public safety department, a public works department, a social welfare department, an economic development and/or urban regeneration department, a local and regional traffic department and so on. In order to protect or enhance these interests they make use of the power that they possess. Power can be exercised if a specific actor is able to control the development, access, distribution or use of specific resources (Pfeffer and Salancik, 1978; Morgan, 1986). Examples of relevant power resources are:

- Material resources, like machines, buildings, infrastructure provisions.
- Financial resources, like money.
- Human resources, like the number of people, their qualities and qualifications in terms of competencies, expertise and experience.
- Information, ICT and knowledge resources, like data and datasets, computer systems and networks, software, registrations.
- Formal resources, like specific rights, tasks, responsibilities and competences that by law have been allocated to a specific actor.
- Social capital resources, like personal contacts and trustful personal relationships.

However, Pfeffer and Salancik (1978:46-47) argue that the powerfulness of these resources is influenced by:

- The criticality of a specific resource. If an actor is really dependent on a specific resource in order to guarantee its survival, then the actor who controls this resource is able to exercise a lot of power. For instance, in many countries, like the Netherlands, municipalities are very dependent on the funds that they receive from central government.
- The degree to which a specific actor is really able to control the access, the distribution and use of resources. For instance, the threat that a central government can postpone the payment of specific subsidies that can be given for the improvement of the vitality of a neighborhood may force a municipality to give in to the additional demands that have been put forward by central government.
- The degree to which alternative resources are available or can be generated. For instance, if local government is able to acquire additional funds by imposing local taxes, this may help to reduce their dependency from central government.

However, in most cases there is no single actor that is able to control all relevant resources. In many cases different resources, which are also vital for the actions and interventions to be considered as possible solutions, are allocated in rather unequal ways among different actors (Pfeffer and Salancik, 1978). As a result all kinds of dependency and interdependency relations between these stakeholders exist, which also generates uncertainty: will a specific actor have access to vital resources that are controlled by other actors. An important challenge for policy makers is to acknowledge these, very often complex and dynamic, (inter) dependency relations between the involved actors play a role in the way power is being exercised (Koppenjan and Klijn, 2004). Within these relations they have to operate.

In order to make use of these power resources all the actors develop strategies to advance their interests and claims. As a result, different games may emerge between the involved actors, games that have different outcomes and generate specific interaction patterns between them. Hence, when developing a policy program, a policy maker has to ask him/herself what kind of game he or she wants to play and how this game relates to the games that other actors play or want to play (Crozier and Friedberg, 1978; Ostrom, Gardner and Walker, 1994). It is this game that explains if and how a dominant definition of the policy problem and the actions that are needed to deal with it, emerges. . .or not. Examples of relevant game-like strategic interactions between actors that are involved in policy making actions are (Scharpf, Reissert and Schnabel, 1976; Scharpf, 1997b):

- *Avoidance.* Actors can interact with each other, by not interacting with each other. In doing so they want to avoid a possible clash of interest and try to create a "stand still" situation, thereby hoping that new circumstances will emerge that change the positions and interests of the involved actors.
- *Competition and conflict.* Actors can also seek to battle with each other, thereby protecting their own interests, putting forward all kinds of (additional) demands and creating all kind of barriers and hurdles (resistance) that have to be taken in order to get possible support. In the end an actor can hope that other actors will give in.
- *Coalition formation.* An actor can also try to advance their own interests and claims, by trying to form a coalition with other actors that to some extent share the same ideas, interests or resources. In doing so they build a coalition of more willing partners that due to its collaboration is able to improve its power in the arena.
- *Competition regulation.* Although actors accept that they compete with each other, they can agree among themselves to reduce the fierceness of the competition by developing a number of common playing rules. For

instance, they can agree that specific information can be accessed by all the involved partners.

- *Consensus development.* Actors can try to develop a shared understanding about how to proceed, by trying to negotiate and to formulate a compromise, in which a possible win–win situation can be achieved. When actors opt to negotiate and to seek a compromise, their intention is that collaboration and co-operation would be a benevolent strategy which could lead to consensus about how to proceed.
- *Coercion.* An actor could, given its dominant position in an arena, force other actors to comply to his definition of a situation.
- *Complexity reduction.* Actors could also try to reduce the complexity of a problem, by splitting up a complex problem into specific parts, thereby seeking to find a solution for a specific part. As such, step-by-step actors try to find a whole range of partial solutions which add up to a more general approach, or limit themselves to only these partial problems of which they know that they are able to work out a solution, thereby bypassing those partial problems which are really hard to deal with.

There is also another concept which is important to understand the political nature of policy development. This concept refers to the notion of a policy network (Koppenjan and Klijn, 2004), which especially focuses on the (inter)dependency relations between the involved actors which are generated by a specific policy problem or the actions that are proposed to deal with these problems (Rhodes, 1985). In the literature several types of dependency are distinguished. A classical distinction has been put forward by Thompson (1967:54):

- *Pooled interdependency.* In such a situation actors make use of the same reservoir of resources to which they all are connected to. For instance, municipalities are all dependent on a central fund, owned by the central government, from which they receive money to fulfill specific tasks. The fact that they are all dependent on this fund implies that they have a shared goal, while on the other hand, central government make use of the joint dependency of the municipalities to influence specific programs on, for instance, crime prevention.
- *Sequential interdependency.* In this situation one specific actor is dependent (in time) on the activities that have previously been executed by another actor. As a result a chain-like sequence of interrelated actions emerges: the output of actor X generates the input for actor Y. For instance, if a local police force wants to develop a more repressive strategy against juvenile crime, this also influences the actions of the other actors. For instance, this increase in activity generates additional

pressure for the prosecutor's office, for the courts, for the (juvenile) prisons, and in the end for the probation organization, which are all different but interlinked tasks in the implementation of this juvenile action program.

● *Reciprocal interdependency*. In this case there are mutual input–output relations between the involved actors: actor X is dependent on actor Y and actor Y is also dependent on actor X. For instance, juvenile prevention teams get money from a municipality in order to deal with and prevent juvenile crime. In doing so they are dependent on the municipality. However, in order to allocate these funds among the teams, the teams have to give specific information which is needed to calculate the budget. However, the information that the municipality needs to receive has to be given by teams.

In the literature regarding the governance of policy networks the willingness and ability of policy makers to recognize dependency and interdependency is viewed as a necessary condition for collaboration and co-operation between a variety of all kinds of public and private actors (Rhodes, 1985; 1997; Kickert, Klijn and Koppenjan, 1997; Koppenjan and Klijn, 2004). As a result all kinds of hybrid arrangements emerge. An example are public–private partnerships, which are drafted when a municipality together with, for instance, real estate development companies and housing companies jointly invest in a new shopping center in order to regenerate a deprived neighborhood. Moreover, these interdependencies underline the idea that the nature of many policy problems is so complex, that governments themselves are not able to deal with these problems on their own. In order to enhance their problem solving capacity they have to seek collaboration with other governments, with companies, with citizens and all kinds of other, societal organizations (Rhodes, 1997; Papadopoulos, 2003; Koppenjan and Klijn, 2004). However, the ability and willingness to embrace these interdependencies is not given. Very often the quality of the relationships, in terms of trust and distrust influence the degree in which different actors are willing to develop a joint approach (Koppenjan and Klijn, 2004; Klijn, Edelenbos and Steijn, 2010). This implies that when policy makers want to develop a specific policy program that touches upon the interests of many different stakeholders, the first step is to look to create and facilitate a safe and trustful environment in which these stakeholders can meet and can explore if there is a common ground that can be used to develop joint actions (de Bruijn and Ten Heuvelhof, 2010).

In order to make a network analysis the framework outlined in Table 4.1 could be used (see also Koppenjan and Klijn, 2004):

Table 4.1 A network analysis table

Characteristics of the network\Actor	Actor A	Actor B	Actor C	Actor D
Task and position				
Interest				
Dominant perception of the problem				
Dominant perception of possible solutions				
Resources at disposal				
Characterization dependency				
Strategy used or expected to be used				

In the way different actors try to protect their interests, given their role and position in the policy networks that surrounds a specific policy problem, actors often develop very different frames, which legitimize the meaning that they attach to what is happening and how to proceed. In doing so a link can be made with the following perspective.

4.4 The cultural perspective: developing appealing frames

In the cultural perspective on policy development the emphasis is put on the development and alignment of appealing and convincing frames which make sense to different groups of different people. In doing so a policy program can be seen as a story or a set of stories that is told about the nature of a specific societal problem and what suitable actions are needed to be implemented in order to deal with this problem (Bekkers and Moody, 2014, 2015). This implies that policy makers should be aware of the expressive nature of a program, because a policy program – in order to survive in the liquid political world of the drama democracy, see also Chapter 1 – is perceived as a legitimate and effective one, if it is able to stimulate a process of identification and shared understanding; not only among relevant stakeholders but also by the wider public. Hence, it is important to pay attention to the symbolic representation of a policy program, in terms of how issues are said, written down and visualized (Stone, 2001:138). The development of a story or storyline that creates a frame of reference that helps people to understand what is happening and what actions should be put forward in order to deal with a specific problematic situation, is an important design issue in the cultural perspective on policy design (Hajer, 2003, 2006; Stone, 2001; Pollitt and Hupe, 2011; Bekkers and Moody, 2014). For instance, Stone (1989) has shown that all kinds of stakeholders develop different causal stories to explain why a societal problem that needs to be dealt with by government, has occurred. For policy makers it is important to develop such an appealing story or storyline to which other stakeholders and groups refer to, when they refer to the nature of the problem and the actions that need to be taken.

When developing a policy program, policy makers can include the following elements into a story or storyline. In doing so, they aim to insert appealing cues into a policy program. Cues are used to influence the interpretation of what is communicated (written down, said or filmed) in a specific way. In doing so policy makers try to influence the discussion around a specific theme and its approach (Bekkers and Moody, 2015):

- It is possible to reduce a rather complex problem by trying to personalize it, by trying to link it to personalized experiences (Stone, 2001). For instance, the actual story of a victim or a hero can be used to illustrate the added value of a policy program in a very prompt way. For instance in relation to the problem of safe neighborhoods, a personal experience of an old lady who is afraid to go on the streets can be used to personalize the problem in this neighborhood. Their story represents in a daily way the necessity that government intervention is needed.
- Another element is the synecdoche (Stone, 2001). This is a figure of speech in which a part is used to represent the whole. This part does not represent a concrete case but it represents the whole. For instance, the bear that is drifting on an ice floe in the sea as has been used in the Al Gore documentary on global warming, not only tells us something about the helplessness of this bear, but also tells us something about the change in our climate that is taking place.
- Metaphors are also elements that can be used (Stone, 2001). Metaphoric reasoning, in which the line between two things is suggested, can also be used. For instance, policy makers make use of metaphors, like "the war on drugs," or "a battle that we need to win" when trying to convince other people to support the measures that they propose when trying to deal with the crime rate in a neighborhood.
- Symbols are another element that can be used (Stone, 2001). For instance, the use of the symbol of a flag can be used to underline that a policy program has a nationwide significance.
- Policy makers can also relate to specific myths that are rooted in a community to improve identification processes (Stone, 2001). Myths can refer to specific stories that for instance refer to a common past or a past experience that are told in a community that can be used to legitimize specific actions. For instance, when dealing with the problem of

immigration in a neighborhood, policy makers can refer to the myth of immigration as "a melting pot".

- Figures can also be used to tell a story (Stone, 2001). They can also be used to express the necessity of a problem by making the problem more quantitative. Very often policy makers play with numbers (small numbers, large numbers, percentages) to reduce or enlarge the scope of a problem and the visual representation of these figures can also be used to stress the importance of a specific message.

- Visualizations (Bekkers and Moody, 2014). A picture often says more than a thousand words. The advantage of visualizations, such as pictures, films but also three dimensional visualization, can help policy makers to stress the importance of a specific program, because, for instance a simulation or animation can help people to understand how the reconstruction of a neighborhood would look like, in a more integrated, and thus transparent way; instead of reading all kinds of plans that only deal with just one or two elements of the reconstruction. The advantage of visualization is that it can represent a possible future in an integrated and coherent way.

- The use of "magic concepts" (Pollitt and Hupe, 2011). Very often policy makers refer to specific policy, management or governance concepts that are quite popular in the political and policy making world, because they refer to change, innovation, renewal and reform. They insert these concepts when drafting specific policy programs in order to enhance their attractiveness. For instance, the idea of the "Big Society" is such a concept that is used by policy makers to legitimize a new distribution of tasks and responsibilities between government and society, in which society and self-organizing communities are in the lead, instead of "big government" when re-defining the welfare state.

4.5　The institutional perspective: playing with different design logics

Many policy problems are multi-faced, because policy makers have to deal with different values that have to be balanced and reconciled. For instance, when dealing with the safety in a neighborhood, it could be argued that CCTV cameras could improve the safety in a neighborhood. Not only because they could help the police in detecting crime, thereby registering what has happened, but also because these cameras may deter people who are thinking of robbing someone. The advantage is also that these cameras are less costly than increasing the number of police officers on the street. But at the same time these cameras not only register the behavior or (intended) criminal behavior, they also collect visual data about innocent people. In doing so they harm their privacy, while though the eyes of the camera, each passer-by is a possible criminal. As such, CCTV cameras also relate to the idea that "Big Brother is watching you." When drafting a policy program, policy makers have to deal with these different values. These different values can be linked to specific rationalities or logics that inherently and explicitly play a role in politics and policy making. These rationalities constitute a world of their own, and have legitimacy in themselves (Snellen, 1987). These rationalities provide a prescriptive framework of reference that policy makers have to use, when formulating policy goals and actions. In doing so specific design logics have to be followed, which are often translated into specific rules, procedures and routines that have to be followed. Together they constitute the normative framework in which they have to operate. For instance, when discussing the role of CCTV cameras policy makers have to take into account a number of legal requirements and fundamental rights which refer to the idea of "Rechtstaat" or the "rule of the law". This can also lead to specific procedures that have to be followed, like an obligation to have a legal check on the proposal by the local or national privacy data protection agency.

According to March and Olsen (1989b) two logics play an important role in developing and implementing public policies. First, they refer to the logic of consequences that have to be taken into consideration. This implies that when drafting a policy program, policy makers have to assess the consequences of a program in terms of effectiveness, efficiency and internal and external coherence. But taking into account the effects of a program is not enough. CCTV cameras could be very effective in terms of crime prevention but when citizens have the feeling that they are a price that they do not want to accept, in terms of always being watched, then there is something wrong. Hence, a program should also be considered as an appropriate one. That is why policy makers have to deal with the so-called logic of appropriateness (March and Olsen, 1989b:23-24). Appropriateness refers to the degree in which a specific program will have enough political and public support, given the dominant political and public support and given the specific problem that needs to be dealt with. At the same time, the way in which these logics and the values that lay behind them are balanced differ per actor, given the interests that are at stake and the claims that are made.

Based on this distinction between these two logics, we are able to put forward four design questions that policy makers need to answer, when drafting a program (Hemerijck, 2001; 2003; see also Fischer, 2003a, 2003b). From an institutional perspective these four questions constitute the boundaries within which policy makers have to operate. The answers to these four questions refer not only to the different sorts of values that have to be taken into consideration, but these answers also point at a number of inherent design dilemmas with which policy makers wrestle. Very often these dilemmas constitute the essence of the political debate. The following questions can be put forward (Hemerijck, 2001; 2003; see also March and Olsen, 1989a, 1989b).

Does it work?

Derived from the logic of consequence, this question forces a policy maker to take into account the possible outcomes of a program, given the goals that have been formulated. Can it be expected that the goals of the program will be achieved in terms of benefits that can be expected? What are possible and relevant costs that have to be taken into consideration? Can something be said, besides the intended consequences, about unintended ones? Are there other programs to be considered that will possibly be harmful? This question relates to the more rational design perspective that we discussed earlier. The answer to this question can be seen as a rational attempt to address and assess the possible outcomes, in terms of effectiveness, efficiency and coherence.

Is it allowed?

This question is also based on the logic of consequence and deals with the legal consequences that have to be taken into consideration. The idea of the "Rechtstaat" implies in western European countries that government policies affect the behavior of citizens in general – being an individual, being a company or being a societal organization, which for instance influence the equity between them or the freedom to act. That is why a government has to take into account a set of obligatory requirements (in terms of rights, obligations and other legal norms), when intervening in society. As a result all government interventions have a legal grounding, have to be based on "the rule of the law" in order to ensure fairness, predictability and equality and to prevent misuse of power.

Is it applicable?

In order to develop a policy program that meets the test of appropriateness, policy makers can ask themselves, is a policy program able to deal with specific circumstances and contingencies in which it is applied. These circumstances can be linked to the concrete support or the concrete resistance that stakeholders may deploy, when being confronted with a specific policy measure. The following is a question that a policy maker has to ask him/herself: what is the reason for this possible lack of commitment? For instance, because the program is not able to deal with the variety of local circumstances, or specific actors that play a role in the implementation do not have enough resources to implement the program. Moreover, this question also relates to the applicability of the measures that are proposed, given the specific circumstances with which they have to deal. For instance, because the actions are too narrowly defined, so that a tailor-made approach is impossible, or because existing procedures, routines and systems are incompatible with the new ways of working as put forward by the policy program.

Is it appropriate?

In order to make a distinction between the local circumstances and the more "generic" circumstances, which are very often defined at the policy sector or "systemic" level, policy makers have also to deal with another type of fit (Fischer, 2003a, 2003b). This type of fit relates to the legitimacy of government and the trust that citizens have in the ability of government to deal with a problem, also in relation to the (changing) needs of citizens, as for instance expressed in public opinion regarding a specific issue. Hence, this aspect of the logic of appropriateness deals with the degree of responsiveness of and trust in government. How appropriate is the policy program?

Although above we discerned four perspectives on how to develop a policy program, we see that in practice policy makers have to follow and have to combine all the design logics. Developing a policy program implies that rational, political, cultural and institutional aspects have to be taken into consideration and have to be balanced. Policy makers need to have a proper understanding about the causes and effects of the policy problem at hand, have to explore what the possible options are and what we really know about these causes, effects, options and possible consequences (rational model). However, at the same time he or she should be aware that causes, effects, options and consequences are related to the specific interests of all kinds of actors, who will push forward specific problem definitions and options as well as make use of all kinds of power resources in order to stimulate or frustrate a specific definition or approach (political model). Sometimes these problem definitions and options are also closely linked to grown practices that specific actors want to preserve or want to go beyond; practices that they embrace or want to leave behind because they are linked to specific values (institutionalized values) that have to be taken into consideration. Given the fact that around many policy problems a network or arena of stakeholders can be discerned which push forward their own definitions of reality, their own definitions of what actions have to be taken, the question remains: which definition of reality is being adopted by the other actors, or: have the involved actors been able to develop a shared definition of the policy problem at hand

and the possible approaches that they want to explore or elaborate? In doing so, not only power and dependency plays a role, but also the way in which these definitions of reality can be framed in a persuasive way, by making use of rhetoric, symbolism and all kinds of visuals (cultural perspective). Persuasive frames are important because they provide a common grammar to the actors involved so that they link their individual interests, motives and beliefs with each other. In doing so, developing a policy program implies that a policy maker has to play chess at different tables. In order to do so policy makers have to be capable of applying knowledge, the understanding and design tools that are linked to each perspective and be able to connect them to each other.

Furthermore, the distinction that has been made between those four perspectives may also function as a check on the quality of the design process. For instance, policy makers can ask themselves, what perspective is dominant in the way in which I approach a problem. A policy maker who is rooted in a more rational tradition, may ask him/herself: did I take into account the different interests that are at stake. While a policy maker that operates as a "political animal" should perhaps ask him or herself the question: what do I really know about the assumptions that I push forward when discussing how to handle a specific policy problem?

Now that we have discussed the four design perspectives that policy makers may use when developing a program, we may switch to the following issue. When exploring the possible actions that governments have to pursue, when dealing with a policy problem, an essential question is, how should I intervene. This issue touches upon the steering capacity of government. Is a government able to intervene in such a way that it can really steer specific developments? When dealing with the safety of a neighborhood, does the combination of more police on the street and a more restrictive, zero-tolerance approach, really enable local government to reduce crime? In the next section we address the development of steering arrangements as a necessary step in the development of policy programs.

4.6   Policy development as the development of different steering arrangements

With the development of a policy program governments try to influence societal developments or problems in a desired and intended way, given a specific context. The ability and willingness to influence societal challenges in a specific context can be defined as an act of steering (Kickert and van Gigch, 1979). As such, a policy program can be seen as a plan to intervene in society.

In the daily practice of policy making, when drafting a program, a policy maker has a number of assumptions in his mind regarding the political desirability and ability to intervene. When dealing with feelings of safety, some questions will pop up in his or her mind. Should government intervene? The question of how to intervene will also be linked to the capacity and ability to intervene. Do we have the legal competences to do so, do we have the knowledge and information to do so? Hence, when talking about steering or intervention, policy makers often adhere to a specific set of implicit or explicit assumptions that together constitute a steering conception or a steering arrangement which very often lies behind a policy program. The following assumptions can be discerned (Bekkers, 1998):

- Assumptions about the political and ideological legitimation to steer or to intervene. Steering is not neutral but the reason for intervention has to be legitimized. Political and ideological doctrines, values and norms legitimize the ways and the extent of government interventions. For instance, the safeguarding of the safety in the street can be seen as a core task of government, which might also influence the freedom of people.
- Assumptions about the steering capacities of the actor that intends to steer and the actor that is being steered. More specifically these assumptions refer to the resources – in terms of capacities and capabilities – that a specific actor has at his disposal and the way these resources are organized. At the same time government is not the only actor that steers. That implies that policy makers may also have assumptions about the possibility of making use of the steering capacities of these other actors. For instance, citizens do possess self-organizing or self-steering capacities that can be used, because citizens can also organize themselves through co-operations, voluntary or grass root organizations that can be seen as possible co-producers of public services. Citizens in a neighborhood can take on responsibility for the vitality of the neighborhood, by exploiting a neighborhood center or a playground, but also by setting up a neighborhood watch or vigilante teams. This implies that policy makers may develop specific assumptions about the relationship between the steering capacities of government and the self-steering capacities that are present in a policy sector, or in society in general. These assumptions about steering and self-steering can be seen as communicating vessels.
- Assumptions about the context and object of steering. Steering always takes place in a specific context and the particularities of this context also influence the ability to steer. Relevant particularities might be the degree of political polarization, the fragmentation of the policy sector or the degree of professionalization. Within this context also the object of steering can be located. A specific intervention is also directed to something or

somebody, for instance the behavior of an individual citizen or company. For instance, the object of steering in a neighborhood could be directed at the hanging around of young people which is perceived as threatening by the inhabitants of the neighborhood. How can we prevent them from hanging around?

- Assumptions about the role of information, knowledge and information and communication technologies. Steering is based on an insight in the nature and course of the development and processes which one tries to influence, while at the same time it is relevant to know if the steering activities that are being pursued really make a difference (in terms of monitoring and evaluation) and that adjustments are necessary. For instance, if we want to intervene on youngsters who hang around, we need to have information about what causes them to hang around.

- Assumptions about the way to intervene and the instruments that can be used. Policy makers may have ideas about how to intervene. Different forms and different instruments can be used. For instance, one can try to regulate the behavior of citizens by making use of all kinds of legal norms that are laid down in rules and regulations. For instance, in terms of hanging around a government can use rules that forbid youngsters from gathering together or the government can deploy all kinds of provisions, like setting up community centers and developing all kinds of leisure and welfare activities that prevent them from hanging around in the street.

These assumptions very often constitute steering arrangements, which lay behind a policy program. For instance, a policy program that tries to prevent crime among youngsters will have another set of assumptions about how to intervene than a program that tries to tackle crime in a more repressive way. Hence, several steering arrangements can be discerned. However, the interesting thing is that these arrangement types are rooted differently in our four perspectives on the policy process. Some (combinations) are more dominant than others. In the next subsection we will describe these arrangements and link them to these different perspectives.

Steering as command and control

The first, and the most traditional way of steering is based on command and control (van Gunsteren, 1976). The idea is that government, structured as a pyramid and organized as a machine in which each cogwheel is smoothly connected to another, from a super-ordinated location in society is able to govern society. In this idea of the "perfect administration" government is operating in a routinized, efficient and reliable and predictable way, based on a well described definition of tasks, responsibilities and competences which are linked to each other by clearly defined lines of communication and coordination (Hood, 1976; Morgan, 1986). Just like government, also society is defined as a machine (Mannheim, 1935). Based on clearly defined policy programs, in which the ends and means are well-defined and adjusted to each other, society – and all the organizations, groups and other actors which constitute society – is willing and able to adjust to the instructions that are laid down in these programs and that are translated in all kinds of laws, regulations and other rules that can be imposed (van Gunsteren, 1976). The idea is that in essence society is compliant to commands that are given, but in order to ensure compliance, the government sets up a monitor and control system to ensure that obedience can be safeguarded (Garrett, 1972; Brown, 1975; Dunsire, 1978). In order to develop these policy programs, special emphasis is paid to the role of information and knowledge. Government is seen as an "information processor" (Zincke, 1990). The assumption is that the availability of extensive and reliable knowledge and information can help governments to plan and program their interventions in a more efficient and effective way, while sophisticated feedback and monitoring information helps the government to adjust and fine-tune their rules and regulations so that they can immediately restrict undesirable outcomes or further impose more desired outcomes (Hood, 1976; Schön, 1971).

In this specific steering arrangement we see that especially the rational and political perspective on the policy process is present. Knowledge and information are seen, together with the competences of government to intervene and to regulate, as very powerful resources that can be used to produce specific and desired outcomes. However, this power is necessary, because it enables government to act rationally in such a way that it can develop and implement well-structured policy programs that are directed to clear and well-defined goals. The super-ordinated position of government toward society and the strong control over knowledge and information is seen as a prerequisite to enhance the planning, programming, regulation and monitoring capacity of government (van Gunsteren, 1976).

Steering as steering on input and output parameters

A second arrangement is steering on input and output parameters (Bekkers, 1998). The idea behind it is that society possesses self-regulation capacities that can be used. This implies that organizations, societal groups but also individual citizens do not act as cogwheels in the machinery of government, but they strive for their own goals and their interests and control specific resources. Steering on input and output tries to make use of these capacities by giving organizations more freedom to develop their own actions and pro-grams. This freedom enables organizations that play a role in the implementation of specific policy programs, to respond more flexibly to a variety of circumstances. However, this freedom is given within a certain framework which refers to specific input and output parameters that have to be met. Very often this framework of parameters is given or imposed, while sometimes the refinement of these parameters is the object of negotiation. For instance, in the fight against crime, which varies from city to city or from region to region, it is easier to give the local police forces a large degree of freedom so that they can think what is the best way to deal with the crime in their city instead of being confronted with "a one size fits all program" that is seen as a "blue print" for all the forces. The power that is given to these police forces is restricted by specific input parameters. These input parameters constitute the budget that these police forces are given to implement a specific policy program. So steering on the input focuses on making use of budgets, that based on specific considerations and calculations add up to a lump sum of money that can be spent. In order to make use of this budget, specific agreements can be made regarding the output or outcomes that have to be realized. For instance, a police force can apply for a budget, while at the same time promising that it will reduce the kind of burglaries (prevention and resolvement) with a specific percentage in a specific time frame. Local police forces have the freedom to develop and implement their own actions and activities, and the budget for financing these activities, as long as the output or outcome goals are met. If these goals are not being achieved, a central intervention may follow, which may lead to adjusted goals or an adjusted budget (in terms of penalties). If the goals have been met, a reward may also be given, for instance in terms of a budget increase. This way of steering is a prominent way of steering, which was embraced by New Public Management (Hood, 1995; Pollitt and Bouckaert, 2004), has led to the introduction of performance management systems in all kinds of sectors, not only in the police, but also in public health and education (Pollitt, 2003). In the slipstream of this steering model, all kinds of budgeting and performance information management systems have emerged, because information is not only necessary to calculate the budget, but also to monitor the output and outcomes that are produced.

When looking at the different perspectives on the policy process, we see that again a combination of the political and rational models is present. From a political perspective, this way of steering acknowledges on the one hand that society cannot be steered from a central point, but actors in society have powerful resources that can be used to obstruct policy programs because they do not fit. Not only because they do not match with specific interests, but also because the variety in society cannot be addressed by a "one size fits all plan". The latter is a rational argument. However, the rational perspective does return to the idea that a system of penalties and rewards – when looking at the output and outcomes that have to be realized – changes the costs and benefits balance of a specific actor. This can be seen as a way to secure compliance to the super-ordinated framework that has been formulated, and which also often – from a political perspective – relates to the dominant position of one actor that defines the input and output parameters.

Steering by making use of incentives

Governments can also use incentives to steer society and societal actors (Schneider and Ingram, 1990). Incentives try to persuade people, organizations and societal organizations to develop a specific kind of behavior that governments want to pursue. A specific stimulus is given, like a subsidy, which tries to change the costs/benefits analysis that a specific actor is making. In doing so, some alternatives are made more attractive than other alternatives, but also the opposite may happen: some alternatives become less attractive, because they will become more costly than others. Steering based on incentives has the advantage that it still allows actors to make their own decisions. It recognizes their autonomy, their interests, frames of reference and resources, while at the same time it is not compulsory. And again, this arrangement acknowledges that society consists of self-regulating actors that are able to make their decisions (Bekkers, 1998). For instance, a municipality that wants to reduce burglary in houses may persuade citizens and companies to invest in better burglary prevention measures (like hinges and locks, and improved lighting) by giving them a small subsidy so that it becomes more attractive to do so.

Traditionally incentive steering has been closely related to the use of especially money-based instruments, focusing on changing the costs/benefits balance of societal actors. Recently the discussion about incentive steering has become popular again, due to the discussion about "nudging" (Thaler and Sunstein, 2008). Nudging tries to change the parameters that citizens take into account, when they make specific decisions, for instance what motivates young people to drink large quantities of alcohol or to eat "junk food." In order to change the decisions that citizens make, nudges try to change the choice architecture of citizens so that specific alternatives get more or less attention (John et al., 2011). Nudges can refer to a large variety of cues that are installed by government, when it tries to influence behavior. These cues act as incentives. In general there are two sets of cues: information driven cues and social norm driven cues (Sunstein, 2016). An example

---

BOX 4.1

NUDGING

Nudging is not only one of the most recently emerged and most discussed steering strategies in policy sciences, but it is also much discussed in government and politics nowadays. Politicians and governments see nudging as a modest and friendly but still effective way of achieving government aims without any element of force or with much government investments. Nudging involves nuanced ways of changing information provision or changing people's choice architectures in order to influence behavior in a certain direction. For instance, asking people not whether they want to be an organ donor, but rather to indicate explicitly that they do not want to be an organ donor, is a clear example of nudging.

Former US President Obama even hired a famous "nudging" professor (Sunstein) as advisor to his administration. His administration introduced various nudges, such as text messages to first-year students during the summer holiday period not to "forget" to complete certain information, which resulted in a much higher enrolment rate than in the years before this nudge. Also in the UK, the Prime Minister's Office has established a team working on "nudging."

---

of information driven cues is the use of default rules, simplifications of the complexity, warnings and graphics that stimulate a specific choice. Social driven norms refer to the normality or abnormality of specific behavior, for instance by saying what most of the people do. However, it is very important that policy makers understand what the decision-making structures of the involved organizations, groups or individuals are: what drives and motivates people in their behavior and what are the possible effects of specific cues that may change their motives?

Although this steering arrangement acknowledges the impossibility of government to control the behavior of actors in society, and thus put its power into perspective (which is related to the political model), this steering arrangement is based on more advanced behavioral insights that try to make use of the degree in which people act rationally (or not). It still tries to influence the cost–benefit assessment of actors, thereby taking into account that these actors act as a "homo economicus," although its rationality is limited. Actors only take into account a limited number of alternatives and make limited costs/benefit analyses, often based on previous experiences and short cuts that fill in their preferences (Simon, 1961).

Steering through the structuration and proceduration of relationships

Government can, again by acknowledging the fact that societal actors are not cogwheels in the machinery of government, try to make use of the self-regulation forces that are present in a societal sector. It can opt to intervene to change the positions that specific actors have when dealing with a policy problem. It can also change the playing rules that these actors should take into account when developing new approaches or set up new service arrangements. In doing so, an arena, or even a "level playing field" can be organized, which on the one hand enables actors to make their own choices, to develop their own strategies or to set up their own collaboration arrangements (Bekkers, 1998). On the other hand this is not a game in which everything is allowed. This arena or playing field is erected in order to achieve specific societal outcomes, in which important values have to be respected by given well-defined specific positions and playing rules. The idea is that through the structuration of the positions and roles of the involved actors and through the proceduration of the interaction between them, specific outcomes may be achieved. This kind of steering has also been described as "institutional design" (Goodin, 1998). A typical example is the creation of a level playing field to enhance the introduction of markets that replace the monopoly of government in service delivery in order to guarantee freedom of choice. For instance, when government want to retreat as the main energy provider, it is important that an energy market emerges in which not only the former national or regional government owned energy provider can profit from this process of liberalization. It is vital that other energy providers have access to the market and that they, on an equal basis, can compete with the former government owned provider. Hence, in order to create a level playing field, the steering interventions can be directed to ensure access and to assure free competition, which makes it also easier for citizens to change from one provider to another one. Furthermore, in order to guarantee this, it is also important that a supervisory body is installed, also to protect "weak interests" (like the access to relevant information that citizens can use to make a more deliberate choice). Another example of this kind of steering is the use of public tenders. When government wants to redevelop a specific area, for instance to improve the vitality of a neighborhood, a public tender can be used to invite all kinds of consortia to formulate plans in order to achieve this goal. In order to ensure that each consortium has an equal chance and to guarantee that specific goals have to be met (for example, houses for the poor, or facilities for young people), specific conditions that relate to each consortium can be formulated. In doing so, a level playing field can be established.

When using our four perspectives, we see that this kind of steering arrangement especially relates to the political and institutional perspective. From a political perspective, it can be argued that this arrangement acknowledges that different actors may have different interests and resources which can be seen as a reservoir for self-regulation, if their interactions can be steered in a specific direction. From an institutional perspective, it can be said in order to develop these new practices, a re-arrangement of positions, relations and playing rules is necessary, thereby leaving all kinds of established path-dependencies behind.

Steering as the development of shared understanding

In the last steering arrangement that can be put forward, the aim is that government tries to bring all relevant stakeholders together, in order to facilitate a process of shared understanding between them (Bekkers, 1998). In doing so, government tries to bring different frames (regarding the dominant definition of the problem as well as possible approaches and solutions) together, which pre-supposes a process of collective or social learning in which – through communication, negotiation and bargaining, but also trial and error – different frames become aligned and a process of re-framing occurs which in the end leads to a shared, common frame of reference that is the basis for collaboration (Weick, 1969). This collaboration is normally the basis for the development and implementation of a joint policy program. This steering arrangement has often been described as a form of network governance (Koppenjan and Klijn, 2004). Network governance has the advantage that based on the recognition of the interdependencies between the involved stakeholders, more and different views are taken into consideration, which may help to explore new problem definitions and approaches that are able to address a variety of needs and interests. Sometimes the role of government is problematic in this arrangement: on the one hand it is one of the involved stakeholders with direct interests, while on the other hand it tries to keep in mind a specific distance, because it wants to facilitate and support (by creating a platform) the communication and negotiation between the involved partners (Sørensen, 2006). This way of steering can often be found in public–private partnerships that are set to regenerate deprived city neighborhoods, which requires the support of many actors. Very often this type of steering is also combined with a government that also tries to protect weak interests, thereby focusing on positions and roles, stipulating specific relationships or giving all kinds of playing rules, like the sharing of information (Koppenjan and Klijn, 2004). Although network governance is very often focused on the collaboration between rather well-organized and institutionalized stakeholders (for example, the local municipality with all its subunits, central government agencies, housing companies, banks and other capital funds, property development companies, schools and so on), also special attention is given in this arrangement to the role of citizens and citizen groups. The literature on "interactive policy making" or "interactive governance" looks especially at how these actors can participate as a co-initiator or co-designer in, for instance, the re-arrangement of the vitality and safety of neighborhoods (Edelenbos and Klijn, 2006). In doing so citizens become co-producers or co-creators in developing and implementing public policy programs (Voorberg, Bekkers and Tummers, 2015). One question is, what motivates citizens to participate, and are they really able to participate?

When we look at this steering arrangement, we see again that the acknowledgement that it is important to take into account the different frames of the involved stakeholders refers to the political perspective. At the same time, the process of trying to develop a common frame of reference, based on a process of re-framing and frame-alignment, shows the influence of the cultural perspective. Also traces of the institutional perspective can be found in this arrangement, if one looks at the emphasis that is put on the questions: who participates (roles and positions) and what are the basic rules of engagement (playing rules).

4.7 Opening Pandora's box: the tools of government

When developing a policy program, it is important to address the steering capacity of government as well as what legitimizes the role of government. It is also important to address the question of how to steer, how to intervene, in terms of the instruments to be used. In the previous section a glance at some of these instruments could be witnessed. For instance, we talked about subsidies, regulations, provisions and so on. Within the public policy literature, this discussion is also known as the tools of government. Which tools has government at its disposal, and how can their application be understood? First, we present several well-known typologies that try to cluster and understand a large variety of tools that governments have in their toolbox. Second, we try to understand the use of these instruments from the four perspectives on the policy process.

When looking at the history of thinking regarding the use of all kinds of policy instruments, we see an interesting shift. Originally we saw that policy instruments were primarily seen as the tools of government, tools that altogether constitute the toolkit of government (Hood, 1983). This conceptualization was strongly rooted in the rational approach of the policy process, in which all kinds of tools, that in essence are neutral, are free and at the disposal of policy makers. Their challenge is to pick those instruments that would contribute to the achievement of specific goals (Bemelmans-Videc, Rist and Vedung, 1998; Schneider and Ingram, 1990). In doing so they have to be aware of the strengths and weaknesses of each instrument, and thereby also take into consideration the context in which they will be applied as well as the features and motives of the target group to which they are directed. At the same time these instruments have to be in accordance with fundamental laws (legality) and have to be democratic (Bemelmans-Videc, Rist and Vedung, 1998). For instance, when considering regulation as an appropriate instrument, it is obvious that regulation has an obligatory nature, because it relies on rights, obligations and norms that can only be made effective when they are enforced. The latter is quite costly. Furthermore, using norms in relation to a target group which has a bad reputation in terms of compliance, makes it even more difficult. Besides, these norms should not violate fundamental rights and obligations, for instance they should respect the constitution or international treaties. In this rational approach, the selection of a policy instrument was considered as a deliberate choice, which rationality could be enhanced if relevant evidence was taken into consideration so that a more informed choice (looking at the efficiency and effectivity of these instruments) could be made. In order to improve the effectivity of the instruments used, policy makers also seek to make combinations of instruments. In doing so they develop a policy instrument mix. For instance, in order to improve the compliance with specific regulations, government information campaigns can be organized to inform a target group that new regulations will be implemented, which will affect them. The idea is that a better informed target group will be more compliant than a non or less informed group.

A typical example of this more rational approach is the distinction between specific families of policy instruments, thereby looking at the similarity between these instruments and the assumptions behind them. The idea is that there are three families (Vedung, 1998; Bemelmans-Videc, Rist and Vedung, 1998).

First, there is a family of legal instruments – also described in terms of "the stick" – that are based on a legal norm setting. These legal norms are obligatory, because they are inserted in a law or because they have been laid down in a contract. Given their obligatory character they function as a stick that can be applied, which stimulates or forces citizens, companies but also other governments to act upon this norm.

Second, there is a family of economic instruments – also framed as the "carrot" – that try to appeal to the cost–benefit assessments that citizens,

Table 4.2 Legal, economic and communicative "families" of instruments

Policy instrument family/aspect	Legal	Economic	Communicative
Constituting	Constitution, state law	Infrastructural works	Education, research
Directing	Instituting a ban, giving commandments	and facilities Fixation of prices	
Individual	License	Fines	Advice
General	Laws and regulations	Fixation of prices	Massa media campaigns
Restricting	Bans, commandments	Taxes, Fines	Propaganda
Enlarging	Contracts	Subsidies	Government information campaigns

companies and societal groups make. For instance, a well-known instrument within this family is the subsidy. By making use of subsidies governments can stimulate behavior in a specific way by making it more attractive, because a carrot is being offered as a present for the kind of behavior government would like to see. For instance, in order to promote solar energy, government can give a subsidy to house owners to help them to install solar panels on the roof. Also the opposite can happen. By making use of fines and penalties as well as raising taxes it becomes more disadvantageous to pursue a specific kind of behavior which government thinks that it should discourage. A classic example is the use of taxes to discourage smoking and drinking.

The third family is called the communicative family of policy instruments – of which the label "the sermon" is used – which try to influence citizens, companies and societal groups, by providing information and setting up a dialogue in order to convince them to develop specific actions. A typical example is government information campaigns that, for instance, try to convince the general public to donate their organs after their death.

In Table 4.2 we list a number of instruments by making use of these three families. When trying to list them we make three distinctions (van der Doelen, 1989). First, we make a distinction between the constituting aspect of the policy instrument, which refers to instruments that rely on the actions that governments themselves have to do, while the directing aspect refers to the behavior action that citizens, companies and other societal groups have to do. Second, we can look at the specificity of the instruments that are used. Some instruments are more focused on influencing specific and individual behavior, while other instruments are more focused on a broader (target) group or at society as a whole. Third, we can also differentiate by looking at the way in which an instrument diminishes or enlarges the freedom of citizens, companies and other groups or their possibilities.

The advantage of this typology is that it tries to cluster specific instruments into categories of different families, which share a number of assumptions. However, reasoning from a more institutional perspective, these families can also be defined as a policy style, which can be linked to a specific tradition of how to influence society, based on shared conventions and grown practices that are present in a specific policy sector or even in a nation (Howlett, 1991), while also the background and the professional training of the involved policy makers may be relevant (Richardson, 1982; Bemelmans-Videc, Rist and Vedung, 1998) because they seem to be biased toward specific instruments.

Nevertheless one can also question the distinctions behind this typology. For instance, in order to regulate prices it is necessary to draft a law. Hence, in practice the use of these instruments are closely intertwined. Furthermore, the distinction between enlarging and restricting is somewhat arbitrary. A contract can also be restricting. Last but not least, we see that this typology has a rather static nature, because new instruments, like the use of computer technology, cannot be linked to these instruments.

When discussing policy instruments Schneider and Ingram (1990) emphasize the importance of the behavioral aspects that are related to the use of these instruments. It is important to look at the behavioral assumptions behind them, because policy tools refer to "attempts to get people to do things that they might not otherwise do, or it enables people to do things that they might not have done (Schneider and Ingram, 1990:513). In order to have an intended impact on society, people in different situations have to decide and act in accordance with the desired policy goals. That is why it is important to match the characteristics of these policy instruments to the behavior of these people (Schneider and Ingram, 1990:153). Six situations can be discerned:

- People believe that the law does not direct them or authorize them to take action. As a result authority tools rely on inherent legitimacy of hierarchical arrangements that grant permission, prohibit or require action under designated circumstances. (Schneider and Ingram, 1990:514, 527)
- People may lack incentive to take action. Incentive tools assume that people are utility maximizers who will change their behavior when net tangible, positive and negative pay-offs will be offered to induce

compliance or encourage utilization. The idea is that people will not be motivated to take policy relevant actions unless they are influenced, encouraged or coerced by manipulation of money, liberty, life or other tangible pay-offs. Examples are inducements, charges, sanctions and the use of force. (Schneider and Ingram, 1990:515, 527)

- People may lack the capacity to take actions. Capacity tools assume that individuals may lack information, training, education and skills to take into account all the alternatives and costs and benefits of these alternatives. People may rely on all kinds of heuristics (shortcuts or rules of thumb, barriers) which restrict their rational behavior, because their rationality is bounded, given the fact that just a limited number of options and alternative actions are taken into consideration, thereby excluding others. Incentives as such are then not enough. Capacity tools assume that the bias and barriers that people encounter can be taken away by providing information, setting up training and education programs. (Schneider and Ingram, 1990:517, 527)

- People may disagree with the values that are implicitly embedded in the policy goals or means that constitute the policy program. Symbolic and hortatory tools assume that people are motivated or demotivated from within, thereby referring to the values and beliefs (about what is right or wrong, what is just and fair) that they adhere to. The idea is that policy instruments can induce the desired behavior by manipulating symbols and influencing values by referring to the beliefs of people. Labeling is, for instance, a tool that can be used, which involves the strategic use of images, symbols and words. Labeling can be found in propaganda but also government communication campaigns, for instance directed at "stop smoking" or "stop drinking" (Schneider and Ingram, 1990:519, 527). Symbolic and hortatory tools can especially be linked to the cultural perspective of the policy process.

- People may encounter high levels of uncertainty so that they do not know what to do, or what is possible to do, which can also lead to disagreement. Learning tools can be used to help them to solve the problems that they are wrestling with or motivate them to solve these problems. Tools are directed on facilitating a learning process in which people can experiment, are given feedback on improving the number and quality of participation but also on consensus building. Examples are hearings and evaluations but also forms of interactive and participatory policy making. (Schneider and Ingram, 1990:521, 527)

In order to understand the application of policy instruments we can also turn to the political perspective on the policy process. The use of a policy instrument can be seen as political intervention in a policy network that changes the power relations within a network. That is why policy instruments constitute a powerful resource that specific actors can use to protect their own interests as well as to influence their relationships with other actors in terms of reducing uncertainty and or increasing or decreasing (inter)dependency (Hood, 1983; de Bruijn and Ten Heuvelhof, 1997; see also Pfeffer and Salancik, 1978). For instance, by making use of a rather permanent stream of subsidies government can make citizens or companies more dependent on them, once a subsidy has been given and has been accepted. In doing so they can control the access to vital resources. For instance, in many countries all kinds of non-profit organizations in the field of health care, youth care, welfare and so on are dependent on the subsidies given by, for instance, local government. This implies that the use of policy instruments can also be seen as a governance strategy in order to influence the positions of actors and relations between them. A related question is how open or closed are these actors in terms of being responsive to external incentives and actions (de Bruijn and Ten Heuvelhof, 1997). The more dependent an actor is the more open he will be. But also, how interdependent are these actors upon each other? For instance, top-down oriented instruments like regulation not only work in situations in which the regulator is dependent on the actors he or she wants to regulate. Last but not least, the number of actors that have to be influenced should be taken into consideration, for instance how scattered or fragmented is a sector (de Bruijn and Ten Heuvelhof, 1997).

A classic typology of instruments that is based on this power resource perspective on policy instruments has been developed by Hood (1983). On the one hand he makes a distinction between effectors and detectors. Effectors are instruments that government can use to try to make an impact on society. Detectors are instruments that government uses for taking in information (Hood, 1983:3). Detecting and effecting instruments are seen as essential capacities that a government should have in order to influence societal developments and policy problems in an effective way. For instance, in order to influence, it is important to understand what is happening in society. On the other hand, governing these detecting and effecting instruments need to have a solid base. So, on what is government to base its instruments? Governments need to have four basic resources at their disposal, when they want to develop detecting and effecting tools.

According to Hood (1983:4) these resources are nodality, treasure, authority and organization. Nodality refers to the property of being in the middle of an information or social network. In doing so governments can try to control the node in a network in which all kinds of information flows and relationships come together. In doing so government is the central actor in a network, given

Table 4.3 Hood's typology of policy instruments

Resource/ instrument	Nodality	Treasure	Authority	Organization
Effectors	Advice to farmers	Grants, loans, subsidies to farmers	Certification of healthy stock, import and export licenses	Marking of subsidized animals, stud farms and artificial insemination; vaccination, quarantine and slaughter of sick animals
Detectors	Surveys	Information from applications	Registration of farms, farm inspection	Laboratories for detecting diseases

the expression that "all roads lead to Rome" (Hood, 1983:4,6). Nodality gives government the ability to gather, process and distribute information in such a way that it is in the lead (ahead of others) or is able to generate the broader picture. The limiting factor is however, credibility of the information it is receiving and processing. Treasure denotes not only the possession of a stock of monies in a narrow sense, but to anything which has a money-like property of "fungibility" like for instance gold, bonds, shares or even intellectual property rights (Hood, 1983:5,6). Treasure gives government the ability to exchange money or other "coins" in order to buy influence, for instance in terms of "check books politics". Authority symbolizes the possession of legal or official, formal power based on the allocation of tasks, competences and responsibilities which enable government to demand, forbid, guarantee or to adjudicate, while organization denotes the possession of a stock of people with whatever skills they may have but also to other related resources like land, materials, equipment and so on (Hood, 1983:5-6). At the same time the authority of government is limited, due to all kinds of legal regulations, while organizational resources in terms of staff and equipment is also limited in terms of available capacity. Based on these distinctions, it is possible to classify the policy instruments that are used in relation to specific policy problems or are being used by an agency. In doing so Hood has applied his typology to different agencies. We will use his example for agricultural services (Table 4.3) (Hood, 1983:124-125).

Later on Hood (2006) and Margetts (1998) especially emphasize that the increased use of information and communication technologies in government also influences the nature and the conditions under which policy instruments can be used. At the same time these technologies influenced the powerfulness of the position that government may take in all kinds of policy networks. Several reasons can be given:

- Information and communication technologies (ICTs) substantially increase the detecting capacity of government, which can be related to the ability to acquire, store and process large quantities of data, while at the same time new data can be acquired through the coupling and linking of data between and within datasets. The idea of "big data" expresses this. As a result, the target groups to which a policy instrument is directed become more transparent, which may facilitate a more contextual and more tailor-made approach of the use of these instruments as well as developing a more advanced mix of instruments to be used (narrow casting). Furthermore the use of CCTV and other surveillance technologies helps government to increase its detecting capacity, while the fact that ICTs are embedded in the vessels of society and are an integral part of the activities that constitute our daily living and working, makes it rather easy to monitor our behavior, all kinds of movements (for example, when we travel) or register specific flows (like water, energy). (Bekkers, 2012)
- Information and communication technologies as a resource increase the nodal position of government in policy networks (in terms of nodality). For instance we see that government agencies through increased exchange of information can be seen as "a spider" in a large information network which enables them to develop a rather panoptical view on what is happening within society, a policy sector or a target group. In doing so it is able to improve its information and knowledge position that facilitates the transparency of for instance a sector but also the specific behavior of people and companies. (Bekkers, 2012)
- Information and communication technologies are increasingly integrated in specific policy instruments. For instance, the application and rendering of subsidies, the collection of fines and taxes but also the rendering of smaller and standard permits has been computerized quite heavily. In doing so ICT functions are the backbone of the application of many tools, given the fact that these tools especially rely on the collection and processing of relevant data that can be automated.
- Information and communication technologies are reflexive technologies, because they are able to generate information about their own use. They possess "informating capacities." (Zuboff, 1988). This implies that the use of these technologies in combination with the application of these policy tools generates information that can be used to learn about how specific tools are being applied and how specific target groups behave. In doing so policy makers can evaluate the strengths and weaknesses of the tools that they use, which can lead to a more fine-tuned instrument mix.

- Information and communication technologies can also improve the access and the handling of information and knowledge, which can be used by citizens. As such they are an instrument on their own. The idea of "open government" and "open data" expresses this. For instance, access to quality information about the output of schools or hospitals may help them to make a more informed choice about where to send their children to school or what hospital to go to in order receive a specific treatment. Furthermore the interactive and communication nature of the technologies may help governments to develop more interactive policy instruments – electronic discussions – but also help them to develop all kinds of feedback and learning processes which help to adjust and fine-tune their policy programs in order to meet the needs of citizens and companies in a better way. In doing so ICT can also be viewed, in terms of Schneider and Ingram (1990) as an important capacity and learning tool to support the decisions and actions of citizens.

When looking at the literature on policy instruments, we see that especially the rational and political perspective seem to be the most dominant perspective, given the fact that instruments are predominantly seen as a tool to achieve goals (rational), while others emphasize the fact that instruments can be seen as powerful resources that also change the power relations between actors (political). The cultural perspective is present but only in the way in which symbols, rhetoric and visualizations are used to frame specific messages. In doing so it is closely related to the use of propaganda and government information campaigns. Elements of the institutional perspective can also be found. Traces of this perspective can be found in the discussion about the influence of state intervention and steering traditions, also related to the political culture of a state, on how governments try to influence societal development (Bemelmans-Videc, Rist and Vedung, 1998; Linder and Peters, 1989). These traditions influence the choice of policy instruments. There seems to be a national or sectoral bias in the selection of specific instruments or adhering to a specific family of instruments (Linder and Peters, 1989; Howlett, 1991). For instance, in western Europe, especially in countries like Sweden and the Netherlands, subsidies are an instrument that are widely used, while in the United States this is not the case. It can also be stated that countries with a strong state tradition like Germany and France, adhere to more intrusive tools that are based on regulation (Bemelmans-Videc, Rist and Vedung, 1998).

4.8   Decision-making

The development of a policy program is just a first step. The next step is to decide upon the concept in order to give it authority. However, this distinction is an ideal one. In the literature about policy processes the phases of policy design and policy determination are often discussed together, because they are closely intertwined. During the design all kinds of decisions are made, while during the decision-making phase all kinds of adjustments are made. In the next section we will discuss a number of decision-making models that help to understand the nature of policy decision-making processes.

The rational perspective: the rational actor model

In the rational perspective policy programs are perceived as the outcome of a rational decision-making process. The rationality of this process is based on the assumption that actors (being individuals, being organizations) act as a homo economicus who makes deliberate choices (Allison and Zelikow, 1999:24-26). As a result, government actions, laid down in a policy program, can be seen as the outcome of choice regarding specific actions that will contribute to achieve the goals that are strived for. In order to make such a deliberate choice, the decision-making process is based on a rather analytical approach of how to proceed. The procedure to be followed is reflected in the behavior of the homo economicus. It is based on the following assumptions:

- A collection of specified goals and values that are considered to be important and that can be translated into a hierarchy of super- and ordinated goals.
- A collection of options, in terms of courses of actions and instruments to be applied, of which it can be expected that they can help to achieve the formulated goals, given the "evidence" that is present or can be collected.
- An assessment of the consequences of each course of action and/or each instrument to be applied in terms of possible costs and benefits. The idea in that an increase in costs of one alternative reduces the likelihood of that option being chosen.
- A choice that is based on value-maximizing, which implies that the homo economicus will select the option whose consequences rank highest in terms of goal accomplishment. (Allison and Zelikow, 1999:24-25)

However, in order to act as a rational actor, it is important that government operates as a unified actor, which just like one single person has one set of goals, one set of options, a single estimation of consequences leading to one choice. Although advocates of this model acknowledge that government is organized in different layers and units, the assumption is that through a clear chain of command, through well-defined coordination and communication procedures, this unity can be achieved (van Gunsteren, 1976; Dunsire, 1978). Another important assumption is that the driver for a government to act is based on external threats and opportunities, which refers to specific societal challenges that need to be addressed at the level of the state as political community, like the fight against crime or urban degeneration (Stone, 2002). For instance, in order to improve the quality of living in a neighborhood, the rational actor model assumes that local government, although organized in many departments, acts as an integrated, unified organization, and will select those options that will really contribute to this goal, given analyses of the possible costs and benefits that are related to each option. It implies that the municipality council, being at the top of the local pyramid, will choose that option that will have largest benefits in terms of goal achievement and the least costs.

However, this model is rather an ideal type model of decision-making. As a result many alternative models have been formulated, thereby addressing the specific shortcomings of this rational and analytical approach. One alternative model has been presented by Herbert Simon (1961). He argues that in the example of the improvement of the quality of living in a neighborhood, local government will only take into account a limited number of options, thereby including options with which they are familiar with, while excluding others. Why is this the case?

Simon (1961) argues that decision-makers are not able to take rational decisions, thereby considering all the options and consequences that are possible in order to make an optimal choice. The rationality of the decision-making process is rather limited, although decision-makers still seek to behave rationally. In doing so he introduces the concept of bounded rationality. This implies that people but also organizations have a limited capacity to gather and process information which seems to be needed to make a comprehensive inventory of possible actions and of possible consequences. It is merely impossible to take all the possible options and consequences into consideration. That is why specific "givens" are take into consideration (Simon, 1961:79). These "givens" lead to a reduction of the information that is needed, because only the information which seems appropriate is taken into account. Hence, in the decision-making process only a limited number of options and a limited number consequences are taken into consideration. Several reasons can be given that account for the rationality of policy makers as being bounded:

- Policy makers and decision-makers know that the knowledge that is needed is fragmented and incomplete;
- That some consequences cannot be known;
- That there is not enough time to consider all relevant options;
- That the staff that is needed to make an inventory or an assessment is limited;
- That the memory of people but also of the organization is limited; and
- That routines and habits play a role, because they are biased toward some actions because these actions are laid down in these routines (Simon, 1961:81-109; Parsons, 1995:277).

This implies that they adhere to options (and the consequences) with which they are already familiar. Furthermore they often formulate goals and objectives with which they are also familiar. In doing so decision-makers strive to make decisions that satisfy, given their bounded rationality.

Although Simon advocates a more realistic appraisal of the rationality of many decision-making processes, he still adheres to the intended rationality of the process. He is still loyal to the procedure to be followed, because he thinks that it is possible to be as a rational as possible. The problem, however, is that, especially in public administration, the reality of decision-making is rather capricious (Hill, 2005:146). In his later work Simon hoped that especially information and communication technologies, new management techniques but also operations research and systems analysis would overcome the limits of bounded rationality (Parsons, 1995:280). Another problem with Simon's approach is that his starting point is still that an organization has clear goals. He still refers to the goals of the organization. The problem in public administration is that goals are sometimes hidden, or that they are subject to continuous dispute and modification (Hill, 2005:146). Another problem is that Simon still defines the organization as a unified actor, although limited in its rationality. This is especially difficult when looking at public administration, given the plurality between the different organizations that constitute government on the one hand and the plurality within these organizations, when looking at all kinds of divisions and organizational units. These critical remarks open the door to present another model which is rooted in the political perspective.

The political perspective: muddling through

In public administration there is another famous concept which tries to deal with the nature of public policy decision-making processes. That is the concept of "incrementalism" which was coined by Charles Lindblom in a number of successive works, alone (Lindblom, 1959, 1965, 1977) or in collaboration with others (for example, Lindblom and Woodhouse, 1993). Just like Herbert Simon, Lindblom challenges the assumption behind the rational actor model – which he calls the "root method" – by looking at the practice of decision-making. This practice can be characterized by a large number of intertwined small steps that decision-makers make. They do not take large decisions, but just small decisions that are based on successive limited comparisons, which he calls the "branch method" (Lindblom, 1959:81). "The branch method involves a process of continually building out of the current situation, step-by-step and by small degrees" (Lindblom, 1959:81). In essence this process can be characterized by a process of "muddling through". In contrast to the rational actor approach, the procedure to be followed is not so needy (Parsons, 1995:284). In contrast to Simon, who still thinks that the rationality of the decision-making process can be improved, Lindblom argues that political decision-making is in essence a capricious and messy process which has not been addressed, when looking at the ideological connotation of the rational actor model (Parsons, 1995:284). The essence of the "muddling through" concept is that political decision-making is about mutual adjustment and negotiation, in which each time new but small, so-called incremental steps are taken. In contrast to the systematic and deliberate procedure that the rational model proposes, many decisions are made by accident, on an ad hoc basis. This also implies that a policy program is constantly being adapted; as such it is not finished because changing circumstances force policy makers to make new adaptive decisions, because they are engaged in a process of "trial and error". Pragmatism prevails, in which daily, rather bottom-up experiences are used instead of rather theory-driven knowledge and information (Lindblom, 1959). As a result goals and means (actions, instruments) are often adapted to each other. Decision-makers formulate goals which they know they can achieve with the instruments that they have at their disposal, while at the same time only those options are chosen because they are fully in line with already existing goals. For instance, a municipality could choose to invest in even more CCTV cameras, because it has already installed some cameras in the neighborhood, because this is in line with the existing actions that have been programmed. The consequence is that policy programs but also decisions build upon each other and that no bigger and larger vision or even blue print can be expected, or that alternative but important possible outcomes, options but also other goals and values are neglected (Lindblom; 1959:81; Parsons, 1995:287).

Two reasons can be given why this is the case. First, Lindblom also embraces the idea of satisfying decision-making (Simon, 1961), because a good decision is a decision which is based on the agreement between the most involved stakeholders, in which goals and interests are mutually adjusted to each other. Decision-making involves a process of bargaining and negotiation, which seldom leads to an optimal decision. It involves compromises, which also challenges the idea that government can be seen as a unified actor, because a unified actor does not need compromises because it is subjected to hierarchical decision-making. That is why Lindblom talks about "partisan mutual adjustment" (Lindblom, 1965). The second reason is that policy making in the public sector involves different and sometimes irreconcilable values which have to be balanced. For instance, in relation to the fight against crime, the use of CCTV implies that security and safety have to be balanced against individual freedom and privacy, while at the same time expected benefits in terms of safety have to be balanced against the costs that have to be paid. The nature of this balancing act implies that compromises have to be made. It implies negotiation and bargaining. As such this can be seen as an intelligent way to deal with rather complicated, wicked problems. That is why Lindblom (1965) talks about the intelligence of democracy, because democracy as a decision-making model enables us to make decisions regarding complicated issues, in which interest and values have to be balanced in such a way that they get societal support.

There is also some critique regarding this approach. The first issue is the emphasis on step-by-step mutual adjustments. When looking at a number of the realities of policy change, it can be stated that there are a large number of changes that are not based on rather incremental changes but on radical changes. That is why Hill (2005:149) argues that it is important to understand decision-making processes in relation to the process of agenda setting and the role that "policy windows" play (see the previous chapter). Lindblom has difficulty in explaining these kinds of changes. The second issue is the inherent ideological connotation of muddling through because it justifies a rather conservative perspective on decision-making. By referring to the incremental nature of a decision-making process, policy makers may use it to legitimize non-decision-making or to postpone decision-making (Parsons, 1995:293). The third issue is that policy makers and decision-makers are not challenged enough to embark on new, and more creative ways of policy making, thereby frustrating policy renewal (Dror, 1964; Etzioni, 1967).

The idea that Lindblom has put forward in terms of partisan mutual adjustment can also be understood from the model in which decision-making can be perceived from the perspective of a government politics perspective (Allison and Zelikow, 1971; later Allison and Zelikow, 1999), in which games are plaid in an arena (Lasswell, 1958; Teisman, 2000). Government is not a monolithic actor, not a unified entity but "it is a constellation of loosely allied organizations on top of which government leaders sit" (Allison and Zelikow, 1999:166). This constellation is also based on the fact that government has to deal with multi-faced problems and for each relevant aspect different organizations or organizational units have been set up. For instance, the vitality of a neighborhood refers to quality of the physical environment (building, streets, houses), but also to safety and security, to the economic capacity of the neighborhood (shops, services) and to the social structure (young versus old, different cultures, loneliness) of a neighborhood. However, the question what to do implies that specific viewpoints and interests will compete with each other. The decisions and actions of governments result from a process of bargaining, conflict and compromise and of confusion of different officials with diverse interests and unequal influence that interact with each other along regularized channels. As a result the organization of government constitutes an arena "in which intricate and subtle, simultaneous, overlapping and often deadly serious games are played among players located in positions in government" (Allison and Zelikow, 1999:295). Very often the hierarchical arrangement of players that constitute government and the regular communication and coordination channels that are used in government, structure the games that are being played. Also all kinds of deadlines that the organization uses, force the involved players to pay attention to specific issues. As a result decision-making can be understood in terms of playing chess: "the moves, the sequences of moves and games (. . .) are thus to be explained in terms of bargaining among players with separate and equal power over particular pieces and with separate objectives in distinguishable subgames" (Allision and Zelikow, 1999:295).

A classic example of such a game is the preparation and decision-making of the annual budgetary processes or the drafting of a major policy program that really wants to make a difference. For instance, the definition of what the vitality issues in terms of problems are will influence the budget and the allocation of the budget among the involved players. If there is an increase in terms of budget, the question will be: who will get the additional budget. If safety and security has been defined as the main issue, the local police would perhaps benefit. If the social issue was nominated as the main issue, then the local welfare department would be the winner. Hence, what you see is that in dividing this larger budget, different players have different interests, because some would win and other would lose. As a result they all try to influence the dominant definition of the problem at stake. This can be seen as a game, while the procedures that are used for the annual determination and allocation of the municipality budget may act as playing rules.

Hence, a specific decision that is made can be seen as the outcome of these games. In order to unravel these games, it is important to ask several questions (Allison and Zelikow, 1999:298-302): Who are the players and what determines their involvement in terms of position and role? How and why do priorities, goals, interests, shape the players' perceptions, their preferences and their standing regarding the issue at hand? What are the stakes in the games to be played? And, what power resource has each player at his disposal to influence the outcomes of the game that is being played? What is the game at stake, but also what are relevant playing rules? At the same time it can be argued that these games are played in different rounds, especially if the compromises that are being accomplished are disputed (Teisman, 2000). By referring to Lindblom, it can be argued that each step in a decision-making process may constitute a new round in which perhaps new players come into the game, or that external circumstances may lead to a re-definition of the stakes that are at hand.

There is, last but not least, another model that can be presented, which also helps us to understand the political nature of the decision-making process, and which has also been discussed in the chapter on agenda setting. The emphasis on arena and games helps to understand the dynamic and complex character of the decision-making process. But sometimes complexity becomes rather chaotic. In order to deal with this chaotic character, we can improve our understanding by looking at the garbage can model of decision-making as formulated by Cohen, March and Olsen (1972). Looking at re-organization processes in an American university they observe that the decision-making processes regarding the content and speed of the re-organization has a rather capricious character. It does not reflect the rational actor model. In the rational actor model the idea is that decision-makers, when confronted with a problem and based on an analysis of this problem, look for a proper solution. Cohen, March and Olsen (1972) observe that the opposite can also be the case. Decision-makers can also go the other way around by matching solutions to problems. Based on this idea they view the decision-making process as a garbage can:

> [I]nto which various problems and solutions are dumped by the participants. The mix of garbage in a single can depends on partly the labels attached to the alternative cans; it also depends on what garbage is being produced at the moment, on the mix of cans that are available, and speed with which garbage is collected and removed from the scene. (Cohen, March and Olsen, 1972:26)

Hence, each participant in a decision-making process carries his own garbage can, his own perception of possible problem definitions, solutions and relevant occurrences. When confronted with a decision they pick from their own garbage can possible relevant definitions and solutions, which will be linked to the definitions and approaches that other participants pick from their garbage can. Timing seems to be very important: when it is opportunistic to put forward a specific problem definition or a specific option. What occurrences stimulate or frustrate a specific connection of a problem to a solution or of a solution to a specific problem? The outcome of this process is that almost any solution can be associated with almost any problem (Cyert and March, 1992). For each new issue that policy makers have to deal with a new garbage can is created: a temporary and loosely coupled set of problem definitions and solutions, because the time seems to be appropriate to make this connection, derived from the definitions that the involved policy makers have in their garbage cans. "What the garbage can idea graphically suggests is that issues, problems and solutions are messy, untidy sorts of things, whose mode of identification by policy makers will depend on the time it was picked up, and the availability of cans to put them in" (Parsons, 1995:302). The ultimate question is, however, are actors able to influence the loose coupling of problems and solutions and vice versa in such a way that there is a chance that a specific combination is being pursued? Hence, what we often see is that the involved decision-makers collaborate with each other, based on compromises and bargaining in order to push forward a specific garbage can. That is why Cyert and March (1963:27-32) stress the importance of looking at what is the dominant coalition in an organization. Organizations can be viewed as comprised of coalitions – groups of individuals pursuing certain interests. Each group attempts to impose its preferences on the organization, on a development of a specific policy program, but no single group will be able to determine the content of a specific decision or policy program. In doing so group members seek to build alliances with other groups, based on making all kinds of "side payments" to secure co-operation and vice versa (Scott, 1995:289). An additional strength of the garbage can model is that it also questions the role of a hierarchy in providing order. Cohen, March and Olsen (1972) talk about organizations as being an organized anarchy: with the order of a hierarchy, rather chaotic and capricious decision-making processes take place, thereby also showing that, in our case, government is not a unified entity, because it consists of a variety of coalitions with different interests that structure the way in which problems are defined and solutions are put forward.

When applying this model to our example of local government dealing with the crime in a neighborhood, it can be argued that the choice to opt for a zero tolerance policy in this neighborhood, which has been rejected for a long time, was stimulated by a series of robberies. These series created a moment in time, which enabled for instance a coalition of the local police force, the mayor and more right-wing parties in the local council to push forward their solution. For the local police force these robberies and the call for a zero tolerance approach implied that their call to the local council to give them more police officers on the street could be accomplished.

The decision-making models that we discussed under the banner of the political perspective on decision-making not only show the importance of looking at the plurality of the involved stakeholders. They also make clear that decision-making takes place in different but linked arenas with different rounds. It is a messy process. Due to this messy nature, the sharp distinction that has been made in the rational model between design and decision-making is also questioned. That is why more political models emphasize the rather intertwined character of design and decision-making.

The cultural perspective: group think

In the cultural perspective we have stressed the importance of framing and the use of frames which are used to give meaning to specific interests, policy problem definitions as well as possible approaches. In relation to the decision-making phase, the role of frames is interesting when we look at the role of group think. Group think can occur when decision-makers during their choice process are subjected to a lot of external pressure, for instance, due to a crisis. A crisis is a stressful situation and stressful situations can lead to a psychological drive to have consensus. Policy makers believe that it is important to think and act as a cohesive group. As a result they tend to suppress dissent frames about what is going on and what should happen and they minimize possible conflicts. In doing so they do not take into consideration alternative problem definitions and other actions that could be worth considering (Allison and Zelikow, 1999:283). Due to this desire to act cohesively under stressful conditions, there is no room for deliberation, for critique. The desire to act cohesively is also influenced when decision-makers under stressful, crisis-like circumstances, feel that they are dependent on each other, because unanimity and conformity is considered as being the only option to deal with the situation. The process that takes place is described by Janis (1982) as bolstering: "exaggerating favourable consequences, downplaying unfavourable consequences, denying uneasy feelings, exaggerating the remoteness of action commitment, downplaying the extent to which others will see what is happening, and downplaying personal responsibility" (Allison and Zelikow, 1999:284). Due to this process of bolstering an inward-looking frame is being developed, which can be seen as being in a tunnel, thereby only seeing the things that one wants to see and excluding all things which do not fit within the adopted frame. This process takes place in small groups in particular.

However, it is not only crisis-like situations that may lead to group think. Group think can also emerge in situations in which there is a severe political polarization between different groups of decision-makers ('t Hart, 1994). This can lead to a dichotomy between "us" and "them". By using stereotypes, and thus closed frames of reference, decision-makers may not have a realistic picture of what is happening or what should be happening. The interpretation of events just follows existing patterns, thereby reinforcing this dichotomy between "us" and "them".

Another aspect which has to be mentioned in relation to the cultural perspective on decision-making refers to the idea that especially in politics and public administration, the decisions that are made do not always have to be substantial. Sometimes decision-makers aim to formulate symbolic decisions (Edelman, 1967, 1977). That is why Edelman (1977) talks about "words that succeeded and policies that fail". The outcome of the decision-making process is to produce decisions that do not aim to have real consequences, by putting things in motion. The desired outcome is to show that policy makers are dealing with the issue and show that they, in a more symbolic way, are doing something, that they pay attention to a specific problem, without solving it, because this is quite difficult or because there is still no consensus among the involved stakeholders about how to deal with the issue. An example of a more symbolic decision is to decide that additional information is needed or that additional investigations are necessary.

The institutional perspective: organizational routines

In the institutional perspective on decision-making, the idea is that decision-making processes are processes that are embedded in all kinds of formal (and also informal) rules that actors are obliged to follow (see also Chapter 2 on the perspectives on the policy process in which we defined rules as the routines, procedures, conventions, roles, strategies, organizational forms and technologies around which political activity is organized (March and Olsen, 1989a:22)). Also, because these rules are imposed to protect specific values which we think are important. For instance, when dealing with crime in a neighborhood we think that it is important that the actions of the police are based on the rule of the law, while from a democratic accountability perspective it is important that local government can be held accountable for the money they spent on, for instance, crime prevention programs that have been developed and the results that have been accomplished. In order to be accountable it is important that specific rules have to be followed. These rules constitute a path that has to be followed in order to make a decision (Pierson, 2000). It also implies that a new decision has a pre-destination, because it is based on already established and grown decision-making practices (see also Chapter 2 on the perspectives). In their famous study on analysing the Cuban missile crisis Allison and Zelikow (1971; later Allison and Zelikow, 1999), show the importance of this model. In their so-called organizational behavior model they show how especially standard operation procedures, programs and repertoires influence the decision-making process and its outcomes. Let's have a closer look at this model.

Allison and Zelikow (1999:164) define governmental actions as outputs of organizations or organizational units. Hence, a specific decision to implement a crime prevention program in a neighborhood is seen as the outcome of a number of organizational actions that have been followed and that are linked to each other. For instance, the mayor has instructed some civil servants to develop a plan. In order to get this plan discussed by the council, all kinds of procedures have to be followed: for instance advice has to be given and consultation has to be organized, a budget has to be drafted and given, staff have to be made available to draft the plan, expertise has to be hired because specific knowledge was not available, and so on. Hence, governmental decisions are dependent on the organizational capacities and capabilities (for example, staff, money, information, knowledge) that are available, how they are organized and the procedures that have to be followed.

Again, in this model government is not viewed as a unified entity. It is a constellation of loosely coupled and allied organizations or organizational units on top of which government leaders sit. Government organizations are inherently fragmented, given the variety and multi-faced nature of the policy problems with which they have to deal. For instance, the vitality of neighborhood not only refers to safety and security, but also to its physical, economic and social quality, for which different and specialized departments have been erected, each of them with their own operational objectives, their own capacities and their own culture. Hence, we have to accept that government has factored problems and fractioned power (Allison and Zelikow, 1999:166). This constellation is only able to act when these different organizations or units follow specific routines in order to overcome fragmentation. These routines facilitate coordination and help to stabilize the organization, by making it more predictable, thereby avoiding uncertainty. Furthermore, these routines are necessary to create some kind of unity in command, given the fragmented and often decentralized organization of government. All routines and procedures are in the end focused on establishing central coordination and control, because in government, the appointed leaders (like an alderman or a minister) have to decide (Allison and Zelikow, 1999:172, 174). Because it is not efficient to develop routines for each new issue which is at hand, governments develop standard operating procedures, programs and repertoires, which also prioritize the things that have to be done (Allison and Zelikow, 1999:169, 177). For instance, the allocation of the budget within a government is linked to all kinds of procedures that have to be followed.

4.9 CHAPTER SUMMARY

The development of a policy program is a rather complicated matter, given the fact that a policy maker needs to play chess at different tables; tables on which another type of game is being played, according to different logics. This metaphor also shows the importance of using different perspectives in the policy process. First, a policy maker needs to have a clear understanding about the relevant causes and effects that are related to a specific policy problem. Moreover, he also needs to have a clear understanding about possible actions and measures and the costs and benefits of these actions. This implies that policy design is primarily a policy analysis challenge in which a policy maker looks for, especially evidence-based, information and knowledge in order to select specific goal/action combinations, given the political assignment that he is given. However, this rational perspective is not enough, because there is another chessboard on which he/she is invited to play. The definition of a specific policy problem and the selection of specific approaches do not take place in a vacuum, because the definition and selection affect the interests, positions and resources of specific actors. Hence, policy design triggers a whole network of relevant stakeholders that try to influence the shaping of a policy design, because some might win and others might lose. That's why policy design is also a political challenge. How to convince other actors that a specific definition of the problem at hand as well as the selection of specific action measures is appropriate, and that it is worth supporting them? This implies strategic behavior, in terms of negotiation, exchange, persuasion, deliberation but also the exercise of power. However, in order to be persuasive, policy makers have to develop strong and appealing frames that help to align the interests of the involved stakeholders as well as the broader public. In doing so policy makers have to be aware of the power that resides in language, rhetoric, symbols, stories and pictures as well as being able to use them. That is why it is important to look at the sensemaking potential of the frames that are being used in the development of a policy program, which as earlier were described as the cultural perspective on the policy processes. The last chessboard on which a policy maker has to play relates to all kinds of informal and formal rules, which very often relate to specific values that have to be respected and that are translated in all kinds of grown practices (routines, procedures, logics, systems, styles) which also create all kinds of path-dependencies. Practice relates to four questions: does it work, is it applicable, is it allowed and is it appropriate? Sometimes a policy maker has to be aware of the existence of these grown practices in order to get support, sometimes it is a deliberate wish of policy makers to question these grown practices. Due to these different design perspectives, which lead to all kinds of different design instructions and criteria, policy development can also be viewed as a balancing act.

This balancing act also relates to the way in which the role of government is defined in the policy programs to be developed. This role, which is not only ideologically and politically determined, also relates to the capacity of government to really influence specific challenges and problems, given the limits of government intervention. Hence, an important challenge for policy makers within a policy program is the design of the specific steering arrangement which a policy maker wants to apply. Furthermore, special attention also needs to be given to the use of policy instruments which a policy maker wants to select in order to steer specific developments in a desired way. And again, the choice for specific instruments also varies depending on which perspective of the policy process a policy maker wants to use.

Following the policy cycle, after the phase of developing a policy program, the phase of decision-making follows, although both are in practice very often intertwined. Reasoning from the rational perspective, decision-making is all about choosing a specific alternative from a broader set of alternatives, based on a comparison of the related costs and benefits of each alternative in relation to specific goals and criteria. But decision-making is also about actors and interests. That is why the political perspective stresses the importance of looking at decision-making from an arena perspective and the struggles (or more politely the games) that take place within this arena. As a result decision-making processes are rather chaotic processes, which take place in different but linked arenas and in different rounds. However, actors that are involved in decision-making processes can also be captured by their own frames that they, due to pressure, embrace (cultural perspective). This can lead to a decision-making process in which group think may occur. Group think processes may hinder a more realistic perspective on how to decide. Last but not least, decision-making processes are also embedded in all kind of routines, standard operating procedures and so on that structure how decisions will be taken. In the institutional perspective on decision-making special attention is being asked for in the role of these organizational practices. The fact that a policy program is formally decided upon opens the door for the next phase that we want to discuss: the implementation. It is this phase which demonstrates if the intended effects that policy makers had in mind when drafting a program or when deciding upon it, will really become true. However, the answer to this question is not as easy as perhaps one might expect.

5

Policy implementation

LEARNING OBJECTIVES

After reading this chapter you should be able to:

- Identify and compare the rational and political perspective on policy implementation.

- Identify and compare different *modes of policy implementation* from a management and organizational perspective.

- Recognize different *types of dependency* within implementation and service delivery supply chains.

- Recognize different logics and tensions in public service delivery settings.

- Understand the importance of *monitoring, supervision and enforcement* in policy processes.

Until the 1970s, the implementation of policy in public administration was somewhat neglected. The idea was that once policy had been adopted, implementing would follow naturally. Particularly research into the effectiveness of policies, however, shows that the way in which the implementation is designed is decisive for the success or failure of policy programs. This lesson is not always followed though. The political and administrative attention still primarily focuses on the design of the policy. At the same time, however, we see that the division between policy development and implementation, particularly as reflected in the creation of quasi-autonomous executive agencies during the 1990s, has led to further emancipation of the implementation.

In this chapter, we take a closer look at a number of doctrines relating to the implementation of policy. In section 5.1 we describe how the scholarly attention on policy implementation has evolved over the past decades in which we recognize the rational and political perspective. In section 5.2 we show that successful policy implementation is a management issue as well, in which it is important to pay attention to the way in which the implementation process is organized in and between organizations. Subsequently, in section 5.3 we describe how the characteristics of implementing bureaucracies have changed, partly because of the far-reaching penetration of technology in implementation processes. A characteristic of implementation is also that successful implementation depends on the extent to which various organizations that play a specific task in, for example, awarding a grant, issuing a license or granting a benefit work together. The nature and course of this collaboration are often described as a chain. In section 5.4 we therefore pay attention to the supply chain approach in policy implementation. A central element in many implementation processes is the service to the citizen as a customer. Section 5.5 therefore elaborates on some insights into public services. We will also show that in this implementation or service, different logics play a role that can provide all kinds of tensions, which can lead to alienation at implementation level. In section 5.6 we focus on the monitoring and enforcement of policy implementation. True to tradition, this chapter ends with a conclusion.

5.1 The foundations of policy implementation research

In this section, we start our exploration of the implementation stage by briefly outlining the way in which policy implementation has been considered from a public administration perspective.

The default of the rational approach: the machinery of government

The first stages of implementation research were based on the idea that the implementation of policy is a mechanistic process that is completely separated from policy making. Once policy is adopted, the implementation of that policy implies the activation of the implementation machine. For a long time, policy implementation was considered as a closed process, which was free from the influence of various social and political-administrative developments and thus unrelated to the context in which it was to be implemented. Implementation was seen as something that had to be carried out: to carry out the actions that were laid down in the policy program in order to achieve specific goals. (Van Meter & Van Horn, 1975:445; Pressman & Wildavsky, 1973). In doing so a rational approach of policy implementation was adopted.

The implementation of policy was considered a process to be designed rationally and centrally controlled. Effective implementation was therefore seen as a planning and programming task that had to be performed from a hierarchical perspective that also related to the primacy of politics (van Gunsteren, 1976). There was a sovereign and unitary steering center in which the policy was formulated and in which one had access to a reliable set of people, resources and other techniques to convey the central message contained in a policy program effectively to all kinds of local units charged with the implementation. It was essential that the message to be transferred could be formulated unambiguously. In addition, local implementation units – often defined as *operating units* – were seen as units located at the periphery of the policy process, but behaving as loyal and willing implementers (Schön 1971:114; van Gunsteren, 1976:21). The idea of *perfect administration* underlies this view of policy implementation (Brown, 1975; Dunsire, 1978). In this perfect system, the implementers not only know what is expected of them, they actually can and want to implement the policy. To achieve this, the following conditions must be observed (Glasbergen 1987:84; Hill, 2005:178):

- There is an explicated work assignment: the objectives of the policy are specified clearly and consistently in operational terms.
- The organization forms a unit with a clear authority structure, consisting of a clear hierarchical structure and an appropriate division of tasks, responsibilities and authorities.
- The organization is differentiated to such an extent that tasks are manageable and can be assigned to specific organizational units, in such a way that this task allocation is clear and consistent.
- The relations with the environment (other organizations, target groups and so on) are specified.
- A communication system ensures the exchange of information; together with the authority structure, it facilitates the regulation of possible conflicts.
- The resources (money, workforce, time) that enable the functioning of the organization are sufficiently available.
- There is a monitoring and control system that monitors the process and measures the performance, for which clear and unambiguous evaluation criteria are developed.
- The organization is self-reflective, which means that it is able to monitor its own activities critically and correct them if necessary.
- A system of positive and negative sanctions (rewarding or punishing) supports this.
- Policy making is disconnected from the implementation, as a policy

implementation that is too close to policy making suffers too much from various disruptive influences.

In the rational perspective the absence of these conditions has long been seen as a key explanation for failing policy implementation. But in the course of the 1970s and 1980s, it became increasingly clear that the idea of a "perfect administration" was at odds with reality. Indeed, other factors also played a role. The following insights contributed to it, which often display an affinity with the political approach of policy.

Policy development in the context of policy implementation

A first important insight concerns the extent to which the policy to be implemented is specified, meaning "fully developed." Not every policy program consists of various specified instructions that concretely stipulate how implementers should act. Sometimes, knowingly or unknowingly, the objectives of the policy are kept vague (to allow compromise formation), these objectives are contradictory, or they conflict with the objectives of other policy programs. This implies that the policy should be adapted to the situation with which the implementers are confronted; that objectives should be adapted in the light of everyday implementation reality. De facto, there is a policy development process that occurs within the phase of implementation (Pressmann & Wildavsky, 1973/1984). The supposed separation between policy making on the one hand and policy implementation on the other hand – as the theory of the policy cycle supposes – is therefore without foundation. The formation of policy is not completed after the policy has formally been adopted. The consequence is that a new phase of exploration and learning occurs in the implementation stage, often with an incremental and evolutionary character. Policy develops further in the implementation, because, for example, objectives and resources are aligned with each other in the light of what is feasible (Pressman and Wildavksy, 1973/1984). Because of this, the implementation gets a much more political and therefore more open character than the rational approach to policy presupposes (Pressman and Wildavsky, 1973:84).

In line with this, the implementation can be seen as a game in which parties seek to strengthen their positions through persuasion, negotiation and manipulation (Bardach, 1977).The implementation of policy is thus a new round with new opportunities. After all, not everything is fixed in the implementation; there is considerable uncertainty that can be exploited politically and that requires a new interpretation, which can even lead to the reformulation of the original program. Here, not only ambitions and goals can be adjusted (perhaps even shifted), one can also choose a different (combination of) policy instruments (Bardach, 1977:56; Barrett and Fudge, 1981:24, 29). A good example is the implementation of EU directives. The implementation of the Birds Directive, which relates to the conservation of all naturally wild birds in the European Union, shows how the space this directive offers to give shape to objectives in light of the specific situation in the member state concerned is used to secure one's own right. In the case of the translation of the Birds Directive into a Flora and Fauna Act in the Netherlands, conflicts of interest (such as the tension between nature conservation, the recreational aspects of hunting and possible damage to agriculture) and conflicting policy styles ensured that the implementation went far from smoothly and became more political than originally thought. This directive also crossed the Dutch policy that was launched earlier and had been reflected in various laws (Bird Act, Hunting Act, Nature Conservation Act). In addition, a number of vague standards included in the Directive (such as Article 9, which refers to "significant damage") gave rise to all kinds of differences in interpretation.

Policy discretion

Another factor that contributes to the dismissal of the ideal of a perfect and neutral implementation stage and that constitutes an explanation for the fact that policy development and implementation are not separate worlds is the existence of policy discretion, also known as discretionary space or discretionary power (Lipsky, 1980). Policy discretion exists because it is impossible to foresee every possible situation when designing a policy. Implementers need to have a certain extent of leeway and thus a choice of certain action alternatives when confronted with unexpected or unspecified situations. Discretion can be found both at the level of the implementing organization or at the level of the individuals that implement policies. The first case is about collective administrative policy discretion and the latter about individual administrative policy discretion. This freedom also contributes to the conclusion above that, in the context of the implementation of policy, the formation of the policy continues still.

The availability of policy discretion is typical of many *street-level bureaucrats* who work in public organizations working on the front line of society, e.g. being a police officer, a teacher or a social care worker (Lipsky, 1980; Maynard-Moody & Musheno, 2000;2003; Hill and Hupe, 2002). On this front line, they are confronted with citizens who request to apply a particular policy program – often contained in laws and regulations – to their specific situation. In this translation process, an interpretation of legal norms takes place. In the decision that follows, the actual content of the policy is determined, especially when standards are (sometimes intentionally) kept vague or conflicting (within the same scheme or between different schemes), which generates additional uncertainty. Sometimes it is necessary to bend the rules (Lipsky, 1980). De facto, these are political decisions because in a specific situation the content of the policy is being changed. One example is the freedom that a police officer has to decide whether or not to stop a car and interrogate its driver (Maynard-Moody & Musheno, 2000; 2003). Another example is the freedom that a tax inspector has when he/she reviews the filed tax returns of a citizen or a company in order to determine whether claimed tax credits and deductions are legal.

The political character of these decisions is strengthened further by the fact that an official is often faced with scarce resources, such as the availability of money and time. This means that one has to set priorities. The availability of policy discretion offers space for further consultation and negotiation. This is reflected in, for example, the manner in which construction permits are sometimes issued. In the so-called "preliminary consultation" between an official of the building and housing inspectorate and the applicant for a permit, often the entrepreneur or project developer, especially in the case of large construction projects, it is negotiated how certain norms should be interpreted and under what conditions the permit is granted, in relation to additional complementary measures for example. This too strengthens the political character of implementation processes.

Policy discretion therefore has advantages and disadvantages (Maynard-Moody & Musheno, 2000;2003; Hill, 2005). Policy discretion is sometimes desirable, because policy programs must be translated into and refined to the individual situation of a citizen. Customization can be realized this way. Additionally, policy discretion provides implementers with an opportunity to adjust the policy to changing or unforeseen circumstances or to anticipate this. Potential problems can be avoided this way. Finally, being able to have policy discretion provides organizations and their employees with the opportunity to gain experience in the implementation of certain measures, so that the policy can be adjusted based on learning experiences.

Yet there are disadvantages too (Maynard-Moody & Musheno, 2000; Hill and Hupe, 2002; Hill, 2005). First, policy discretion can contribute to legal inequality and legal uncertainty. After all, will all similar cases be treated equally and all dissimilar cases unequally? Especially in relation to using stereotypes (like in ethnic profiling) this issue has drawn considerable attention in the United States, but also in other countries. Do Afro-Americans or Arab looking people have a greater chance to get inspected by for instance a police officer when he/she pulls over a car (Maynard-Moody & Musheno, 2003). Second, policy discretion can be used to frustrate the objectives of the policy and discretionary powers often act as a power source for resistance, especially when implementers disagree with the content of the policy to be implemented. Third, the allocation of policy discretion can be used to go out of the way of certain sensitive decisions that actually had to be made in the formation of the policy for the time being. This shifts the ball to implementation. For instance, this is the case when the formation of the policy is based on vague compromises. The way in which a compromise works out in practice is then primarily a puzzle to be solved in the implementation.

Conflicting objectives and standards

The contested character of implementation also increases when, in the implementation of policy, it shows that the policy is inconsistent with the objectives of other policy programs (Pressmann & Wildavsky, 1973/1984). Conflicting objectives and standards are often also the result of the densification of rules that implementing organizations face. This densification is the result of an increase in the scope of the number of rules that must be implemented: the interweaving of rules due to all kinds of cross-references and due to the further refinement and detail of the rules to be implemented. We often see that implementation problems in turn give rise to additional rules and instructions. The result is that choices need to be made in the implementation and that compromises must be made.

Multilayer problems

Another criticism of the traditional approach to policy implementation is rooted in the so-called multilayer problems, especially when it comes to federal states like the United States, Germany or the European Union. The implementation of policy implies that the implementation not only occurs within one tier of government, but that several tiers of government (such as Europe, State, province and municipality) with various jurisdictions (in terms of tasks, responsibilities and powers) play a role in the implementation, in which they can often use other policy instruments. The result is that the implementation gets a network character, wherein the success of the implementation is also determined by the quality of the interactions (in terms of collaboration and coordination) between the levels of administration involved and the extent to which they are able to recognize their mutual dependencies (Mayntz, 1980:239). That is why Pressman and Wildavsky (1984) lament that "great expectations in Washington are dashed in Oakland," according to the subtitle of their book.

For successful implementation across multiple layers, it is therefore necessary that the various implementers at the various levels have the same idea about the use and necessity of a given measure and that they are aware of their interdependency, which is partly due to an unequal distribution of resources among the actors involved in the implementation (Mayntz, 1980; Scharpf, Reissert and Schnabel, 1976). If this idea is missing, resistance is often the result. For instance, in the implementation of the deal between the European Union and the Turkish government regarding how to regulate and stop the influx of refugees that want to immigrate to the European Union, we see that within the European Union this deal has to be implemented by a variety of organizations that act on different layers of government, while at the same time throughout the EU the involved administrative systems also differ (Hill, 2005). This does not only lead to all kinds of different interpretations (also given specific interests and competences that are at stake) between the EU countries but also within a country differences occur between for instance central government, all kinds of executive agencies and the involved municipalities.

Target group orientation

In the implementation of policy, the target group or the target groups on which the policy focuses explicitly come(s) into the picture. The reactions of these target groups thus partly determine the success of the implementation and therefore the policy; nevertheless, here too, these target groups do not conform to the objectives of the policy in advance. It is naive to assume that they will behave loyally. The reactions of these target groups on the policy to be implemented will vary from support, passive resistance to actual objection. It is therefore important to take into account the characteristics of these target groups explicitly in the implementation of the policy (Glasbergen 1987:89; Mayntz, 1980:246). As these target groups are harder to define, this is more difficult. Who should be addressed, for instance? The degree of organization of a target group is relevant too. Is it a well-organized target group or, on the contrary, a poorly organized target group? Relevant information is less readily available in such a case. The question whether the representatives of the target group are sufficiently representative of the whole group and sufficiently authoritative can also be asked in this regard. The experiences gained from previous policy programs can be decisive for the support they give to the implementation. Bad experiences lead to distrust and consequently undermine the support.

The bottom-up model of policy implementation

The criticism inspired by the political character of policy implementation in the rational model of policy implementation has led to the well-known distinction between the so-called top-down and bottom-up model of policy implementation. Here, the top-down model shows strong affinity with the previously presented rational model of policy implementation. As an alternative and response to that, the so-called bottom-up model is put forward. Instead of seeing implementers (people and organizations) as cogs in a machine or as links in a chain of command, it is advisable to see the formation and implementation of policy as a process of *backward mapping*, which is in contrast to the top-down model that can be seen as a form of *forward mapping* (Elmore, 1980).

Backward mapping begins with the recipients or target groups of the policy, and then raises the question of what actions and measures should be taken to ensure that the characteristics and behavior of the "recipients of policy" are taken into account as much as possible. This means that possible bottlenecks and tensions are signalled in advance. This is only possible, however, if consultations and negotiations take place with the "recipients" of the policy at an early stage in order to reach an agreement; this also applies to *street level bureaucrats*, who play an important role in the "endpoint" of the policy.

The consequence of this bottom-up approach is that it is accepted that policy objectives are vague and sometimes contradictory, and that those organizations playing a role in the implementation (as well as the target groups of the policy) can also pursue other interests that run counter to the intentions of the policy to be implemented. The challenge, therefore, lies not in enforcing compliance and loyalty to the established policy. It is more important to assess how possible conflicts that might arise in the implementation can be mitigated or solved through consultation and negotiation. This creates a workable common implementation practice that is supported by all relevant parties rather than an imposed and enforced practice.

The previous distinction between top-down and bottom-up approaches to policy implementation, however, should not be exaggerated. Furthermore, it should definitely not be defined in terms of a normative choice that must be made. Sometimes, there are policy programs starting from narrowly defined objectives; sometimes, a start is made with vague goals and a program gets more form and content in implementation; sometimes, both approaches occur simultaneously or alternately (Hill, 2005:185; Birkland, 2001:184-185). This also depends on the nature of the policy problem.

Tamed problems lend themselves much better to a performance practice based on a more top-down approach, while a bottom-up type of performance practice often better serves untamed political problems. The latter is also the case if more programs focus on the same problem, albeit from different angles. Practice shows that it is about following instructions as well as negotiation and dialogue in the implementation (Birkland, 2001:185). It is often no choice of either-or.

The choice of a more top-down or bottom-up approach is also seen in a new light when we bring two different perspectives to the fore. First, the implementation of policy can also be understood as the ability to learn from the actions undertaken in the implementation stage. However, this learning ability is not limited to a specific organization or a specific part of the organization. Since more actors often play a role in the implementation of policy, it is about the question of how collective learning processes can be organized: within a policy sector or policy network for example. This is necessary, because the successful implementation of policy is not only determined by the bottom-up or top-down nature of the implementation, but also by the ability to translate changing circumstances in the policy implementation into necessary adjustments (Parsons, 1995:486). We will come back to it in Chapter 8, where we discuss the so-called *Advocacy Coalition Framework* (Sabatier and Jenkins-Smith, 1988, 1993).

A second perspective mainly draws attention to the relationship between the implementation of policy and the organization and management of the implementation, especially when it comes to the steering effect that all kinds of organizational rules, routines, procedures and other practices have on the success of the policy implementation (see also Allison and Zelikow, 1971; Parsons, 1995; Hill, 2005). This is an observation that we have already encountered in the institutional approach to policy. The quality of the organization and management of the policy implementation process thus determines the success of the policy implementation.

5.2 Policy implementation from a management and organizational perspective

When we look at policy implementation from a management perspective, it is mostly about "policy introduction" or "policy fine-tuning." What is the organizational framework within which an effective implementation can take place? To what extent can the policy to be implemented be translated and programmed into operational policies, such as various work orders, instructions, routines and procedures? This is important, because the implementation of policy is normally taken up by organizations, which touches upon the institutional perspective on policy implementation, given its emphasis on the role that "rules" (e.g. routines, procedures and systems) play. Characteristics of organizations therefore also affect the way in which policy is implemented (Parsons, 1995; Hill, 2005). One of those characteristics is the bureaucratic character of many implementing organizations. Understanding policy implementation presupposes that policy makers are able to understand how and why bureaucracy works as it works. How should we value the character of bureaucracy?

Bureaucracy

A common complaint about the implementation of policy is the accusation of bureaucracy, which is partly reflected in inefficiency, poor consultations, compartmentalization and/or poor quality of service. In some cases, this complaint is justified, but to understand the implementation and the role that implementing organizations take on in this process, it is essential to reflect on the concept of bureaucracy.

The bureaucracy is the embodiment of what Weber (1922/1928) called rational-legal authority relations. This means that the action of the State is bound to objectified rules laid down in legislation that is made known to everyone, and that have to ensure that "all similar cases are treated equally" and "all dissimilar cases are treated unequally" when such rules are implemented and applied. This way, legal equality and legal certainty are offered, while arbitrariness in the activities of the government is prevented. These values also affect the conduct of a government bureaucracy, because they show that bureaucracy is the embodiment of the rule of law.

With this, rational-legal authority relationships differ from traditional and charismatic authority relations, in which there is always an element of arbitrariness in the exercise of authority. In the case of traditional authority relationships, this arbitrariness is the consequence of the fact that the authority is exerted by a certain family, often based on succession (as in the case of royal families). In the case of charismatic authority relationships, the authority is based on the charisma of a certain person who is considered a "leader."

Consequently, in order to prevent arbitrariness, government bureaucracies are characterized first by a high degree of standardization and formalization. This means that the implementation of tasks is programmed and recorded in all kinds of procedures, rules and routines that give instructions on how certain tasks, in the implementation of various types of social insurance for example, should be implemented in order to be able to ensure legal certainty and legal equality. A characteristic of bureaucracies is the importance attached to operational policy that specifies concretely who should do what to contribute to the achievement of the objectives laid down in an act or program, such as when it comes to granting special assistance in individual situations; this policy is usually characterized by fairly detailed instructions, procedures and routines.

Second, government bureaucracies are characterized by a high degree of centralization. This is the result of the consideration that in a rule of law, it must also be possible to hold directors accountable for the functioning of the organization concerned in relation to the implementation of the policy, which is, after all, politically ratified by the legislature or parliament. Yet accountability on the performances delivered, and thus on the way in which tasks are performed, is only possible if one has clear lines of authority based on a system of capacity and subordination (hierarchy). If such a hierarchy is missing, accountability is a complicated process, because of the risk that the responsible directors or managers continuously blame someone else.

In short, formalization, standardization and centralization are therefore characteristics inherent to the implementation of policy by bureaucracies in a democratic rule of law. The question is when this is functional and when perverse effects occur. Perverse effects can occur when these regulations, instructions, procedures and routines start to lead a life of their own and become ends in themselves. In that case, they are no longer a means to ensure reliable implementation and application of laws and other rules.

Mechanistic and organic regimes

Earlier, it was stated that an important factor in the assessment of policy implementation is the ability to adapt to changing circumstances. Are implementing organizations capable of that, given the importance attached to standardization, formalization and centralization?

From a management and organizational perspective, it is essential that an implementation organization is able to adapt to changing circumstances. This adaptability will be put to the test if it appears that the assumptions on which a certain policy program or particular laws and regulations are based are not founded on a realistic assessment of the implementation practice, or a variety thereof. Many government organizations are characterized by (logically so, given the remark just made) a mechanistic regime. Characteristic of

Table 5.1 Mechanistic and organic organizational regimes

Mechanistic regime	Organic regime
Own task is regarded separately from the overall task setting of the organization	Own task is seen in the context of the overall task setting of the organization
Coordination of these individual tasks by close and higher chief	Mutual adaptation and revision of individual tasks through mutual interaction and communication
Separation of performance of tasks on the one hand, and authorities and responsibilities on the other hand	Greater personal responsibility for the performance of tasks and associated responsibilities
Emphasis on precise definition of everyone's rights and duties associated with the performance of tasks	Distributing responsibilities among each other rather than passing the buck to each other
One sees oneself as "contract partner" of the organization (represented by its chief)	One sees oneself as a joint owner in the organization (organization as working and living community)
Interactions are mostly vertical in nature (meaning up and down), thus creating a hierarchical structure of authority	Both many "vertical" and "horizontal" interactions (meaning up, down and sideways), creating a network-like structure of authority
Activities are determined by instructions and decisions from the chief	Activities are determined by information and advice from the chief rather than by instructions
Emphasis on loyalty and obedience as conditions for the "membership" of the organization	Emphasis on commitment to the overall task setting and to a "technological ethos" focused on progress and expansion as conditions for membership of the organization, and less on loyalty

Sources: Burns and Stalker, 1961:120–122; Lammers, 1978; Mintzberg, 1979:87.

mechanistic regimes is that, unlike organic regimes, they adapt to changing circumstances less easily, Burns and Stalker argue (1961:120-122; see also Mintzberg, 1979:87). Indeed, standardization and formalization limit the necessary flexibility. Standardization and formalization do not need to be a problem as long as an organization moves in a stable and simple environment. However, if an organization moves in a dynamic environment, an organic regime offers more solace, precisely because there is less emphasis on standardization and formalization. In Table 5.1 we list the characteristics of both regimes.

It should be remembered though that the distinction mentioned is an ideal-typical reconstruction of certain organizational characteristics. In practice, we see that elements of both regimes occur in implementing organizations. Thus, it is possible that one part of the organization is more similar to the mechanistic regime, while another part is marked by an organic regime. For example, a department that focuses on the application of certain laws and regulations to "difficult cases" is likely to have an organic character, because the complexity of the application requires more consultation between high-quality professionals. On the other hand, a department dealing with the standard cases, to which certain rules can be applied relatively easy, will be marked by a rather mechanistic regime.

Apart from that, the list also clarifies that when government bureaucracies face a more dynamic environment, a predominantly mechanistic regime is a handicap in this adjustment process. The sketch of a number of relevant social and political-administrative developments that we have given in the introduction to this book shows that the environment in which many implementing organizations operate is increasingly more dynamic and complex. Hence, the distinction also provides insight into the possible capacity for change of government institutions in relation to the mechanistic or organic nature of these organizations.

The changes that implementing organizations are facing are also determined by the amount of legislation and regulations that must be considered and their complexity. That is why the absorption capacity of an implementing organization is a special point of attention.

Absorption capacity and the implementation of policy

Another important aspect of managing the implementation is about the introduction of a policy program, so that it can then be implemented. Central questions in the introduction are (Glasbergen, 1987:80):

- Do the implementers *know* what is expected of them? This question predominantly refers to the knowledge and information about the specific program to be implemented.
- *Can* they actually implement the policy? This question refers to the various types of resources (such as knowledge, information, and experience) that are required to implement the program.
- Do they also actually *want* to implement the policy? This question refers to the willingness to implement the program or to the support that exists at the implementers.

Successful implementation depends on the extent to which the implementing organizations actually have the people and resources to implement the policy. Lack of adequate resources and too little time are complaints regularly put forward from the implementation world as the cause of problems in implementation (Simonis, 1983:84). These problems increase as an organization is faced with policy or legislative changes that follow each other rapidly, so that adjustments quickly need to follow. Problems also arise when implementing organizations face several programs that have to be introduced and implemented at the same time. The absorption capacity of an implementing organization thus also affects the way in which programs can actually be picked up successfully.

The large influx of refugees in the European Union in 2015 and 2016 especially demonstrated how the absorption capacity of the involved organizations that all perform specific tasks in giving asylum and shelter to these refugees, was changed. Not only the involved (border) police forces, but also the immigration services had to deal with thousands and thousands of applications which had to be checked and scrutinized, while at the same time these files had to be processed forward to other involved agencies. Furthermore, shelter had to be provided, while at the same time the existing capacity was limited. As a result all kinds of temporary housing facilities were established, e.g. by making use of abandoned office buildings or schools or establishing a temporary camp of tents.

Quality systems and the implementation of policy

The extent to which an implementing organization is in a position to carry out policy also depends on the quality of the organization. Hence, implementing organizations pay close attention to the introduction of various quality systems that aim to make the organization more transparent and manageable, and give the performances of the organization better accountability. This is reflected, among other things, in describing business processes better and more explicitly, and then linking these processes more explicitly to the performance of the organization. An example is the throughput of a file from the moment a request for a grant or benefit is made to when the actual decision on the request is made.

On the one hand, business processes can relate to the primary process, meaning all processes in the organization that contribute to the implementation of the policy program or legislation. On the other hand, business processes can also relate to all kinds of supporting processes, being human resources, finance, information and ICT, communications and housing and facility services. In order to improve the quality of the primary process as well as the different business supporting processes government organizations may adopt all kinds of internationally accepted quality standards and norms that relate to certified organization-wide quality models, like ISO (International Standards Organization) 9000 norms.

5.3 Characteristics and changes in implementing bureaucracies

So far, we have talked about the "implementing organization" or "implementing bureaucracy" in general terms, but these organizations also come in different shapes and sizes. The extent to which they differ from each other is partly related to the nature of the tasks they perform, the way in which these tasks are programmed, and the extent to which officials have discretion in the workplace. However, this discretion is coming under increasing pressure due to the high degree of automation or computerization of implementation tasks that is taking place.

Implementing bureaucracies in shapes and sizes

Broadly speaking, the following types of implementing bureaucracies can be distinguished (WRR, 2004:68-69; see also Mintzberg, 1979):

1. The selection bureaucracy;
2. The mass services organization;
3. The professional services organization;
4. Care arrangements; and
5. The volunteer organization.

Ad 1   *The selection bureaucracy*

The selection bureaucracy is focused on the selection of clients who, as they meet certain criteria or as they can be categorized in a certain way, are eligible for certain rights and obligations. These selection bureaucracies are reflected particularly in the sphere of social security, relocation or employment services. In many cases, it involves involuntary services provided on a large scale, because one needs a job, a home or benefits. The interventions, ultimately aimed at assigning rights and duties, are often administrative or referring in nature: the completed application for benefits is forwarded, an agreement is made with an employer or training institution, or one is redirected to a proprietor.

The core values that play a role in this bureaucracy are mainly legal equality and legal certainty, which are realized by implementing uniform rules and procedures. Individual implementing officials often have limited control in this, because the selection process and the allocation of rights and duties occur largely in an automated way. In many countries the local welfare agency, that selects and determines which person is needed in order to render him/her a social benefit, is an example of such a selection bureaucracy. Selection also takes place when for instance a refugee is given asylum.

Ad 2 *The mass services organization*

The mass services organization is focused on the provision of mass services products that, despite a personal service aspect, are based on the implementation of standard programs founded on specialist and professional knowledge. Standardization of the offer, especially organized at a large scale, provides all kinds of efficiency benefits. Examples include hospitals, nursing homes, child care organizations and educational institutions. Efficiency and maximization of profitability are core values in this type of organization. This often involves civil society organizations funded by the government for the implementation of certain semi-public goods such as education and health care.

Ad 3 *The professional services organization*

The professional services organization does not have the scope of the previous two types of implementing organizations. Characteristic of the professional services organization is that it is about highly educated professionals who are often self-managing. Their work is focused on helping specific individuals instead of a large group of people. It concerns the application of advanced knowledge – often based on certain professional practices and standards – founded on a high degree of freedom. The relationships between the professionals are usually horizontal in nature and are determined by a high degree of professional ethos, with quality as a core value of paramount importance. Examples of this are partnerships of medical specialists, lawyers or engineers. Also, institutions in the field of outpatient youth services and clinics for the placement under a hospital order are examples of the professional services organization.

Ad 4 *Care arrangements*

The care arrangement is a type of organization that is also found in various social services sectors, and that often stems from a private initiative. Care arrangements, however, are government-related due to all kinds of subsidy relationships and a system of (quality) supervision. This is because they play a role in the realization of certain semi-public goods that we as a society consider important. Examples are psychiatric institutions, addiction institutions, child custody institutions, nursing homes or institutions for social care for homeless people. In this type of organization, dependent residents or their representatives (guardians, parents) can rely on continuous care, nursing and attention. Here too, care is provided by highly qualified professionals. Core value of this arrangement is to provide continuity and security.

Ad 5   *The volunteer organization*

The volunteer organization is a type that can also play a role in the implementation of policy. Both the implementers of the policy and the clients are volunteers. An example can be found in sports and recreational clubs that, in the context of the local welfare or youth policy, take on tasks arising from the local social policy or the local youth policy. They do this by, for example, paying more attention to immigrant youth and by providing them with additional services and activities. Another example is informal care, where volunteers play an important role in providing help, support and care where, for example, the home care organization is no longer able to do so. The core value is not only voluntariness, but also that this voluntariness is motivated by the wish to contribute to certain "values" (such as solidarity, care for the weak and needy).

Many organizations playing a role in the implementation of policy are selection bureaucracies, which is about assigning legally established rights and duties to citizens who meet certain criteria. Based on this, tax is levied, housing subsidy is granted or a benefit is paid. When we take a closer look at the historical development of these organizations, we see that an interesting transformation unfolds.

The implementing organization as process bureaucracy

The transformation experienced by many implementing bureaucracies is primarily attributable to the extensive penetration of IT in the primary process, where the actual application of laws and regulations – meaning the decisions made – largely occurs using automated systems. In recent years, we see that the relationship between legislation, system development and organizational development has fundamentally changed as a result (Zouridis, 2000; Bovens and Zouridis, 2002). Let us illustrate this with reference to a Dutch example (Zouridis, 2000).

When the Dutch Ministry of Education, Culture and Science took on student finance (at the beginning of the twentieth century), the former legislation was concerned with the awarding of scholarships to students. Under this

Act, a separate organizational unit was created that was part of the Ministry of Education, Culture and Science. With the act in hand and on grounds of all kinds of implementing rules and instructions, awarding officials determined – and based on the discretion granted to them by the act – which students were eligible for student finance as well as what the amount of the scholarships would be, carefully considering the personal circumstances of the student involved. The implementing organization for student finance consequently was a true *street level bureaucracy*. It was the law that was leading in the development of this implementing organizational unit.

In the mid-1960s, the administration of student finance was mechanized. The first computers were installed. Initially, computers were mainly used to take over a number of supporting activities, such as storing information about a student or printing the decisions of the awarding officials. Gradually, however, computers were taking over more and more functions. As a result, the emphasis shifted to the formalization and standardization of work processes, because formalization and standardization are necessary conditions for the use of computers; after all, computers need accurately and unambiguously defined steps to take decisions. Consequently, computers increasingly took over decisions from the decision official. In practice, decision officials pushed a button, indicating to agree to the draft decision for a particular request as proposed by the computer. Formally, an official could still deviate from this, so that one's discretion remained intact. Materially, however, there was a large decline in the discretionary power of the awarding official.

The introduction of the new Student Finance Act, formally taking place in 1986, confirms and reinforces this development. The interesting thing is that this act is designed in such a way that computers can best perform it. The act was drawn up in such a way that it enabled computers to make detailed decisions. This meant a break with the previous practice, in which the legislative process was leading to system development. Normally, an act would come first, which would then be turned into decision software. However, this can only work if there is a binary code and thus a binary allocation process. Vague concepts therefore do not have a place in this. To prevent this, the legislative process and the system development process were linked to each other. The aim was to develop an act that would pave the way for the development of an automated decision system as error-free as possible. That is why system development and legislation went hand-in-hand, and why they were developed in parallel and in conjunction with each other; this way, the act to be drawn up could optimally be translated into computer software. Based on this, the organization was then redesigned, whereby so-called *screen level* bureaucrats replaced the original awarding officers, focusing mainly on entering the necessary data without making a single decision themselves. Subsequently, the *street level bureaucracy* turned into a *screen level bureaucracy*.

Around 1996, we see yet another transformation, in which the *screen level* bureaucrats disappear too. The possibilities of modern information technology are so great that filling the necessary data files also predominantly takes place digitally. For example, students add data directly to the student finance file via the Internet and the website of the then IB Group (now DUO), and the IB Group increasingly uses information that is already available elsewhere, such as at the Dutch Tax and Customs Administration. This information is therefore no longer collected by the organization itself. This results in an organization-wide information system that not only directs the organizational development, but also makes demands on existing legislation. In this case, we see how the logic of the system development is leading, to the detriment of the primacy of legislation and of the implementing organization. The initial parallelism between legislation and system development is replaced by the primacy of the system development, creating a so-called *system level* bureaucracy. The members of the organization are no longer concerned with individual cases, but they mainly focus on fine-tuning the production process that has become an information-gathering and editing process going beyond its own implementing organization and extending to the sharing of information with other organizations, such as the municipal social services. The result is fully automatic decision-making on requests for student finance, in which there is only room for decisions based on policy discretion in very rare cases. The transactions arising from this are subsequently also performed in a fully automated way.

The selection bureaucracy that student finance initially was, has turned into a process bureaucracy bearing a strong resemblance to an oil-refining factory. That too involves completely automated production processes in which the human hand is no longer involved or hardly so. All attention is paid to the logistics of the refining process or the awarding process. Zuurmond (1994) describes this latest development differently: in terms of the transition from the traditional bureaucracy to the so-called infocracy, in which the IT infrastructure within a policy sector is increasingly coordinating the actions of individual officials and their organizations. This coordination takes place, because they all use the same infrastructure with the associated data files, data definitions and data processing procedures.

In Table 5.2 we outline once again this development, following the example of Bovens and Zouridis (2002:71).

Table 5.2 Technological transformation of implementing bureaucracies

Type of implementing organization	Street level bureaucracy	Screen level bureaucracy	System level bureaucracy
Role of IT	Supporting	Leading	Decisive
Function of IT	Registration data	Assessment and a virtual assembly line of requests	Implementation, monitoring, external communications
Human interference with individual cases	Full	Partial	Absent
Key figures within the organization	Implementing officials	Production managers	System designers
Organizational boundaries	Strict between organizations	Strict, both within and between organizations	Fluid, both within and between organizations
Legal regime	Open, much discretion	Closed, little discretion	Closed, no discretion
Legal reach	Some articles in the law	Comprehensive law	Various laws and legal domains
Relationship legislation, system development and organizational development	Primacy of legislation	Parallel development of legislation and system development	Primacy of system development

Source: Bovens and Zouridis, 2002:71.

The development of a system bureaucracy shows that it is a characteristic of the implementation that implementing organizations collaborate more and more in order to share vital information with each other. Organizational boundaries seem to blur. As a result all kinds of service delivery networks and supply chains emerge which collaborate in order to implement specific or interrelated policy programs.

5.4   Collaborative public service governance

An important development in the implementation of policy is the growing collaboration between implementing organizations which has been an impetus for many government reforms. In the literature this development has been described in terms of collaborative public service governance (Ansell & Gash, 2007), joined up government (Ling, 2002), holistic governance (Perri 6 et al, 2002), or as new public governance (Osborne, 2006). All these concepts try to bring forward that in delivering public services, when dealing with rather complex problems and related target groups, a whole person approach is needed. The latter, however, presupposes that the involved agencies as well as involved (non-state) societal and private organizations, have to collaborate because each of the involved actors adds specific knowledge, information and expertise, given the individual tasks they have to fulfill. It also presupposes that they organize their work as well as the sharing of vital resources, from a common frame of reference. A related concept is digital era governance, in which especially the role of ICT has been pushed forward as a vital factor that facilitates collaboration across organizational boundaries and jurisdictions (Dunleavy et al, 2005) First we address why this need to collaborate has been pushed forward. Secondly, we address the question of which different types of dependencies play a role in public service delivery and the question of which coordination mechanisms may emerge in the wake of these dependencies. The latter question is important because the willingness to collaborate depends on the mutual recognition of (inter) dependency between the involved implementing organizations (Ansell & Gash, 2007; Emerson et al, 2011)

The recognition of dependency in collaborative public services

Underlying the emergence of collaborative public services are the growing dependencies between organizations. On the one hand, this is related to a process of specialization that has taken place, which has led to fragmentation (see also Chapter 1). For instance, the number of specializations and departments in a modern hospital and between these hospitals has exploded in the last 50 years. Furthermore, due to the introduction of more market-based incentives the financial management and accounting systems of these hospitals require processes of internal pricing and recalculation, which stimulates a rather inward looking perspective (see Dunleavy et al., 2005). However, the needs of these patients require that several departments have to collaborate on the same patient. This requires processes of communication and exchange of information. But we could easily extend this example beyond the walls of the hospital. The patient needs to be referred to the hospital by a GP. In an insurance-based system of health care information about the coverage of the patient is needed. And upon dismissal, the formal or informal home care network should be on stand-by to assist the patient with some daily tasks if necessary. The well-being and recovery of the patient depends on the performance of each of the actors in this process. Hence, we could consider this as a supply chain of activities performed by different individuals and organizations. The chain metaphor underlines that an unambiguous or formal hierarchical relationship between the parties concerned is often lacking. There is no central authority; on the contrary, the authority relationships are often diffuse. In principle, each link determines its own policy more or less. The tragedy of chains is that this sometimes leads to no one being responsible for the operation of the chain as a whole. This implies that not only dependency but also autonomy is an important characteristic of service delivery chains. That is why a collaborative public service arrangement in which a chain-like approach is being pursued is dominated by the search for a balance between the recognition of dependency on the one hand and the giving up of a part of one's autonomy on the other hand.

Broadly speaking, the following types of ideal-typical dependencies are distinguished, as based on the work of Thompson (1967) and Grijpink (1997) (Figure 5.1):

In the case of *pooled dependency*, the resulting dependency is the product of the fact that organizations use the same reservoir of resources that can also be seen as a "common pool" (Thompson, 1967). The organization that controls the access to this pool or that controls the distribution of resources from this pool and is put in a central position within a collaborative service arrangement. An interesting example can be found in the Netherlands where the Dutch Vehicle Registration Agency (RDW) is the legal owner of the vehicle license information. Other organizations that want to make use of this information are forbidden to develop their own registrations. For instance, organizations like the Tax and Custom Administration, the police, private car insurance companies, but also garages that inspect the safety of a car, have access to this registration, when they want to check specific information (e.g. who is the owner of a car) or when they want to add new information regarding specific topics (e.g. care safety issues), and are obliged to make use of this registration.

In the case of *sequential dependency*, there really is a chain, with each link in the chain passing the baton to another link (Thompson, 1967). The activities performed by each link follow each other in time. A classic example is the criminal justice system. When the police have traced a person suspected of a criminal offense, a second phase follows: the phase of the prosecution, which is taken up by the Public Prosecutor. Then, the suspect appears in court. That is where the next phase, the trial, takes place. Based on the implementation of the judgment, the person is then transferred to jail, to be put behind bars for some time. Finally, after the person has served his sentence, rehabilitation takes place, which is taken up by the probation service.

There may also be *parallel sequentiality*, meaning that a given stream is split in separate flows that run parallel, and then put together again. For instance, this process can very often be witnessed when somebody applies for a social

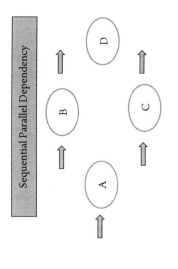

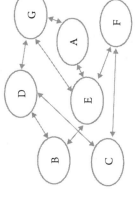
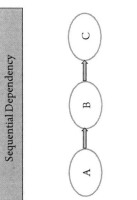

Sources: Thompson, 1967; Grijpink, 1997.

Figure 5.1 Types of dependency

benefit, because he or she is unemployed for some time. When an application is made, specific elements from this application are separated from each other, e.g. personal and social circumstances are separated from the more financial and tax related aspects. These aspects are taken care of by different organizations or organizational units, because their assessment requires different and specialized knowledge, information and expertise. When these different organizations have looked at them, the relevant information is put together again, in order to make a decision.

Within a chain, there may also be forward and backward processes (*reciprocal interdependency*) between the links in the chain. For example, a file is not only passed to the next link, but when this next link performs certain actions, feedback on the observed findings, for instance, is also given to the previous link. We can illustrate this by using the referral from a general practitioner to a medical specialist. First, the general practitioner provides a referral note for the specialist, then the specialist gives feedback to the general practitioner (by means of a discharge letter for instance) on what causes underlie a certain disorder, what interventions or treatments the specialist will use and the effects achieved as well as advice on the follow-up by the general practitioner.

Finally, there is also *networked dependency*. Not only are there forward and backward processes of activities, knowledge and information, but the sequence of certain actions is lost too. An example of networked dependency can be found in an approach that is called "family conferencing", which is being used when offering help and support for families and children who are in need. The idea behind this approach (developed in Australia but also adopted in other countries) is that in order to deliver more tailor-made services, the whole network of supporting actors to which this family or these children are connected may have to be mobilized, ranging from next of kin, the neighbors, school, social care, the police or child protection etc. This process of mobilization starts with the organization of a family conference, in which a family tries to express what kind of difficulties and needs it experiences. Information, knowledge, expertise, support and assistance is being exchanged between the involved and supporting actors. The interdependencies that are being mobilized correlate with the changing needs and circumstances of this family.

Models of coordination in collaborative services

The previous section has shown that in many implementation and service delivery processes, dependencies between organizations exist. To ensure the adequate collaboration between these organizations, coordination might be necessary. However, coordination implies a loss of organizational autonomy. Therefore, models of coordination tend to balance between direction and organization autonomy. In essence, the aim is to create conditions for better collaboration between relatively (mutual) dependent actors to better fulfill a certain common task (the collaborative service assignment) in a context of organizational autonomy. The idea of working with a "family conferencing" can be seen as the manifestation of this common task or assignment: bringing together all the parties around a specific family together in order to mobilize their support that is necessary to address the needs of this family. This direction role can be shaped in various ways (Provan and Kenis, 2008):

1. *Direction as a form of self-management.* In this case, there is a collaborative service arrangement that manages itself. Within this chain, there is no separate management unit. The autonomy of participating organizations is paramount. Management of common activities is done by the individual organizations that form the chain together. Decisions related to the functioning of the chain are made collectively or by organizations that want to work on certain aspects together, such as regarding the sharing of information, knowledge or expertise. Collaboration often occurs on an ad hoc basis. For this purpose, bilateral or multilateral agreements are usually made. The advantage of this type of chain direction is that the involvement of the parties may be relatively large. Another advantage is that this form of collaboration and direction gets form and content based on voluntariness and concrete needs. The downside is that no clear coordination structure exists and that everyone communicates with everyone. It may also be that such a chain has no face to the outside world, causing the chain not to have any point of contact. Additionally, none of the organizations involved is accountable for the performance of the chain as a whole.

2. *Direction by the leader of the chain.* In this case, the formation of direction occurs by giving a particular organization in the chain a relatively higher-level position. As well as implementing, this leading organization also directs the chain. The director's role may be allocated from above (for example, under certain statutory powers or based on a subsidizing task). An example of this is the position that the earlier described Dutch Vehicle Registration Agency (RDW) performs in running all kinds of public service delivery chains in which license number information plays an important role, such as the MOT for cars. The RDW can take on that leadership role, because it has a legal monopoly on the registration of license number data, on which other parties depend. In addition, that leadership role can be allocated from below. In such a case, the

parties collaborating in a chain assign one of them the leading role for the functioning of the chain as a whole. The manner in which this leading organization can then do its work partly depends on how much power the other organizations are willing to give up. The leading organization makes the most important (usually operational) decisions, while the leading organization also coordinates the activities within the chain. This leading organization may also provide certain administrative support. The advantage of this method of chain direction is that there is coordination and an unambiguous face or point of contact. The downside is that the interests and viewpoints of the leader may not always be consistent with those of the other organizations, causing the so-called chain interest to be dominated by the interests of the leading organization. Essential for the functioning of this type of direction is therefore the degree to which the chain partners see the leading organization as legitimate.

3. *Direction by an independent, external chain director.* In this case, there is a third and often independent party that acts as an intermediary or broker between the parties. This party is responsible for the coordination within the chain and its task is to monitor and direct the performance of the chain as a whole. Contrary to the role in the form as referred to under (2), this director does not perform any tasks in the chain. It is necessary though for the organizations concerned to give this independent director the mandate to act as chain coordinator. An example of such a form of chain direction is found in social security in many western countries. The director functions as an independent broker between all kinds of different organizations that are involved in administering and implementing social benefits. These organizations do not exchange information directly with each other; this is done through the broker. This ensures the autonomy of the participating parties without damaging the quality of the information exchange. To safeguard the quality of this exchange, this broker may make specific demands on how information should be exchanged. Sometimes, this third independent party acts as a *third trusted partner*. As a solicitor does when buying and selling a house, this external director makes sure the exchange– in the form of information exchange – between two or more parties happens in an orderly manner and sees to it that each party adheres to the agreements made.

Chain collaboration is often mentioned together with improving the service to citizens. Chain collaboration helps to make sure that citizens are not sent from pillar to post. This brings us to another aspect that is of importance in the context of implementing policy: the service aspect.

5.5   Service as aspect of the implementation

In many respects, the implementation of policy is an important phase that affects the position and appreciation of the government in society. First, the organization and quality of the implementation process contribute to the efficiency and effectiveness of the policy. Second, the quality of the implementation also affects the legitimacy of the government and the confidence that citizens and businesses have in governments. For many citizens and businesses, the government only truly gets a face when certain rules and programs are applied, and rights and obligations are actually allocated to individual citizens and businesses. In these cases, there is actual interaction between government and citizens. The manner in which governments, citizens and businesses treat each other in these encounters thereby greatly determines the appreciation of the government. Therefore, the process of service delivery may be considered as an important element in the implementation process.

Focus on service

For a long time, the thinking about service was dominated by a supply-oriented approach resulting from a fairly mechanistic notion of policy implementation. A number of developments increasingly pressured this supply-oriented approach (Bekkers and Zouridis, 1999):

- Due to the increased *individualization* of society and the related fragmentation of all kinds of target groups, it is essential that citizens are increasingly approached on an individual basis, requiring customization in order to take all relevant aspects into account (for example, when it comes to providing welfare payments). This customization can only be provided if citizens are not "sent from pillar to post" and getting lost in the maze of a splintered government, but if they can rely on an integrated approach to their question, request or situation.
- Due to the increased *assertiveness of citizens*, they have a less passive attitude regarding the performances delivered by governments. Citizens and businesses become critical consumers who expect that governments deliver the same quality as is customary in business.
- Due to the *decreasing turnout of citizens in elections*, especially in the municipal elections, the gap between citizens and government is increasingly discussed. Improving the quality of services is seen as a strategy to bridge this gap.
- Due to the rise of *New Public Management* (Hood, 1991) and the discussion on *Reinventing Government* (Osborne and Gaebler, 1992), more and more attention is drawn to the actual performance of a government.

This performance is particularly evident in the quality of the services provided. Attention is also drawn to the efficiency of the implementation and service, with the result that more and more value is attached to the control of unnecessary administrative burdens. Citizens and businesses need to get *value for money* in their contacts with the government.

- Due to the possibilities of IT, especially of network technology, it is increasingly clear that *IT* can improve the quality of service. We can think of the linking of files and the sharing of information and knowledge, even if it is stored in various locations within the public administration. This supports integral types of service that transcend organizational boundaries. IT also contributes to the development of virtual forms of service that, in principle, are accessible 24 hours a day, 7 days a week.

Types of service

Broadly speaking, the following services are distinguished in the context of implementation, which can be offered both physically and digitally (Bekkers & Homburg 2007):

- *Information services*, aimed at providing information. In many cases, there is no real interaction between the information providing government and the asking citizens; a leaflet holder in the foyer of a city hall and downloading brochures or policy documents are relevant examples.
- On the other hand, *contact services*, aimed at asking questions and getting answers, have a higher degree of interaction. Examples of these services include reporting on litter or filing a complaint.
- *Transaction services*, aimed at assigning individual rights and obligations to citizens. For this, a certain amount of money (such as a fee) is sometimes charged. An example of a transaction service is acquiring a certificate of conduct or birth certificate. Paying fines is another example.

The aforementioned services are increasingly offered and processed digitally. This form of digital service is also called e-government. E-government can be defined as supporting or redesigning the (existing and potential) relationships and related (information and communication) processes that a government has with relevant parties in its environment to offer certain added value by using IT. This added value may lie in improving the quality of services (such as 7 days a week, 24 hours a day), improving the accessibility and transparency of public administration, improving the efficiency of these processes (by, for example, shortening them or skipping steps), or strengthening the participation of citizens (in relation to processes of interactive policy for example). Relevant groups are citizens, companies, civil society organizations and other governments (Bekkers & Homburg, 2007).

Shifts in service

The result is that a number of fundamental changes unfold within the service, which can be summarized as follows (Ling, 2002; Perri 6 et al., 2002; Bovaird, 2007; Osborne et al., 2012):

- From *supply-oriented to demand-oriented service*, in which the focus will increasingly be on the ability to design the service to the needs of citizens as customers. The earlier mentioned example of the use of family conferencing in youth care and protection can be seen as an example of setting up more need-oriented public service arrangements.
- From functionally *fragmented to integrated and holistic service*, in which the overall demand pattern of a citizen is taken into account (how one actually experiences this in one's daily life and work), instead of being confronted with the compartmentalized offer of all kinds of isolated services that implement various types or parts of all sorts of laws and regulations, mostly carried out by rather autonomous organizational units (often talked about in terms of silos). Questions of citizens arising from their personal situation should be treated as a coherent and interrelated whole rather than as separate questions. And again, the family conferencing example can be seen as a way to organize more integrated, holistic services.
- From *reactive to proactive service*, in which governments approach citizens and businesses actively and on their own initiative, and point out certain rights or obligations. For instance, many municipalities inform holders of a passport and/or driver's license of the fact that the validity is about to expire in advance.
- From *one point of contact to "multi-channeling,"* in which citizens have access to a wider range of points of contact and communication channels for obtaining certain services than just one physical counter. In addition to the counter in, for example, the city hall, call centers, websites and social media are also used, while it is also possible to send a text message with a particular request. This means that increasingly, a shift occurs from *physical services to digital and virtual forms of service.*
- From *collective to individual services*, in which more and more customization is delivered rather than mass services for large groups. Sometimes, this is not necessary, but a certain degree of customization in the context of the mass service is still pursued. We call this mass customization.
- From *specialist to generalist service.* Counters with a specific theme offering

interrelated services are increasingly used, such as the counter of building and living or the counter of health and welfare. This minimizes the referral to specialist services. In this context, a distinction is made between the so-called *front office* and the *back office*. In the front office, the actual contact with the customer takes place, questions are answered, information is provided and data are entered, for example. The back office refers to the administrative handling of, for example, an application for a grant or a request for welfare payment and the associated information processing processes. The submitted data are checked, while other data too – often from other services – are included in the subsequent decision. Then, for example, one proceeds to payment or a permit is issued. The difficult cases are often handled in specialized parts of the back office.

- From *passive customer participation to active customer participation and engagement*. Citizens and businesses are increasingly involved in the design and organization of services that are important to them as well as given some tasks in the execution of these services or even the management of these services. This development has also been described in terms of coproduction. For instance, citizens are given a say in the development and maintenance of the neighbourhood in which they live. They may for instance receive a budget for the creation and maintenance of a playing ground.

We have seen that the quality of implementation and service delivery is important for the appreciation of the government. At the same time, we see that various logics interact in this implementation which influence the appreciation of the involved citizens as well as the appreciation of the involved civil servants, being often street level bureaucrats or professionals. Tensions and dilemmas are often the result. These logics represent different worlds and values (WRR, 2004). Thinking in terms of logics fits into the previously described institutional approach to policy. The logics come forward, if for instance a doctor is forced to comply with all kinds of legal or managerial demands, while his primary goal is to help people by providing him/her the proper care that really addresses his/her needs.

First, there is the *institutional logic*. This logic refers to the demands made on the implementation under laws and regulations. These demands may relate to all kinds of substantive and procedural norms to be followed. Second, there is the *provision logic*. This logic focuses on the demands an implementing organization makes on the way in which the implementation should be organized and the service to the citizen should take place. For instance, implementing organizations increasingly work with all kinds of objectives or targets to be achieved, due to the introduction of all kinds of performance management systems. A "production" must be made, such as the demands made on the quantity of files that must be dealt with at a given throughput and the paper work that has to be filled in. Third, there is the *professional logic*. This logic results from the professionalism of the implementing official, because one as a professional is educated in a certain way, and one is deemed to observe certain professional values and standards, treatment programs, codes of conduct and so on, because one is a doctor, a teacher or lawyer for example. Finally, there is the *demand logic*, which stems from the wishes, needs and interests a citizen seeks to put forward in one's contacts with the government, because one applies for a certain benefit for example. All these logics make different demands on the implementation; these demands cannot always be reconciled with each other and thus affect the extent to which implementers and citizens can identify with the policies in which they play a certain role.

However, these tensions and dilemmas can be rather intense so that the involved civil servants have difficulty identifying themselves with the policies they have to implement. This phenomenon can be described as policy alienation (Tummers et al, 2009). Policy alienation is especially influenced by two factors. The first factor refers to degree of powerlessness that public professionals or street level bureaucrats experience when they are confronted with the tensions between these four logics, during the implementing of a policy program. For instance, if they do not have some discretion to soften these tensions, the degree of alienation will increase. The second factor refers to the degree of meaninglessness that these professionals experience during implementation. When implementing policies these professionals fundamentally question the degree in which society, specific target groups or individual citizens or companies really benefit from the policies implemented, looking at the degree in which the outcomes of these policies really contribute to societal, group or individual needs. If this contribution is lacking then the degree of alienation increases. Furthermore, these feelings of meaninglessness increase if these public professionals do not have the power or discretion to implement more tailor made decisions (Tummers et al, 2009). Moreover, these feelings of alienation are also more experienced, if public professionals such as teachers or doctors are confronted with a continuing process of policy accumulation, in which the policies to be implemented are changed almost constantly (Van Engen et al., 2016).

5.6   Monitoring, supervision and enforcement

In addition to the discovery of the crucial role of the implementation process for the performance of public policy in the 1970s and 1980s, many countries experienced the importance of monitoring, inspection, supervision and enforcement since the 1990s (see Hood et al., 1999; Sparrow, 2011; Hood, Rothstein and Baldwin, 2001). Three reasons may be given for this increased attention.

First, in many countries the shortcomings of the implementation process were learned the hard way. For instance, the explosion of a fireworks company in the Netherlands or a textile manufacturing company in Bangladesh had in common that the existing policy framework may have been sufficient to prevent these disasters, *if it had been implemented correctly* (see Box 5.1). But

---

BOX 5.1

DISASTERS AND ENFORCEMENT

Case 1: SE Fireworks – Enschede, the Netherlands
On May 13, 2000, a dramatic explosion in the grounds of the SE Fireworks company shocked the otherwise rather tranquil city of Enschede, in the eastern part of the Netherlands. The disaster left 23 deaths, almost 1000 injured people, 200 destroyed houses and 1250 people homeless (NOS, 2015). This tragedy led to research about the neglect of regulations. Live camera footage shows the impact of the explosion. In the aftermath of the events, investigations showed that SE Fireworks as well as the government were responsible for these tragic events. Even though the legal framework should have prevented this disaster from occurring, it had occurred. The Evaluation Committee that investigated this disaster specifically criticized the lack of supervision from various government agencies once permits had been granted (Commissie-Oosting, 2001). This has led to intensification of supervision capacity in the Netherlands.

Case 2: Tazreen Fashion Factory – Dhaka, Bangladesh
The fire that almost fully burnt down the Tazreen Fashion Factory in the city of Dhaka (Bangladesh) on November 24, 2012 was not the first, nor the last, in a series of tragic accidents and disasters in the Bangladesh clothing industry. Over 100 people lost their lives and more than 200 people were injured (BBC, 2012). Although it is still unclear what precisely caused the fire, it is clear that overcrowding, lax safety standards and poor wiring played a role in it. But again, the Bangladesh government, under the pressure of western clothing companies (in their turn under the pressure of their consumers), had invested in improving the legal framework that regulates occupational safety and labor conditions. As a consequence of this fire, not only the safety regulations were further improved, but perhaps even more importantly, more and better qualified workplace inspectors were assigned (Zain Al-Mahmoud, 2013).

If the implementation of the different policies or legal obligations were done correctly, the incidents could have been prevented. As a result, these two incidents have intensified the importance of enforcement, monitoring and supervision.

also in less tragic cases, policy makers have concluded that the full impact of a policy may only be witnessed if the implementing agencies adequately implement the tasks, responsibilities and powers that have been assigned to them.

Second, the intensified attention for enforcement, monitoring and supervision follows from the radical restructuring that many governments have experienced under the label of *new public management* since the 1980s. With the move toward privatization and autonomization of many governmental tasks, the issue of information asymmetry needed to be solved. Information asymmetry occurs when a principal assigns tasks to an agent. In general, the agent has more knowledge about the way it implements these tasks than the principal, even though the principal may be politically responsible for it. In this regard, monitoring and supervision are tools to limit the information gap between the principal and the agent.

Finally, the rise of monitoring, enforcement and supervision is related to what Majone (1997) has labeled as the shift from the positive to the regulatory state. In the positive state, governments try to reach their goals by directly interfering in societal processes through taxing and spending. In the positive state, parliaments, ministerial departments, nationalized firms and welfare services are the main actors through which governments try to reach their goals. In the regulatory state, governments do not directly tax or spend, but only design rules to reach preferred societal outcomes. Here, parliamentary committees, independent agencies, supervisors and regulators are the key actors. Ensuring that agencies play their part is more important in the regulatory state than it used to be in the positive state.

These three reasons highlight the importance of monitoring the ways implementation agencies operate at regular intervals. The monitoring process includes the question to what extent the agency follows the obligations and has translated the legal framework into operation procedures – the so-called legality – as well as the effectiveness and efficiency of the policy in practice. With this regard, enforcement, monitoring and supervision form a bridge between the stages of policy design and policy implementation. Insight in the performance of a policy may lead to the adjustment, refinement or even ending of a policy. In this section, we discuss three issues that are related to monitoring, supervision and enforcement. First, we will provide conceptual clarity about these three concepts. Second, we discuss three different modes of monitoring and enforcement and discuss their differences and similarities. Third, we discuss a number of dilemmas that are involved with designing monitoring and enforcement arrangements.

Monitoring, supervision and enforcement: definitions

In policy processes, the concepts of monitoring, supervision and enforcement are used as interchangeable concepts. However, these concepts are clearly distinct from each other, as they pursue different targets in the policy process and have different impacts on policy processes.

Monitoring can be considered as the "lightest" form of the three. According to Waterman and Wood (1993) policy monitoring allows policy makers and interested actors to systematically examine the process of creating a policy, implementing it, and evaluating its effects. Dunn (2004) considers policy monitoring primarily as a tool for policy analysts by defining monitoring as an analytic procedure that produces information on causes and consequences of public policies. When considering monitoring as a substage of the implementation stage, Sapru (2010) seems to be the most helpful. He considers monitoring as the process of observing the policy implementation progress and resource utilization and anticipating deviations from expected policy outcomes. In doing so, policy monitoring should also include the identification of operational policy barriers that can be addressed through policy and program reform, and findings can support improved implementation of existing policies (Hardee et al., 2012). Monitoring can be performed by all kinds of actors, varying from civil servants directly involved in designing the policy and overseeing its implementation to independent policy analysts or independent agencies. In all cases, monitoring involves the systematic collection of data at regular intervals and the systematized feedback of these data into the policy process. This distinguishes monitoring from ad hoc forms of policy evaluation.

Supervision is a concept that can be found in many branches of literature. Its popularity is most common in management literature, where it refers to the relation between a manager (the supervisor) and his employees (the subordinates). In a public policy context, however, supervision relates to potential or actual interactions between public bodies with specifically defined roles, tasks and responsibilities. The supervisor has the authority to assess the supervisee's actual and intended activities and has the possibility to influence the behavior of the supervisee. Moreover, communication takes place at regular intervals (De Ridder, 1990:39). In comparison with monitoring, the roles and tasks in a process of supervision are usually better defined, as also follows from this definition. According to the Dutch Scientific Council, it is the task of government supervisory bodies (inspectorates, market regulators) to ensure a satisfactory level of compliance, risk management and quality assurance (WRR, 2013).

Enforcement is the narrowest of the three concepts. For some authors, enforcement is part of the supervision process, specifically in the responsive regulation approach (see Ayres and Braithwaite, 1992). In this book, we consider enforcement as a strategy that is aimed at ensuring that legally binding regulations are followed in practice by applying the means of private law, public law or criminal law. Compliance to the legal framework is the desired outcome of the enforcement process.

Three modes of supervision

In the previous section, we have argued that the concepts of monitoring, supervision and enforcement have different meanings. We have also made clear that "supervision" seems to be the most inclusive of the three. Therefore, in this section we distinguish three ideal-typical forms of supervision. The way supervision is considered from this perspective also determines its relation to the concepts of monitoring and enforcement. These three ideal types are based on the institutional positions and roles of the supervisors and the supervisees. We distinguish between repressive supervision, supportive supervision and polycentric supervision (Bekkers & Homburg, 2002).

Repressive supervision

The first ideal type of supervision is repressive supervision. This form may be considered as the traditional mode of supervision. This form of supervision is primarily based on the rational approach of the policy processes, a cybernetic model of control and the so-called principal–agent theory (see Eisenhardt, 1989). In the principal–agent model, there is a principal that hires an agent to perform specific tasks for him. The principal is hierarchically superior to the agent, usually based on agreements or other legally binding frameworks. Usually, these frameworks specify the number, the type and the quality level of the services that the agent delivers. The agent has a certain degree of discretion because it has more information about the services it delivers than the principal. A major challenge for both the principal and the agent is that they do not pursue the same interests and that they may hold different interpretations of their common interests. Moreover, both operate under different conditions. The characteristics of the internal organizations may differ, as well as the legal framework under which both operate. Consequently, problems may arise in meeting the performance requirements that both parties agreed upon. Sometimes these requirements cannot be fulfilled by the agent, sometimes the agent does not want to (fully) fulfill the requirements, and in addition during the execution process the interests and the preferences of the agent may evolve. For these reasons, supervision is important, but also very difficult. By organizing inspection at the site, developing protocols, designing performance management systems and using indicators, the principal tries to assess whether the agent still adheres to the agreements made. Through these instruments and systems, the principal tries to influence the agent so that it adheres to the objectives pursued by the principal and does not conceal actions or hide information. The repressive model of supervision relies on a cybernetic model of control. This model allows a comparison of the actual state of affairs – for example by the use of inspections and monitoring – with the previously stated policy objectives or standards in laws and regulations. Following from this cybernetic model, the mode through which the supervisor tries to affect the behavior of the supervisee can be considered as single-loop learning. The supervised party should align its operations with the standards set by the regulator. These standards are a given and cannot be questioned. The learning process on the part of the regulator focuses on the rationalization of the existing supervision process. This primarily concerns the refinement of the accounting standards and instruments, as well as the refinement of the existing feedback process information.

Supportive supervision

The second ideal type of supervision does not start from the differences in the interests of the supervisor and the supervisee but from their joint interests. This is also known as the stewardship approach (see Schillemans, 2013). The aim is to exchange knowledge, information and experiences between supervisor and supervised party to create a collective learning process (Zeef, 1994). This ideal type follows the political and cultural perspectives on policy. In this form of supervision, the supervisor and supervisee recognize and act upon their interconnectedness and interdependence (in't Veld, Bruijn and Ten Heuvelhof, 1998). Supervision can be considered as a process of collaboration between supervisor and supervisee with the goal to improve policy performance. This implies that knowledge, information, expertise and experiences need to be shared, allowing both parties to gain a better understanding of the implementation of the policy and the pitfalls that occur here. The formal distance pursued in the repressive style in order to ensure independent supervision will be exchanged for a more professional distance.

In this ideal type of supervision, the development of supervision criteria is a joint operation of supervisor and supervisee. These criteria reflect the complexity of the policy field in which they operate, and also provide a reference for professional interaction with each other. The development of criteria involves an ongoing development process. The supervisor takes the role of a "coach" that tries to improve the performance of his pupil (Sparrow, 2011). Instead of the "vertical" relation that characterizes the relation between supervisor and supervisee in the repressive mode, the relation becomes horizontal. An example of this may be found in the relation between the Dutch tax authority and medium- and large-size companies. As the Dutch secretary of state phrases:

> Horizontal monitoring refers to mutual trust between the taxpayer and the Netherlands Tax and Customs Administration, the more precise specification of each other's responsibilities and options available to enforce the law and the setting out and fulfillment of mutual agreements. In so doing, the mutual relationships and communications between citizens and the government shift toward a more equal position. Horizontal monitoring is also compatible with social developments in which the citizen's personal responsibility is accompanied by the feeling that the enforcement of the law is of great value. In addition, the horizontal monitoring concept also implies that enforcement is feasible in today's complex and rapidly changing society solely when use is made of society's knowledge. (DGB, 2005/1109)

In this mode of supervision, learning takes place through processes of double-loop learning. Double-loop learning allows a critical reflection on the appropriate policies and supervision criteria: it refers not to instrumental learning to better reach the goals but it questions the assumptions that underlie the goals. This critical perspective on the assumptions can be considered as a prerequisite for the development and adaptation of the professional standards and regulatory criteria that the supervisor and supervisee (intend to) use in the interactions. The development of professional standards can only take place if information, knowledge, expertise and experiences are shared and exchanged, resulting in a process of alignment of perceptions of the professional standards within a sector between supervisor and supervisee.

Polycentric supervision

The third ideal-typical form of supervision does not take the relationship between supervisor and supervisee as its starting-point, but embeds the process of supervision within the broader network of stakeholders involved in a specific implementation process. The supervision process is not in the hands of a central supervisory authority but in the hands of the network of stakeholders that deal with the supervisee. Supervision is much more about installing adequate checks and balances, and therefore fits within the political and institutional perspective on public policy as it has been developed throughout this book. Agencies may be confronted with multiple supervisors and even with competition among multiple supervisors.

A supervisor may invest in positioning adequate checks and balances that monitor the behavior of the supervisee, but it may also publish information about the performance of the organization and thereby mobilize the target group of the organization. This is also known as "naming and shaming". In the latter case, citizens are emphatically mobilized as co-supervisor, for example by giving them a better informed position. For example, by publishing information about the quality of a school on the Internet (as the Dutch Inspectorate for Education does), or by making information on the quality of food in cafes and restaurants accessible in a transparent manner (as the Danish Food Authority does) citizens become co-supervisors and the supervision process socializes.

This type of supervision can be found in processes that are easy to monitor for outsiders, like food quality or school performance. But also in settings in which the process is complex and rather high-risk, polycentric supervision may be used. When different supervisors with different professional backgrounds and different perspectives monitor the organizations, risks may be minimized (see Koolhaas and Olsthoorn, 1993). For instance, when monitoring the safety of chemical factories, occupational safety, environmental safety and product safety require totally different forms of supervision, even though they are closely intertwined.

The background of this polycentric arrangement is the idea that the complexity and dynamics of society are such that it is impossible to oversee these processes from one position or one perspective. Variety in the types of supervision and supervisors is desirable, even though this may lead to contrasting norms and criteria in some cases. In polycentric supervision, policy performance improves because different norms and criteria clash, interact and collaborate. Organizations learn from each other and continuously adapt their learning strategies. This form of learning in polycentric supervision may be labeled as triple loop learning: the ability to learn how to learn (see Flood and Romm, 1996).

Dilemmas in monitoring, supervision and enforcement

From analyses of the ways monitoring, enforcement and supervision work in practice, we may identify three dilemmas that are related to the design, the position and the implementation of monitoring, enforcement and supervision. First, there is the dilemma related to the way in which the supervising body positions itself vis-à-vis the supervisee. Second, there is a dilemma related to the moral hazard of supervisees. And finally, there is a dilemma related to attitude of the supervisor.

Position: close or distant?

There is a lot of variety in institutional positions of supervisors. Some supervisors collaborate with supervisees in formulating quality criteria that the supervisee should strive for and that also serve as supervision criteria. Other supervisors even advise the organizations that they supervise about the measures they implement or should implement to increase their compliance to the supervision criteria. But there are also supervising agents that articulate their independent positions and refuse to interact and communicate with their supervisees.

It gets even more confusing when a supervisor is part of a larger agency that also has other tasks than supervising. In many countries, local governments for instance are responsible for policy formulation, for decisions about permits based on these policies and for the supervision of the conditions of these permits. This can be observed for instance in the area of construction. In many municipalities, the permits for construction activities on large construction sites are formulated in negotiation and collaboration with the entrepreneur, the constructor or the real estate agency, specifically when the construction activities benefit the local community or economy and are desired by the municipality. Even though national and local regulations stipulate the conditions for the permit, usually there are a lot of minor decisions related to the specificities of the site that are open to interpretation by the permitting body. At the same time, the department is responsible for supervising the compliance to the conditions for the permit. In case of non-compliance, a renewed discussion may emerge in which the department for construction may be held co-responsible for the non-compliance.

Role: interventionist or non-interventionist

Moral hazard occurs when organizations or individuals do not (fully) experience the consequences of their behavior. Because this is the case, they are more willing to take risks than they would do when they had experienced the full consequences of their activities. Moral hazard for instance is one of the reasons why lease riders are more involved in car accidents than car owners (see for instance Arrow, 1971; Holmstrom, 1979; Johnson and Waldman, 2010). Similarly, supervision, monitoring and enforcement can undermine the self-responsibility of citizens and organizations. They may rely on the supervisor to identify risks and suggest responses to them. For instance, citizens wanting to invest their money in stock investments may be inclined to invest in products of which they cannot fully assess the risks once the supervisor has stated a label of approval for this product. But in contrast, a supervisor that does not actively assess risks and respond to them may be held at least partially responsible if things go wrong.

Attitude: trust or distrust

In principle, the relation between supervisor and supervisee is based on distrust; if the supervisee was to be trusted, supervision would not have been necessary. However, when distrust is the supervisor's leading attitude in interactions with the supervisee, this may affect the latter's behavior in two directions. The first option is that the supervisee is more inclined to perform the expected – but undesired – behavior. There is no moral appeal to show the desired behavior as distrust is the default attitude anyway. So the chance of getting caught and sanctioned when performing undesired behavior is the only factor that prevents the supervisee to perform undesired behavior. The only tool a supervisor has is communicating that there is a chance of getting caught and being sanctioned, thus deepening the vicious cycle of distrust. A second option is that the supervisee is extremely aware of the supervisor's distrust and tries to safeguard himself from this distrust by explicating and following extensive procedures, formalizing his own actions and sharing this with the supervisor. The result is an overload of formal, bureaucratic, procedural information from the supervisee to the supervisor that not necessarily reflects the real actions of the supervisee, but only provides a symbolic reality of which the only goal is to still the supervisor's hunger for control.

5.7 CHAPTER SUMMARY

In this chapter, we have examined the implementation of policy. In many cases, the implementation phase is the most important phase in the policy cycle as it ultimately determines the success or failure of policy. The potential failure of a policy program can be explained, among other things, by the fact that policy makers are not always aware of the fact that implementation is more than the activation of a machine. The implementation of policy has a political character as well. The support that exists for a particular program within a society and within the organizations responsible for the implementation becomes particularly visible in the implementation. This means that the implementation of policy implies a new round of steering the policy in a certain direction. Hence, the distinction between policy development and implementation in the practice of public administration is not as absolute as some suggest.

The success of a program is also determined by the extent to which an implementing organization is organized. Hence, it is important to pay attention to the management and organizational aspects. The success of the implementation is also determined by the fact that the implementation of policy is usually not limited to a single implementing organization, but that it mobilizes an entire network of organizations. That is why the extent to which these organizations are willing and able to collaborate with each other also plays a role in the successful implementation of a policy program. Usually, one makes the use and necessity of collaboration visible by talking about service delivery chains. The judgment of the degree of success, moreover, is determined by the way in which the actual interaction between government and citizens or businesses takes place in the actual, individual application of an act, for instance. This includes some interesting service aspects. That is why attention should be paid to services in a chapter on implementation. Furthermore, we have shown that in delivering these services various logics interact. As a result, the involved implementing public professionals may experience feelings of policy alienation, when being confronted with these tensions.

One element that may also contribute to the successful implementation of policies is the degree in which this implementation process is being monitored and supervised, in order to ensure compliance. However, the degree in which compliance is assured differs with the kind of supervision model that is being applied.

6
Evaluating public policy

LEARNING OBJECTIVES

After reading this chapter you should be able to:

- Recognize different *types of evaluation studies,* focusing on different aspects of policies or policy processes.

- Compare and apply different perspectives on *policy evaluation*, based on the rationalist, culturalist, institutionalist and political perspectives.

- Recognize and identify different *types of utilization* of evaluation studies.

- Understand the relation between *policy evaluation and accountability.*

Following the terrorist attacks on New York and Washington on September 11, 2001, President George W. Bush established a National Commission on Terrorist Attacks Upon the United States, also described as the 9/11 Commission. This commission with many high-level experts on board was given the challenging task of finding out what happened, why it happened and how it could be prevented in the future. After hearing over 1200 stakeholders and analysing more than 2.5 million documents, the committee came with firm criticism on the role of intelligence agencies FBI and CIA that had not communicated sufficiency with security agencies on the risk of a terrorist attack. It also came with numerous recommendations, some calling for more policies on the root causes of terrorism in different parts of the world, some on better coordination between intelligence agencies and government administration, and some on the need for coalition building in international relations. This committee has provided key building blocks for the US anti-terrorism policies until today. However, not all recommendations were implemented, and the committee itself also received significant criticism, amongst others due to the alleged partisan status of some of its members.

The example of the 9/11 Commission shows how evaluation fulfills a central role in the policy process, but also shows how contentious this stage can be. Policy evaluation is all about determining the content, implementation and impact of policies. This involves not just the most obvious evaluation question: "does the policy work as it was intended to do." Evaluation also concerns questions such as whether the policy has been effectively implemented at all, how do policy measures work in practice, what intended as well as unintended consequences does the policy have, to what extent do the policy stakeholders perceive the policy as effective and legitimate, and what lessons can be drawn for designing better policies. This makes evaluation an essential stage in the policy cycle, providing the foundation for the next stage of policy change.

Evaluation has been at the heart of the rational analytical movement in public policy studies. As Radin (2000) shows in her book *Beyond Machiavelli: Policy Analysis Comes of Age*, policy analysis in general and policy evaluation have for a long time been driven by a firm belief in the possibilities of measuring policy effects and casting rational judgments on a policy's success or failure. As a reflection of the belief in rational societal steering (see Chapters 1, 2 and 4), there was a strong belief in rational policy evaluation as well, which was even to fulfill a crucial role in the policy cycle where evaluation was to be the key motor of policy adjustments or change. And it must be recognized that this rational analytical movement continues to play a key role in the study of public policy today. It has contributed to significant understanding of methods of monitoring policies and policy effects, auditing, cost–benefit analyses and to what is nowadays described as "evidence-based policy making." However, it has also triggered criticism for the technocratic role it prescribes for the analyst who is doing the policy evaluation.

However, in line with the evolution of the different theoretical perspectives that are explored in this book, approaches of policy evaluation have diversified as well. In their famous work on policy evaluation, Guba and Lincoln (1989) describe how policy evaluation develops over different "generations" of evaluation studies. What they describe as the "first generation of evaluation" focused on policy evaluation as a technical approach to rationally determining whether a policy works or not. The second generation was more modest in not so much determining whether a policy works or not but rather describing how a policy works in practice and what (expected and unexpected) effects it generates. The third generation cast judgment on how far a policy lives up to its stated formal objectives. And finally, Guba and Lincoln describe a fourth generation of evaluation studies, which focuses more on the policy process with its multiple actors and multiple beliefs and interests involved.

These generations of evaluation show that evaluation can have very different meanings in different settings. The rational approach, or the "first generation" continues to prove its usefulness in many cases even today. Where policies are made and budget is spent to achieve policy aims, there will always be a desire to measure policy effects. At the same time, processes such as mediatization and politicization have made evaluation an increasingly contested process. This broadens the role of policy evaluations beyond that of being instrumental to policy change; policy evaluation has increasingly become a central element of public judgment about policies and about the stakeholders involved in these policies. Evaluations can have repercussions for the legitimacy of policies and policy stakeholders; negative as well as positive for instance when an evaluation report proves that a policy is successful. At the same time, the findings of evaluations are more and more often publicly contested. Sometimes the integration of the evaluation method is questioned or the credibility of the evaluators is put on the line, or there are multiple evaluation reports that do not arrive at similar conclusions.

In this chapter, we first discuss what different types of policy evaluation can be distinguished (section 6.1). Subsequently (section 6.2), we show how the evaluation of policy in terms of success or failure depends on the evaluation criteria and the method of data collection and analysis that are applied. This includes a discussion of how such methods and criteria are defined differently in rational, political, cultural and institutional approaches to public policy. Also, we address how policy evaluations relate to judgment about policies and about the stakeholders involved in these policies (section 6.3). Finally, we address different facets of the impact of evaluation on the policy process. This includes a discussion of evaluation as a means for public accountability for policies (section 6.4) as well as evaluation as a source for policy learning (section 6.5). We wrap up with some conclusions (section 6.6).

6.1 Types of evaluation

Policies can be evaluated in different ways. This can involve different sorts of evaluation tools and strategies, depending on the different functions that evaluation may have. Examples include evaluation studies, program-evaluations, audits, policy monitors, budget monitors, impact assessments and investigative committees. Evaluation usually serves two purposes:

1. Evaluation as a condition for learning, with the aim of enhancing the quality and the impact of policy; and
2. Evaluation as a condition for public accountability for what has been achieved with a policy.

Systematic and *ad hoc* evaluations

A distinction can be made between systematic and ad hoc evaluations. The goals of learning and accountability can be achieved systematically and periodically, which means that the implementation and the outcomes of policies are structurally and frequently followed. Think about how the European Court of Auditors constantly evaluates EU policies and budgets, as do courts of audit in most countries (as well as most regional and local authorities). Often such systematic evaluations also have a clear consequence in the policy process, as they are structural and predictable.

Evaluations can also be ad hoc, for instance in response to specific events. Objective indicators, such as monitors that show that little progress is made in a specific area can give rise to ad hoc policy evaluations. For instance, here the example of the OECD comes in (Box 6.1), as its monitors have frequently been causes for governments to evaluate their social and economic policies after the OECD had pinpointed "problem areas." Also, the occurrence of incidents can give rise to evaluation studies. For instance, after the terrorist attacks that struck Madrid in 2004 and London in 2005, extensive evaluations were done of the intelligence efforts that should have prevented these attacks. In some cases, ad hoc evaluations also clearly show the political nature of evaluations, especially as the call for evaluations can be driven by strategies of different actors with specific interests to get a specific topic on the agenda. For instance, many NGOs and interest groups frequently make evaluations of policies in order to set specific topics or specific concerns on the agenda.

Ex ante and *ex post* evaluations

A distinction can be drawn between evaluations that are done before (*ex ante*) a policy is implemented, as well as after implementation (*ex post*). Often, *ex ante* evaluations are primarily aimed at establishing the feasibility of a policy program so as to prevent problems in the implementation stage. *Ex post* evaluations are aimed at policies that have already been implemented and are evaluated in terms of their outcomes or in terms of how they were actually implemented in practice.

Objects of evaluation

Different types of evaluation studies can be distinguished in terms of objects of evaluation. In general, a distinction is made between the following types (Howlett, Ramesh and Perl, 1995:171):

BOX 6.1

DISTINGUISHING BETWEEN "EVALUATIONS" AND "MONITORS"

It is also important to distinguish "evaluation" from "monitoring", although the two can and often are clearly related. Monitoring refers to the collection of information and data on policy indicators. Think for instance of an organization like the OECD that is constantly collecting data on social and economic developments in member countries, such as about poverty, discrimination, average income and even happiness. Evaluation goes a step further in always connecting this information and data to policies. In this sense it adds an element of judgment, which also makes evaluation more contentious than monitoring. For instance, an evaluation study when focusing on poverty would try to establish the relation between poverty indicators and policy efforts that have been made. However, monitors in practice often tend to be mistakenly interpreted as evaluations. For instance, if the OECD indicates that poverty in one country has increased more significantly than in another, this often tends to be interpreted as a consequence of policies. That does clearly involve a misreading of a monitor as an evaluation study, although it also shows how evaluation itself has increasingly become part of public debate and accountability as well.

Input evaluations: this involves evaluations of the resources and efforts that have to be put into a policy in order to achieve certain aims. This can include different types of resources, such as financial means, human resources, materials but also knowledge, information and sometimes other immaterial resources such as time or leadership. Also, input evaluations can be oriented at the quantity of input, as well as the quality of the required input; for instance, is the quality of available knowledge sufficient to implement the policy?

Goal achievement evaluations: this involves evaluations of the extent to which the stated policy objectives have been met. Here it is important to differentiate between the *output* of policies and the *outcomes* or effects of policies. Goal achievement evaluations are about whether the output of policies is in line with the objectives, such as whether the number of teachers before the class or the number of police officers in the street have been increased in accordance with the goals. It is not about the broader outcomes of these policies, for instance whether the teaching results have improved as well, or whether people now indeed feel safer on the streets.

Effectiveness evaluations: this involves evaluations that do take the (broader) *outcomes* of a policy as objects of evaluation. For instance, did more police officers on the street decrease crime and increase feelings of security? In this respect, a distinction can be made between summative and formative evaluations (see also Patton 1994, 2008). Summative evaluations focus solely on whether the formal goals and effects have been achieved. Formative evaluations take the broader outcomes of a policy in to consideration in order to provide an answer to why the goals and effects have or have not been achieved. These broader outcomes can involve many more factors than just the policy efforts that have been made, such as efforts by the neighborhood to make the street safer, incidents that might have increased feelings of insecurity, and so on. This can, in a formative sense, contribute to lesson drawing by stakeholders involved in the policy concerned.

Efficiency evaluations: these are evaluations of the costs in relation to the benefits of a specific program, so a cost–benefit analysis. This can involve actual as well as anticipated costs or benefits. Here the achievement of effects is not the object of evaluation per se, but rather whether the ways in which these effects were achieved have been efficient.

Process evaluations: these are evaluations of different processes involved in a policy. This can include an evaluation of how a policy has come about, as well as how it has been implemented, how different actors are involved or how it is being monitored. For instance, are procedures clear, efficient and transparent enough? What obstacles can be found in the different processes that may obstruct the implementation of a policy?

Internal and external evaluations

Finally, a distinction can be made between internal evaluations and external evaluations. Internal evaluations involve evaluations that are performed by organizations that are also involved in the implementation of the policy that is being evaluated. For instance, when an organization evaluates internal processes in the implementation of a specific policy, or when the output or outcomes of a policy are evaluated by the policy actors responsible for the implementation. External evaluations are performed by evaluators that are not themselves stakeholders in the policy that is being evaluated. This can be an important way to give the evaluation a more impartial or independent status, which can boost the impact of the evaluation study as well as avoid "group think" amongst those already involved in the status quo of a specific policy field.

6.2   Evaluation criteria

For the evaluation of policy programs, it is necessary that politicians and policy makers define clear criteria or measurements for evaluation. The formulation of these criteria is in itself a political choice. Which policy is successful, is that the policy that receives the broadest possible support, the policy that achieves aims in the most efficient way or the policy that is most effective? In defining these criteria, the different policy perspectives can be associated with different sets of criteria, which will be discussed in depth in this section.

The rational approach: effectiveness, efficiency and coherency

In the rational approach, evaluation is all about "learning about the consequences of public policy" (Dye 1976: 351). It is assumed to play a key role in the policy cycle; by rational evaluation, policies should learn about how to improve instruments or adjust goals, which should feed back into the stages of agenda setting and policy formulation and thus eventually contribute to improving policies. As such, Sanderson (2002) sees rational evaluation as a crucial part of "evidence based policymaking."

The rational approach puts all emphasis on the goals of policy, as these goals are supposed to give direction to the input of means and resources, such as funding in the form of subsidies or the passing of new regulations. The success of this input is measured by means of three criteria (see also Ringeling 1993 and Dunn 2004): effectiveness, efficiency and coherency. First of all, *effectiveness* refers to the extent to which the measures and means that have been taken have managed to achieve the output or outcomes that had been set. This involves at least two questions. How do the actual output and outcomes compare to the output and outcomes that had been aimed for? And what has been the contribution of policy (measures, means) to achieving these outputs and outcomes? The answer to these questions depends on a number of conditions. Have the policy aims been formulated in concrete and measurable units? For instance, an increase in the number of police officers on the street is easy to measure, but a reduction of poverty is much more complex to measure as the definition of what counts as poverty is highly contentious. Are effects triggered by a purposeful and targeted deployment of specific measures and instruments? This means that there should be a well-articulated "policy theory" that connects policy measures, consequences and aims (see Chapter 4). And, can a distinction be made between the output and the outcomes of policy, and how certain is it that outcomes are really due to policy and not to other factors?

The second criterion, *efficiency*, refers to the extent to which policy is able to achieve output and outcomes against the lowest possible costs in terms of (different types of) resources. This implies that evaluators are able to precisely measure these costs and attribute them to specific policy measures or activities. This may be more difficult to achieve in practice than it seems. Especially large infrastructural projects such as road, bridge and train line constructions are known for the lack of precision in *ex ante* evaluations, as such projects often encounter so many unforeseen costs that the actual budget sometimes turns out to be double the original budget. However, also for *ex post* evaluations, efficiency may be difficult to establish when more immaterial or difficult to measure costs are involved. Furthermore, efficiency may mean different things to different stakeholders; what counts as a benefit to one stakeholder may count as a cost to another.

Finally, the criterion of *consistency* is closely associated with the idea of government as "perfect administration." If the government wishes to operate like a machine, then it is necessary that all the subparts of the administrative machinery are well aligned. For policy evaluation, this means that policy should be consistent, internally as well as externally. Internal consistency means for instance that all the stakeholders involved in a policy know what is expected from them, or in other words, what their positions and roles are in the broader policy setting. External consistency means that one policy does not contradict other policies. For instance, if one policy tries to raise the retirement age and another policy tries to discourage elderly people from participating in the labor market so as to make way for young people, the external consistency of these policies can be said to be weak. Consistency also refers to the need to combine policy instruments in an optimal way, where instruments do not contradict but rather reinforce each other. An example is how anti-radicalization policies usually involve a mix of preventive instruments and more repressive instruments, where the need to prevent these two types of instruments conflicting with each other is very obvious.

The political perspective: the politics of evaluation

The role of evaluation in the political perspective is all about actors positioning themselves and protecting their interests. Actor judgments on a policy as either a success or a failure will to a great extent be framed in terms of whether it has contributed to either a strengthening or a weakening of their position and their interests. Hence, the political perspective expects differences in how different actors evaluate a specific policy. Furthermore, it expects that the policy that manages to take a broad range of interests into account, for instance by giving actors a voice in the formulation or implementation of policies, will receive the widest support. Policy is successful if it manages to be accepted by a sufficiently broad range of actors.

The political perspective clearly connects evaluation to the interests of coalitions of actors. In some policy areas, there is a "dominant coalition" that has vested interests in a specific policy. This can involve a variety of different types of actors, such as government organizations, business interests, NGOs and even advisory bodies, but who share a common interest in maintaining a specific policy as their interests are aligned with that policy. These vested interests inescapably "color" these actors' evaluation of the policy (Cyert and March, 1963:27-32), which clearly challenges the more objectivist interpretation of evaluation as in the rationalist approach.

In the political perspective, evaluation is an inherently political practice, leading to what can be described as the "politics of evaluation" (Bovens a.o. 2006, Fischer 1995). In fact, there are plenty of examples of evaluation studies that have been commissioned by dominant coalitions and can be understood as efforts to substantiate and legitimate the dominant coalition rather than to critically examine it. For instance, the cigarette producing industry continued until very recently to produce evaluations that showed that smoking as a cause of lung cancer could not be singled out from other causes. The same goes for "advocacy coalitions" that challenge a dominant coalition and their vested interests. For instance, environmental movements throughout the world have had a large impact on government policies through their evaluations of environmental impacts of government policies.

This political nature of evaluation also explains why in some cases governments do not pursue evaluations at all. For instance, the role of the OECD has been carefully restricted to monitoring social and economic trends rather than really evaluating the policies that supposedly contributed to these trends. Governments would be far more reluctant to support an international and independent organization that could evaluate their policies, which would turn this organization into a powerful political force to be reckoned with. Hence, confining the role of the OECD to policy monitoring is a way to prevent this politics of evaluation, while still being able to make use of the information provided by the OECD. However, as mentioned before, in the reality of public and political debate, the differences between policy monitoring and policy evaluation are not always respected.

The cultural approach: evaluation as the creation of a shared policy story

The cultural approach focuses on how evaluation studies create a shared meaning or interpretation of a specific policy. This perspective does not focus on the objective measurements of effectiveness, efficiency and consistency or the serving of vested interests of a dominant coalition that determine a policy's successfulness, but rather the extent to which it manages to create a shared image or "story" about the purpose and need for a specific policy (see a.o. Fischer 2003a, Haas 2004, Hoppe 1999). Policy evaluation, especially when done by authoritative experts, can have an important impact on how people understand a policy and interpret its successes or failures. In this sense, there is more to evaluation then evaluation methods or taking specific interests into account, it is also about language, communication and setting a shared frame of reality that many actors can relate to (Fischer and Forester 1993). According to this approach, this also does justice to the fact that what actors see as effective or efficient is highly subjective and cannot be simply uncovered with objective methods (Guba and Lincoln, 1989). Also, what actors see as their interests is also seen as subjective in this approach; rather, it depends on how actors perceive a policy and interpret it as either successful or not that they may redefine their role in this policy (Bovens a.o. 2006).

Take for instance the impact of the 9/11 Commission on the framing of the US war against terror, within the US as well as at various places across the world. Although the commission itself was later revealed as being divided on important points and in various cases also not allowed to reveal some of its sources, it did create a story of the US being under attack and the US in need of tightening security controls for instance at airports and needing to intensify its intelligence efforts. This is a very different story than set by experts in various other countries, who stressed that terrorism can only be partially prevented by education and social inclusion and that it is almost impossible to stop terrorism while not trampling on basic privacy rights and that even then it is practically impossible to control all terrorist activities. These are two different stories that each would have very different consequences in terms of policy and international relations. With the 9/11 Commission the security and control story largely won the day, and would impact policies in a profound manner.

The institutional approach: policy evaluation as multi-rationality

In many ways, the institutional approach combines elements of the other approaches when it comes to policy evaluation. An institutional approach recognizes the multiple "rationalities" that can be institutionalized into a policy field. Depending on the institutional setting in which a policy is being evaluated, one or many of these rationalities may surface (Hemerijck, 2003, 2013). One of these rationalities focuses indeed on whether policy works; whether it is effective, efficient and consistent. Another rationality focuses on the feasibility of a policy. This includes not only the more technical and organizational aspects of feasibility, but also whether a policy has sufficient support. Is the policy feasible in a political sense? But also, can the policy target groups be expected to respond and co-operate in the way that is anticipated?

However, the institutional approach also focuses on the institutional embedding of a policy; does the policy fit in a broader legal setting, is it seen as legitimate? This includes the principle of legality, whether a policy fits in the broader legal setting or whether it conflicts with specific laws or regulations, at different levels of government (local, regional, national, international). For instance, when the European financial and economic crisis began in 2007, many European governments attempted to adjust their policies to protect industries, such as the French automobile industries of Peugeot, Citroen and Renault. However, the legality of these policies was contested, and their scope eventually constrained, in the context of European regulations regarding the internal market and regarding market competition.

Finally, the focus on the institutional embedding of policy not only involves the legal embedding but also the more social embedding in terms of legitimacy. Does a policy do justice to the preferences of society and does it contribute to the functioning of the political system and to trust in government in politics?

Taking together the different criteria for evaluation shows how varied and contested evaluation can be. Importantly, this means that simple judgments about policies in terms of success or failure should be carefully avoided. Any time you hear someone discarding policy as a failure or you read a newspaper article that claims a policy has failed, try to find out what criteria are involved and what perspective seems to drive the evaluation. You will find that in almost all cases there can be serious debate about whether the criteria were appropriate, and as a consequence, whether the claims about policy success or failure are appropriate.

6.3   Designing policy evaluation

We have seen that evaluation can be approached very differently from different perspectives and with different (sets of) criteria. This also has consequences for the design of the evaluation process. In the following we will discuss for each perspective what the most important design issues are.

The rational approach: measuring effects

In the rational approach, evaluation means (objective) measuring. By measuring the actual results of a policy, policy makers are enabled to cast an objective judgment on the success or failure of policy. The strength of a policy evaluation would, in this perspective, be primarily determined by the strength of the methods used (see also Dunn 2004, Dye 1976). Sometimes this can even involve quasi-experimental evaluation designs (see Cook and Campbell, 1979). Several issues have to be taken into account when designing policy evaluation according to the rationalist approach.

Reconstructing the "policy theory"

The first step is to reconstruct the "policy theory" on which a policy is based. Sometimes, and this is to be preferred in a rationalist approach, there is an explicit policy theory. In fact, the rationalist approach toward policy formulation presupposes that an articulated policy theory is in place (see Chapter 4). In reality however, a policy theory may turn out to be much more complex, unclear and even uncertain and contested. Here it is an important task of the rational evaluator to reconstruct the policy theory, as without an articulated policy theory an evaluation "rationalist style" would be impossible.

The policy evaluator should try to put her or himself as best as possible in the shoes of the policy designers, to reconstruct the causal, final and normative assumptions they had in mind when designing the policy to be evaluated. What cause–effect relations were assumed, such as "too high levels of mortgages can lead to a bank crisis"? What means–goals relations were assumed, such as "lowering the mortgage–income ratio per household will decrease the risks of too high loan dependency"? What normative assumptions were in place, such as "the banking system should be as stable as possible without government support"?

However, the evaluator must also be aware of the discrepancies that may exist between the policy theory as it was when the policy was being designed and the policy theory as it is at the time of evaluation. There may be various causes of such discrepancies. In some cases, there may have been tacit or hidden policy goals underlying the original policy design, or the original policy goals may have been unrealistic or even symbolic in nature. In some cases governments just want to make clear to the public that they take a concern very seriously by designing a "tough" policy approach in spite (or rather because) of its unrealistic ambitions. For instance, many mayors have announced that they would ban the use of all hard drugs in their cities, which may have been very satisfying to their electorates, but no mayor has ever actually achieved this goal!

Goal displacement can be another factor behind the discrepancy between original and actual policy theory. In many cases, goals "shift" over time when a policy is put to practice, without the original policy theory being formulated or adjusted. For instance, some goals, such as banning all crime in a city, may turn out to be unrealistic in practice and replaced by a more workable policy goal of cutting off financial streams of gangs and increasing subjective feelings of safety by putting more police officers on the streets. It is important to take such goal displacements into account, as it allows for a more balanced policy evaluation.

Measuring effects

Another important concern in a rational policy evaluation is how to measure effects. Rational measurement of policy effects comes with a number of issues. First of all, how to determine whether the changes that are measured are actually the effects of policy? For instance, when a decrease of levels of unemployment is observed, this can be the effect of policy efforts to increase employment but it can also be a consequence of broader economic developments that increase demand for labor, the coincidental opening up of new markets abroad, the decrease of the labor population in itself, and many other factors. This is why it is important for a rational policy evaluation to have a well-informed and well-articulated causal model. This provides the evaluator with good insight of what factors may be responsible for specific changes or effects. This point of indeterminacy of cause–effect relations is, however, one of the key points of divergence with other approaches to policy evaluation, as we will see later on.

Another issue concerns the distinction between intended and unintended or inadvertent effects. A rational policy evaluator is first of all interested in the presence or absence of intended effects. This goes for the positive as well as the negative effects that have been anticipated in the policy design. But it may very well be that an evaluation also reveals other effects or consequences, not anticipated in the policy design. Once again, this may include positive as well as negative inadvertent effects. For instance, some studies have identified an unintended negative effect of welfare state policies that were put in place to help weaker groups in society but inadvertently also contributed to higher state dependency of these groups.

Third, some policy efforts (intended as well as unintended) may only become manifest after longer periods of time. Policies often need some time for "incubation" before any effects may become manifest. Think for example of processes of environmental change that often take decades to change, or social processes such as migrant integration which often take more than a generation to materialize. Here a rationalist evaluation that takes account of the periods that policies need to work out in practice often conflicts with a political logic that is bound to an election cycle of often four or five years. This creates an inherent "political impatience" to change or discard policies even before any effects could have been manifested.

A fourth issue concerns the actual measurement of effects itself. In a pure rationalist perspective, there should always be clear and measurable indicators to define policy effects. In management jargon, this is often phrased as SMART formulation of policy goals: specific, measurable, assignable, realistic and time-related. However, in some cases it may be hard to identify clear and measurable indicators. For instance, the degree of safety and security in a city cannot be simply defined in terms of objective figures on the number of crimes committed in a city, it is as much a subjective notion referring to how people experience being safe or not. In fact, there have been many studies that showed that while objective crime figures decreased, feelings of unsafety increased. Furthermore, measurement methods may be contested as well. In spite of a rational belief in positivist methods to measure effects, such methods may be difficult to implement in practice or may be contested by other actors (where the rationalist approach meets the political approach to evaluation). Think about the fierce political conflicts that have, and continue to, revolve around the so-called Kyoto Protocol for environmental protection, where measurements determine the effects of policy on the gap in the ozone layer, carbon dioxide emissions and global warming.

A final concern in policy evaluation is the objectivity of the evaluation, or the extent to which the evaluation (and the evaluator) are seen as value free. Here it is important to be aware that evaluation always has a normative dimension; policies are always related to specific political values, such as freedom, security, justice and equality. In fact, normative assumptions are, as observed above, part of a policy theory. Therefore they can, and should, be part of a rational policy evaluation. To what extent have the normative ideals that were set in the original policy design been advanced?

In dealing with this normative dimension of policy evaluation from a rational perspective, it is important that any normative elements for evaluation are stated explicitly and are clearly derived from the actual policy design itself. This is to make sure that the normative evaluation is based on the policy designers' normative assumptions rather than those of the evaluator itself. However, this inherent normative dimension of policies and policy evaluation is one of the key points of divergence with other perspectives, especially the cultural and political perspectives.

BOX 6.2

"MULTICULTURALISM HAS FAILED"

A key challenge in the rationalist approach to policy evaluation is how to define policy aims and how to measure to what extent policy efforts have contributed to achieving these aims. However, in many policy areas it may be difficult to clearly define what the policy aims were in the first place. Take the example of migrant integration policies, which have been developed in many countries in response to growing levels of immigration since the 1950s. It is very difficult to define what migrant integration is in the first place; when is a migrant sufficiently integrated? Is it when the migrant has found work and goes to school, speaks the native language, feels "at home" and abides by the norms and values of the host society, and so on.

Nonetheless, in early 2011, the leaders of the three largest EU member states each stated that "multiculturalism had failed." However, from a rational perspective, this "evaluation" can be criticized on several accounts. First of all, what multiculturalism means has remained rather vague; whereas the British referred primarily to "race relations", the Germans rather spoke of participation and the French of assimilation (and in fact rarely using the term multiculturalism itself). So what has failed precisely? Second, where is the evidence that it (whatever it is) has failed. In fact, there was quite a lot of contestation in all three countries where the public mood and politicization triggered concerns about a lack of integration and growing radicalization, whereas objective indicators in all three countries showed that over a generation quite a lot of progress had been made primarily in terms of socio-economic participation (in housing, schooling, work). Third, isn't it too early to tell? Integration often takes decades if not several generations to materialize. Most migrants had arrived in the 1960s and 1970s so were in their second generation, but there has been a constant inflow of new arrivals as well. Perhaps multiculturalism would have been more successful if it had been consistently pursued over a longer period of time.

The political approach: evaluation as the measurement of support

In the political approach, evaluation is all about the support that a policy can mobilize. A policy is successful if it managed to mobilize sufficient support amongst relevant stakeholders, providing the policy with sufficient (material and immaterial) resources. A policy becomes unsuccessful if it loses such support. Therefore, in a political approach, it is important to map the network of actors within such support which needs to be mobilized.

A network analysis is a much used method for mapping the constellation of actors and stakeholders within which a policy is designed and implemented. A first step of a network analysis (see also Chapter 6) is to identify the relevant actors involved and to define the network of positions, interests and dependencies within the network. Subsequently, for an evaluation study such a network analysis should also address these actors' perceptions and interpretations of a policy's success or failure. Here, in a sense, a policy evaluation is based on how involved actors evaluate the policy, rather than on the evaluator's objective methods and approach.

A key issue in using a network analysis for policy evaluation is defining relevant actors or stakeholders. Some policy fields are relatively "simple" and involve a limited number of clearly identifiable actors. However, in some cases the network of actors will be much more complex and fragmented, with many interlocking interdependencies and potentially also hidden interests. Furthermore, organizations (such as government departments or political parties) cannot always be defined as unitary actors; often, within an organization different fragments hold different positions and have different interests. Consequently, a network analysis can become a very laborious activity. For instance, an evaluation of neighborhood service centers, often providing multiple public services to a specific community in an integrated manner, will have to take account of the highly complex environment in which these centers operate. Their success depends not only on how clearly their targets are defined and whether they have sufficient material and immaterial resources, but also on their interaction with other actors from the neighborhood such as local businesses, schools, housing corporations, labor recruitment agencies and NGOs. Furthermore, within a neighborhood center, there may also be different "actors", such as professionals with different backgrounds or frontline and back-office workers that need to co-operate.

The aim of the network analysis is to define the basis of support for a policy, as well as to define possible bottlenecks in a network that may obstruct the effectiveness of a policy. Here it is not only important what position an actor holds in a network, but also how important the resources are that this actor provides to a policy (material as well as immaterial). Some actors are strongly organized and, if mobilized, can be an important support (or obstacle) to a policy. Although their influence appears somewhat weakening, labor unions were traditionally perceived as very well organized and powerful actors that could potentially disturb the economy to a significant extent. However, there are also actors (and interests) that are weakly mobilized. For instance, due to a lack of knowledge as well as due to their weak position, migrant communities often tend to be weakly organized, and consequently also only marginally involved in the development and evaluation of policies that may concern them.

The orientation of the political approach on the broader network of actors is also seen as a condition for the findings of an evaluation to be actually used by these actors. By actively taking the perceptions and interests of involved actors into account, the evaluation outcomes will also be more likely to be usable to these actors involved (Patton, 1997:23). In fact, the political approach to evaluation also advocates the involvement of such actors in the formulation of an evaluation study, the choice of evaluation questions and methods, and the monitoring of the evaluation proceedings. If done properly, this will (in full accordance with the political approach) also promote the support and legitimacy of the evaluation study and its findings itself.

Cultural approach: evaluation as interpretation

Whereas evaluation in the rational approach is all about objective measurement of effects and in the political approach all about determining a policy's level of support and resources, the cultural approach sees evaluation more as a form of interpretation. This involves a strongly subjectivist approach to evaluation. Although the political approach is also subjectivist in its focus on actors, the cultural approach focuses more on the stories that actors tell about a policy than on the actors' interests and resources. This cultural approach represents what Guba and Lincoln (1989) describe as the "fourth generation of evaluation."

Actors' interpretations of a policy's success or failure depend on the specific context in which an actor is situated, his history and frame of reference, and can differ strongly between actors. Evaluation then involves the construction of a common story that involves a form of judgment about a policy. In contrast to the political approach that emphasizes the role of power and resources in evaluation, in this approach the construction of a common story evolves much more around language and social interaction. It is about the construction of an intersubjective story that is convincing and that makes sense to the actors involved, regardless of their (perceived) interests and regardless of objective indicators of whether the story is actually "true".

The construction of such intersubjective stories or interpretations of a policy takes place in a process of social interaction. Language or framing can play an important role in this interaction and shaping of a collective story. It is not uncommon that policies that lack evidence for concrete effects are framed as a success through the use of persuasive language. Edelman (2013) has described this paradoxical situation as "words that succeed, and policies that fail." For instance, the failure of policies can be "masked" by referring to other countries where the situation may be much worse, thus contributing to a story that the policy is not so bad after all. The other way around, extensive policies can be brought down by single incidents that manage to attract broad attention and have a determining influence on the collective story. Increasingly, the media plays an important role in shaping collective stories of success or failure. This involves traditional as well as new media.

Designing evaluation as social interaction

For the design of evaluation in the cultural approach, the process of interaction between actors (citizens, policy makers, politicians, NGOs) is key. The goal of the interaction should be to create a shared interpretation of a policy reality (Guba and Lincoln, 1989). This means, first of all, that a process needs to be created that allows for meaningful interaction between involved stakeholders. The art is then to connect the different actors' stories in a common evaluation. Like in the political approach, this involves a multi stakeholder approach where the stakeholders' perceptions are central to the evaluation. However, here the aim is not to draw a network analysis and analyse interdependencies and resources, but rather to create one palette out of the different stories. These represent different perspectives on a specific policy. The goal is then to develop a mutual understanding in the form of a common story or narrative, through a process of social interaction and dialogue between actors that feel involved and treated as equals. This dialogue and construction of a common story can then provide the basis for policy learning and the adjustment of policies. Hence, this form of evaluation is sometimes also described as "responsive evaluation" (Abma, 2001:239).

A second element that needs to be taken into account in a culturalist evaluation design is identifying and addressing any potential barriers that may exist and obstruct the dialogue between actors. The evaluator must identify such potential barriers, which may obstruct a fair and free exchange of thoughts and introduce a bias in the policy evaluation. For instance, are all relevant voices represented, are some actors unaware or unable to contribute to a policy evaluation, are there actors that are unwilling to participate? In a sense, the evaluator must make sure that the setting in which actors convene resembles as much as possible the Habermasian ideal type of an "ideal speech situation", or a situation where all actors are involved and feel free to speak out as they wish and engage in dialogues on an equal playing field. Schön and Rein (1994) identify a number of conditions that need to be satisfied for creating such an ideal situation; participants should trust each other, must be willing to enter dialogue with others, they must be aware of their own views but also willing to put themselves in the shoes of other actors. In such an ideal situation actors are stimulated to reflect on their "frames" and to jointly construct a story on a policy situation.

A third element concerns value pluralism. Whereas the rationalist perspective assumes a clear ordering of normative premises on which a policy theory is based, the culturalist perspective assumes that policies are always based on a plurality of normative perspectives. So, policies are considered to be based not simply on one value, say "freedom", but always involve a blend of values. Furthermore, it assumes that in practice such values are difficult to disentangle. What one actor considers "freedom" may be interpreted very differently by other actors. Take for instance the very normative issue of migration. International organizations have often stated that the regulation of international migration is itself an infringement on the principle of individual freedom and sustains inequality between individuals living in different places of the world. On the other hand, nation-states often legitimize the regulation of (international) migration by the principle of national sovereignty allowing the state to be a place of equality of all citizens (in contrast to non-citizens) and guaranteeing the freedom of its citizens.

The evaluator as coach

The cultural perspective differs from other perspectives regarding the role that the evaluator should take in the evaluation itself. In the rationalist perspective, the evaluator should be as independent and objective as possible, preferably keeping a certain distance from the actual policy stakeholders. In the political perspective, the evaluator is more like a chief negotiator standing in between stakeholders. In the culturalist perspective, the evaluator becomes one of the actors in the evaluation, who has to work with the actors in the construction of a common policy story. This also implies that the evaluator is not "objective" in a traditional sense, but becomes engaged in the policy evaluation itself and is also responsible (also in a normative sense) for the outcomes of the evaluation.

In this respect, there are two major challenges to the role of the evaluator in the culturalist perspective. These speak to two of the main criticisms of the culturalist perspective on evaluation. First, the evaluator should try to promote the "ideal speech situation" described above, in which all actors are involved and feel free to speak out. However, as the notion of ideal type already suggests, such a situation may be very hard to establish in practice. What about structural imbalances between different actors in terms of knowledge and skills in framing their story? What if an actor does not want to put himself in the shoes of another, or to adapt its frame if necessary? Second, a key challenge is to address value relativism. Especially from a rationalist perspective, a much heard criticism is that the culturalist approach can lead to nihilism as it does not have methods for determining a hierarchy of values. Especially if conflicting values are involved, this introduces a risk of policy stalemate or inaction (Bovens and 't Hart, 1993:155).

Fischer's multi-layered approach to policy evaluation

A framework for the study of policy evaluation that offers the evaluator tools for averting relativism and structuring the dialogue between actors to promote a common story has been developed by Frank Fischer (2003a). This framework has been widely used in academia for the study of evaluations (or "meta-evaluations"), but also offers structuring principles for a culturalist evaluator, while combining important elements of the rational, political and cultural perspectives. Fischer renounces the idea that evaluation involves a pure calculation of inputs and effects. Rather, he defines various levels of "discursive practices" that in practice are often strongly entwined but that should be distinguished on an analytical level. The four layers that Fischer distinguishes (program verification, situational validation, societal vindication and social choice) can facilitate the process of dialogue and communication that is so essential to the cultural approach. Each of these levels involves a specific type of policy evaluation. He describes this process as:

> The goal is not to "plug in" answers to specific questions or to fulfil pre-specified methodological requirements. It is to engage an open and flexible exploration of the kinds of concerns raised in various discursive phases of the problem. In this regard the questions do not constitute a complex set of rules or fixed requirements that must be dealt with in any formal way. Within the framework of discourse, the deliberation may follow its own course in the pursuit of understanding and consensus. (Fischer, 2003a:193)

Program verification: the first layer of policy evaluation involves primarily what Fischer describes as "technical-analytical discourse" (Fischer, 2003a:193). In fact, this level comes close to what we have described as the rationalist approach to policy evaluation. This level involves what Fischer describes as "conventional policy analysis" addressed at questions like whether a policy has achieved its objectives (did it work?) and whether the policy was the most efficient way for achieving the goals that had been set.

Situational validation: this second layer involves "contextual discourse", addressing to what extent a policy still fits a specific problem situation. Is the policy (still) relevant to the problem situation? Has there been a change of circumstances that may require a change in objectives and tools?

Societal vindication: the third layer puts a policy in a broader evaluative perspective, involving what Fischer describes as "system discourse." This means whether a policy fits the broader political and social choices that have been made, does it fit in the prevailing political and social system? Is the policy considered valuable to society as a whole? Does it contribute something that is considered of value?

Social choice: finally, the fourth and most abstract layer involves ideological discourse, or the choice for the very social order on which a policy is based. This turns attention to the very basic ideological principles on which a policy is based (choice for a social system). Are the basic social and political values that underlie a policy still relevant and acceptable? Is it important, or is it the right thing to do? This includes ideological principles regarding society as well as regarding the role of government in this society and the relation between government and citizenry.

Fischer's model shows that policy evaluation is, in the end, always based on some form of (political normative) social choice. In this sense, it also reflects important elements of a more political perspective. However, Fischer's model has also been criticized for its lack of attention to political processes of negotiation, bargaining and conflict at the different levels of evaluation.

The institutional approach: evaluation as dealing with multi-rationality

The institutional approach to evaluation questions the possibility for casting a single judgment about policy success or failure. However, in this perspective it is not the actors' interests or their problem perspectives that would account for different evaluations, but rather the different institutional

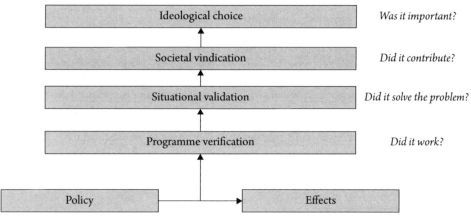

Figure 6.1 Schematic overview of Fischer's multi-layered approach to policy evaluation

---

BOX 6.3

RETHINKING THE WELFARE STATE AT TIMES OF ECONOMIC CRISIS

During the financial and economic crisis that struck Europe (and many other parts of the world) between about 2007 and 2014, many European countries saw the need to evaluate and reconsider their welfare state policies. Here, the crisis was a trigger for an evaluation of policies that clearly involved all four levels of Fischer's framework.

At the level of program verification, this involved a systematic inquiry of the cost-efficiency of various welfare state schemes, such as unemployment benefits, support for disabled persons and early retirement schemes. Which schemes have turned out much more costly than expected? Are there schemes that inadvertently may have contributed to forms of welfare dependency? Subsequently, at the level of situational validation, the question was asked whether the different welfare state schemes were still relevant to the problem situation in the countries examined. For instance, with the growing ageing of the population (amongst others due to the increase of life expectancy), are early-retirement schemes still necessary?

At the level of societal vindication, the welfare state reform involved a rethinking of whether social policies still fitted in the rapidly changing social and political settings of European countries in the late 2000s. Because of a liberalization of economies in various countries as well as a growing internationalization of labor supply, the value of a welfare state was put in a different perspective. Finally, the economic crisis was also a trigger to rethink the very fundamental ideological principles on which the welfare state was based. What should be the relation between citizens and the state, what level of social protection should the state provide (especially at times of crisis), where are the boundaries of individual responsibility?

settings in which actors operate. Whereas some actors will be more concerned about the legal appropriateness of a policy, others (such as street level bureaucrats) may focus more on practical feasibility. This means that the four questions that are key to the institutional approach in general (see Chapter 2: "is it applicable", "does it work", "is it appropriate" and "is it allowed") do also apply to evaluation. In addressing these four questions, a policy evaluation does justice to the multiple rationality that characterizes policy according to the institutional approach. As we will see below, this actually combines elements of the rationalist, political and culturalist perspectives.

Does it work?

Addressing the "does it work?" question primarily concerns whether the goals and outcomes that had been set by the original policy have actually been met. Here the evaluation incorporates elements (and challenges) of the rationalist approach to evaluation. Is policy effective, efficient and consistent (Hemerijck, 2003:34-37)?

Is it applicable?

This question reflects ideas from the political perspective. It focuses on whether the policy that is being evaluated can rely on sufficient support from stakeholders (with key resources), or whether there is resistance (mobilization) against the policy (Hemerijck, 2003:38-41). The extent of support or resistance will determine the applicability of a policy.

Is it allowed?

This question brings in a more legalistic perspective on policy evaluation, a dimension that is considered of key importance in the institutionalist perspective and perhaps somewhat forgotten in the other perspectives. However, as discussed in earlier chapters, the legal context can have an important effect on policy in general and policy evaluation in particular. This involves not just the assessment of whether policies are or are not "allowed" in a strict legal sense, but also the broader legal implications of a policy for generic principles of parliamentary democracy and rule of law (Hemerijck, 2003:41-44).

Is it appropriate?

Whereas the "is it allowed" question addresses the legal fit of a policy, the "is it appropriate" question addresses the broader social and institutional fit of a policy. Does a policy, according to the stakeholders involved, fit their interests, ideas, expectations, values and norms? The extent to which policy is seen as appropriate will also influence trust of citizens in policy, and the institutions that are involved. If a government pursues policies that are considered not to be appropriate, this may result in problems of credibility (Hemerijck, 2003:44-47).

A challenge in an institutionalist evaluation is not only to address all four of these evaluation questions, but also to deal with potential ambiguities and contradictions that may arise when addressing all four questions. There may be tensions, trade-offs or clear conflicts between the different questions. For instance, a policy may be very effective, but not legally allowed. Or it may be considered very appropriate, but not effective. Take for instance the work of intelligence agencies, who constantly have to cope with trade-offs between secret service methods (such as infiltration, bugging mobile telephones or even the "staging" of criminal activities to catch specific persons) that may be very effective, may at times acquire sufficient political support and may even be considered appropriate by large parts of the population, but conflict with basic legal principles such as privacy and freedom. In the institutionalist perspective, it is the role of the evaluator to address all four questions and identify possible discrepancies or conflicts, not to cast a final judgment based on these questions on the success or failure of policy. As such, the evaluator does justice to the multiple (institutional) rationality that characterizes policy.

6.4 Utilization of evaluation studies

Although evaluation is a key element of the policy process, this does not mean that evaluation studies will always be used. Sometimes evaluation studies are ignored, for instance when they bring an unwelcome message or when the political timing is not right. In fact, sometimes the establishment of an evaluation committee can even be interpreted as an effort to cool down political debate and, for the time being, remove a contested topic from the political agenda. But it is also possible that the publication of an evaluation study opens a window of opportunity and provides a key incentive for policy change. Take for instance the 9/11 Commission whose report triggered debate not just in the US but all over the world. Whereas in the next chapter we will deal with the topic of policy change, in this section we will look at the dissemination and utilization of evaluation studies, as a factor that could later potentially contribute to policy change.

Discussing the impact of evaluation studies speaks to a broader body of literature on how knowledge and expertise, such as in evaluation reports but also in academic research, advisory reports and expert committees, make their way into the policy process (Lester and Wilds, 1990; Jasanoff, 1995; Oh and Rich, 1996; Rich, 1997; Shulba and Cousins, 1997; Gieryn, 1999; Hoppe, 2005; Halffman, 2003; Scholten, 2011). This literature makes clear that there is very little consensus on how and why knowledge does impact policy in one situation and not in another. In fact, the term "impact" has become very contested in this literature, as it is very difficult to prove that "knowledge" or "information" has a specific "impact" or "influence." For instance, even for the 9/11 Commission, it could also be that the changes in policies for intelligence agencies such as the CIA and FBI would have been taken also without this committee report, or perhaps these changes were already considered before the committee began but then only formulated more precisely and authoritatively by the committee. The reality of impact of knowledge is often "*ambiguous, amorphus, incremental and meandering*" (Webber, 1991:15).

Therefore, rather than speaking of "impact" or "influence" there is a preference for "knowledge utilization", which can be much more clearly defined, operationalized and studied (Rich, 1997; Boswell, 2009). This allows for a more empirical study of who utilizes knowledge and in what way knowledge is utilized. For instance, how is the relation between knowledge producer (such as the evaluator) and knowledge utilizer (for instance a government agency) organized? And in what way is knowledge being utilized, for instance in the context of setting a concern on the agenda, formulating policy alternatives, or perhaps rather for symbolic purposes such as supporting a specific policy argument or legitimizing someone's position in a specific policy field?

Models of research–policy relations

In the literature, a distinction is made between different models of the relationship between knowledge producer and knowledge utilizer. Some of these models relate more closely to the rational perspective that prescribes a direct linear relationship between producer and utilizer of knowledge, whereas others see this relationship as a more interactive one. Hoppe (2005) has distinguished several ideal typical research–policy relationships, which can be fruitfully applied to evaluation studies as well. The four types differ on two dimensions. First, whether there is a primacy of research or policy in the mutual relationship. For instance, do political actors have primacy in determining evaluation questions and addressing (or suppressing) issues to be evaluated in the first place, or do researchers have primacy in determining their research agenda as well as the approach used in the evaluation study. Second, whether there is a clear differentiation of roles between researcher and policy maker. Jasanoff (1990) and Gieryn (1999) refer to this second

Table 6.1 Overview of models of research–policy relations

		Relative primacy	
		Primacy of research	Primacy of policy
Differentiation of roles	Sharp boundaries	Enlightenment	Bureaucracy
	Diffuse boundaries	Technocracy	Engineering

Source: Hoppe, 2011.

dimension in terms of "boundary work"; whether there are clear defined boundaries between science and politics, or whether the roles of both realms converge and intertwine. This leads to the definition of four models: enlightenment, technocracy, bureaucracy and engineering model.

In the *enlightenment model* the researcher, or evaluator, stays at a distance from the policy realm. The evaluator, or the agency of which he or she is part, determines what is evaluated, when, how and why. This can be for instance out of professional or academic interest, not necessarily connected to any policy purpose per se. For instance, when associations of doctors decide to evaluate euthanasia practices out of a professional interest in gaining more knowledge about application and to preserve the integrity of the profession. It can also be out of a desire to trigger broader attention to a specific concern, and put an issue on the societal agenda. Think for example of early evaluation studies of experiments with fracking, or the extraction of gas and oil from natural shales, which eventually put fracking centrally on the political agenda as an alternative to conventional energy sources. This enlightenment model puts most emphasis on the "push" factor of knowledge as a source of new ideas and insights that may (or may not) make their way into the policy process (Hanney et al., 2003). Often, if knowledge makes its way into policy at all, this will be done in a rather indirect way, which has been described by Weiss (1980) as the "knowledge creep." Whether knowledge "creeps" into the policy process often depends on a variety of factors, including timing, framing, venues of dissemination, and so on.

This indirect relationship between producer and utilizer of knowledge is a key difference with another model, the technocratic model. In this model, there is a very direct relationship between producers and utilizers of knowledge. In fact, in radical models of technocracy, the knowledge producer takes over the seat of the policy makers. Here, evaluation studies are to have a clear policy orientation and to provide concrete lessons and recommendations to policy. The researcher, or evaluator, maintains primacy in this relationship. This usually leads to a rather technical and depoliticized conception of the mutual relation. Policies are in this model often directly founded on knowledge or expert advice. Some countries, like the UK in particular, have developed an institutional practice of establishing high level committees in which experts come together to jointly shape policies. For instance, after the terrorist attacks in London in 2005, a high-level Committee on Integration and Cohesion was established that was to provide the building blocks for a new approach toward integration and against radicalization.

In a third model there is primacy for policy in the mutual relationship, which often means that actors from the policy and political fields will determine what is being evaluated, when, how and why. In the bureaucratic model, this relative primacy is associated with a clear separation of roles. This means that the knowledge producer produces knowledge "on demand" and does absolutely no more than just provide knowledge, so without any policy orientation per se. For instance, many governments have established statistical agencies for providing data on economic performance and clear societal trends; this provides input in the broader policy process, based on which policy makers can take policy decisions. An evaluation study, in this model, is to provide information into the policy process to allow policy makers to take actions wherever they are needed, rather than bringing policy alternatives in itself.

Finally, in the engineering model, policy also has primacy but the roles between research and policy are more convergent than in the bureaucratic model. Knowledge or research in this model provides a marketplace full of ideas and policy-relevant suggestions from which policy makers can happily select and choose. In this sense, policy makers can select from the marketplace of research to support the design or engineering of new policies. This also means that policy makers can choose to ignore an evaluation study if they see fit, or for instance commission an alternative study if the results of the first study are seen as unsatisfactory. In the same way, actors that oppose a policy status quo may be eager to use critical evaluation studies and take them as a starting point for demands for change. Consequently, the engineering model carries an important risk of research being used as "ammunition" in the broader political process. This also brings us to the patterns of knowledge utilization that may follow out of these models of research–policy relations.

Patterns of knowledge utilization

Besides the relation between knowledge producer and utilizer, a distinction can also be made between different patterns of knowledge utilization. The form of utilization that is most commonly referred to, but perhaps not always equally manifest in practice, is instrumental knowledge utilization. This

involves direct forms of using knowledge, such as the findings of an evaluation committee, for filling gaps of knowledge in a policy theory and designing
specific policy initiatives. According to Boswell (2009), such instrumental
knowledge utilization is most likely when the actors involved also recognize
uncertainty and the need for knowledge to enhance their functioning. It is
this type of knowledge utilization that is assumed in the technocratic and
bureaucratic types in particular.

In contrast, Boswell (2009) describes two kinds of *symbolic knowledge
utilization*. In both modes it is the symbolic meaning of knowledge that is
being put to purpose rather than the actual knowledge at an epistemological
level itself. One mode of symbolic knowledge utilization refers to the sub-
stantiation of specific policy (or organizational) discourses with reference
to knowledge and expertise. Here it is the symbolic meaning of research that
supports policy programs or discourses that have already been developed,
rather than being utilized to design or develop these programs per se. For
instance, an often found form of symbolic knowledge utilization is when
policy makers selectively pick and choose those elements from an evaluation report that support their policies and help them defer pressure to policy
change, while ignoring possibly more critical elements. In another form of
symbolic knowledge utilization research is utilized primarily to legitimize the
involvement of a specific actor or institution in a policy field. Whereas in substantiating knowledge utilization it is still the narrative of an evaluation study
that supports a specific policy, in the legitimizing form it is the mere fact of
(letting do) research that boosts the authority of an actor or institution.

Finally, there is also the possibility of *non-utilization of knowledge*. In fact,
there is so much research, and there are so many evaluations done by so many
different institutions, that non-utilization is almost unavoidable. Sometimes
non-utilization involves an unwelcome message from an evaluation study
that is consciously being ignored. However, non-utilization can just as well be
a consequence of misplaced timing of a report (after the closing of a window
of opportunity) or a lack of knowledge or understanding of a report (for
instance when a report is too technical to be understood or when it is simply
not sufficiently disseminated).

6.5   Evaluation as a form of accountability

The importance of evaluation does not just involve its role in policy change
and policy learning. Evaluation also has an important function in terms of
(public) accountability. It provides a means for holding policy actors (not
just governments) accountable for their policies and the effects that they

have achieved. Accountability is closely related to responsibility. When an actor, such as a minister or a mayor, is responsible for a specific policy, it is a basic democratic principle to be publicly held accountable for his or her actions, efforts, achievements and consequences (or a lack thereof). Being held accountable has a legal as well as a political and social dimension. A minister can be held responsible in a legal sense, for instance when policies violate specific legal principles. However, in a democracy accountability also has a political and a social dimension. Even if a policy meets all legal requirements, democratic institutions such as parliaments can still hold ministers accountable in a political sense, and dismiss a minister if political reality dictates so. In a mediatized world, social accountability has been gaining increased importance as well.

Evaluation can be an important means for holding officials accountable. In a technical sense, it provides a method for objectifying policy input, output and outcomes. Sometimes, this can also have legal or political implications, for instance if an evaluation reveals any unlawful activities or if it captures media attention. The independence of an evaluation matters significantly in terms of accountability. If an evaluation is perceived as not fully independent, it will not be considered legitimate material for accountability in a legal or political sense. This independence not only involves the use of objective methods of evaluation, but also the biographies and networks of the persons involved in the evaluation, and the leadership over establishing and formulating an evaluation study in the first place. Remember for instance how the 9/11 Commission became contested in media controversies on personal connections of one of the members with a law firm and on the appointment of a former minister that was supposedly involved in the policies that the commission was now to evaluate (this minister, Henry Kissinger, stepped down after a couple of weeks).

As a clear manifestation of how evaluation contributes to accountability, many democracies have procedures for the establishment of special commissions in cases where parliament considers further investigation is required. Sometimes this involves formal parliamentary inquiries where a committee is established that has formal competencies to interrogate persons under oath. Sometimes it involves more informal commissions without such formal competencies, but whose political impact can nonetheless be very significant as well. Whereas the formal commissions are often composed of members of parliament, the more informal commissions can be composed of various actors (such as the UK practice of establishing high-level committees with experts from various parts of society). To strengthen democratic control, such commissions often combine the two purposes of evaluation: promoting

---

BOX 6.4

THE IMPEACHMENT PROCESS OF BILL CLINTON

In a democracy, everyone can be held accountable, even the highest executive powers. Therefore, many democracies have enshrined into their constitutions a special procedure for cases where presidents or prime ministers are to be held accountable. These are referred to as "impeachment" procedures. In most cases, such procedures give parliament the right to initiate an impeachment procedure, call for an investigation or hearing, and remove (impeach) an official from office (often after a vote, and often requiring a two-thirds majority).

One of the most recent and well-known impeachment cases concerned the former US president Bill Clinton. The US House of Representatives had initiated an impeachment procedure in 1998 because of perjury and obstruction of justice around a case of sexual harassment (Paula Jones) and a case of sexual relations with a former White House intern (Monica Lewinsky). This led to very lively debates in the House as well as in the Senate, and created an immense media hype in which the tiniest details of Bill Clinton's personal life were exposed. The Senate in the end acquitted Bill Clinton, as it did not manage the two-thirds majority required for impeachment, which was attained in the House of Representatives (as a clear example of the political nature of evaluation). However, in a political sense, Clinton's reputation had been ruined, something that would haunt the Clinton family until the plans by Hillary Clinton to run for Presidential office.

---

learning and strengthening accountability. Perhaps the ultimate form of accountability involves the so-called impeachment procedure where a president or prime minister can be held accountable (see Box 6.4).

Accountability is in many cases connected to the concept of responsibility (Bovens and 't Hart, 1995). This applies in particular to cases where an evaluation study shows that a specific "norm" has been violated. This can be in the form of a direct conclusion of an evaluation study (that also assessed the normative dimension of policy, so not the rationalist approach to evaluation), or when in the public interpretation of the evaluation study the conclusion is drawn that a norm has been violated. In such cases, the debate can move on to who is responsible for this norm violation, and who is responsible for the consequences. This can involve economic consequences, as well as personal consequences (such as loss of life due to police intervention), ecological consequences or political-administrative consequences (such as decrease of trust in public office).

Responsibility can be conceptualized in different ways. A distinction can be made between active and passive responsibility (Bovens, 1990:34-35). Passive responsibility refers to those cases where someone is held accountable *ex post* for something that may have happened as a consequence of specific policies. For instance, referring to the 9/11 Commission, passive responsibility was assessed for the fact that US intelligence agencies had been unable to spot terrorists that enjoyed flight training in the US and airport security services that had been unable to stop the terrorists from boarding planes. In a political sense, such passive forms of responsibility are often indirect, for instance when a Minister of Justice is held responsible for any activities by agencies that fall under this Minister's formal responsibility. Active responsibility refers to whether someone has made sufficient effort *ex ante* to prevent a certain situation from occurring. For the example of the 9/11 Commission, this refers to whether the CIA and FBI were sufficiently aware of the risk of terrorist attacks, and whether at airports sufficient safety structures and adequate protocols were in place in case suspected terrorists wanted to board a plane.

Furthermore, a distinction should be made between five different forms of (active or passive) responsibility (Bovens, 1990). First of all, responsibility as *cause*. Here responsibility means that a specific action (or absence thereof) is seen as the cause of a situation. For instance, Bill Clinton's "perjury" before the Supreme House was considered a direct cause of the impeachment procedure regarding his presidential office. Sometimes causality can be easily inferred when there is clear political or administrative failure, especially when there is a clear "problem owner" in terms of a specific actor, individual or (part of an) organization. However, in many cases causality may be much more difficult to infer, especially when there is a complex network of actors involved in a specific problem area and when there are clear interdependencies between these actors.

Second, responsibility as *liability*. Here an individual or organization is held accountable for the consequences of specific actions (or the absence thereof). This can involve liability in a legal sense, but also in a moral or a political sense. For instance, the CIA was not considered liable in a legal sense for the 9/11 attacks, but morally and politically it was. However, just as for establishing responsibility as cause, establishing liability is in practice often difficult, especially when a complex network of actors is involved in a policy area. Also, especially when highly technical situations are involved, it can be concluded that although an actor has been the cause of the situation it could not be expected for the actor to be able to foresee the situation at the time in question.

Third, responsibility as *capacity*. This refers to the qualities that are required for bearing responsibility in the first place. For instance, did the CIA have sufficient resources (material and immaterial) to bear responsibility for the terrorist attacks? However, as we have seen earlier, contemporary government is increasingly faced with problems (social and technological) that cannot be controlled; so-called uncontrollable "risks." For instance, the financial and economic crisis that raged at the end of the 2000s could not be controlled by a single government due to the high degree of interdependence between different national economies. Also, in some cases one can plainly speak of political or administrative "misfortune" rather than "failure", especially when faced with a situation that is neither controllable nor foreseeable.

Fourth, responsibility as *task*. Here a coupling is made between tasks, responsibility and competencies. Was it really the task of the CIA to monitor these terrorist preparations, or was this more the task of the FBI?

Finally, responsibility as *virtue*. This goes beyond responsibility in a legal sense, referring more to what extent a person or organization has really taken its formal responsibilities seriously and has been sufficiently aware of the work needed to live up to this responsibility. For instance, was it really fair of the US Executive to expect from the CIA to be able to monitor and control terrorist activities in the US to this extent?

In practice, these different forms of responsibility work in a cumulative way. When an evaluation shows that a person or individual is responsible for the cause of a situation, can be considered liable, had the capacity and also the task to prevent the situation and can also normatively be held responsible, then consequences in terms of being held accountable will be unavertable. However, it may be very difficult to infer responsibility on all five counts, especially as contemporary governments are increasingly faced with complex or "wicked" policy problems.

At the same time, politicization and mediatization have increased the use of evaluation studies for public accountability of individuals and organizations. On the one hand, politicization has increased the use of democratic fora such as parliament, but also parliamentary commissions and inquiries, for evaluation and accountability. On the other hand, we see that accountability is increasingly taking place in broader society. The media plays a key role in this respect, as well as the Internet (and so-called new media). More than ever, old and new media make accountability a public process. Anyone can now have access to and participate in debates on evaluation reports, and mobilize to hold someone or some organization accountable. Increasingly, such public accountability does not only involve "top-down" initiatives from established organizations but also mobilizations "from below" where (self) organizations of emancipated citizens call for more accountability. Consider for instance how in the US, after various incidents with police violence regarding black Americans, spontaneous mobilizations of (white and black) citizens called successfully for more accountability for lack of diversity within the police organization.

6.6 CHAPTER SUMMARY

This chapter discussed a facet of the policy process that has become increasingly prominent: evaluation. It shows how evaluation can be done in various ways and can have different implications. The chapter calls for caution in evaluating policies plainly in terms of success or failure. It is questionable whether there are objectifiable methods for inferring success or failure. There can be many criteria for evaluation, including effectiveness, efficiency, consistency, feasibility, support, legality, legitimacy and learning capacity. In practice, evaluation methods can be contested and the interpretation of evaluation results can vary strongly between different actors. In the end the definition of policy success or failure is part of political judgment. Therefore, this chapter has also elaborated political, culturalist and institutionalist perspectives on policy evaluation, providing the evaluator with a more differentiated set of evaluation methods and tools.

In spite of the inherent limitations to objective or "rationalist" evaluation, the role of evaluation in the policy process has become increasingly prominent. Partly, this is a consequence of politicization and mediatization which have made evaluation and accountability increasingly public. Whereas until not long ago, evaluation was something done within relatively narrow and closed political and administrative circles, nowadays it takes place in the open in broader society. This speaks to a broader trend in the "shift of politics" from political arenas in the narrow sense to broader society including old and new media, NGOs and innovative new ways of citizen engagement and mobilization with contemporary policies.

However, the growing manifestation of evaluation also raises questions about whether this has helped improve policies. In this chapter we have already seen that evaluation studies can be utilized in different ways, including symbolic as well as instrumental forms of utilization. In the next chapter we will turn our attention to whether the output of evaluation is also used for policy learning; is learning an outcome of evaluation? And what other sources are there of policy learning?

7

Policy dynamics: learning, change and innovation

LEARNING OBJECTIVES

After reading this chapter you should be able to:

- Define policy learning and appreciate the complexity of the relation between *policy learning* and *policy change*.

- Recognize and identify different sorts of *policy dynamics*, and recognize the complexity of factors that contribute to policy dynamics.

- Compare and apply the different theoretical perspectives (rationalism, culturalism, institutionalism, political perspective) to *policy dynamics*.

- Define *policy innovation* and appreciate the factors that lead to or impede policy innovation.

7.1   Introduction

Policies are dynamic. Even when there are no observable changes, forces have to be at work to keep a policy in place, and to defend it wherever necessary against challenges. Sometimes policies change in a big bang, usually associated with a great extent of political and media controversy. Sometimes they change only very gradually, accommodating lessons and experiences to refine policies rather than to adopt an entirely different policy approach. A thorough understanding of what changes policies therefore goes hand-in-hand with a thorough understanding of what keeps them in place.

Such policy dynamics can be driven by a variety of factors. Learning is only one of them. Indeed, under specific circumstances policies can indeed change in response to the availability of new knowledge, information and experiences, for instance formulated in an evaluation study. However, change may also be politically driven, for instance when there is a political shift of power. Or driven by changes in the public framing of a problem, for instance due to media reporting. Or it may be driven by developments in the institutional context, such as macro-institutional developments as government retrench-ment or spin-offs from other policy areas.

These factors often blend in concrete cases. Take for instance climate adapta-tion as a process of policy change. Here we can clearly see that the availabil-ity of knowledge and information per se is not sufficient for policy change. The Nobel-prize winning Intergovernmental Panel on Climate Change (IPCC), whose work has also been brought to the broader public with Al Gore's movie *An Inconvenient Truth*, made an unprecedented effort to bring together data and research on climate change. Also, it managed to put climate change on the public agenda with the help of Al Gore. Nonetheless, in many countries political and institutional constraints were in place that restricted opportunities for adequate policy responses. Furthermore, when a global financial and economic crisis broke loose in the late 2000s, attention to climate change diminished again. In contrast, in places where incidents took place, such as the flooding due to Hurricane Sandy in New York in 2012, policy changes for dealing with the consequences of climate change were much swifter. Clearly, there is much more at play in policy dynamics than policy learning.

Furthermore, policy change does not necessarily mean that better policies are being produced, in terms of being more effective, efficient or more legiti-mate. This means that policy change, or policy learning, cannot be equated with "policy innovation." Especially in the private sector there has been a strong trend toward innovation in open networks. This idea has recently also emerged in the public sector, referring to "social innovation." However, to many critics there is a contradiction between the idea of innovation and the logic of the public sector. Is there a way for the public sector to engage in and organize "social innovation"?

Explaining policy dynamics has been at the heart of the policy sciences lit-erature. Several policy theories have emerged that provide accounts for why policy changes as well as for why (most of the time) policies remain stable. These include widely used theories such as the Multiple Streams approach developed by Kingdon (1984), the Advocacy Coalition Framework developed by Sabatier (1988), the punctuated equilibrium framework devel-oped by Baumgartner and Jones (1993, 2005) and the Institutional Analysis and Development framework developed by Ostrom, Gardner and Walker (1994).

These frameworks theorize policy dynamics in a way that embraces various policy stages. Some put most emphasis on the dynamics of agenda setting as an explanation for policy change, others on political struggles in the decision-making stage, or on the feedback effects of policy evaluation on policy formulation. In this sense, policy change should not be seen as a separate or final stage of the policy process; rather it refers to patterns of dynamics in all stages of the policy process.

In section 7.2 we will first conceptualize policy change and policy learning. As core concepts in the policy sciences they have received much attention in the literature, but this has not always benefited a clear conceptualization. A distinction is made between different types of policy dynamics, for which the frameworks then offer specific explanations. Also, very different methodologies are employed for operationalizing and measuring policy dynamics. Policy learning is perhaps an even more contested concept. Whereas the concept is widely used in particularly the rationalist approach for accounting for policy change, other perspectives see much more limited opportunities for policy learning, or even criticize the idea of learning per se. Subsequently, in sections 7.3-7.6 we will discuss how policy learning and dynamics are theorized from the four different perspectives, including the relation between learning and change. For every perspective, we will discuss at least one theoretical framework that accounts for policy dynamics as a process that encompasses all stages of the policy process. Finally, in 7.7 we discuss the concept "policy innovation", and discuss the main theoretical frameworks that account for policy innovation and provide methods and tools for promoting policy innovation.

7.2 Conceptualizing policy dynamics and policy learning

Policy dynamics and learning are at the heart of many heuristic accounts of the policy process. Whereas the following sections deal with the different theoretizations of learning and change in the literature, this section will first offer a discussion of how policy dynamics and learning are conceptualized in the literature.

Policy dynamics

Policy dynamics refers to policy change as well as policy stability. It addresses factors and processes that can lead policies to change as well as that help keep policy in place. In the literature, a distinction is made between "*positive feedback*" that involves processes that increase the tendency of policies to change, and "*negative feedback*" that involves processes that promote stability and help neutralize challenges to the status quo (Baumgartner and Jones 1993). For instance, a key event such as Hurricane Sandy in New York had a catalyzing effect on policy change in the state of New York in terms of flood protection, thus being a source of "positive feedback." On the other hand, the circumstance that many countries did not have budget to spare for climate policies during the global financial economic crisis of the late 2000s can be understood as a source of "negative feedback" preventing policy change and promoting the status quo. As we will see in section 7.6, the institutionalist perspective has made much work out of theorizing how the institutional context of policies often has a dampening effect on policy change, thus leading to what is described as "path-dependency." It is the interplay of positive and negative feedback that eventually determines whether policies change or not. In a given policy area, there will always be actors that advocate change (thus mobilizing positive feedback), and others whose interests are more served by preserving the status quo or who are just not convinced of the need for change (thus mobilizing negative feedback).

When negative feedback is dominant, it can be expected that policy stability is maintained. However, if positive feedback prevails, change can occur. Here, a distinction is made between incremental and non-incremental change. *Incremental policy change* involves relatively gradual and marginal policy adjustments. This involves both a relatively slow pace of change, as well as a relatively low degree of change. For instance, the decision to heighten the dikes in response to Hurricane Sandy should be seen as an incremental policy change, as it does not alter the fundamental ideas behind flood protection and it also does not disrupt the network of stakeholders involved in this field. In contrast, *non-incremental policy change* does disrupt stakeholder networks and challenges the ideas on which a policy is based. Non-incremental change usually involves both rapid change as well as fundamental change. Non-incremental change leads to what is described in the literature as "paradigm shifts", "policy breakthroughs" or "policy punctuations." For instance, the September 11 attacks on the US triggered a non-incremental change or "paradigm shift" in US policies in the areas of defense and international relations.

In practice, the distinction between incremental and non-incremental change may not always be easy to make. Therefore, in a standard work on policy dynamics, Hogwood and Peters (1983) further differentiate between different types of policy dynamics. Some of these types of dynamics are less incremental than others. Hogwood and Peters define four types:

1. *Policy innovation.* This involves "new policy" not just at the level of policy instruments and settings, but also at the fundamental level of policy

ideas. Such new policies can be created in new policy areas that are being developed, for instance when new situations have emerged that ask for policy intervention. However, it can also concern policy areas where a non-incremental change has taken place, where a new paradigm has been adopted, and a new policy has to be developed.

2. *Policy succession.* Succession involves the replacement of one policy by another policy, which is however not entirely new but rather elaborates on policies from the past. There is "change", but this change is a consequence of and is inspired by policies and policy experiences from the past. Fundamental policy ideas are not adjusted, but operationalized and implemented in a different way. For instance, diversity policies have been developed in the past for gender relations in particular, but have gradually absorbed more target groups, such as ethnic and racial minorities, disabled and elderly, all under the banner of a diversity policy.

3. *Policy maintenance.* As a clear example of incrementalism, this type usually involves only secondary adjustments to an established policy. Such adjustments are rather marginal, which also speaks for the budget that is applied and the target groups that are being served.

4. *Policy termination.* This involves the deconstruction of a policy. This can be because it has been so successful that it has become obsolete, but also because it has failed or no longer fits with (new) legal regulations. It depends on the situation whether termination is incremental or non-incremental. In some cases, policies lose relevance in a very gradual way, for instance when the problem that a policy is supposed to address gradually fades. In some cases policy termination is a more sudden process, for instance if legal or political developments demand termination.

Although these types almost give the impression of a succession between types – from innovation, to succession, maintenance and eventually termination – a number of critical observations have to be made in relation to Hogwood and Peters' typology. First of all, they ignore the dynamics behind what we could define as a fifth type: policy stability, or policy stasis. This involves situations where the status quo successfully manages to defend and maintain a policy (even without adjustments) or where there is simply a lack of agreement on the direction that change should take (a stalemate). In some cases this will lead to strategies of keeping a policy under the radar, depoliticization and the prevention of agenda setting (all forms of negative feedback).

Second, even this differentiation between types may be difficult to draw in practice. For instance, institutionalists will doubt whether real policy innovation in the sense that new policy is created without any reference to past policies (which would be policy succession) does ever take place. Furthermore, what one actor will see as policy succession could be seen as policy maintenance by another actor with a different perspective and a different set of interests. Institutionalists have also argued that policy termination is rather unlikely; policies create interests and institutional legacies that tend to ensure their own survival rather than to terminate.

A key question that drives this chapter is how and why these different types of policy dynamics emerge. This also brings us to a second concept that requires further conceptualization: policy learning.

Conceptualizing policy learning

Policy learning should be considered as one of the factors that accounts for policy change. However, it is a very pertinent one, as learning carries in it the promise of improving policies based on knowledge, ideas and experiences. Especially in a rapidly changing societal context that is increasingly characterized by complexity, it is expected that policies not just change but also learn in response to new situations and new experiences in order to adapt and be responsive to this changing context. From a rational perspective, learning is a condition for policies to be (and to remain) efficient and effective. From a political perspective, it can promote support for a policy, whereas from an institutional perspective it is seen as a key factor in institutional survival and in maintaining legitimacy. Finally, from a culturalist perspective, the concept of learning is approached more critically because of its cognitivist bias, but here too ideas of learning are key to understanding how common policy stories can be produced as well as reproduced.

Defining policy learning is very difficult, and contested in the policy science literature (Jolly, 2003:16-19). Learning can but does not necessarily have to lead to policy change; it can strengthen the conviction that a policy should not change, but it can also call for non-incremental policy change. There is some consensus that policy learning has something to do with cognition; it approximates *"puzzling"* rather than "powering." This can involve the way we make sense of policy situations, but also how we make sense of policy tools and methods. There is also some consensus that learning often takes place on the basis of (new) *knowledge, information or experiences*. This can involve knowledge and information brought in by experts, but also so-called lay expertise or experiences from policies in the past or even lessons that can be drawn out of comparisons between different policies. Here it must be observed that in practice learning is a context-dependent process, rooted in specific local (social) practices and networks of actors (Brown and Duguid,

2000). Finally, learning is mostly defined as an *iterative process* that takes place constantly throughout the policy process and often involves much trial and error. Sometimes this involves explicit efforts of policy learning, such as in the context of evaluation studies. Many times it involves more implicit and embedded processes "along the way" during different parts of the policy process (Jolly, 2003:19-20; Heclo, 1974:306; Hall, 1993:278). For instance, street-level bureaucrats also "learn" by acquiring experiences while putting policy into practice, or by exchanging lessons with others.

But who learns? First of all, learning can take place at the individual level. However, it is doubtful whether individual learning can be considered policy learning. Even if an individual adapts his or her policy beliefs, for policy learning to occur this individual must be able to convince sufficient other policy stakeholders as well in order to be able to make a difference. Learning can also take place at the organizational level, for instance contributing to the capacity of an organization to adapt to a changing policy environment and to improve and strengthen its role in a certain policy area (Argyris and Schön, 1978). Also at this organizational level, learning can be about many things; it can be about specific functions of the organization, for instance by means of market research or technological innovation, it can be about human resource management in the organization, about "organizational culture" or about how to respond to external challenges or opportunities. Third, learning can take place at the level of policy sectors, also described as "policy subsystems." For instance, Sabatier (1988) argues that learning can take place at the level of advocacy coalitions that define policies in specific policy sectors. He defines policy learning then as "relatively enduring alterations of thought or behavioural intentions which result from experience and which are concerned with the attainment or revision of policy objectives" (Sabatier, 1988:133).

Furthermore, there can be various degrees of learning, or put differently, different levels at which learning takes place. The social scientist Peter Hall (1993:278) has made a distinction between first, second and third order learning, which has been widely used throughout the social sciences. *First order learning* (Hall, 1993:281) is learning oriented at improving policy instruments. This means that neither the choice of instruments nor the policy targets are at stake, but rather how these instruments are put to practice. For instance, after the September 11 attacks it became evident that although airport security checks are in place, they are often inadequate due to lack of technology to scan luggage, which was addressed by making new scan technology more widely available. Learning at this level is most likely to contribute to "policy maintenance."

Second order learning involves learning that does address the choice and selection of policy instruments, while not discussing the fundamental policy aims and priorities. For instance, new instruments are adopted to achieve a specific policy aim, or previous instruments are abandoned. For instance, after the September 11 attacks, new instruments were added to airport security control as well, including new regulations concerning hand luggage (no liquids!). Second order learning is most likely to contribute to "policy succession."

Finally, *third order learning* does put the aims and priorities of policies at stake. This involves learning at the level of policy paradigms, or as Sabatier (1988) describes it, policy beliefs. This involves a fundamental reconsideration of how the policy problem is defined, what policy theory should be employed, what the role of policy could and should be and what actors should be involved. This also means that third order learning is likely to affect the roles and positions of actors involved in the policy as well, thus challenging the status quo. Furthermore, when policy ideas change, it is highly likely that policy instruments will change as well. When learning takes place at this level, it is most likely to contribute to policy innovation or policy termination, in both cases most likely involving non-incremental policy change.

Whereas there is relatively little debate that first and second order learning occur relatively often, there is considerable debate whether and under what conditions third order learning takes place. On the one hand there are scholars who believe that such fundamental policy changes will always be triggered by external events and breakthroughs rather than by learning by involved actors themselves (Sabatier 1998). On the other hand, there are scholars (Schon and Rein 1994) who believe that under the right conditions, third order learning can take place, for instance in the form of "critical frame reflection."

To develop a better understanding of how and why different kinds of learning appear to take place under specific circumstances, Dunlop and Radaelli (2013) have developed a typology that connects types of learning to two key factors. First, problem tractability, or the level of uncertainty that is involved in a specific policy issue. This relates to the distinction between types of public problems that has been discussed in Chapter 1 and links to the levels of learning distinguished by Hall. If a problem is intractable, uncertainty is high, and learning is likely to take place at a higher level (second/third order). If a problem is relatively tractable and well structured, uncertainty is low, and learning is likely to take place a lower level (first/second order). Second, Dunlop and Radaelli address the actors involved in the learning process:

BOX 7.1

POWERING AND PUZZLING

In a standard work on policy change, Heclo (1974) distinguishes "powering" and "puzzling" as two alternative sources of policy dynamics. Powering refers not only to the political logic of decision-making, but also to the interest-driven nature of policy making, with actors competing for resources. At the time of Heclo's writing, there was still a dominant preoccupation in policy literature with political decision-making. The field of policy sciences and public policy studies had only just started to emerge. Heclo contrasts "powering" to "puzzling", or "policy making as a form of collective puzzlement on society's behalf."

In a study of social politics in the UK and in Sweden, Heclo showed that policy change sometimes resulted from trial-and-error learning by policy experiments, or by the deliberate effort to collect a better understanding of problem causes and policy interventions. Especially in the context of a broad consensus in the 1970s about Keynesian economic policies and about the social function of welfare states, Heclo revealed that many aspects of social policy making in the UK and Sweden were not political at all, but involved an informed and sometimes almost technical quest for solving public problems.

A lot has changed since Heclo's times. The Keynesian consensus has collapsed, welfare state policies have been transformed, and politics has gained rather than lost importance as the key arena for public policy making. However, Heclo's distinction between powering and puzzling remains a very useful heuristic for understanding that learning, or "puzzling", can be an important source of policy dynamics. But it also shows that learning is rarely the only source of policy dynamics.

---

what kind of actors are promoting the learning process? Sometimes learning involves highly certified actors, such as experts, authoritative advisory bodies and think tanks, or others that enjoy a certain legitimacy and authority derived from their institutional roles. Sometimes learning takes place in a very open environment in which many different sorts of actors participate, also including NGOs, social movements, lay expertise, lobby organizations and so on. Whereas in the former case the level of certification of actors is high, in the latter case the level of certification is low or of no relevance at all to the learning process.

Combining these two dimensions (problem tractability and certification of actors), leads to the definition of four "ideal types" of policy learning (Figure 7.1). First, *reflexive learning* involves an open process of learning where fundamental policy ideas are discussed (first/second order learning). This can involve for instance interactive or deliberative modes of learning where multiple types of actors engage in critical dialogues, or experimental

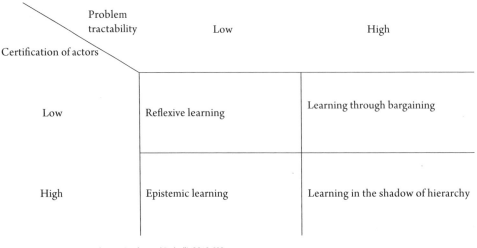

Source: Dunlop and Radaelli, 2013:603.

Figure 7.1 Typology of policy learning

and trial and error modes of learning when fully new policies are at stake. Second, *epistemic learning* also addresses fundamental policy ideas, but here the learning is promoted by certified actors such as experts or advisory bodies. This type of learning speaks closely to the role of knowledge elites or "epistemic communities" that will be discussed in more detail later. Also when problem tractability is high, learning will take place, but often at Hall's first and second order rather than the third order. The third type involves *learning through bargaining*, when tractability is high and multiple actors have access to the learning process. Here knowledge is often used as a strategic source ("ammunition") transferred between actors in processes of political and social interaction ("policy transfer"). Finally, *learning in the shadow of hierarchy* takes place when tractability is high and the certification of actors is also high, for instance in clear bureaucratic settings. In this type of learning, knowledge elites are involved, but politics remains clearly "on top" and the experts "on tap."

This brings us to the following section where the relation between learning and change is discussed in-depth for each of the four different perspectives that have been adopted in this book.

7.3 Rational perspective: learning as the motor of policy change

Knowledge and information are at the core of the policy process in the rational perspective. Therefore, the acquisition of new knowledge and information is also considered the key motor of policy dynamics in this perspective. In an ideal rationalist (or "positivist") world, unhampered by interests, subjective interpretation and institutional legacies, policy dynamics would be a direct response to learning or the organized production and collection of knowledge and information. That is also why this perspective tends to be associated with a technocratic organization of the policy process. Technocracy involves a technical organization of the policy process where knowledge producers take the seat of the policy maker and keep politics out in order to avoid normative bias: "politics spoils good policies."

In current rationalist literature, the "radical" idea of full rationality has been abandoned for a more realistic conceptualization of "bounded rationality" (Simon, 1982; see also Chapters 2 and 4). It is in this mild form that rationalism continues to add significantly to contemporary debates on policy dynamics. In fact, the popularity of the notion "policy learning" as such already shows the continued relevancy of rationalism. A very contemporary "framing" of this rationalist influence involves "evidence-based policy making" (Sanderson, 2002), which we will discuss in more detail later. Another growing body of literature that speaks closely to the ideas of rationalism concerns policy transfer (Dolowitz, 2000). Like rationalism, the policy transfer literature stresses the importance of knowledge and information in policy making, primarily involving lesson drawing from other cases (Rose, 1993).

Incrementalism and the science of muddling through

One modest rationalist who worked out the implications of bounded rationality for policy dynamics was Charles Lindblom (1959). He criticized the idea that knowledge and information could be the single drivers of policy change, as assumed in what he described as the "comprehensive rationalist model." Such a model would ignore the complexity of many policy issues (which has become even more pertinent with the developments since the time of Lindblom's writings), overestimate the capacity to map all policy alternatives and have full information on the consequences of these alternatives, while underestimating the social and political context in which policy making takes place.

Lindblom defines a method of "incrementalism" as a more realistic alternative to the "comprehensive rational model." He describes incrementalism as a "science of muddling through", making clear that a rational "scientific" approach to policy analysis continues to be relevant but will at best only result in small step-by-step changes. Policies are not redesigned all over again once new knowledge and information become available, but rather adjusted by small degrees in the context of bounded rationality but also because of the broader social and political context in which policy change takes place.

Incrementalism takes the shape of "successive limited comparisons" in Lindblom's approach. This means that when policies are changed, knowledge and information is acquired only on marginal policy adjustments; the consideration of fully new policy alternatives (policy innovation) would be unlikely, at least based on knowledge and information. Furthermore, the knowledge and information that is being acquired and the adjustments that are being considered are always incomplete. Often this would happen not so much out of a deliberate choice to ignore alternatives, but rather by accident or ignorance. Lindblom also argues that incrementalism in the form of "trial and error" learning is necessary for gradually improving policies; incrementalism would, in his view, be much better than a "futile attempt at superhuman comprehensiveness" (Lindblom, 1959:85).

Evidence-based policy making and cybernetic learning

Potentially a distant legacy of Lindblom's incrementalism is the contemporary hype of interest in "evidence-based policy making." Although perhaps less used in academic literature on policy analysis, the notion of evidence-based policy making is widely used in policy-oriented research in many European countries. It commonly refers to the relevancy of knowledge of "what works" in the evaluation and subsequent redesign of policies (Sanderson, 2002). With reference to the policy cycle heuristic, it emphasizes the importance of (*ex ante* and *ex post*) evaluation in order to acquire the necessary knowledge and information to improve policies; in order for the policy cycle to be rationalist, the evaluation stage has to feed back into the agenda setting and policy formulation stages. As a model of policy dynamics, evidence policy making therefore assumes a constant testing, monitoring, evaluation and adjustment of policies. Like in Lindblom's approach, such constant collection of evidence and policy adjustment in response to evidence is likely to lead to incremental rather than non-incremental policy changes.

Although there are very different interpretations of what constitutes "evidence-based policy making", three characteristics seem to stand out. First of all, the belief that acquiring knowledge of what works and why it works is not only important for solving policy problems in increasingly complex

---

BOX 7.2

POLICY ANALYSIS COMES OF AGE (RADIN, 2000)

In a standard work on the transformation of the role of policy analysis (*Policy Analysis Comes of Age: Beyond Machiavelli*), Radin (2000) argues that the simple image of policy analysis as an advisor to the ruler, as in Machiavellian times, is outdone by the complexity of contemporary society. However, this does not mean that policy analysis is any less relevant than before; rather, she argues that policy analysis has diversified and has become used more widespread in policy processes.

There are several reasons why, according to Radin, policy analysis "has come of age." One is that policy making and decision-making in contemporary society have become much more complex, involving many more actors than the idea of a single ruler in need of advice. Also, even if objectivity and scientific method are still pursued, there is political contestation over appropriate methods and there is an overload of information. Furthermore, policy making has become much more politicized, with multiple coalitions competing for influence, which has increased rather than decreased the demand for policy analysis.

In this more complex policy setting, policy analysis nowadays plays various roles (which Radin illustrates by various fictitious cases). Sometimes policy analysts "measure", for instance when making monitors or evaluations reports to be used by actors in the policy making process. Sometimes they provide descriptions that help actors and coalitions define their positions, for instance by writing briefings, state-of-the-art problem scans, fact-scans or fact-checks, and so on. And sometimes they provide "judgments", for instance by making process evaluations that allow actors to improve their performance or by providing normative advice to actors and coalitions as to how they should take appropriate action.

This diversification of policy analysis involves an expansion of its role that should, according to Radin, also be reflected in policy analysis training. Besides objective methods of policy analysis, policy analysts should be trained in a variety of methods, but also in political analysis, in techniques of advising and "lobbying", in techniques of presentation and reporting, and so on.

---

social systems, but also for accountability and legitimacy of policies. The public expects policies to "work" and therefore expects policy makers to do their best to make policy decisions based on available knowledge and information, to monitor and evaluate their policies and to prove to the public that policies did indeed make a difference. Second, evidence-based policy making is associated with an apolitical and sometimes even pragmatic or trial and error approach to policy change. Evidence-based policy making rarely seems to address the level of policy beliefs, or what we have described as "third order learning." Third, the popularity of evidence-based policy making is also associated with a revival of interest in (positivist) research and evaluation methods, emphasizing validity and reliability of quantitative methods. This also involves the exploration of relatively new methods such as policy piloting and experimentation, or the testing of policy alternatives as a form of *ex ante* evaluation.

In terms of policy learning, evidence-based policy making speaks closely to the notion of *"cybernetic learning."* This refers to learning within a specific system (such as a policy field) or an organization (such as a policy department) by means of building feedback mechanisms that monitor the efforts made by specific actors (input) as well as the contribution to achieving the policy goals (in terms of output and outcomes) (Jolly, 2003:24). These feedback mechanisms allow policy makers to pinpoint problems or errors and to make corrections wherever required, in order to make sure that the original goals are achieved. This can be compared to a dashboard on which policy makers can measure and monitor relevant information from within the system or organization, based on which they can decide to take action wherever appropriate. In practice, such cybernetic feedback mechanisms may work out less ideally, for instance when there is a lack of clear indicators, when measurement tools fail, or when communication of measurements is distorted (compare with a faulty dashboard or a dashboard that is unreadable or simply not understandable to the policy maker).

In this cybernetic approach, a distinction is made between two levels of learning, each involving different feedback mechanisms. The first level is described as *"single loop learning."* This involves the most simple feedback mechanism where policy results (output and outcomes) are measured in relation to policy aims. When a discrepancy is observed, interventions or instruments are improved or new instruments are developed in order to make sure the original goals are achieved after all. For instance, more resources (manpower, budget) are made available, or implementation manuals are refined, or mechanisms for control are enhanced. Each of these involves learning of the second and the first order at most.

Second, *"double loop learning"* also includes a feedback mechanism to adjust the goals and norms wherever necessary. This involves "third order learning", where policy assumptions are put at stake and adjusted, for instance in cases where new information has led to the definition of different norms or to a different problem understanding (Argyris and Schön, 1978).

The rationalism of policy transfer

Finally, another strand of literature that bears traces of the rationalist approach and has been receiving growing attention in contemporary policy sciences concerns policy transfer or policy diffusion. Policy transfer involves a mode of policy learning by social interaction and comparison. It involves the "travel" of policy ideas, programs or experiences from one setting to another. Dolowitz and Marsh (2000: 5) define policy transfer as "a process by which knowledge about policies, administrative arrangements, institutions and ideas in one political system (past or present) is used in the development of policies, administrative arrangements, institutions and ideas in another political system."

Although policy transfer in itself cannot be considered a new phenomenon, the relevancy of transfer has increased in contemporary society. In the context of globalization and internationalization, many more interdependencies have emerged bringing about more intensive contacts and relations between nations across the globe. This has strongly increased opportunities for policy transfer. Furthermore, technological advancement facilitates policy transfer as well. The Internet and new communication technologies, including new media, have provided new opportunities for exploring policy alternatives and for communication as a means for policy transfer.

Policy transfer comes in very different forms. First, a distinction can be made between coercive and voluntary transfer. Coercive transfer refers to those cases where the transposition of a specific policy is a requirement, such as was the case for many Central and Eastern European countries that joined the European Union in the 2000s and had to implement the so-called "acquis communautaire". Voluntary transfer can also be described as lesson drawing. Second, what is transferred can differ as well. In some cases policies are transferred, such as the transfer of anti-discrimination law from the UK and the Netherlands to the European Union. However, in many cases, transfer involves specific policy programs, such as tools for monitoring compliancy to anti-discrimination policies, or policy experiences in a broader sense, such as the experience of "naming and shaming" by revealing the results of diversity policies by major businesses can be an even more effective tool for policy coordination than legal regulation of diversity policies. There are also multiple possibilities regarding who is involved in transfer and at what level transfer takes place. In some cases, transfer takes place between nations, but it can also take place between organizations, or between cities even when in different countries.

There can also be various degrees of policy transfer. Sometimes, a whole policy or policy program is "copied." However, such copying is rare, although again the EU enlargement provides a clear example where copying did take place on a large scale. Often, there will be institutional constraints that inhibit copying, or policies may be too complex to "travel" from one setting to another. More common is what Dolowitz and Marsh (2000) refer to as emulation, where policies are imitated but also adjusted to fit in the new policy setting. For instance, if a country decides to adopt anti-discrimination policies similar to those in the UK and the Netherlands, it may be necessary to adjust this policy to the country-specific legal setting or to the target group constructions that have already been inscribed in related policies. Finally, it is also possible that transfer simply refers to one policy inspiring the development of another. This means for instance that the idea for having anti-discrimination policies inspires another country, but that this country develops in its own way rather than by copying.

However, as Dolowitz and Marsh argue, transfer is not always successful. When a transfer fails for some reason, this may result in policy failure in the borrowing country. For instance, a transfer may have been ill informed, with insufficient knowledge and information on how to best copy or emulate a policy. Or, there can be an incomplete transfer, where some parts have been transferred but precisely those aspects that made a policy a success have not been transferred. Finally, sometimes a transfer may turn out to have been inappropriate, for instance when the transferred policy does not fit in the context of the borrowing country.

7.4 Political perspective: between powering and puzzling

Whereas the rational perspective emphasizes the role of knowledge, information and experiences as motors of policy dynamics, the political perspective emphasizes the role of power, interests and conflict. Heclo (1974) created a famous dichotomy between "puzzling" and "powering", with the political perspective concerned primarily with the second one. In his study of pension reform in Sweden, Heclo showed that the availability of new knowledge and information, or "puzzling", is neither a necessary nor a sufficient condition for policy change. Other factors are at play, such as interest-driven actors that compete for influence and opportunities to change policies in accordance with their beliefs and interests. In this competition or conflict for influence, resources play a key role; such as what actor has the most (formal) decision power, what financial resources an actor has available, but also immaterial resources such as authority, manpower and even time can play a role.

Although widely used, Heclo's dichotomy is hard to apply in practice. The distinction between puzzling and powering is very difficult to make, as both are closely intertwined. For instance, knowledge is also power; having information and expertise can give an actor more authority and more say in policy dynamics. Also, actors often act not simply based on their interests, but based on what they perceive and believe to be their interests. In practice, rather than a dichotomy, there seems to be an interplay of powering and puzzling. A key question then is how and why does powering or puzzling, or framed differently "policy learning," get the upper hand in policy dynamics in specific cases?

Learning in the Advocacy Coalition Framework

This brings us to one of the most broadly applied political perspectives on the policy process with a very specific understanding of the role of policy learning in policy dynamics: the Advocacy Coalition Framework developed by Sabatier and Jenkins-Smith. This perspective has already been introduced in some detail, when we introduced the notion of "*policy subsystems*," which involve relatively demarcated networks of actors operating in relation to a specific policy topic. In the view of ACF, this subsystem level is particularly important for understanding both learning and change, as we will see below. Furthermore, we introduced the notion of "*advocacy coalitions*", or actors who share specific policy ideas or "beliefs" and share resources (material as well as immaterial) in efforts to achieve those beliefs. We learnt that agenda setting involved a struggle between advocacy coalitions who tried to get an issue from the subsystem level onto the political agenda and advocacy coalitions who were best served by the status quo and tried to prevent agenda setting.

Policy belief systems form the glue that holds together advocacy coalitions, and hold the key for understanding the role of learning in the ACF. A policy belief system includes "value priorities, perceptions of important causal relationships, perceptions of world states (including the magnitude of the problem), and perceptions/assumptions concerning the efficacy of various policy instruments" (Heclo, 1974:99). Sabatier distinguishes several "levels" within policy belief system, which have different implications in terms of the likelihood of policy change and the opportunities for policy learning. At the most fundamental level, the "deep core", a policy belief system involves fundamental beliefs and norms that are highly resistant to change. This includes fundamental beliefs about the relation between state–society–individual, about equality and freedom, and so on. The second level, the "policy core", includes beliefs that are specific to a policy problem or issue, such as the problem definition, causal theories, choice of policy strategies, and so on. Within a policy system, it is this level that binds together an advocacy coalition. Finally, on a third level, there are "secondary aspects" that have a more instrumental character, referring to the choice and setting of instruments and the applications of specific means (such as budget). Often, there can exist differences even within an advocacy coalition on this level.

As an example, in the policy subsystem of migrant incorporation there are often several advocacy coalitions including one around a policy belief system of multiculturalism. On a deep core level, multiculturalism is based on a strong belief in equality and in the need for state intervention to promote and guarantee equality. On this level, actors that adhere to multiculturalism often also tend to advocate equality and an active role of the state in other policy areas such as social policy and education policies. On a policy core level, multiculturalism involves a belief in a group-specific approach to promote the social-cultural emancipation and social-economic participation of specific ethnic, cultural and racial groups. It is this approach that had long been manifest in British race relations policies and in Dutch ethnic minorities policies, and that continues to play a key role in for instance Swedish migrant integration policies. On the level of secondary aspects, multicultural policies often involve support and subsidies for (ethnic, cultural or racial) group organizations, targeted measures in educational policies such as providing more support to schools with many migrant children, and equal treatment measures such as positive discrimination laws.

Opportunities for change and *policy learning* differ strongly between these levels of policy belief systems. Change at the level of deep core beliefs is considered highly unlikely. Sabatier compares this to religious conversion. Largely the same applies to the policy core, which tends to be highly resistant to policy learning as well. According to Sabatier, "coalition members will resist information suggesting that their deep core or policy core beliefs may be invalid and/or unattainable, and they will use formal policy analysis to buttress and elaborate those beliefs (or attack their opponents)" (Sabatier and Jenkins-Smith, 1988:123). A multiculturalist is unlikely to turn into an assimilationist overnight, Learning is considered to play a key role at the level of secondary aspects. Sabatier: "members of various coalitions seek to better understand the world in order to further their policy objectives" (Sabatier and Jenkins-Smith, 1988:123). Consequently, Sabatier defines policy learning as "relatively enduring alterations of thought or behavioural intentions that result from experience and which are concerned with the attainment or revision of the precepts of the belief system of individuals or collectivities such as Advocacy Coalitions" (Sabatier, 1993:42).

Policy learning can thus lead to incremental policy change (or "policy adjustments"), especially on the level of secondary policy aspects. Here the interaction between advocacy coalitions, but also within advocacy coalitions, plays a key role. In confrontation with others, there is a constant quest for information, knowledge and experiences that can help the advocacy to achieve its policy goals. Conflict and competition therefore have an important function in the ACF: they are triggers for advocacy coalitions not to change their beliefs, but to defend and sharpen their understanding of how to best achieve their aims.

Relative policy stability (allowing mostly for incremental policy adjustments rather than fundamental policy change) is further sustained by *relatively stable parameters* that structure a policy subsystem and are unlikely to change easily. For instance, problem parameters such as numbers of migrants present in a country and the public attitudes toward migrants are unlikely to change overnight. Furthermore, generic legal principles (such as a constitution) but also the distribution of resources promote relative stability; the principle of non-discrimination based on religion, sex, color or ethnicity is in many countries included in the constitution and therefore unlikely to change easily.

Non-incremental policy change can occur in the Advocacy Coalition Framework, but is unlikely to be the consequence of policy learning. Rather, Sabatier speaks of the need for external perturbations in order to trigger major policy change. This involves large external changes to a policy subsystem that do change the "balance of power" between advocacy coalitions. This can involve major political or economic events or spin-offs from other policy areas. For instance, a new government (coalition) coming to power may have a tremendous effect on the resources of advocacy coalitions in many policy subsystems. Also, as we have seen with the global financial and economic crisis at the end of the 2000s, a crisis can disturb the balance between advocacy coalitions as well. Following the work of Kingdon (1995), Sabatier also recognizes the opportunity of "trigger" or "focus events", and the opportunity of such events triggering rather sudden "swings" in the public mood. Dramatic events such as the terrorist attacks in New York, Washington, Madrid, London and Paris, especially when strongly mediatized, can trigger sudden changes in a highly unpredictable and unforeseeable way.

Policy analysts can contribute to policy dynamics in the ACF in different ways. A common role of policy analysts is to be part of specific advocacy coalitions, engaging in research and evaluation that lends support to and contributes to the refinement of a policy belief system. This can take the form of research as a form of "political ammunition" (see Chapter 6), but as

---

BOX 7.3

ADVOCACY COALITIONS AND LEARNING; HOW THE HYBRID CAR WAS OBSTRUCTED

Advocacy coalitions can be a source as well as an impediment to policy learning. A clear example of how advocacy coalitions may impede policy learning and policy change is the development of the electric or hybrid car. In the US, car industries have an important economic position, which they developed historically as a key provider of jobs in key areas of the US (such as Detroit). This position is strongly connected with oil companies that produce the fuel that makes these cars run.

This interdependency between car and oil manufacturers created the foundation for an extremely powerful advocacy coalition. This advocacy coalition has been very powerful not only in influencing US industrial policies, but also environmental policies, social policies and even research and innovation. The example of the Ford industry shows how sometimes it was a source of experimentation and innovation, not just in production technologies but also in social policies.

However, the example of the electric and/or hybrid car shows how this advocacy coalition in this case managed to inhibit learning and innovation. Already in the 1990s, technologies for constructing hybrid and electric cars were available. Also, several oil companies and car manufacturers held key patents of parts of this technology. However, they refrained from applying these technologies, presumably to defend the position of the traditional fuel-consuming car business. Eventually, Japanese car manufacturers such as Toyota were first to start mass production of electric and hybrid cars, out of fear that US industries would be ahead of them. In the end, an external perturbation in the form of the global economic crisis and government help to several industries provided an incentive to invest more heavily in mass production of electric and hybrid cars.

---

evaluation contribution to first and second order learning. Sometimes, policy analysts can fulfill the role of policy brokers in between different advocacy coalitions. Here the aim of policy analysis can be to bring together advocacy coalitions, for instance by exploring policy alternatives and instruments that may relate well to different advocacy coalitions. Third, policy analysts can also contribute to what we have described in Chapter 7 as "enlightenment", especially by exploring subsystem parameters or changes in the subsystem environment (such as macropolitical or economic changes, or specific disasters or trigger events). However, as stated clearly by Sabatier, the latter role may have an impact on the shaping of policy belief systems in the longer term, they rarely lead directly to non-incremental policy change (Figure 7.2).

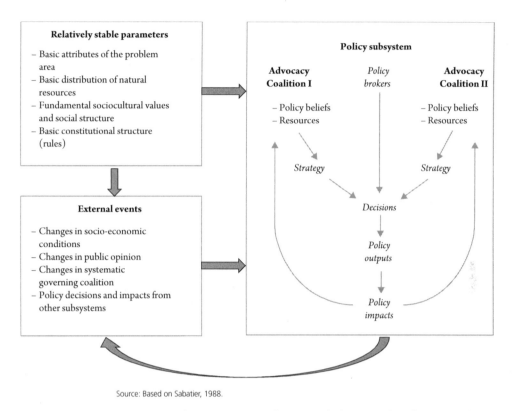

Source: Based on Sabatier, 1988.

Figure 7.2 Schematic overview of conceptual relations in the Advocacy Coalition Framework

7.5 Cultural perspective: epistemic communities, discourses and critical frame reflection

Whereas the political perspective is already rather critical of the opportunities for policy learning, the culturalist perspective largely refrains from using the notion policy learning at all. Learning, especially as originally conceptualized in the rational approach, has a cognitivist connotation, which is rejected or at least nuanced in the culturalist perspective. Rather than speaking of knowledge, culturalists tend to speak of ideas, discourses or beliefs (see also Scholten 2017). Rather than speaking of power and conflict, culturalists tend to look at how ideas persuade and spread and eventually structure the process of policy formulation.

In the culturalist approach, learning is therefore seen as a process of construction, which is an inherently social activity (Brown and Duguid, 2000). Learning involves the development of a shared language, which allows actors to understand each other. This shared language enables actors to create a shared frame of reference for defining specific phenomena and developing a shared interpretation of a situation. This involves a blend of information, knowledge, experiences, thoughts, opinions and interests. The distinction between knowledge and ideas is problematized in the culturalist perspective. So is the distinction between interests and ideas; according to the culturalist perspective, actors often have no objective way of defining their own interests; their interests are what they perceive them to be.

The benefit of learning in the culturalist approach is the social interaction it involves in developing a shared interpretation of a situation. Such a shared interpretation is a necessary basis for collective action, or policy making. Without such social learning, only individual interpretations would remain, leading to relativism and policy stalemate. The interaction that is required for this learning requires that actors meet, engage in creative competition, in which ideas are exchanged, discussed and wherever combined to shape new policy approaches. As we saw earlier, it is this requirement of a free and open exchange between actors that is often criticized from other perspectives as being unrealistic. It demands from actors that they surpass the institutional environments in which they operate and that they are aware of and able to reflect on their own ideas and beliefs. Furthermore, as objected from the political perspective, it requires that the exchange can take place on a level playing field, which in practice can prove hard to achieve.

The culturalist perspective puts much emphasis on plurality, or the multiplicity of ideas in policy fields (or organizations) as a source of creativity and innovation. Here it resembles the political perspective that focuses on the competition between belief systems, but contrasts sharply with the rationalist approach that emphasizes the objectivity of knowledge claims and the institutionalist approach too emphasizes processes of negative and positive feedback. When an organization or policy area allows for a varied range of problem perspectives, definitions and approaches to emerge, a process of creative competition can emerge where new combinations of problem constructs and policy approaches emerge. Such a creative process could lead to what we have defined as third order learning. An often used example in this regard is the virtual Linux community that without a clear "center of command" has evolved through the efforts of many individual members of the community making contributions to the operating system Linux. This learning mechanism is also described as "Given enough eyeballs, all bugs are shallow" (Bekkers, 2000).

This creativity can be a very important and functional source for policy dynamics and innovation as well. How social problems manifest themselves is often also strongly context-dependent. Local circumstances often define policy situations, for instance the presence of specific infrastructures (such as a harbor), a specific demographic or socio-economic composition of the population (in terms of age, education, income, origin, sex) or specific histories of a place. For instance, fighting crime will mean very different things in New York than in Davos, Switzerland. Pluralism can therefore be an important source to create innovation in diverse settings, with actors exchanging ideas and learning from each other (Brown and Duguid, 2000). However, taking a rational perspective on pluralism, this can also come at a cost in terms of efficiency. For instance, whereas centralization can (sometimes) introduce more efficiency or at least cut costs, it can also diminish sources of creativity and opportunities for trial and error learning in specific local settings. For instance, in the context of the global financial and economic crisis of the late 2000s, many nations (including but not limited to Greece) "complained" that European economic and monetary integration had rid them of key opportunities for creative responses to specific local (or national) financial and economic concerns.

In this section, we will discuss three frameworks that can be positioned within the culturalist perspective. Some of them also combine important elements of other perspectives with culturalism. The perspectives share a culturalist understanding of the role of ideas in policy dynamics, but they vary in their perspectives on learning.

Epistemic communities

The epistemic communities approach approximates the rationalist perspective in its emphasis on the role of knowledge and beliefs in the policy process. Furthermore, it borrows elements of the political perspective in its emphasis on knowledge being developed in and propagated by communities, defined as "epistemic communities." However, it rejects the rationalist idea that it is the objectivity of knowledge claims that defines their relevance to policy making. It defines knowledge as "epistemic beliefs" that can persuade and have impact on many different grounds than their "objectivity." This would do more justice to the reality that knowledge is often "uncertain", especially when complex problems are involved. It also discards the political perspective's preoccupation with conflict and competition between advocacy coalitions, emphasizing that there is a great variety of ways in which epistemic communities can acquire and hold on to influence on the decision-making process.

From a culturalist perspective, the epistemic communities approach emphasizes the key role of experts, as unified in epistemic communities, play in the policy process. Haas (1992:3) defines an epistemic community as "a network of professionals with recognized expertise and competence in a particular domain and an authoritative claim to policy-relevant knowledge within that domain or issue-area." This puts much more emphasis on the role of professionals, or the knowledge elite, than the notion of advocacy coalitions. An epistemic community is held together by a "shared set of normative and principled beliefs" and "shared causal beliefs", which can be reasonably compared to Sabatier's deep core and policy core beliefs. Validity has an important meaning in epistemic communities, but in a very different way than for rationalists; epistemic communities have their own notions of validity, which are intersubjectively shared and which contribute to the persuasiveness of epistemic claims. Finally, an epistemic community usually also engages in a "common policy enterprise" (Haas, 1992:3), which can take the form of a shared professional approach to a specific policy issue, or rather in some cases even professional organizations or "think tanks" that can be mobilized to expand an epistemic community's influence.

A much used example of an epistemic community refers to the Keynesian and monetarist epistemic communities in economic and monetary policies. More than objective realities or conflicts between advocacy coalitions, the competition between these two communities involves a struggle between professionals and experts defined by different epistemic beliefs about how the economy could and should be run. The Euro crisis proved that this almost ancient opposition between epistemic communities continues to be relevant. Another example of how epistemic communities contribute to policy dynamics involves the role of experts in the transformation of US foreign and defense policies in the late 1990s. After the end of the Cold War, uncertainty had grown as to where US priorities would lie in these policy areas. An epistemic community emerged with a neo-conservative background that defined the US as a cultural defender of what was described as "western civilization." In a very influential piece (and later in a book), public intellectual Samuel Huntington referred to a "clash of civilizations" that would define US policies, especially when engaging in cultural fault lines such as between the West, China and the Muslim world. In co-operation with think tanks such as the neo-conservative American Enterprise Institute, an epistemic community emerged around this idea of the clash of civilizations that would exert significant influence on US politics, even before the 9/11 attacks in 2001.

According to Haas, epistemic communities do seek influence on the policy process. This does not necessarily involve "learning" of a cognitive kind, but rather that "the claim to truth being advanced must be more persuasive to the dominant political decision makers than some other claims" (Haas, 1992:42). This means that professionals and experts, besides proving the "validity" of their knowledge claims, have to make sure that their knowledge claims are framed in persuasive terms, that experts engage in dialogues with policy makers to disseminate and apply their epistemic beliefs, and that wherever necessary they need to defend their epistemic beliefs when challenged. Idea brokers in this sense not so much broker between different types of ideas, but rather broker between a specific epistemic community and political coalitions. This accounts for the development of, what Fischer (1990) has described as, advocacy think tanks, such as the American Enterprise Institute in the abovementioned example. A successful epistemic community will be able to build an "alliance" with the dominant political coalition, and "monopolize access to strategic decision-making positions."

Learning as critical frame reflection

Another constructivist perspective does allow for learning, if the right conditions are met; the critical frame analysis approach (which was already introduced in some detail in Chapter 3). Critical frame policy analysis has become a very popular approach in the policy sciences, as well as beyond. One of the reasons for its popularity is that it combines a culturalist approach to how policies and policy problems are "framed" with a perspective on how reason or cognition can play a role in changing such frames. Rather than speaking of "learning", the approach speaks of "reflection", or "critical frame reflection."

In Chapter 3 we defined *policy frames* as "underlying structures of belief, perception and appreciation" (Rein and Schön, 1994:23). Consequently, a *frame-shift* constitutes a non-incremental policy change as it alters the fundamental underlying problem perceptions and policy prescriptions. Rein and Schön (1994) believe that learning, or as they define it, critical reflection can be a source of such frame shifts. In fact, they see critical frame reflection as an important strategy for avoiding "the relativist trap", or a radical constructivist interpretation where all meaning is seen as subjective. Critical frame reflection does not involve learning in the sense of addressing the objectivity of claims, but rather addressing the consistency and coherence of frames, the relation between frames and the evidence that should fit the frames, and a critical confrontation of different frames. By engaging in critical frame reflection, Rein and Schön argue that policy actors can "learn in action": "We believe that hope for human reason in the chaotic, conflictual world of policy-making lies in a view of policy rationality that gives a central place to this human capability for reflection 'within the game'" (Rein and Schön, 1994:37-38).

In order to allow for critical frame reflection, specific conditions have to be met. Rein and Schön frame this as *design rationality*. Whether design rationality can be achieved depends on the institutional setting in which frame reflection takes place. Reflection is therefore always "situated." First of all, they posit a "communicative imperative", which means that actors must at least be willing and able to engage in dialogue and to engage in interaction and a free exchange of ideas about how to address a problem situation. Second, actors must be able to "put themselves in the shoes of another", in order to assess potential alternative frames. Third, they must be aware of their own frames, through introspection. Only when aware of your own frame, can an actor critically assess a frame in terms of consistency and coherency. Fourth, and connected to some of the preceding points, actors must also be willing to alter their frame when reflection reveals that this may be necessary. Finally, there must be a certain degree of trust between actors; without trust, a free and equal exchange of ideas becomes impossible. However, as we have already seen in Chapter 7 there has been much criticism as to the extent to which the conditions of design rationality can be met in reality.

However, critical reflection is not the only cause of policy change or "frame-shifts" frame analysis approach. Snow and Benford (1988:198) argue that the development of a shared interpretation and definition of a specific problem situation often involves a process of *frame alignment*. This involves a process of linking between frames in order to create resonance between different frames, thus creating a more broadly shared interpretation of the situation and providing the basis for mobilization or collective action. For instance, in the field of environmental policies, a frame of "sustainable development" emerged through alignment between an economic development and an environmental sustainability frame (see Box 7.4). Such frame alignment can take place in four different ways (also conceptualized as framing strategies). First, "*frame bridging*" involves the linking and merging of two frames into one more broadly shared frame. "*Frame amplification*" involves the "clarification and invigoration" of a specific frame to give it more resonance amongst a broader group, for instance by articulating specific values that have a broader appeal. Third, "*frame extensions*" involve the expansion of a frame by incorporating problem definitions and beliefs of other actors, for instance in the extension of the "diversity frame" from gender to include also religion, ethnicity, culture, disability, sexuality, and so on. Finally, "*frame transformation*" may take place when a frame fails to resonate and needs to be reformulated or "transformed" in order to acquire more support and offer a more adequate interpretation of a problem situation, for instance when the US foreign policy and defense frame from the Cold War period was transformed into a frame that put stress on the "clash of civilizations" and the fight against terrorism.

BOX 7.4

"SUSTAINABLE GROWTH"

One of the processes behind policy change can be frame alignment, which creates more broadly shared and supported frames as a foundation for policy making. An illustration of frame alignment is the development of the "sustainable growth" frame that connects environmental and economic policies. This alignment involved a "bridging" of two frames, one about economic growth and one about environmental protection. The idea of allowing for economic growth only when the environmental consequences are neutral resonates amongst actors from both frames. Thus, "sustainable growth" created a shared language and interpretation that resonated broadly. As a consequence, it provided a more broadly shared foundation for the development of new economic and environmental policies.

Discourse structuration and institutionalization

A third culturalist framework that will be discussed involves a more discursive approach to policy dynamics; the discourse coalition framework (DCF). In contrast to the epistemic communities approach and the frame reflective approach, the DCF puts much less confidence in the role of knowledge and cognition. The DCF sees policy dynamics as evolving around specific policy discourses. A policy discourse is "an ensemble of ideas, concepts and categories through which meaning is given to phenomena" (Hajer and Fisher, 1999:46). Such discourses are supported by what Hajer describes as "discourse coalitions", or "an ensemble of a set of storylines, the actors that utter these story lines and the practices that confirm to these story lines, all organized around a discourse" (Hajer and Fischer, 1999:45). Although there is some similarity here with the notion of advocacy coalition, there are at least two key differences. First, discourse coalitions are held together by language and storylines, rather than by interests and belief systems on a cognitive level. Thus a discourse coalition may involve actors with different interests, but who have been "persuaded" by a discourse. This persuasion does not so much evolve around the objectivity of a discourse, but rather by what Hajer describes as "*discursive affinity*," or the extent to which an actor recognizes and feels familiar with a specific discourse. Second, there does not have to be a clear degree of organization in a discourse coalition. Rather than by shared mobilization and advocacy, a discourse coalition spreads by the diffusion of a specific discourse on a problem situation.

Discourses can change or "shift", but learning is unlikely to be a cause of it (Hajer, 1995). Adopting a distinctly constructivist point of view, Hajer argues that discourses represent such fundamental ways of perceiving reality that actors will rarely be able to make these explicit, reflect upon them and change them. Even if new information emerges, this tends to be "framed" or interpreted through the lens of a specific discourse. Consequently, discourses tend to be deeply resistant to change.

Hajer discusses two mechanisms through which discourses can become dominant or embedded, which speak to the institutionalist perspective that will be discussed more in depth in the next section. First, *discourse structuration* involves a process in which "a discourse starts to dominate the way a society conceptualizes the world" (Hajer, 1995:42). This process can take place tacitly, for instance when a new discourse is used in the media (such as "fight against terror") or when experts authoritatively bring in a new discourse that is more broadly accepted (such as "global warming"). Knowledge and expertise can play a role in this process of discourse structuration, but not because of their objective input but rather because their claims have authority in persuading and convincing others to adopt a specific frame.

Second, once a discourse has started to structure the way a specific problem situation is defined, a process of "*discourse institutionalization*" will further reinforce the influence of a specific discourse. Discourse institutionalization involves a process where discourses "solidify into an institution, sometimes as organizational practices, sometimes as traditional way of reasoning" (Hajer, 1995:46). For instance, discourse institutionalization takes place when a discourse becomes part of "official policy." An illustration of discourse institutionalization is how the discourse on "migrant integration" that emerged in many European countries in the 1990s as a successor to more multicultural ideas about "minority policies", eventually became institutionalized in "integration policies." Institutionalization may also take the shape of "socialization", for instance when a discourse becomes embedded in schooling and training programs.

Discourse structuration and institutionalization are mutually reinforcing processes. Once a discourse starts to structure problem perceptions, institutionalization will become more likely; and the other way around, once a discourse is institutionalized, it will be able to structure problem perceptions even more profoundly. In this sense, the discourse coalition framework provides a bridge between the culturalist perspective and the institutionalist perspective, which is discussed in more depth in the following section.

7.6 Institutional perspective: institutional path-dependency and punctuated equilibrium

The fourth perspective, institutionalism, defines specific constraints as well as opportunities for learning and change. On the one hand, institutionalists show how the institutional setting of policies (such as rules, routines, normalized relations and problem understandings) constrains opportunities for policy change. The institutional setting can be an important source of "negative feedback", or feedback that helps neutralize any challenge and thus promote policy stability or incremental change rather than non-incremental change. On the other hand, the institutional setting may under specific conditions also provide opportunities for change. This can trigger "positive feedback", or a process where actors that manage to create an institutional breakthrough face "increasing returns to scale" in their efforts to challenge the status quo. Such positive feedback processes are mostly associated with non-incremental policy change. Whereas learning is considered, like in several of the other perspectives, a key source of incremental change, its role in non-incremental change is considered much more limited. In this section we discuss the notions of negative and positive feedback, and discuss the punctuated equilibrium framework that brings together both processes in a single heuristic framework of the policy process (Baumgartner and Jones, 1993).

Negative feedback and institutional path-dependency

Even when there is policy stability, or only marginal "incremental" policy change, dynamic forces have to be at work to preserve this (relative) stability. Stability is maintained as long as the forces that promote stability are stronger than the forces that challenge the status quo and promote change. Institutionalists refer to such forces promoting stability and equilibrium as "*negative feedback.*" This can involve actions that explicitly maintain stability, as well as practices that have stability as an implicit consequence.

In the institutionalist literature, such a situation where negative feedback prevails over positive feedback will lead to a situation of "*institutional path dependency.*" This does not mean that there can be no change, but rather that change is likely to be incremental rather than non-incremental, and that the direction of change follows out of past decisions and developments or out of established institutional repertoires or practices. Institutions, such as historically developed practices and rules or decisions that have been taken before and have become standardized in routines, procedures and systems, play a key role in creating institutional path-dependency. These institutions define how actors perceive reality and approach specific policy situations (Thelen,

2003). In the broadly developed institutionalism literature, various causes of institutional path-dependency are distinguished, of which we will discuss the main ones.

Pierson (2000) is an institutionalist that emphasizes in particular how past policies define the playing field on which actors take decisions and define future policies: "*policies create new politics*" (Pierson, 1993: 595). Once policies are established, they create specific "opportunity structures" that may constrain or rather enable actors in specific ways. They can define resources and incentives in such a way that capacity building takes place to sustain a specific policy (or policy institution), for instance by socialization, training, or subsidies. Also, past-decisions may create *lock-in* effects; for instance when huge investments have been made to start developing a specific policy instrument or program, which cannot be easily reverted (economists refer to this as "sunk costs"). Also, past policies have interpretative implications; they are sources of information and meaning that affect future decisions. For instance, the introduction of the euro was not just a monetary action, but also a symbolic action to reinforce European identity, which will affect many future decisions related to European integration.

Mahoney (2000) adopts a more historical sociological perspective on path-dependency. Rather than focusing on how institutions "lock in" future decisions, Mahoney focuses on how policy decisions follow from very specific *historic sequences of events*. Taking the notion of path-dependency quite literally, Mahoney shows that policies develop according to specific paths. For instance, a decision to install an investigation committee on euthanasia at T1 may lead to the availability of knowledge and information on the practical implementation of and techniques for euthanasia at T2, which can lead to formation of a political consensus on specific techniques and circumstances for euthanasia to be applied at T3, and so on. Critical junctures can emerge when historic sequences intersect, for instance when the historic sequence leading to knowledge and information on how euthanasia could be applied conjures with another historical sequence in which illegal application of euthanasia at T1 leads to a tragic suicide of a mentally ill person at T2 and to mass media attention and mobilization calling for appropriate action to prevent such tragic events at T3. Mahoney's conceptualization of critical junctures shows that path-dependency does not always lead to incremental changes only, but sometimes can lead to non-incremental change when different parts collide at specific moments.

Another source of path-dependency is "*group think*" ('t Hart, 1990:59). Group think involves a relatively high degree of cohesion within a specific group of policy makers or decision-makers concerning the definition and interpretation of a policy situation. It can lead to a so-called "tunnel vision" when new information and knowledge emerges and is ignored or misinterpreted. The tendency toward group think increases to the extent that policy makers share a similar background or "esprit des corps" and participate in networks that are clearly demarcated. Also when there are strong interdependencies between actors, the likelihood of group think in order not to disturb these interdependencies increases. This can contribute to a "monopolization of reality", which becomes embedded not only in shared beliefs but also in institutions and routines that further stabilize a problem understanding. Finally, group think may also be promoted by "group polarization" ('t Hart, 1990:59). This involves a sharpening of specific policy understanding in confrontation or conflict with others, leading to (dysfunctional) stereotyping and dichotomization ("them" versus "us"). Especially when this involves the institutionalization of different world views in different networks and organizations, group polarization can be difficult to punctuate.

Finally, a source that is closely related to group think is "*self-referentiality*" or "autopoiesis." Whereas group think is an element of social interaction, self-referentiality is a characteristic of the social system in which policy making takes place. It is developed as part of the autopoietic social systems theory (Luhmann, 1984a; Bekkers, 1994). Autopoietic means "referring to oneself". Social systems theory emphasizes the importance of social differentiation (see Chapter 1), which involves a differentiation of society in different "systems" such as law, economics, politics and social security. Each of these systems are designed based on their own perception of reality, which is institutionalized and maintained through various rules, repertoires, and routines within the system itself. Such systems can react to outside challenges, such as political or economic developments, but without questioning the identity of the system, or the "code" of the system (Willke, 1991).

As a consequence of self-referentiality, the outside world is perceived and interpreted selectively. The reproduction of the social system is ensured by constantly referring to a system's code when decisions or actions are taken, and establishing appropriate ways for implementing and sustaining the code to preserve the identity of the social system. Even if a social system may involve actors with different interests, they will derive their identity largely from the existence of the social system in the first place and the position and role this attributes to them. Examples include social policy areas that have developed over long periods of time and have developed a stable institutional position in dealing with a specific social problem. Such self-referential social systems are an important source of negative feedback to external challenges or interventions. A social system usually involves strong interests and deeply embedded problem understandings that once established are difficult to change or to influence. Actor coalitions will mobilize when a social system, and thus their interests, are challenged.

For instance, the treatment of disabled people usually involves an extensive industry of actors and organizations who each fulfill very specific roles that are strongly interdependent in the much broader context of disabled policies and that often have their own channels of socialization (education, training), a shared language (problem framing) and channels of information (professional organizations, journals, centers of expertise, and so on). To some extent, the state itself can also be seen as a self-referential system. It has its own codes in terms of democracy, legitimacy and rationality. Also, a state has its own channels of formation (such as public policy training), institutional procedures (bureaucracy) and culture (problem solving and societal steering) that can be difficult to alter. For instance, as Boswell (2009) and Scott (1998) argue, rational societal steering has always been at the heart of the identity of the state, or what the state thinks it ought to do. This self-referential logic of rational steering has however also led to an overestimation of the state capacity and sometimes to centralization in problem areas where much local knowledge was required for policy formulation and implementation. For instance, development aid has in many western countries often been developed from a state-centric perspective, with very little consideration for the local knowledge but also local ideas, interests and resources available in the "development countries" themselves.

Path-dependency can involve very specific forms of policy learning. Mostly, this involves learning on what we have described earlier as secondary policy aspects, or single loop learning. First of all, learning can take the form of "*institutional layering*" (Thelen, 2002:222). This involves the questioning of only specific parts of an institutional practice, while leaving other elements intact. This leads to a process of accommodation (policy adjustment), without the core of the institutional practice and the associated policy values and norms being affected (Thelen, 2002:224). This can be done by absorbing elements of change, in order to prevent pressure for larger change; being flexible to accommodate challenges and prevent the system from reaching a breaking point. For instance, in response to the euro crisis, the convention of financial and economic ministers of EU member states (ECOFIN) adopted various accommodating responses, to prevent the need for more drastic changes such as more far reaching political integration. Another form of learning in the context of path-dependency involves *institutional conversion* (Thelen, 2002:224). This does not involve a change in parts of an institutional practice, but rather a change in procedures, the position of specific actors or a redistribution of resources in order to change a policy's course.

Positive feedback and punctuated equilibrium

We earlier discussed the punctuated equilibrium framework in some detail. Policy change plays a central role in this framework. Baumgartner and Jones (1993) argue that policy dynamics tends to follow a pattern of punctuated equilibrium; long periods of relative stability interrupted by moments of dramatic policy change. As we saw earlier, the concept of "*negative feedback*" also plays a key role in the punctuated equilibrium framework, especially in accounting for the periods of relative stability. Like in the abovementioned literature on path-dependency, negative feedback refers to feedback that negates any challenge that tries to bring a specific policy off its path of development. It is negative not in a normative sense, but in the sense that challengers face "diminishing returns to scale" for their efforts to press for change. The result will be incremental change and preservation of the position of the incumbent *policy monopoly*.

However, when this negative feedback is overcome, then major non-incremental change is likely to be the effect. When a topic for some reason does emerge on the agenda in spite of the efforts by the policy monopoly to mobilize negative feedback, then a positive feedback process will emerge that brings increasing returns to scale for challengers to the status quo. As we saw earlier, sources of such positive feedback can be strategies of issue manipulation, venue shopping or the occurrence of focus events that trigger attention to a policy topic.

Whereas the concept of change is central to the punctuated equilibrium framework, the concept of learning is more problematic in this framework. Similar to various other perspectives, learning is expected to take place especially during periods of relative stability as a factor in negative feedback and incremental policy change. Policy monopolies are expected to learn by refining (rather than adjusting) their policy images in response to new information and by improving programs and methods for implementing the policies they advocate. As such, learning can be an important source of negative feedback, holding off challenges and preserving the status quo. However, there is very limited room for learning during processes of positive feedback. Here the logic of the politics of attention applies. Knowledge and information can play an important role in positive feedback processes as well, but often more as ammunition and to boost the authority of specific claim makers (or as "substantiating" and "legitimating" knowledge utilization, see Chapter 6), rather than as using knowledge and information instrumentally for policy learning.

7.7 Policy innovation

Societies are wrestling with all kinds of societal challenges that challenge the problem solving capacity of governments. In many cases, when dealing with a growing ageing of the population, climate change, energy transformation, urban and rural regeneration or the declining trust in efficiency and performance of governments themselves, new approaches that fundamentally represent a discontinuity with the past are needed (Osborne and Brown, 2011). When dealing with these challenges governments, often in close cooperation with other governments, companies, societal organizations as well as citizens, explore new concepts, new technologies, new organizational set-ups. These efforts are often labeled in terms of embarking on the public sector innovation journey (Van de Ven et al., 2008). An innovation is often defined as "an idea, practice or object that is perceived as new by an individual or a unit of adoption" (Rogers, 2003:12).

An innovative public sector: a contradiction in terms

Sometimes it is stated that innovation in the public sector is "a contra dictionary in terminis", especially if the public sector is compared with the private sector. The most important argument in favor of this statement is that the public sector lacks competition and competition is being viewed as a necessary condition for innovation. According to Schumpeter (1934) a basic trait of capitalism is that the desire to gain profit forces entrepreneurs and companies to explore and exploit new opportunities; opportunities in terms of new products and services, new production methods and new markets. In order to survive companies have to develop a competitive advantage which can be realized if they are able to conquer new markets with new products. In the public sector hardly any competition can be found (Bekkers et al., 2011a).

However, some arguments can be made against this statement. First there is an empirical argument. If we look at the practice of innovation in the public sector, we see that the public sector has a long-lasting tradition of innovation. It was the public sector that put a man on the moon, it was the public sector that invented the Internet. And, when looking at the last thirty years, we see that new service management and organization models (more integrated, more tailor-made, more pro-active, more digital and Internet driven) have been developed and adopted, new policy intervention strategies have been developed, and citizens have been given the opportunity to participate in the development of their neighborhood through the introduction of interactive governance.

Second, the perspective that we want to take into account also makes a difference. For instance, if we look at the changes that have been carried out in the kind of services and kind of policy programs that have been developed in social care, social security, education and health care, we see how fundamentally the welfare state has changed during the last sixty years; a change process which is still taking place (Thelen, 1999, 2003). Hence, if we especially adopt a more historical and evolutionary approach to public sector innovation, we see that the changes that have been made often consist of a long-lasting series of smaller steps that have resulted in a fundamental transition; this fundamental transition can only be seen if we are able to have a longer-lasting look over our shoulder.

Third, an important source of public sector innovation is the changing societal and political demands with which governments are confronted with and that not only challenge their efficiency and effectiveness but also their legitimacy. What we see is that governments are increasingly confronted with questions regarding their ability to perform, given the changing needs and wicked problems with which they are confronted. Increasingly we also witness that these societal and political demands also generate a lot of media attention (not only by traditional media but also by social media) which increases the external pressure on government and politics (de Vries, Bekkers and Tummers, 2016).

Fourth, and related to the previous argument, we see that the demands that are put forward are also related to the existence of "wicked problems" like the growing ageing of the population, the deprivation of neighborhoods or the fight against obesity; demands that refer to the rising demands of citizens that expect that governments are able to deal with them, while at the same time politicians, public managers as well as other policy makers suggest that they are also able to solve them, also in order to get elected or re-elected (Lindblom, 1977; Sørensen and Torfing, 2011). The complex and also dynamic nature of these wicked policy problems forces governments, often in close co-operation with other relevant stakeholders, to look for new approaches or to re-frame existing problem definitions in new ones so that new perspectives and new bodies of knowledge can be linked to it (Sørensen and Torfing, 2011).

Fifth, in the private sector the added value of innovation can be calculated in terms of profit share or market share. This does not imply that there is no added value in the public sector. In the public sector innovations also generate added value. However, in the public sector economic values like efficiency and effectiveness are not the only values that stimulate government to embark on the innovation journey. In the public sector also other values can act as a stimulus for innovation, like more political, democratic and legal ("Rechtstaat") values that have to be achieved. For instance political values refer to the nature of the political process, which refers to how to deal with challenges that societies as being political communities are confronted with and which cannot be dealt with in a satisfactory way by the market (Stone, 2001). Democratic values refer to how to respond to the changing needs in society and how to give society a say in defining these needs and the ways in which they can be accomplished, for instance in terms of access, participation, accountability and transparency. Legal values, which refer to fundamental values of the rule of law and that have to be applied in terms of legal security, lack of arbitrariness but also fundamental rights like privacy. The way in which governments are able to meet these other values will also contribute to their legitimacy (Moore, 1995; Bekkers et al., 2011a; see also Chapter 8). The way in which these other values are being accomplished also influences the identity of government. The degree to which governments are capable of preservation by adapting their identity (in changing times) can also be seen as a driver for innovation (March and Olsen, 1986).

Last but not least, it can also be argued that increasingly we also see that countries, regions and cities are increasingly competing with each other as being the most attractive place to work, to live, to study and so on. This type of competition also acts as a driver for innovation. When doing so they also want to make use of the best practices that are developed elsewhere, in the public but also in the private sector. Hence, we see that learning from these practices and copying them also contributes to the innovativeness of the public sector (Pollitt and Bouckaert, 2004; de Vries, Bekkers and Tummers, 2016).

Now that we have argued that the public sector is much more innovative than we perhaps thought, we will discuss especially the concept of innovation.

The concept of innovation: types and process

Innovation is rather a fuzzy concept, because it is often perceived as a "magic concept" which is gladly embraced by politicians, policy makers, public managers as well as citizens, given its rhetorical and inspiring power (Pollitt and Hupe, 2011). One reason is that innovation is often considered as a normative concept. Innovation is perceived as "something good" which prevents policy makers and scholars from developing a more critical approach in order to understand the substance of social innovation (Osborne and Brown, 2011).

However, when looking at the concept of innovation a distinction can be made between the manifestations of different innovations and the process of innovation. The literature on innovation provides various classifications of different types of innovation (see also Fagerberg, 2005; Moore and Hartley, 2008; Bekkers et al., 2011a; de Vries, Bekkers and Tummers, 2016).

- *Service-oriented innovations*, aimed at creating new public services or products. For instance, in the Netherlands an example of a service innovation is the development of the Integrated Environmental Licence ("omgevingsvergunning"). Different environmental permits, which deal with different legal obligations, derived from different laws and regulations, are integrated in one single, umbrella-like license when for instance a citizen or company wants to build a new residence or wants to start a company. This prevents him or her from going from one office to another, while being confronted with often contrasting norms.
- *Process-oriented innovations*, aimed at designing or redesigning administrative processes within government and between governments and citizens or companies. An example of this kind of innovation is the digital assessment of taxes. Another example is the use of specific datasets (like residential or tax information) that are used for different purposes. This has the advantage that, when applying for a specific service, citizens and companies do not have to give the same information over and over again. By making use of this "common pool" services can become easier and more efficient.
- *Technological innovations*, aimed at the application of new technologies. The use of the Internet, the introduction of social media (like Twitter, Facebook, Instagram) and most recently the idea of "big data" and DNA and visual technologies can be seen as examples of technological innovations that can be by government for all kinds of different purposes. For instance, governments can use large datasets and three dimensional visualizations to develop scenarios about the rising of the sea level in order to support complicated policy discussions.
- *Organizational innovations*, aimed at introducing new organization and management models, working methods and new techniques. An example is the development of so-called "shared service centers", in which governments share specific services (such as ICT, human resource, training), can be seen as an organizational innovation. Another example is the use

of "one stop shops", in which different services around a specific theme are integrated, in order to prevent citizens and companies from having to visit different government shelters at different locations.

- *Conceptual innovations*, for instance aimed at developing new ideas or concepts, leading to a different definition and approach of specific policy problems. For instance, the reframing of welfare states into "participation societies" or "big societies" has stimulated the development of all kinds of co-operatives (co-ops), trusts and charities that have replaced traditional public service arrangements in the field of social care, health and urban and rural regeneration. Another example is the concept of participatory budgeting, in which citizens are given a say in how to spend public money when dealing with the challenges of their neighborhood.
- *Governance innovations*, aimed at the development of new forms of steering, thereby making use of the self-regulating capacities that are present in society. For instance, public–private partnerships can be seen as an innovation in which government and companies collaborate while dealing with the reconstruction of, for instance, a socially and economically deprived city area.

In practice the types of innovations are often intertwined. For instance, new technologies very often stimulate the development of new concepts that are being used to redesign specific administrative processes or to develop new organizational arrangements. Network technologies make it possible to share data, stemming from different sources, so that more tailor-made, integrated services can be developed in which for instance citizens are requested to participate in parts of the service delivery process (Dunleavy et al., 2006).

Despite these different types of innovation, scholars emphasize that, when talking about public sector innovation, it is important to look at the process of innovation. It is the process that seems to count. One of the founding fathers of modern innovation theory, Joseph Schumpeter (1934) defined innovation as "a process of creative destruction" in which "new combinations of existing resources" are achieved. This process of creative destruction is sometimes considered as following a specific cycle: the innovation cycle. This cycle consists of a number different stages or sub-processes (Sørensen and Torfing, 2011) which are defined in Figure 7.3.

This linear model is rather dominant in many normative and prescriptive innovation models (for example, Mulgan, 2007; Bason, 2010). However, scholars argue that innovation processes do not resemble such a simple and linear model, in which an innovation goes through different stages. Innovation processes are a rather messy and complex progress of events

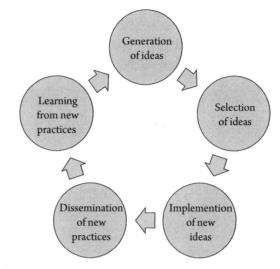

Source: Adapted from Sørensen and Torfing, 2011.

Figure 7.3 The innovation cycle

which goes in all kinds of directions and contains all kinds of different feed-back loops (Fagerberg, 2006). For instance, when organizations adopt and implement an innovation, a process of re-invention and re-innovation takes place, because in order to make an innovation work, it has to be molded into the specific challenges and characteristics of the organization which also requires a learning process.

Hence, innovation processes are shaped in all kinds of complicated and highly dynamic interactions. These interactions can be defined as learning processes. However, one important question is how transformative is this learning process. Innovation requires change and the willingness to learn, but change is not always necessarily innovative, while a learning process does not always turn into new ideas or practices (Lundvall and Lam, 1992; Rashman and Hartley, 2002; Downe, Hartley and Rashman, 2004; Korteland and Bekkers, 2008). Therefore, Osborne and Brown (2005:121) argue that the issue of discontinuity with the past is an essential distinction in order to understand the nature of innovation, both in terms of the transformation of an idea into reality and also in terms of its impact upon the host organization, the existing policy sector or a community. That is why it is important to make a distinction between organizational development and service improvements on the one hand and innovations on the other hand (Osborne and Brown, 2005). Both lead to changes but in the case of an innovation the change is more radical, more transformative, because an innovation changes the paradigm which people and organizations use: in doing so a paradigm shift of newness is being accomplished. For instance, a Dutch example is the personalized budgets that are given to parents with disabled children. These budgets allow them to buy tailor-made and specific health care. However, when the involved parents were putting these budgets together, they were able to create a completely new health care arrangement, called Thomas houses (named after one child, Thomas, whose father developed this new arrangement). In this house a limited number of children (often with the same disability) receive professional care that could not be given by the traditional, very often large-scale operating and standardized health institutions, nor by making use of the individual budgets that were provided to individual parents. In doing so a new service arrangement was developed that substantially challenged existing care practices.

Furthermore, these paradigm shifts are also often related to the introduction of new technologies which offer the possibility of creating new business models (Mulgan and Albury, 2003; Osborne and Brown, 2005; Drechsler, Kattel and Reinert, 2009). For instance, the penetration of the Internet, web, social media and app technologies has really changed the way in which we receive public services, the way in which governments communicate with citizens and companies and vice versa.

An open or ecological perspective on innovation

We have argued above that it is important to conceive public sector innovation as a transformative learning process in which ideas are being generated, selected and implemented. However, this learning process does not take place in a vacuum. First, innovation as process takes place within a specific environment. The environment can be considered as an important input for the process of innovation, given the needs that are present in this environment. Based on the systematic review of de Vries, Bekkers and Tummers (2016) on drivers and barriers behind innovation in the public sector, we know that especially societal needs, in combination with media and political pressure, are an important source of public sector innovation. At the same time the outcomes of this innovation process, for instance in terms of new services and new organizational models, are given back to the environment because they are adopted by all kinds of organizations that operate in this environment. That is why scholars stress to define innovation from an open systems perspective (Osborne and Brown, 2011) or even an ecological perspective (Brown and Duguid, 2000; Greenhalgh et al., 2004; Walker, 2007; Bason, 2010; Osborne and Brown, 2011). This implies that this innovation process is a locally embedded process which takes place in a specific context (for an overview, see Fagerberg, 2005; see also Osborne and Brown, 2005; Bekkers et al., 2011a). Given this local embeddedness, innovation processes and outcomes are contingent ones (Walker, 2007). Innovations processes are shaped by the local, and thus contingent, as well as institutionally embedded interactions of relevant stakeholders who attach different meanings to innovation; meanings that reflect the specific interests and values of the involved actors and/or that stem from different (political, economic, sociocultural, technological) environments (Bekkers and Homburg, 2005; Dunleavy et al., 2006). In doing so innovation can be seen as a process in which ideas and interests co-evolve. The adoption of this ecological perspective also enables us to take into account the different governance traditions in various countries, which also touches upon the institutional perspective on the policy process that we have discerned in this book. For instance, the way in which citizens are considered as being a vital resource for innovation depends on the dominant state or governance tradition in a country or within a specific policy sector.

Second, nowadays innovation theory stresses the open character of innovation as being a (radical) learning process (Chesbrough, 2003a, 2003b, 2006; Von Hippel, 1976, 2005, 2007). Innovation is not something that can only be attributed to the capacities and capabilities of a specific person (the entrepreneur as Schumpeter presumed), or a systematic process of research and development that has been institutionalized in a laboratory or a R&D department (Drucker, 1985). The study of innovation practices shows that innovation processes require the ability and willingness of relevant actors to co-operate and to link and share ideas, knowledge and experience beyond traditional organizational boundaries, as well as to exchange vital resources such as staff. It refers to the rather free and interactive exchange of knowledge, information and experiences, in which new ideas and concepts are discussed in intra- and inter-organizational networks (Chesbrough 2003a, 2003b, 2006; Von Hippel 1976, 2005, 2007). Moreover, it requires the existence of an open culture and a safe context in which "trial and error", "reflection" and "learning" can take place without one being penalized for making "mistakes" or not realizing immediate results. Hence the importance of a free and open exchange of resources, based on a shared understanding about the challenge that has to be dealt with, relates to especially the political and cultural perspective on the policy process. That is why in several countries so-called city labs (for example, Barcelona) are being erected in which relevant stakeholders collaborate in a "living lab" environment. Typical for a living lab is that through a process of (rapid) prototyping, consisting of short cycles of experimentation, learning, evaluation and redesign (based on trial and error, re-trial and error) stakeholders try to develop approaches that really address the needs of citizens or citizen groups.

Third, the fact that public innovation processes around "wicked problems" (like ageing, unemployment or climate adaptation) presupposes the willingness and ability of relevant stakeholders to exchange and share relevant resources, also implies that innovation processes in the public sector take place in arrangements that facilitate and support collaboration. Hence, modern innovation theory stresses the importance of viewing innovation in the public sector as a governance challenge and explores under what conditions these stakeholders can be involved and if and when they are willing to share resources (Sørensen and Torfing, 2011; Torfing, 2016).

Fourth, this idea of collaboration also touches upon the role of citizens and citizen groups in public sector innovation. In public sector innovation theory citizens are given a more active role in public sector innovation. For instance, citizens are increasingly being viewed as a valuable source of innovation, given their needs but also the knowledge that they possess. In doing so they are defined as a co-creator in public sector innovation (Voorberg, Bekkers and Tummers, 2015). For instance, citizens can be viewed as being initiators of innovation, for instance because they put forward specific ideas about how to establish more climate-resilient neighborhoods which are picked up and supported by government; or they are viewed as an important co-designer, because their input is being asked for when government wants to re-design a neighborhood in order to become more climate resilient.

Last but not least, some scholars also argue that the innovation process itself can be considered as a virtue on its own, and therefore does not have to result in new ideas, products or services (Feller, 1981). It is the process itself that matters and can be labeled as innovative. This process of innovation refers to a process of sense-making. Innovation is perceived as valuable to the people and organizations who are involved in the process of generating, selecting, implementing, adopting and learning from new ideas (Weick, 1969). By getting involved in the process of innovation, an organization or people in an organization seek to adapt to changing circumstances, thereby seeking to acquire legitimacy (Feller, 1981; Meyer and Rowan, 1977). The importance of this notion is also put forward in the systematic review of de Vries, Bekkers and Tummers (2016). When looking at the empirical studies of public sector innovation they concluded that limited attention was paid to the outcomes of the specific innovations studied, in terms of being more efficient, more effective, more client-friendly and so on. They conclude that the innovation process as such was considered as a value on its own. This also relates to the cultural perspective on policy making that we have discerned in this book, stressing the importance of symbolism in the public policy process. Embarking on the innovation journey can be seen as an important symbolic, sense-making action of governments by which they show their willingness to adapt in order to strengthen the trust that people have in government.

7.8 CHAPTER SUMMARY

This chapter has discussed varying perspectives on policy dynamics, involving processes of policy learning as well as policy innovation. Although the various perspectives have very different ways of conceptualizing and theorizing learning and change, there does seem to be a consensus or at least convergence between the perspectives on a number of specific elements.

One point of convergence appears to be the recognition that policy dynamics most of the time involves only incremental change. This situation of "relative stability" is interpreted in different ways from the various perspectives, such as "muddling through," "institutional path-dependency," "frame alignment" or "negative feedback." This incrementalism is expected to involve changes only at the level of "secondary policy aspects." Furthermore, the perspectives agree that this stability tends to be maintained by some sort of (more or less institutionalized) network of actors, defined as "epistemic communities," "advocacy coalitions," "discourse coalitions" or "policy monopolies." This speaks closely to the fact that many of the frameworks discussed in this chapter seem to focus on "policy subsystems" as the key unit of analysis, rather than focusing on macropolitical developments or for instance on specific actors or organizations.

It is in the context of such incremental processes that all perspectives see most opportunities for learning. This appears to be a second point of convergence between the four perspectives. Learning apparently requires a stable interpretative framework within which learning can take place. This frame of reference can be defined as a "policy frame," "policy image," a "belief system" or a "discourse." Learning will lead to adaptations or adjustments within this interpretative framework, rather than changing the interpretative framework itself. This involves adjustments in "secondary aspects" of the belief system, "single loop learning" or "first order learning." As we have seen, even the rationalist idea of "evidence-based policy making" requires a stable interpretative framework that allows evidence-based policy making to take place in an apolitical and almost technical manner.

A third point of convergence is that non-incremental change is addressed in all four perspectives, but is expected to be more rare. A rationalist would view non-incremental change primarily as a form of policy innovation. The political perspective sees external perturbations of the power balance in a policy field as triggers of non-incremental change. Institutionalists are perhaps more skeptical of opportunities for non-incremental change, but do see critical junctures as a likely cause of path-dependent but also non-incremental change. Finally, culturalists also believe that "frame shifts" or "punctuations" can take place, but only under very specific circumstances.

Learning is unlikely to be a source of non-incremental change, according to almost all perspectives discussed in this chapter. Only the framing perspective claims that under the right (institutional) conditions critical reflection at the level of framing could lead to frame shifts. However, many perspectives recognize that knowledge and information, also in non-incremental changes, tends to operate within a specific interpretative framework and within the network of actors associated with this framework. They can be important "political ammunition" for advocacy coalitions, contribute to "discourses structuration" and "discourse institutionalization," or "substantiate" and "legitimate" the role of specific actors in a policy field.

8

The reflective policy maker

LEARNING OBJECTIVES

After reading this chapter you should be able to:

- Understand how and why a firm intellectual grasp of the multiplicity of perspectives (rationalism, culturalism, institutionalism, political perspective) on public policy contributes to *reflexivity* on the part of policy makers.

- Appreciate the sources and implications of *legitimacy* for the policy process and for institutions.

- Appreciate the complexity of the role of *knowledge* in contemporary policy processes.

8.1   Introduction

Imagine that you are a policy maker who works for the European Commission in Brussels and you are responsible for finding approaches to deal with the large amounts of immigrants that try to reach the countries of the European Union. Immigrants who leave their country, like Syria, because civil war, displacement and destruction have reigned. Immigrants who sometimes take up their belongings because there is no future in their country because of bad economic circumstances, which is very often the case in some parts of Africa. This enormous flow not only challenges the existing absorption capacity of the national governments in terms of the number of civil servants that have to be involved in order to help settle these immigrants. Not only are extra immigrant officers needed but also refugee centers have to be built. Also established practices have to be set aside or have to be altered because existing procedures, routines and systems are not able to deal with these large amounts of immigrants. Furthermore, this enormous flow of immigrants also challenges the willingness of citizens to accept these people. A willingness that is put under pressure because sometimes anxiety rules. Anxiety regarding the clash of cultures that might take place and that would (allegedly) threaten the identity of people. Anxiety that is, furthermore, related to the perceived competition that might emerge, given the scarce amount of jobs and houses that are available. Anxiety which also may lead to anger, given the fact that many citizens do not feel represented by their traditional politicians, political parties and government, when dealing with these issues. As such this refugee crisis not only defies the effectiveness of national and European immigrant and integration policies, but it also challenges the legitimacy of politics in the EU, at the international (EU), the national (member state) as well as the local and regional (for example, when discussing the establishment of a refugee center in a municipality) levels. As such, and also due to the emergence of popular politics and popular politicians, the vitality of the existing institutions of representative democracy in dealing with this issue in such a way, that the solutions that are put forward are being considered by the people as acceptable. For instance, the idea of spreading the refugees among the EU member states, based on a specific set of allocation rules, was not considered by several member states (for example, Hungary, Poland, the Baltic states) as the most appropriate way to deal with this issue, while others were in favor (for example, Belgium, the Netherlands and Germany). Interests clashed. For instance, some member states said that they had already done enough, that their absorption capacity has been reached, while pointing the finger at other, more reluctant member states. Others were afraid that that the identity and/or culture of a country would be subjected to a lot of pressure.

The refugee crisis of 2014-2016 is an example of an arena in which policy makers have to operate. How to develop and implement policy programs that are not only being considered as efficient and effective, but are also being perceived as doing the right thing given the current circumstances. This presupposes reflective policy makers that acknowledge that legitimacy is the invisible hand that guides reflective policy processes. Therefore we discuss the multi-faced concept of legitimacy in sections 8.2 and 8.3.

Given this challenge to contribute to legitimate policy processes and outcomes, it is important to address why society and public administration need reflective policy makers. Reflective policy makers can be defined as policy makers that are able to learn, by critically looking at the assumptions regarding the activities that have to be performed when being engaged in all kinds of policy processes, like the development of a policy program. In doing so he or she is able to organize feedback and forward loops that enable him to make use of relevant theoretical concepts and research as well as practical experiences. In doing so he or she is able to understand the multi-faced complexity and dynamics of policy processes (see also Chapter 7; Schön,

1983). The first step in being a reflective policy maker relates to the ability to use the four perspectives on the policy process as sketched throughout this book. The second step is to acknowledge that the ultimate test for a policy maker is to get in involved in policy processes that are being perceived as being legitimate. However, this concept is also a multi-faced concept. The third step is that, in order to develop and implement legitimate policies, a reflective policy maker possesses the ability to operate in different worlds: an inside world which is constituted by the bureaucracy in which he or she works and which is closely related to the world of institutionalized politics; and an outside world, which relates to the policy network or arena in which he also needs to operate and in which he meets other relevant and powerful actors.

In section 8.5 we will address these two worlds and the role that political polarization and mediatization of politics and policy making increasingly play in both worlds. Moreover these processes also influence the role of knowledge in policy processes, because especially in bureaucracy knowledge is very often used as an important source of legitimacy (especially in relation to the rational perspective on the policy process). Policy makers are increasingly confronted with competing knowledge claims to which they have to respond. In section 8.6 we address this issue. The fact that reflective policy makers very often work on the boundaries of this inside and outside world makes them also vulnerable which might also endanger their integrity. That is why in section 8.7 the ethical aspect of being a reflective policy maker is discussed.

8.2 Legitimacy: the invisible hand in policy making

Who gets what when and how? This is a famous description that has been used by Harold Lasswell (1936, 1958) when he tried to understand the nature of politics. In his definition politics refers to the allocation of goods, services, resources and values among the members and groups in a community. Politics and policies are about communities that try to deal with all kinds of challenges with which these communities are wrestling, like how to deal with the large influx of refugees, how to deal with unemployment or how to deal with the growing ageing of the population (Stone, 2002). However, the allocation within a community is always controversial, not only in terms of values that have to be balanced with each other, but also because there is always scarcity: the amount of resources, especially financial resources, is limited. For instance, when a city or region is forced to offer shelter to large amounts of refugees, extra money is needed for housing, education, welfare and security. Sometimes the national government can help, but in many cases the funds that they provide are insufficient. In such a situation the expenditures for these refugees compete with other intended expenditures. Furthermore, a specific city or region could also be critical about the number of people that it has to absorb in comparison to other cities and regions, while some cities might even get more costs funded than others.

Thus, the controversial nature of the allocation of values within a community, being a political community, adds a fourth question to Lasswell's definition. Politics is not only about who gets what, when and how but also the question: *why?* This question refers to the justification of the political decisions that are made regarding the policies that are formulated and implemented, also because power is used to enforce them. That is why David Easton (1965:278) in his description of politics not only refers to politics as the allocation of values for society as a whole, but also to the binding allocation of values. Binding implies that although controversial, the members of a political community are willing to accept the decisions and policies that lay behind this allocation. This also refers to the validity of the authority that is being used to make these decisions.

In relation to our example we see that in many European countries, the authority of the national government and the European Union is fundamentally discussed when dealing with the refugee crisis, for example, when looking at the resistance that can be noticed in many countries. The rise of populist parties and politicians in countries like, for instance, Germany (Alternative fur Deutschland) but also the exit by the United Kingdom out of the European Union (the so-called Brexit) can be seen as illustrations of the decreased authority of the involved governments.

The quest for developing and implementing policies that are considered legitimate can be seen as the most important challenge for policy makers. That is why a reflective policy maker should always try to explain to him or herself (but also to the outside world) why he or she is doing things that he or she is doing.

Legitimacy as invisible hand

Just as the market has an "invisible hand" that guides the match between supply and demand, a political system also has an "invisible hand" (Bekkers and Edwards, 2007:36-39). In a political system this is *legitimacy*. Typical for legitimacy as an invisible hand is that we know that it exists as a force that holds communities together, but we cannot give satisfactory explanations of how to create it, or why it is sometimes strong and why it sometimes seems to disappear (Stone, 2002:285). However, let us try to explore what the nature of legitimacy is.

A good starting point for understanding legitimacy is to relate it to the notion of authority, because these two are interrelated concepts. Legitimacy pre-supposes authority. A legitimate authority is one that is recognized as valid or justified by those to whom it applies. If this is the case, the decisions that have been made will be perceived as binding, as authoritative (Easton, 1965:107). An example of the opposite can be found in the referendum in 2016 that led to the exit of the United Kingdom out of the European Union. Fifty-two percent of the people who participated in the referendum did not perceive the European Union and its institutions as being authoritative enough. Phrases like "we want our country back," "Europe is a failed state," or when proclaiming the victory in the referendum in terms of celebrating "independence day," illustrate this lack of legitimacy. In this campaign, the anxiety about the large influx of immigrants into the United Kingdom played an important role when illustrating the lack of power of the EU to deal with this issue. Hence, in the legitimation of political decisions, which are often laid down in a policy program, two issues play an important role. According to Morris (1998:102) legitimacy can be considered as being lawful, just or rightful. Not only should a political decision be based on: (a) the "rule of the law", it should also be recognized as (b) being "a good decision", because it seems right. Let's explore these two issues in more detail.

Legitimacy is closely related to *legality*. Legitimacy is derived from the Latin word lex, which refers to the law. It implies that one interpretation of legiti-macy especially looks valid if a political decision or a policy program is in accordance with the law. In western democratic countries legitimacy is always rooted in the concept of the democratic "Rechtstaat", in which the rule of the law prevails. As such the idea of the "Rechtstaat" can be seen as a solid res-ervoir of well-established norms, rules and procedures (Morris, 1998:103). This implies that interventions in a society by government should always be based on well-known and well-described rules and regulations that contrib-ute to fairness and equality before the law and contribute to (legal) predict-ability and stability. For instance, the legitimacy of European asylum policy is based on the fact that despite the country in which a refugee seeks asylum, each country uses the same norms in determining if a refugee can be given the asylum seeker status; norms that apply to everybody in the same way, because these norms are well-defined and well-known to everybody who has to use them. This example not only shows that the content of the norms that have to be applied adds to the legitimacy of a policy program, but also the way in which they are applied. This implies that first it has to be established what makes an asylum seeker an asylum seeker. An asylum seeker is a person who has fled their own country and applied for protection as a refugee. The United Nations Convention relating to the Status of Refugees (the so-called Refugee Convention), defines who is a refugee and sets out the basic rights that countries should guarantee to refugees. According to the Convention, a refugee is a person who is outside their own country and is unable or unwilling to return due to a well-founded fear of being persecuted because of their race, religion, nationality, membership of a particular social group or political opinion. But the legitimacy of a policy program is not only based on the content of these norms, it is also based on how the norms are applied. The latter means that we also have to look at the procedures that are being used to establish if the protection needs of an asylum seeker as refugee are genuine. If these procedures are rather capricious, this does not add to the legitimacy of the asylum seekers program. That is why Luhmann (1969:28) emphasizes the importance of procedural legitimacy: how to safeguard a fair decision-making process.

However, when talking about legitimacy as being considered to be right or just, it is also important to understand that legitimacy refers to the expression of the will of a political community, which is based on shared beliefs regarding rights, duties and liabilities as well as to a certain status (Morris, 1998:104, Beetham, 1991:20). However, these shared beliefs are not imposed or enforced but they are based on something like free will (Kim, 1966:225). This implies that when political decisions or policy programs express the will of a society, they are considered to be more legitimate than programs which systematically and fundamentally neglect the shared beliefs in a society. That is why legitimacy also refers to the degree of support that a policy program might encounter. As a result policy makers need to be responsive toward the (changing) needs of a society in relation to the question of how these needs converge or diverge with specific beliefs in a society. The societal and public upheaval that the EU refugee policies encounter in many European countries refers to some extent to this issue, to the lack of support among large groups in society. However, one important challenge is that especially in relation to problems that are quite controversial and for which no one size fits all solution is at hand, it is difficult to develop an approach which is in line with the shared beliefs in a country, and there is a tension between the general interest and all kinds of particular interests.

In such a situation, the notion of *procedural legitimacy* might help (Luhman, 1969). This concept implies that the legitimacy of political decisions and the drafting of controversial policy programs may benefit if the procedures (used to develop a program and to decide on a program) refer to procedural values and norms that are based on shared beliefs about how to make these kinds of decisions. That is why Friedrich (1963:223) says that legitimacy as such is inferior to the process of legitimation. It is the process that especially seems to matter. For instance, when trying to determine the location of homes for asylum seekers, some Dutch local municipalities imposed this decision upon the local community. Fierce debates followed, because the inhabitants of these local communities did not feel heard. Local inhabitants very often understood that the establishment of such a home could not be stopped, but they wanted to have an opportunity to express their anxieties and to have the opportunity to explore how these anxieties could be softened. Hence, procedural norms in terms of being given the opportunity to participate, to express interests and views, to have an open and transparent decision-making process may also help to acquire legitimacy. Hence, although people perhaps do not support the content of a decision that is made, they are supportive toward the way in which this decision has been made and power has been exercised in this process (Friedrich, 1963:223). This implies that the process in which legitimation is sought, adds to the legitimacy of a policy program. If this process has an arbitrary and unfair nature, or when it touches upon the integrity of the people (in terms of corruptive behavior) that are involved, then it will undermine the legitimacy of a policy program and the trust in the political system that produced this program (Beetham, 1991:141)

Sources of legitimacy

In the literature on legitimacy, several sources have been described that enable political systems to legitimize the exercise of power to take binding decisions for society as whole (Bekkers and Edwards, 2007:39-40). A seminal piece is the work of Max Weber (1922/1928) who describes three ideal types of authority systems that are founded on different sources of legitimacy. In practice they are often mixed. He makes a distinction between legitimacy that is based on charisma, tradition and rational-legality. *Charismatic legitimacy* is based on the independent belief in the personal competences of the authorities involved and the values that are embodied in this person (Easton, 1965:287). In Weber's account, this could be a religious or political leader who is able to develop appealing and convincing beliefs and views that people adhere to. The legitimacy of an authority can also be based on tradition: *traditional legitimacy*. The authority of a king is very often rooted in a tradition in which one family has held power for a long time and where the power to rule has been transferred from one generation to a new generation. However, especially in modern societies authority is not based on personal qualities or tradition but is based on the conviction that the stability in a society is served if power is exercised along the lines of general, rationally designed, transparent and logically ordered rules that offer security, fairness and predictability in order to prevent capriciousness and arbitrariness which is typical of more personal and traditional authority regimes. As such *rational legality* refers to the earlier mentioned idea of the "Rechtsstaat" which refers to three fundamental issues. First, the rule of law applies which entails that all the decisions which are taken by government refer to well-known and well-described rules in which the competences and responsibilities are defined of the authority that takes a decision as well as how decisions should be made and how they are implemented by making use of the law. Second, the "Rechtstaat" refers to fundamental rights and obligations with which governments and citizens have to comply. Third, in order to prevent misuse of power it is important to have distribution of power, in which, for instance, a distinction is made between legislative, judiciary and administrative powers, in order to create a system of checks and balances. The bureaucracy is defined as being an instrument of the "Rechtstaat".

The idea of the "Rechtstaat" refers to something which Easton (1965:287) has called *structural legitimacy*. Structural legitimacy refers to an independent belief in the validity of the structure and the norms of a political system and the roles that are fulfilled in this system. It refers to the institutional embeddedness of the use of authority to take binding decisions for society as a whole. The way a government is organized in terms of being a bureaucracy – with clear lines of command, well-defined roles that have to be fulfilled and formalized procedures and routines that have to be followed when applying all kinds of rules and regulations – can be seen as the expression of structural legitimacy. At the same time structural legitimacy does not solely refer to formal rules that structure the decision-making processes. It may also refer to grown habits and informal convictions and traditions which may add to the legitimacy of a policy program. For instance, in many European countries there is a close collaboration between government, employers and employees to develop joint approaches toward socio-economic challenges and issues. In the literature this is referred to as (neo-) corporatist ways of decision-making. The legitimacy of all kinds of socio-economic decisions that are achieved in relation to, for instance, wages, health insurance, unemployment and disability provisions are rooted in the participation of labor organizations as well as employers' organizations in all kinds of decision-making processes (Schmitter and Lehmbruch, 1979; Low, 1991). Their participation is seen as a way of establishing more binding policy programs, given the conflict of interests that are at stake. Giving room to vested interests to participate in wicked decision-making processes and giving them a say in the development of policy programs about the development of a country or economy also touches upon the dominant state and governance model that has been used in countries in order to generate legitimacy (Streeck and Schmitter, 1985). It is this state and governance model which can also be seen as a source of structural legitimacy.

Very often this state and governance model also touches upon the dominant *democracy model* that is being used. For instance, the strong involvement of interest groups such as employers and employees fits very well into a pluralistic democracy model, in which competition, conflicts, negotiations and compromises between these interest groups and with the state (which is often seen as a neutral mediator or arbiter) generate a set of checks and balances within the political system so that one-sidedness does not prevail (Dahl, 1965). A democracy model is in essence a decision-making procedure that societies can use to develop binding decisions for society as a whole (Held, 1996). By following specific procedures a binding decision is made. For instance, in a direct democracy model, in which citizens have the authority to decide about specific policy proposals, the legitimacy of a verdict that is created when people have the power to vote for or against a proposal is based on the idea that a referendum can be seen as an expression of the (majority) of the will of the people in which the influence of each person is equal to each other. However, in a representative democracy model the legitimacy of the decisions that are made is based on the fact that elected officials are given a mandate by the people of a country to decide on their behalf, thereby independently taking all pros and cons into consideration. The legitimacy of the mandate is based on having free elections. Hence, when trying to assess the legitimacy of a policy program, it is also important to take into account how the (combination of) democracy models might add to the structural legitimacy of political systems (Held, 1996; Saward, 2001).

Easton (1965) separates structural legitimacy from personal and ideological legitimacy. *Personal legitimacy* refers to the qualities of a person as being the reservoir that can be tapped to enhance the legitimacy of decisions. For instance, because a specific person stands for specific values, norms or convictions, people adhere to them because of the charisma that the person has (Easton 1965:287). *Ideological legitimacy* refers to the shared moral convictions about the validity of a political regime or certain authority roles, the role of politics (Easton, 1965:287). Sometimes these convictions refer to specific partisan ideologies, like the role of the communist party and the values that communism stands for. For instance, in China the legitimacy of policy programs are to some extent based on the moral superiority of the role of the Chinese Communist Party in how to develop and guide China. Sometimes these convictions may also refer to shared beliefs about how a political system inherently should function. For instance, the earlier discussed theory of "Rechtstaat" can also be seen as a moral set of convictions that is based on specific normative political and legal theories that especially in western countries are broadly accepted (Easton, 1965:291).

Legitimacy as a corner stone for the reflective policy maker

Reflective policy making presupposes that policy makers should be aware of the fact that in the end, the ultimate corner stone when assessing the quality of a policy program is the perceived legitimacy of a policy program. Not only in terms of how lawful a program is but also how rightful and just it is. This implies that a reflective policy maker should always take into consideration that:

- A policy program should take into account the values and procedures that are represented by the Rechtstaat and especially the rule of law. The latter being seen as an important source of legitimacy in order to create equity, stability and predictability, fairness and lack of arbitrariness. This implies that a reflective policy maker should look at the lawfulness of his/her plan and his/her decisions by looking at the legal authority base and taking into account that he/she needs to draft a plan that is based on well-defined and non-arbitrary rules.
- A policy program should be responsive toward the shared beliefs, convictions, traditions, values and norms and changes within them, within a community. If this is the case it adds to the rightness of a program. These beliefs are not only substantial but can also be procedural in terms of beliefs that indicate how to take decisions that are perceived as just.
- Policy makers should be sensitive toward the way in which they organize the development of a policy program and the decision-making process that is related to it, because the perceived qualities of the procedure used (for example, fairness, openness, arbitrariness) might stimulate or frustrate the legitimacy of a program. As such, a reflective policy maker should be aware of how important the process of legitimizing is, because it is the processes of seeking support itself that adds to socially and politically accepted political decisions and policy programs. (Beetham and Lord, 1998)
- Policy makers should be sensitive regarding the way in which the dominant state and governance as well as democracy models in which decision-making procedures are embedded may stimulate or frustrate the legitimacy of policy programs. The characteristics of these state, governance and democracy models really influence the process of legitimizing. A reflective policy maker should be sensitive regarding the strengths and weaknesses of these models, in terms of how well they function.

8.3 Legitimacy: a system analysis

In the previous section we revealed the multi-faced nature of the concept of legitimacy. But we can go one step further by looking at how specific values that play in different phases in policy making, influence the legitimacy of a policy program. And, again these different values represent a rather complex balancing act which a policy maker has to perform. For instance, when policy makers are confronted with a large influx of immigrants, when legitimizing their policies, they can point at the effectiveness of the operations fulfilled, because they were able to scrutinize these refugees properly, they were able to find houses and other places to stay, they organized courses in which they were able to learn the language, and so on. However, despite these remarkable successes the legitimacy of the policy program that organized this can be very low, because the inhabitants of a city or region in which these refugees were given shelter did not have a say in the discussion of how many people could be given shelter and where they should be located. In order to deal with this complexity a reflective policy maker should be aware of the fact that in different stages of the policy-making process different values play a different role. Hence, it is important to analyse how these different values at different stages are accomplished.

In order to make this analysis, we use a classical distinction that is made by David Easton (1957) which helps us to unravel the legitimacy concept. In doing so Easton uses an open system perspective on analysing political systems and political decision-making processes. Typical for an open system approach is that a political system that is focused on taking binding decisions for society as a whole is embedded in an environment. Between the environment and the political systems all kinds of interactions take place. These interactions can be understood in terms of *input*. For instance, inputs are the demands and wishes that citizens put forward and to which the political systems have to respond, as well as the support that is given. Elections are a way of voicing these demands and wishes. Interactions also take place in terms of *output*. These are the decisions, the policy programs and laws and regulations that the political system formulates and which are binding for society and can be imposed on the environment. These programs create all kinds of *outcomes* that try to meet the wishes and demands of citizens in the environment of the political systems. What are the results that have been established? The matching of how successful these results are in relation to the wishes and needs of citizens can be described in terms of *feedback*. Last but not least the conversion of needs and wishes from the environment into decisions, policy programs and laws and regulations, can be described as a *throughput*. This model is visualized in Figure 8.1.

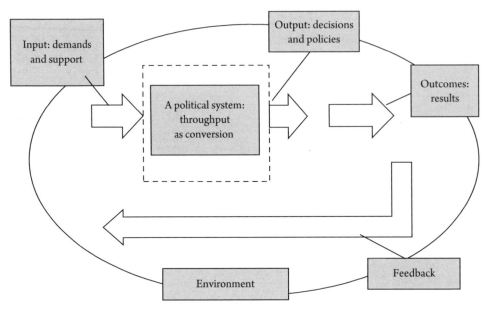

Note: A system analysis model of political decision-making, adapted from Easton, 1957:384.

Figure 8.1 An open system model of political life and policy making

Not only Easton (1965) but also other scholars like Scharpf (1998), when discussing the legitimacy of governing Europe, have used these insights to analyse how legitimacy and the values to which it refers can be operationalized. Following this model a distinction can be made between input, throughput, output/outcomes and feedback legitimacy.

Input legitimacy

Input legitimacy refers to the political values and norms that tell us something about how the input of demands, wishes, claims as well as support takes place and how the interaction between a political system and its environment at this side of the model occurs. We see that especially values like openness and access seem to be important. The following indicators can be formulated to assess the input legitimacy of the political decision-making process that lies behind the drafting of a policy program (Scharpf, 1998:6-7; de Jonghe and Bursens, 2003:8; Engelen and Sie Dhian Ho, 2004:20):

- *The degree in which there where opportunities for (citizen) participation,* so that citizens and other groups have been able to voice their wishes, desires, claims and interests. In a classical representative democracy elections play an important role in voicing these demands or in expressing support. But a question is, for instance, how equally are people to express their voice. For instance, how equal are men and women in having the opportunity to vote? However, opportunities are not only restricted to elections. Governments may also use public hearings but also digital fora as channels that citizens can use to raise their voice.

- *The quality of the representation of the interests and demands that are voiced.* For instance, in a representative democracy political parties and politicians represent specific interests, but do they really represent their district or their group of people? While for instance, in public hearings and all kinds of interactive policy making processes in which citizens are asked to come up with ideas and approaches, the question can be asked: how representative are the people that participate and their voices for the needs of their neighborhood? And, what about "weak" interests? The latter is relevant because research shows that especially white, well-educated and well-to-do people seem to participate. (Voorberg, Bekkers and Tummers, 2015)

- *The degree in which there is an open agenda setting process.* As discussed in Chapter 3 an important issue in the articulation of demands is the degree in which specific concerns are able to acquire a certain status so that they are part of the political agenda. This process is not always an open process, because it is often biased toward specific problem solutions and approaches, which can even lead to a blocked agenda setting process. (Schattschneider, 1960; Bachrach and Baratz, 1970)

Throughput legitimacy

This type of legitimacy refers to the conversion of demands, interest claims and support into specific political decisions that have an impact on society because they are binding, given the authority of the institutions whose task it is to take these decisions. One can think of the role of political and legislative bodies like a parliament or a municipal council. But also the interaction between the elected politicians, ministers and secretaries, mayors and aldermen with civil servants, while working in the administrative world of the political system can be taken into consideration. In the open system model this process is often described as being a "black box" (Easton, 1957). However, if we want to assess the legitimacy of this conversion and decision-making process, we have to break open the black box. What are values and norms that tell us something about the quality of the decision-making process and will formation that takes place (Engelen and Sie Dhian Ho, 2004:20; Scharpf, 1998:13-22)? The transparency of the organization of this process, for instance in terms of how to achieve decisions, as well as the way in which power is exercised in this process, tell us something about the legitimacy of this process:

1. *The way in which collective decision-making and will formation is being pursued.* For instance, one can take a decision by using a majority rule or one can try to establish a collective decision by making use of compromises and exchange, thereby focusing on creating a win–win. In the first case you have clear winners and losers, while in the second case everybody wins or loses a little bit. Or when political decisions are made by making use of a referendum, the majority takes it all. This also refers to the degree in which there seems to be a rather fair balance between winning and losing and the way in which possible losses are compensated. Also the question of how to deal with outspoken minorities and minority issues and how to respect them is an issue that says something about the legitimacy of the decision-making process.

2. *The quality of the participation in the collective decision-making and will formation processes.* In relation to this point questions can be asked about how, for instance, politicians in a representative democracy, while acting in parliament or in a municipality, make use of the mandate that they acquired because they were elected. How strong is their mandate? But also, are they able to renew their mandate because they are engaged in continuous discussions with the people in his/her constituency? Another issue is, for instance, the degree to which the people who participate in political decision-making processes have access to relevant knowledge and information, in order to make informed decisions.

3. The degree to which "checks and balances" are built into the decision-making and will formation process and the degree to which they really do their job. In decision-making processes power is always present and people will use this power to protect their interests and claims. This is inevitable, but vital is how this power is exercised in terms of possible misuse which may lead to arbitrariness. That is why it is important that these decision-making processes are transparent processes and the use of power is subject to scrutiny and accountability, for instance because it can be controlled or balanced.

Output/outcome legitimacy

Legitimacy also refers to the actual decisions and programs that are produced by a political system (in terms of output) and the results that these decisions and programs actually achieve (in terms of outcomes). As such output and outcome legitimacy is achieved in the implementation stage of policy making. Do the results that are being established really meet the wishes and needs of society? That is why Abraham Lincoln in his famous Gettysburg Address on November 19, 1863 talked about "government for the people"; besides his aim that government should also be government of people and by the people (which mainly refers to the input and throughput legitimacy of government). How far have results that have been promised really been achieved? How meticulously have all kinds of resources, especially money, been used to achieve these results? But also what is the support for these results among society? The following indicators tell us something about the output/outcome legitimacy of a policy program (Engelen and Sie Dhian Ho, 2004:23-26; Scharpf, 1997a:153-154; Scharpf, 1998:13-22; Beetham, 1991:145):

1. The degree in which the intended results have been actually achieved by looking at their consequences in terms of *effectiveness and efficiency* (see also the earlier reference to March and Olsen's (1989b), logic of consequentiality). Effectivity relates to the degree in which the goals that are stated in a decision or in a policy program have really been met, while looking at the output that is promised and the outcomes that are promised. Efficiency relates to the balance between costs and benefits. What costs have been made to realize specific outcomes and was this in accordance with the budget?

2. The degree in which the realized results have been responsive toward the original or changed demands and wishes of society. *Responsiveness* relates to the question if the outcomes that have been accomplished were able to meet the (changing) wishes and demands of society. In doing so the question could be raised regarding the so-called appropriateness of a policy program: did it really fit with the original changes and demands in society (see also the logic of appropriateness as framed by March and Olsen, 1989b). This also implies that the actions that are laid down in a policy program have been able to deal with a variety of (changing) circumstances, that they can be made applicable in different contexts.

3. The degree in which the realized results have gained *societal support*. A policy program can be very effective, for instance because it is forced upon society, while at the same time there seems to be a lack of societal support. That is why the degree of resistance can also be seen as an important indicator for the legitimacy of a policy program, which also touches upon the appropriateness of a policy program (see March and Olsen, 1989b).

4. The degree in which a program is in *accordance with the law*. This issue relates to the earlier point that was made when discussing the lawfulness of a policy program. When a policy program is in conflict with established rules and regulations, sometimes because fundamental rights are being violated, then it lacks legitimacy. Also the applicability of actions and norms that are laid down in the program in specific circumstances,

thereby recognizing that equal cases should be treated as equal cases and unequal cases as unequal cases, does tell us something about the lawfulness of a program, and thus about its appropriateness. (March and Olsen, 1989b)

Feedback legitimacy

In Easton's system analysis of political life, it is also important to understand how the learning process takes place if the results that have been achieved are translated in new demands, in support and other claims. Hence, the quality of the feedback process can teach us something about the legitimacy of a policy program (Engelen and Sie Dhian Ho, 2004:20).

1. The way in which policy makers can be held *accountable* for the results that have been achieved. How is the responsibility for these outcomes being organized? It is important to know who is responsible for what, and who can be held accountable for what and by whom. It is also essential that the process of being accountable is transparent to everybody concerned and that all involved actors know which steps have to be taken and which norms have to be taken into consideration. (Meijer and Bovens, 2005)
2. The degree in which the outcomes of a policy program can be used as a source of knowledge to develop new policies or adjust existing policies. As such this also touches upon the *responsiveness* and the learning capacity of policy makers and their organizations (see also Chapter 7).

Legitimacy in multi-level governance arrangements

Up to now, when assessing the multi-faced nature of the legitimacy concept from an open system analysis perspective, we have assumed that there is one political system that is involved in producing a policy program. However, the reality is sometimes more complicated. For instance, when looking at the refugee problem in Europe we see that different political systems that operate at different layers in society and that relate to corresponding governments are involved. At the European Union level we see that policies are developed and decided upon by the European institutions which involve the European Commission, the European Council and the European Parliament. Hence, it is interesting to see what the input, throughput and output legitimacy of this decision-making process looks like. But at the same time the decisions at the European level have to be implemented at the national level and will also be translated in new programs at the level of the member states, which involves the participation of other and different members of parliament. At the same time national ministers and prime ministers operate at the EU and national level: while national parliaments have not always been consulted, these parliaments have to draft programs in accordance with decisions made at the EU level.

What does this imply for the legitimacy of their handling? Again, we can go one step further. Local municipalities and their councils have to take all kinds of measures, for instance in terms of offering housing, education, and welfare services, which really affect the local community, but the community did not have a say, as the decisions are made at the national or EU level. This example shows that many policy programs are multi-level arrangements, in which a "legitimacy deficit" might occur (Scharpf, 1988, 1998). For instance, when confronted with an EU program a local municipality is not able to ask questions about how the interests of the municipality, when confronted with a large influx of refugees, are represented at the national and EU level. As such they have been represented in an indirect way: by the minister as a representative of a nation, which also implies that he represents the collection of municipalities that constitute his nation. That is why in the literature a distinction is made between direct and indirect legitimacy (de Jonghe and Bursens, 2003; Bekkers and Edwards, 2007). Furthermore, these examples show how legitimacy issues at one level have implications for legitimacy at another level. They are intertwined, which really makes it difficult to establish how legitimate a specific program is.

Hence, this exercise shows that the quest for legitimacy is quite complex, because policy makers should be aware that legitimacy can be strengthened as well as weakened in the input, throughput, output/outcome and feedback stages. One reason for this complexity is that these stages are connected to each other. For instance, a lack of support or a lack of response could perhaps be linked to the participation of relevant stakeholders in the input or throughput stage. Another reason is that legitimacy refers to rather wideranging sets of values and critical issues that have to be taken into consideration. And again policy makers should be aware that acquiring legitimacy implies that they have to play chess at a different table, in different but connected playing fields (relating to input, throughput, output/outcome and feedback processes that add to the legitimacy of a policy program).

8.4   Operating in a different world: inside and outside

Up to now we have argued that a reflective policy maker is able to make use of four perspectives on how policy processes are shaped. A rational perspective which focuses on goals, and means and knowledge; a political perspective that teaches us how important a multi-actor perspective is, thereby taking into account interests, dependencies and power resources; a cultural perspective in which framing plays an important role, while embracing the persuasive power of language, symbols and visuality; and an institutional perspective which draws our attention to the role of grown practices that become manifest in routines, procedures, logics and systems. This generates complexity but this complexity becomes even bigger if we take into account the inside and the outside world in which a policy maker has to operate. For instance, a policy maker in the Ministry of the Interior who is involved in refugee policies not only has to take into consideration the interests that are at stake of the involved municipalities, the police, the immigration service agency, or the interests of other involved ministries. He also has to take into account the interests of other units in the department, not only because they have a different view on how to handle this influx, but also because these units have to give in on their budget claims. Hence, we see that policy makers have to balance between the specific internal and external dynamics. This implies that a reflective policy maker should always look over his shoulder, while trying to understand what is happening in the organization or organizational unit that he or she represents. So he/she has to be aware of organizing his/her own internal back up and support. The opposite is also true: policy makers who are completely internally focused may present approaches that do not find much support in the outside world. Hence, a reflective policy maker should be aware of the fact that in many cases he or she is fulfilling a *boundary spanning role* between these two worlds. On the one hand this enforces his position in terms of being a gate keeper, because he can influence the exchange of views, frames, claims, information and knowledge in terms of being selective in what to pass through (thereby including or excluding specific elements, but also in terms of the timing of what is passing through). In doing so they try to control the process of giving meaning to what is happening in the inside world as well as what is happening in the outside world (Pfeffer and Salancik, 1978). On the other hand his position is also vulnerable, because he has to deal with competing demands.

This boundary spanning role becomes even more interesting if we look at two developments in the western political systems that especially influence the outside world. The first development refers to the increased *political polarization* around policy problems which can be noticed in many countries. To some extent this can be explained by the decline of traditional political parties which very often operate at the center of the political system and which integrate and moderate different views and claims. In combination with this development we also see the emergence of rather populist parties and populist political leaders, which try to express the "view of the people" (Canovan, 1999; Mudde, 2004). As a result, ministers, deputy ministers but also aldermen and mayors have to deal with these issues, because it influences their authority, and thus the legitimacy of the policy processes in which they fulfill a role.

The second development refers to the fact that we live in a *"mediated democracy"*. Politics and democracy have become mediated politics and mediated democracies, which also influence the content, shape and dynamics of public policy processes (Bennett and Entman, 2000:5). Media logic plays a vital role in the way politics is represented and portrayed by the media and how politicians make use of the media logic in terms of trying to strategically influence the image that they want to communicate (Bennett, 2007). The Belgian philosopher Elchardus (2003:49) has described the growing influence of the media logic and strategic communication in the political process as the emergence of the so-called "drama democracy". Politics is being portrayed as a theater and politicians seem to be the actors on stage, while citizens are defined as the watching and rather passive audience that needs to be entertained. Entertainment is being created by presenting policy issues in terms of drama, in terms of a game, with winners and losers, with good and bad guys that try to stimulate our emotions in a way that appeals to our personal life and experiences, thereby reducing complexity by not telling the overall story but by picking one or two appealing elements out of this story (Bennett, 2007; Mudde, 2004). Hence, policy makers should be aware they also fulfill a role in this theater (perhaps behind the curtains) and they should be aware of how the "drama democracy" functions. Furthermore, the penetration of especially social media in society adds a new dimension to it. Social media enables citizens and citizen groups to mobilize themselves around specific issues very rapidly (in terms of speed) and on a rather massive scale, and sometimes out of sight of policy makers and politicians (Bekkers, Moody and Edwards, 2011b). Also the crossover effects that can be witnessed between these new media and the traditional media add to the speed and scale of the mobilization process, which also contributes to feelings of polarization. As a result of these two developments, policy issues can rapidly grow into "strategic issues" that have to be managed because they influence the legitimacy of the involved policy program, the involved organizations and the involved policy makers (Bekkers, Moody and Edwards, 2011b). In this process the importance of the cultural perspective on the policy process comes forward, given the role that is attached to framing by making use of appealing rhetoric, symbols and visuals (like videos and photos) (Bekkers and Moody, 2015). An example of a strategic issue that really influenced the refugee debate in Europe (but also around the world) was the picture of the dead body of 3-year-old child (called Aylan Kurdi) from Kobai (Syria) who was found on the beach of Bodrum in Turkey. The silent atrocity of this picture showed not only the despair of having to flee, but also the ineffectiveness of the existing refugee policy regime which triggered the European and Turkish governments in the Autumn and Winter of 2015-2016 to set up an arrangement in order to prevent such things from happening again.

Hence, policy makers should be aware that the increased polarization and mediatization of policy issues and processes generates a lot of pressure under which they have to operate, which also influences their boundary spanning role between the inside and outside world of policy making. This also implies that within governments new systems and new procedures are developed that facilitate policy makers to deal with these issues. An example is the systematic scanning of the media environment, in which the monitoring of social media outlets is taken into consideration to enhance the responsiveness of public policy processes (Bekkers, de Kool and Edwards, 2013). As such these developments also influence the role of knowledge which becomes increasingly contested.

8.5 Contested knowledge

Traditionally knowledge has played an important role in policy making and other policy processes, because knowledge is often used to legitimize the interventions and programs that governments want to pursue. In the drafting of a policy program, but also evaluating it, knowledge plays a vital part. Knowledge cannot only be seen as a resource that is used to make rational decisions, but is it also perceived as a powerful resource that can be used to protect specific interests and claims as well as a resource that can be used to develop persuasive frames. However, we witness that policy makers are increasingly confronted with different knowledge claims that have their own source of legitimacy. Knowledge controversies repeatedly play a role in policy processes. That is why policy makers should be able to recognize these controversies and the legitimacy debates that are related to them.

First, there is a call for policies to be evidence-based, which is strongly rooted in the rationalist approach and which emphasizes the traditional view of science as the producer of relevant, non-disputed and *authoritative knowledge* about what works and what does not (see also Chapter 4). Evidence-based policy making is based on the question of what approach works and how can we make use of the evidence that has been gathered, when dealing with similar policy challenges (Pawson, 2006).

The second trend refers to looking beyond well-established bodies of knowledge and looking at alternative bodies of knowledge, like the *"laymen's knowledge"* as opposed to expert knowledge (Fischer, 2000) or the "wisdom of crowds" (Surowiecki, 2004). The possibilities that the Internet and online social networks offer to help citizens create their own knowledge base can be called "commons knowledge" (Lievrouw, 2011). Commons knowledge "provides an alternative and complement to the expert-driven, disciplinary, institutionalized and authoritative process of knowledge creation, distribution, and gatekeeping" in modern societies (Lievrouw, 2011:178). Online social networks not only play an increasing role in sharing and facilitating different forms of knowledge in our society, but also the open access and flexible character of digitally stored knowledge makes it possible to produce new knowledge. Users are not only consumers of this knowledge by they are also co-producers of this knowledge: they add new knowledge, they discuss it and they change it. Since every user can add knowledge and may perform the role of a potential expert, this implies that online forums can be centers of debate about the reliability of knowledge and trustworthiness of sources (Lievrouw, 2011). An important aspect of knowledge sharing in social networks is that boundaries between ordinary knowledge and scientific knowledge ("theoretical knowledge") are becoming vague (Lievrouw and Livingstone, 2006). Knowledge from sources with a somewhat ambiguous academic status, for instance, are referred to as "alternative sources" with an expert status. We see that "commons knowledge" especially plays a role in the "wicked problems" and in the definition of the risks that evolve from those wicked problems. To some extent the development of this "commons knowledge" can also be seen as a new way of "speaking truth power" (Wildavksy, 1989). However, at the same time fundamental questions can be raised regarding the quality of these alternative bodies. Some even talk about the "the cult of the amateur" (Keen, 2007).

The last trend is called *"fact free politics."* In this trend the idea is embraced that policy making is about visions, about beliefs and choices to be made that are based on these beliefs while at the same time it is the task of politicians to formulate these visions and to make these choices, given the fact that "government is of the people, for the people and by the people" (Canovan, 1999:10). In doing so fact free politics is closely related to a more populist view on politics and policy making, thereby stressing the "redemptive" instead of a more pragmatic dimension of democracy as well as the need to make use of personalized political leadership (Canovan, 1999). The redemptive dimension refers to a set of ideas in which salvation is brought through politics and that people (defined as a unity) are the only source of legitimate authority. Salvation is promised when people are able to take charge of their own lives and are not subjected to all kinds of institutions and rules that embrace rationality as an elite value and rely on expert elites and expert knowledge that limit their power, suffer spontaneous action, political enthusiasm and directedness, and neglect common sense (Canovan, 1999; Mudde, 2004). The pragmatic idea which democracy also represents, in which rationally designed rules and institutes support people to re-conceal different views, ideas and interests in a peaceful way, is perceived as an alienating one. This also influences the role of knowledge. Knowledge is considered as being relevant as it expresses the will of the people (Mudde, 2004). So-called "facts" that are produced by organizations that are established to support rational policy making processes are suspect, because these organizations are considered as representing elite interests. This type of knowledge is not considered as relevant because it is considered as not being representative of the will of the people. Hence, perceptions seem to be more important than facts (Mudde, 2004:553). In the articulation and mobilization of these perceptions media plays an important role.

If we relate these three different perspectives on the policy process we see that the first trend, which is rooted in the rational perspective on policy making, embraces the idea that effective policy making is evidence-based policy making, while at the same time, in order to acquire knowledge, specific procedures and routines have to be followed (institutional policy making perspective). In this discourse the emphasis is placed on the *primacy of science* as the dominant institution which has the monopoly on delivery of evidence-based knowledge (Hoppe, 2005). The second trend refers to the fact that citizens and all kinds of societal organizations, single issue and other social movements are able to acquire competing knowledge that can be used to pursue specific interests and to advance specific views. By making use of the open knowledge and information reservoir of the Internet which represents an alternative powerful resource (political perspective), well-established knowledge producing organizations can be bypassed (institutional perspective). In this second discourse the emphasis is put on the *primacy of society*. The third trend questions this assumption and argues that policy making is about politics and that effective policy making is about "fact free politics", about political sense-making, thereby trying to link to the will of the people. "Fact free politics" is therefore primarily rooted in the political perspective as well in the cultural perspective on policy making, while at the same time it also relates to the institutional perspective, thereby stressing the alienating effect that all kinds of knowledge producing institutions have. In this trend the emphasis is laid on the *primacy of politics* and the primacy of society (Hoppe, 2005).

An important challenge for policy makers is that they should try to bridge these different knowledge sources and see how they can link these different legitimacy claims. For instance, when dealing with the migrant and refugee issue, governments are often confronted with conflicting knowledge claims coming from science, politics and society (Geddes and Scholten, 2016). Many academics have argued that immigration is of a structural nature and that governments can best try to open up immigration policies for those migrants that can contribute to their economies rather than restricting immigration altogether, which provides incentives for irregular migration or for "bogus" asylum seekers. This conflicts, however, with a layman's perceptions and political beliefs that migration in general should and also can be restricted. As a consequence, governments have to engage in a careful and dangerous balancing act between different knowledge sources. When they risk tipping over too much to one side, this may have serious repercussions. For instance, various EU countries had delegated migrant integration policy making to a large extent to experts, in an effort to depoliticize this policy issue. In most cases this eventually backfired on these governments, who were blamed for being undemocratic and ignoring "the voice from the street." Often this also led to a public questioning of the credibility of the experts involved in policy making in the past, who were, for instance, seen as biased toward the multicultural policy paradigm that is nowadays so widely rejected.

8.6   Integrity and responsibility

The fact that policy makers, when involved in all kinds of policy processes, have been forced to play chess at different tables (according to the four perspectives on the policy process), have to deal with different kinds of legitimacy and bridge the internal political-administrative world of bureaucracy with the external world of society and the media, which implies that they are brought into a delicate position; a delicacy which makes them vulnerable. This vulnerability also touches upon their integrity. For instance, how to deal with external societal, media and political pressure if you know that the claims that are put forward by specific politicians and societal groups are in sharp contrast with what we know about a specific policy program or regarding the results that have been achieved? Or, knowing that the interests behind a specific policy program do not match with the interests and needs that specific groups of citizens have. That these interests have been pushed aside in favor of the specific interests of the dominant coalition in, for instance, a municipality, because each department wins with the continuation of the existing status quo. It implies that a reflective policy maker should always be a responsible policy maker. He or she should be aware of the fact that, when moving around these chessboards, ethical aspects are at stake; ethical aspects that are inherently related to the nature of the policy process, because this process generates internal and external roles, interest and values conflict. Policy makers are forced to negotiate permanently with themselves (and their consciousness), given the social bargains that he or she has to make with all kinds of groups because of the permanent need to co-operate with other actors (inside and outside) (Cooper, 2006:106; Banton, 1965:2). However, an important step is that policy makers do not perceive these conflicts as practical issues, but that they recognize them as being ethical issues, because they touch upon different very often competing roles that have to be fulfilled, different interests that have to be met as well as different values which have to be balanced (Cooper, 2006:106). However recognition is just one step, the next step is that the organization in which he/she operates possesses an open culture in which these issues can be discussed and that there is a formal or informal procedure that can be followed so that these issues, the conflicts they generate and the evolving dilemmas that are faced, can be debated (Cooper, 2006).

8.7   Toward a reflective policy practice

In this book we have argued that the practice of policy making in public administration has become more complicated, when compared to 30 or 40 years ago. This also influences the role and competences that policy makers have to possess when dealing with this complexity. One solution is to enhance the reflectiveness of these practices. It is important that policy makers are critical toward the content, course and outcome of policy processes and the assumptions that lay behind these processes. As argued in the chapter on policy learning (Chapter 7), reflection implies that the conditions to learn are available. However, learning not only refers to the ability and willingness to adjust the goals in relation to changed circumstances that have not been foreseen, when drafting a policy program. Learning goes beyond the question, if the set of actions that are pursued, or the instruments that are being applied, will contribute to the achievement of the proclaimed goals and to the corresponding question that changes have to be made. A reflective policy practice also presupposes the willingness and the ability to question the assumptions behind a policy program, to discuss the core of a program and the interests and values that shaped this core (Sabatier, 1987, 1988). It also implies that policy makers should be rather critical toward the established and grown policy practices. In order to facilitate these reflective policy practices, we have elaborated a number of steps that could be followed; steps that have been described in this book.

First, we have argued that it is important to acknowledge that policy processes are in essence *political processes*, because they deal with the allocation of values for society as whole in such a way that this process of allocation is perceived as binding. Policy programs address the question of who gets what and how, given the challenges that a society – being a political community – faces (Stone, 2002; Easton, 1965; Dahl, 1961). A reflective policy practice should acknowledge its political roots, which also implies that policy makers should be aware of the specific logics that play a role in the political realm of society (see Chapter 1).

Second, policy processes can strengthen their *reflexivity*, if the involved policy makers opt for an outside-in perspective. This implies that it is important to understand how fundamental transformations in the political, economic, sociocultural and technological realm of society influence the content, course and outcomes of these policy processes. Transformations that also influence the role and position of government and politics in society. As such this could lead to a more responsive policy practice, because the adoption of a more inside-out perspective would lead to the opposite. When dealing with the challenges and needs of society it is important to understand these needs, instead of approaching these challenges and needs by sticking to vested interests and vested ways of looking at things (see Chapter 2).

Third, the complicated nature of policy processes implies that we have to acknowledge its *complexity* instead of trying to fit into one single model or one super-ordinated approach. That is why we opt for a multi-focal approach in order to enhance the reflexivity of policy making practices. By adopting four different perspectives on the policy process we are able to understand how different forces shape the content, course and outcomes of the policy process. In doing so we have distinguished a rational, political, cultural and institutional perspective. The advantage of this distinction is that we are able to analyse the complexity of policy processes by putting on a different lens, while at the same time this distinction helps to understand the trade-offs and dilemmas that policy makers face, when they have to meet different requirements. That is why we have argued that policy makers should be aware that they play chess at different tables. Each table has different players, with different stakes and different playing rules. At the rational table policy making is about goals and means and the information that is needed to formulate evidence-based goal–means combinations. At the political table it is about how to safeguard specific interests, given the variety of stakeholders that are involved and the dependency relations between them as well as how to find a common ground to act. At the cultural table the stakes are based on the desire to develop persuasive programs by making use of powerful and appealing frames (in terms of language, symbols and visuals). At the institutional table it is established formal and informal rules – which become visible in specific logics that have to be followed and which stress the importance of specific values to be taken into consideration. Behind them lay specific routines, procedures and systems that influence the content and course of policy processes that have to be recognized, while at the same time the major challenge is how to change these grown practices (Chapter 2-7).

Fourth, we have argued (in this chapter) that the ultimate test for a reflective policy practice is the perceived *legitimacy* of a policy program and the processes that are followed to draft, implement and evaluate them. In doing so policy makers also add to the legitimacy of the political system. Here again, we have argued that legitimacy is a multi-faced concept, because it relates to different but interlinked processes (input, throughput, output, outcome and feedback) and to different values (for example, effectiveness, efficiency, support, responsiveness, openness, transparency, representation and so on) which also generate all kinds of trade-offs and dilemmas. Furthermore a reflective policy practice should also take into account the importance of the "Rechtstaat" (the rule of law) as a shared set of beliefs that should be taken into consideration when drafting and implementing policy programs. This legality aspect refers to another set of more legal values that should be taken into consideration (legal security, legal equality and predictability as well as the control of power by making use of all kinds of checks and balances). Last but not least a reflective policy maker should also be aware of the fact that the way in which relevant processes are organized (the procedures that are followed) substantially contributes to the legitimacy of a policy program and of government (procedural legitimacy).

Fifth, we have argued (in this chapter) that a reflective policy maker is often part of two worlds which he/she also has to connect: *an inside and outside world.* In doing so policy makers operate at the boundaries of government, which also generate all kinds of complicated puzzles in how to deal with different values, interests, roles and rules that can be found in both worlds and that mutually influence each other. At the same time, we see that that this boundary spanning role is subjected to a lot of pressure, which is based on the increased political polarization and mediatization of the involved policy processes. This also influences the role of knowledge, because different knowledge claims are put forward that have a legitimacy of their own. Furthermore, operating at the boundaries implies that reflective policy makers possess a vulnerable position, because conflicting interests, rules, roles and values generate all kinds of ethical issues that touch upon someone's integrity.

This book has made an effort to provide conceptual and intellectual tools for such reflective policy practice. We have "trained" the reader to understand and to be able to switch between multiple perspectives on public policy: rationalism, culturalism, institutionalism and the political perspective. Rather than stating that one of these perspectives would be "better" or "worse" or would hold more or less "explanatory leverage", we argue that a deep understanding of public policy requires a deep understanding of all four perspectives. This will help to make sense of the complexity of public policy rather than reducing complexity and trying to simplify what drives public policy. This will help in understanding why public policy is not only driven by knowledge, but is also an inherently political phenomenon in which meanings are contested and institutions are constantly being produced and reproduced. It will help in understanding the various sources of legitimacy that sustain public policy. It will help in understanding how and why public policies have to engage in careful balancing acts between different and sometimes conflicting sources of knowledge, be it authoritative scientific knowledge or laymen's knowledge or more politically substantiated claims. Finally, it will help understanding of how policies can be responsive (or "reflexive") when faced with new situations or specific needs for innovation.

References

Abma, T. (2001). Variaties in beleidsevaluaties: meten, beoordelen en onderhandelen, in T. Abma and R.J. in't Veld (eds) *Handboek beleidswetenschap* (pp. 311-321). Boom: Amsterdam.

Abma, T. and R. in't Veld (2001). *Handboek beleidswetenschap*. Amsterdam: Boom.

Allison, G. and P. Zelikow (1971). *The Essence of Decisions: Explaining the Cuban Missile Crises.* Boston: Little Brown & Co.

Allison, G. and P. Zelikow (1999). *Essence of Decision: Explaining the Cuban Missile Crisis.* New Jersey: Pearson Education.

Anderson, J. (2003). *Public Policy Making* (5th edition). Boston: Houghton Mifflin.

Ansell, C. and A. Gash (2007). Collaborative Governance in Theory and Practice. *Journal of Public Administration Research & Theory*, 18(4): 543–571.

Argyris, C. and D.A. Schön (1978). *Organizational Learning*. Reading, MA: Addison.

Arrow, K. (1971). *Essays in the Theory of Risk- Bearing*. Chicago: Markham.

Arthur, B.W. (1994). *Increasing Returns and Path Dependence in the Economy*. Ann Arbor, MI: University of Michigan Press.

Ayres, I. and J. Braithwaite (1992). *Responsive Regulation. Transcending the Deregulation Debate.* New York: Oxford University Press.

Bachrach, P. and M.S. Baratz (1963). Decisions and nondecisions: an analytical framework. *American Political Science Review*, 57(3): 632-642.

Bachrach, P.S. and M.S. Baratz (1970). *Power and Poverty. Theory and Practice.* New York: Oxford University Press.

Banton, M. (1965). *Roles. An Introduction to the Study of Social Relations.* New York: Basic Books.

Barber, B. (1984). *Strong Democracy*. Berkeley, CA: University of California Press.

Barber, B. (2013). *If Mayors Ruled the World. Dysfunctional Nationas*, Vital Cities. New Haven: Yale University Press.

Bardach, E. (1977). *The Implementation Game: What Happens After a Bill Becomes a Law.* Cambridge, MA: MIT Press.

Barrett, S. and C. Fudge (1981). *Policy and Action: Essays on the Implementation of Public Policy.* London: Methuen, 249-278.

Bason, C. (2010). *Leading Public Sector Innovation*. Bristol: Policy Press.

Bauman, Z. (2000). *Liquid Modernity*. Cambridge: Polity Press.

Bauman, Z. (2010). *Hermeneutics and Social Science: Approaches to Understanding.* London: Hutchinson & Co.

Baumgartner, F. and B. Jones (1993). *Agendas and Instability in American Politics.* Chicago, IL: Chicago of University Press.

Baumgartner, F.R. and B.D. Jones (2002). *Policy Dynamics*. Chicago, IL: University of Chicago Press.

Baumgartner, F.R. and B.D. Jones (2005). *The Politics of Attention: How Government Prioritizes Problems.* Chicago. IL: University of Chicago Press.

BBC (2012). *Press coverage of Dhaka fire on 25 November*, retrieved November 1, 2016.

Beck, U. (1999). *World Risk Society*. Cambridge: Polity Press.

Beetham, D. (1991). *The Legitimation of Power*. London: Macmillan.

Beetham, D. and C. Lord (1998). *Legitimacy and the European Union*. London/New York: Longman.

Bekkers, V. (2012). Why does e-government looks as it looks? Looking beyond the explanatory emptiness of the e-government concept. *Information Polity*, 17 (3-4): 329-342.

Bekkers, V. and M. Fenger (2007). The governance concept in public administration, in V. Bekkers, G. Dijkstra, A. Edwards and M. Fenger (eds) *Governance and the Democratic Deficit* (pp. 13-35). London: Sage.

Bekkers, V. and V. Homburg (2002). Administrative supervision and information relations. *The Information Polity*, 7 (2/3): 129–142.

Bekkers, V. and V. Homburg (2005). E-government as an information ecology, in V. Bekkers and V. Homburg (eds) *The Information Ecology of E-Government* (pp. 1-20). Amsterdam: IOS Press.

Bekkers, V. and V. Homburg (2007). The Myths of E-Government: Looking Beyond the Assumptions of a New and Better Government. *The Information Society*, 23(5): 373–382.

Bekkers, V. and R. Moody (2014). Accountability and the framing power of visual technology. How do visual reconstructions of incidents influence public and political accountability discussions. *The Information Society*, 30 (2): 144-158.

Bekkers, V. and R. Moody (2015). *Visual Culture and Public Policy. Towards a Visual Polity?* London: Routledge.

Bekkers, V. and S. Zouridis (1999). Electronic service delivery in public administration: Some trends and issues. *International Review of Administrative Sciences*, 65 (2): 183-195.

Bekkers, V., A. Edwards and D. de Kool, (2013). Social media monitoring: responsive governance in the shadow of surveillance. *Government Information Quarterly*, 30 (4): 335-342.

Bekkers, V., R. Moody and A. Edwards (2011b). Micro-mobilization, social media and coping strategies: some Dutch experiences. *Policy & Internet*, 3(4): 1-29.

Bekkers, V., A. Edwards, R. Moody and H. Beunders (2011a). Micro-mobilization, new media and the management of strategic surprises. *Public Management Review*, 13 (7): 1003-1022.

Bekkers, V.J.J.M. (1998). New forms of steering and the ambivalency of transparency, in I.T.M. Snellen and W.B.J.H. van de Donk (eds) *Public Administration In An Information Age* (pp. 341-358). Amsterdam/Berlin/Oxford/Tokyo/Washington: IOS Press.

Bekkers, V.J.J.M. (1994). *Nieuwe vormen van sturing en informatisering*. Delft: Eburon.

Bekkers, V.J.J.M. (2000). Keteninformatisering en het management van organisatiegrenzen: organisatorische en institutionele implicaties, in H. van Duivenbodem, M. van Twist, M. Veldhuizen and R. in't Veld (eds) *Ketenmanagement in de publieke sector* (pp. 147-160). Utrecht: Lemma.

Bekkers, V.J.J.M. (2001a). Virtuele beleidsgemeenschappen. Over responsieve democratie en digitale participatie. Bestuurskunde, 252-262.

Bekkers, V.J.J.M. (2001b). De mythen van de elektronische overheid. Over retoriek en realiteit. Bestuurswetenschappen, 277-295.

Bekkers, V.J.J.M. and A.R. Edwards (2007). Legitimacy and democracy: A conceptual framework for assessing governance practices, in V. Bekkers, G. Dijkstra, A. Edwards and M. Fenger (eds) *Governance and the Democratic Deficit: Assessing the Democratic Legitimacy of Governance Practices* (pp. 36-60). Aldershot: Ashgate.

Bekkers, V.J.J.M., H. van Duivenboden and A.M. Lips (2004). ICT en publieke dienstverlening, in A.B.M. Lips, V.J.J.M. Bekkers and A. Zuurmond (eds), *ICT en openbaar bestuur. Implicaties en uitdagingen van technologische toepassingen voor de overheid* (pp. 237-256). Utrecht: Lemma.

Béland, D. and M. Howlett (2016). The role and impact of the multiple-streams approach in comparative analysis. *Journal of Comparative Policy Analysis*, 18(3): 221–227.

Bemelmans-Videc, L., R. Rist and E. Vedung (1998). *Carrots, Sticks and Sermons: Policy Instruments and Their Evaluation*. Piscataway, NJ: Transaction Publishing.

Bennett, W.L. (2007). *News. The Politics of Illusion* (7th edition). New York: Pearson.

Bennett, W.L. and R. Entman (2000). *Mediated Politics: Communication in the Future of Democracy: Communication, Society and Politics.* Cambridge: Cambridge University Press.

Bennett, W.L. and R. Entman (eds) (2001). Mediated politics: an introduction, in L. Bennett and R. Entman (eds) *Mediated Politics. Communication in the Future of Democracy* (pp. 1-29). Cambridge. Cambridge University Press.

Berger, P. and T. Luckmann (1966). *The Social Construction of Reality.* New York: Penguin.

Birkland, T. (2001). *Policy Process: Theories, Concepts, and Models of Public Policy Making.* Armonk, NY: Sharpe.

Blom-Hansen, J. (1997). A "new institutional" perspective on policy networks, *Public Administration*, 75: 669-693.

Bobrow, D.B. and J.S. Dryzek (1987). *Policy Analysis by Design.* Pittsburgh, PA: University of Pittsburgh Press.

Bonoli, G. and P. Trein (2015). Best practice report on policy learning infrastructures in innovative labour market policies. INSPIRES Working Paper 2015 no. 4, Rotterdam: Erasmus University Rotterdam.

Börzel, T. and T. Risse (2010). Governance without a state: can it work? *Regulation and Governance*, 4: 113–134.

Boswell, C. (2009). *The Political Uses Of Expert Knowledge: Immigration Policy and Social Research.* Cambridge: Cambridge University Press.

Boutelier, H. (2004). De veiligheidsutopie: hedendaags onbehagen en verlangen rond misdaad en straf. Den Haag: Boom Juridische Uitgevers.

Bovens, M.A.P. (1990). *Verantwoordelijkheid en organisatie: beschouwingen over aansprakelijkheid, institutioneel burgerschap en ambtelijke ongehoorzaamheid.* Zwolle: WEJ Tjeenk Willink.

Bovens M. and P. 't Hart (1995). Frame multiplicity and policy fiascos: limits to explanation. *Knowledge and Policy*, 8(4): 61–82.

Bovens, M.A.P. and P. 't Hart (1993). Succes en falen van beleid: de sociale constructie van beleidsfiasco's, in M. van Twist and O. van Heffen (eds) *Beleid en wetenschap: Hedendaagse bestuurskundige beschouwingen.* Alphen aan den Rijn: Samsom.

Bovens, M., P. 't Hart and Kuipers, S. (2006). The politics of policy evaluation, in Goodin, Moran and Rein (eds), *Oxford Handbook of Public Policy.* Oxford: Oxford University Press.

Bovens, M.A.P. and S. Zouridis (2002). From street level to system level bureaucracies. How ICT is transforming administrative discretion and constitutional control. *Public Administration Review*, 62(2): 174-183.

Brown J. and P. Duguid (2000). Balancing act: how to capture knowledge without killing it. *Harvard Business Review*, 78(3): 73-80.

Brown, R. (1975). *The Management of Welfare*, London: Tavistock.

Bruijn, J.A. de and E. Ten Heuvelhof (1997). Instruments for network management, in W.J.M. Kickert, E.H. Klijn and J.F.M. Koppenjan (eds) *Managing Complex Networks* (pp. 1119-1136). London: Sage.

Bruijn, J.A. de and E. Ten Heuvelhof (2010). *Process Management: Why Project Management Fails in Complex Decision Making Processes.* New York: Springer.

Burns, T.E. and G.M. Stalker (1961). *The Management of Innovation.* London: Routledge.

Burrell, G. and G. Morgan (1979). *Sociological Paradigms and Organizational Analysis.* Aldershot: Gower.

Campbell, T. (1981). *Seven Theories of Human Society.* Oxford: Clarendon Press.

Canovan, M. (1999). Trust the people! Populism and the two faces of democracy. *Political Studies*, XLVII: 2-16.

Castells, M. (1996). *The Rise of the Network Society: The Information Age: Economy, Society, and Culture.* Oxford: Blackwell Publishers.

Castells, M. (1997). *The Power of Identity*. Cambridge: Blackwell publishers.

Castells, M. (1998). *End of Millennium*. Cambridge: Blackwell Publishers.

Castells, M. (2009). *Communication Power*. New York: Oxford University Press.

Chesbrough, H. (2003a). The era of open innovation. *MIT Sloan Management Review*, 44 (3): 35-42.

Chesbrough, H. (2003b). *Open Innovation: The New Imperative for Creating and Profiting from Technology*. Harvard: Harvard Business School Press.

Chesbrough, H. (2006). Open innovation: a new paradigm for understanding industrial innovation, in H. Chesbrough, W. Vanhaverbeke and J. West (eds) *Open Innovation: Researching a New Paradigm* (pp. 43-62). Oxford: Oxford University Press.

Cleveland, H. (1986), Government is information (but not vice versa). *Public Administration Review*, 46(6): 605-607.

Cobb, R.W. and C.D. Elder (1971). The politics of agenda-building: an alternative perspective for modern democratic theory. *The Journal of Politics*, 33(4): 892-915.

Cobb, R.W. and C.D. Elder (1972). *Participation in American Politics: The Dynamics of Agenda Building*. Boston, MA: Allyn & Bacon.

Cobb, R., J.K. Ross and M.H. Ross (1976). Agenda building as a comparative political process. *The American Political Science Review*, 70(1): 126-138.

Cochran, C.L. and E.F. Malone (1995). *Public Policy: Perspectives and Choices*. New York: McGraw Hill.

Cohen, M.D., J.G. March and J. Olsen (1972). A garbage can model of organizational choice. *Administrative Science Quarterly*, 17(1): 1-25.

Colebatch, H.K. (2009). *Policy (Concepts in the Social Sciences)*. Maidenhead: Open University Press.

Commissie-Oosting. 2001. *De vuurwerkramp: Eindrapport*. Retrieved on October 31, 2016 from https://www.enschede.nl/inhoud/commissie-oosting.

Cooper, T. (2006). *The Responsible Administrator. An Approach to Ethics for the Administrative Role*. San Francisco: Jossey-Bass.

Cook, T. D., Campbell, D. T. (1979). *Quasi-experimentation: Design & analysis issues for field settings* (Vol. 351). Boston: Houghton Mifflin.

Crenson, M.A. (1971). *The Un-politics of Air Pollution*. Baltimore/London: John Hopkins University Press.

Crick, B. (1992). *In Defense of Politics*. Chicago, IL: The University Chicago Press.

Crozier, M. and E. Friedberg (1980). *Actors and Systems*. Chicago/London: Chicago University Press.

Crozier, M. and E. Friedberg (1978). Attore sociale e sistema. *Sociologia dell'azione organizzata*. Italy: Etas.

Cyert, R.M. and J.G. March (1963). *A Behavorial Theory of the Firm*. Englewood Cliffs, NJ: Prentice Hall.

Cyert, R. and J.G. March (1992). *A Behavioral Theory of the Firm* (2nd edition). London: Wiley-Blackwell.

Dahl, R. (1961). *Who Governs?* New Haven: Yale University Press.

Dahl, R. (1965). Reflections on opposition in western democracies. *Government and Opposition*, 1: 7-24.

Dahlgren, P. (2009). *Media and Political Engagement: Citizens, Communication, and Democracy*. Cambridge: Cambridge University Press.

DeLeon, P. (1997). Afterward: the once and future state of policy termination. *International Journal of Public Administration*, 20(12): 2195-2212.

De Ridder, J. (1990). *Toezicht in de ruimtelijke ordening. Een empirische studie naar de intergouver-*

mentele betrekkingen tussen provincie en gemeente in het kader van het planologisch toezicht. Alphen aan den Rijn: Kluwer.

Deuze, M. (2007). Convergence culture in the creative industries. *International Journal of Cultural Studies*, 10(2): 243-263.

DGB (2005). *Brief staatssecretaris van Financiën van 8 april 2005*, nr. DGB 2005/1109, VN 2005/21.3.

DiMaggio, P. and W.W. Powell (1983). The iron cage revisited: institutional isomorphism and collective rationality in organizational fields. *American Sociological Review*, 48(2): 147-160.

DiMaggio, P.J. and W.W. Powell (eds) (1991). *The New Institutionalism in Organizational Analysis* (Vol. 17). Chicago, IL: University of Chicago Press.

Doelen, F. van der (1989). *Beleidsinstrumenten en energiebesparing*. Enschede: Universiteit Twente.

Dolowitz, D.P. (2000). *Policy Transfer and British social policy: learning from the USA?*. Maidenhead: Open University Press.

Dolowitz, D.P. and D. Marsh (2000). Learning from abroad: the role of policy transfer in contemporary policy-making. *Governance*, 13(1): 5-23.

Douglas, M. (1992). Risk and danger, in M. Douglas (ed.) *Risk and Blame-Essays in Cultural Theory* (pp. 38-54). London/New York: Routledge.

Douglas, M. and A. Wildavsky (1983). *Risk and Culture: An Essay on the Selection of Technological and Environmental Dangers*. Oakland, CA: University of California Press.

Downe, J., J. Hartley and L. Rashman (2004). Evaluating the extent of interorganizational learning and change through the Beacon Council Scheme. *Public Management Review*, 6: 531-553.

Downs, A. (1972). *The issue-attention cycle and the political economy of improving our environment. The Political Economy of Environmental Control*. Berkeley, CA: University of California Press, 9-34.

Drechsler, W., R. Kattel and E. Reinert (2009). *Techno-Economic Paradigms: Essays in Honour of Carlota Perez*. London: Anthem.

Dror, Y. (1964). Muddling through – science or inertia. *Public Administration Review*, 24: 153-157.

Drucker, P (1985). *Innovation and Entrepreneurship*. London: Heinemann.

Dunleavy, P., H. Margetts, S. Bastow and J. Tinkler (2006). New Public Management is dead – long live digital-era governance. *Journal of Public Administration Research and Theory*, 16(3): 467–494.

Dunlop, C.A. and C.M. Radaelli (2013). Systematising policy learning: from monolith to dimensions. *Political Studies*, 61(3): 599-619.

Dunn, W.N. (1991). Assessing the impact of policy analysis: the functions of usable ignorance. *Knowledge and Policy*, 4(4): 36-55.

Dunn, W.N. (1994). *Public Policy Analysis* (2nd edition). Upper Saddle River, NJ: Prentice Hall.

Dunn, W.N. (2004). *Public Policy Analysis. An Introduction*. Upper Saddle River, NJ: Pearson Prentice Hall.

Dunsire, A. (1978). *The Execution Process, Implementation in a Bureaucracy*. Oxford: Oxford University Press.

Durant, R.F. and A.L. Warber (2001). Networking in the shadow of hierarchy: public policy, the administrative presidency, and the neo-administrative state. *Presidential Studies Quarterly*, 31(2): 221-244.

Dutton, B. and J. Danziger (1982). Computer and politics, in J. Danziger, W. Dutton, R. Kling and K. Kraemer (eds) *Computer and Politics* (pp. 1-21). New York: Columbia University Press.

Dye, T.R. (1976). *What governments do, why they do it, what difference it makes*. Tuscaloo: University of Alabama Press.

Easton, D. (1957). An approach to the analysis of political systems. *World Politics*, 9(3): 383-400.

Easton, D. (1965). *A System Analysis of Political Life*. London: Wiley.

Edelenbos, J. and E-H. Klijn (2006). Managing stakeholder involvement in decision-making: a comparative analysis of six interactive processes in the Netherlands. *Journal of Public Administration Theory and Practice*, 16(3): 417-446.

Edelman, M. (1967). *The Symbolic Use of Politics*. Urbana, IL: University of Illinois Press.

Edelman, M. (1977). *Political Language. Words that Succeed and Policies that Fail*. New York: Academic Press.

Edelman, M. (2013). *Political language: Words that succeed and policies that fail*. Amsterdam: Elsevier.

Eisenhardt, K. (1989). Agency Theory: An Assessment and Review. *The Academy of Management Review*, 14(1): 57–74.

Elchardus, M, (2003). *De dramademocratie*. Tielt: Lannoo.

Elmore, R.F. (1980). *Complexity and control: What legislators and administrators can do about implementing public policy*. US Department of Education, Office of Educational Research and Improvement, National Institute of Education.

Engelen, E.R. and M. Sie Dhian Ho (2004). Democratische vernieuwing. Luxe of noodzaak? In E.R. Engelen and M. Sie Dhian Ho (eds) *De staat van de democratie. Democratie voorbij de staat* (pp. 17-37). Amsterdam: Amsterdam University Press.

Etzioni, A. (1967). Mixed scanning: a third approach to decision-making. *Public Administration Review*, 27: 385-392.

Fagerberg, J. (2005). *The Oxford Handbook of Innovation*. Oxford: Oxford University Press.

Fagerberg, J. (2006). Innovation: a guide to the literature, in J. Fagerberg, D.C. Mowery and R. Nelson (eds) *Oxford Handbook of Innovation* (pp. 1-26). Oxford: Oxford University Press.

Feldman, M. and J. March (1981). Information in organizations as signal and symbol. *Administrative Science Quarterly*, 26: 171-186.

Feller, I. (1981). Public sector innovation as conspicuous production. *Policy Analysis*, 7(1): 1-20.

Fischer, F. (1990). *Technocracy and the Politics of Expertise*. Newbury Park, CA: Sage.

Fischer, F. (2000). *Citizens, Experts, and the Environment: The Politics of Local Knowledge*. Durham, NC: Duke University Press.

Fischer, F. (2005). *Evaluating Public Policy*. London: Wadsworth Publishing.

Fischer, F. (2003a). Policy analysis as discursive practice: the argumentative turn, in F. Fischer (ed.) *Reframing Public Policy* (pp. 181-202). Oxford: Oxford University Press.

Fischer, F. (2003b). *Reframing Public Policy. Discursive Politics and Deliberative Practices*. Oxford: Oxford University Press.

Fischer, F. and J. Forester (1993). *The Argumentative Turn in Policy Analysis and Planning*. Durham/London: Duke University Press, pp. 43-75.

Flood, R.L. and N.R.A. Romm (1996). *Diversity Management: Triple Loop Learning*, Chichester: Wiley.

Friedrich, C.J. (1963). *Man and His Government*. New York: McGraw Hill Duke University Press.

Garrett, J. (1972). *The Management of Government*. Harmondsworth: Penguin.

Geddes, A. and P. Scholten (2016). *The Politics of Migration and Immigration in Europe*. London: Sage.

Giddens, A. (1979). *Central Problems in Social Theory*. London and Basingstoke: Macmillan.

Gieryn, T.F. (1999). *Cultural Boundaries of Science: Credibility on the Line*. Chicago, IL: University of Chicago Press.

Glasbergen, P. (1987). Beleidsuitvoering als probleem: oorzaken en perspectieven. In P.B. Lehning and J.B.D. Simonis (eds) *Handboek beleidswetenschap* (pp. 80-93). Meppel/Amsterdam: Uitgeverij Boom.

Goodin, R. (1998). *The Theory of Institutional Design*. Cambridge: Cambridge University Press.

Goodin, R., M. Rein and M. Moran (eds) (2006). *Handbook of Public Policy*. Oxford: Oxford University Press.

Greenhalgh, T., G. Robert, F. MacFarlane, P. Bate and O. Kyriakidou (2004). Diffusion of innovations in service organizations: systematic review and recommendations. *The Milbank Quarterly*, 82(4): 581-629.

Grijpink, J.H.A.M. (1997). *Keteninformatisering met toepassing op de justitiële bedrijfsketen: een informatie-infrastructurele aanpak voor communicatie tussen zelfstandige organisaties*. Retrieved on April 16, 2017 from https://pure.tue.nl/ws/files/3552881/475610.pdf.

Guba, E.G. and Y.S. Lincoln (1989). *Fourth Generation Evaluation*. London: Sage.

Guiraudon, V. (1999). The Marshallian triptych re-ordered: the role of courts and bureaucracies in furthering migrant social rights. *European Institute-European Forum Papers*, 99(1).

Guldbrandsson, K. and B. Fossum (2009). An exploration of the theoretical concepts policy windows and policy entrepreneurs at the Swedish public health arena. *Health Promotion International*, 24(4): 434–444.

Gunsteren, H., van (1976). *The Quest for Control*. London: Wiley.

Haas, P.M. (1992). Introduction: epistemic communities and international policy coordination. *International Organization*, 46(1): 1-35.

Haas, P. (2004). When does power listen to truth? A constructivist approach to the policy process. *Journal of European public policy*, 11(4), 569–592.

Habermas, J. (1981). *Theorie des kommunikativen Handelns* (Bd.1: Handlungsrationalität und gesellschaftliche Rationalisierung, Bd. 2: Zur Kritik der funktionalistischen Vernunft). Frankfurt am Main: Suhrkamp.

Hajer, M.A. (1993). Discourse coalitions and the institutionalization of practice. The case of acid rain in Great Britain, in F. Fischer and J. Forester (eds) *The Argumentative Turn in Policy Analysis and Planning* (pp. 43-75). Durham, NC/London: Duke University Press.

Hajer, M.A. (1995). *The Politics of Environmental Discourse: Ecological Modernization and the Policy Process* (p. 40). Oxford: Clarendon Press.

Hajer, M.A. (2003). A frame in the fields: policymaking and the reinvention of politics, in M.A. Hajer and H. Wagenaar (eds) *Deliberative Policy Analysis* (pp. 88-112). Cambridge: Cambridge University Press.

Hajer, M.A. (2006). Doing discourse analysis: coalitions, practices, meaning. *Koninklijk Nederlands Aardrijkskundig Genootschap*, 65-74.

Hajer, M.A. and F. Fischer (1999). *Living with Nature: Environmental Politics as Cultural Discourse*. Oxford: Oxford University Press.

Hajer, M.A. and D. Laws (2006). Ordering through discourse, in R. Goodin, M. Rein and M. Moran (eds) *Handbook of Public Policy* (pp. 250-268). Oxford: Oxford University Press.

Hajer, M.A. and H. Wagenaar, (2003). *Deliberative Policy Analysis: Understanding Governance in the Network Society*. Cambridge: Cambridge University Press.

Halffman, W. (2003). Boundaries of regulatory science. University of Twente: PHD Thesis.

Hall, P.A. (1993). Policy paradigms, social learning, and the state: the case of economic policymaking in Britain. *Comparative Politics*, 275-296.

Hanney, S.R., M.A. Gonzalez-Block, M.J. Buxton and M. Kogan (2003). The utilisation of health research in policy-making: concepts, examples and methods of assessment. *Health Research Policy and Systems*, 1(1): 2.

Hardee, K., L. Irani, R. MacInnis and M. Hamilton (2012). Linking Health Policy with Health Systems and Health Outcomes: A Conceptual Framework. Washington, DC: Futures Group, Health Policy Project. Retrieved on October 19, 2016 from http://www.healthpolicyproject.com/pubs/186_HealthPolicySystemOutcomesConceptualALDec.pdf.

Hart, P.'t. (1990). *Groupthink in Government: A Study of Small Groups and Policy Failure.* The Netherlands: Swets & Zeitlinger Publishers.

Hart, P.'t (1994). *Groupthink in Government: A Study of Small Groups and Policy Failure.* Baltimore, MD: John Hopkins University Press.

Head, B. (2008). Three lenses of evidence based policy. *Australian Journal of Public Administration,* 67(1): 1-11.

Heclo, H. (1974). *Social policy in Britain and Sweden.* New Haven, NJ: Princeton University Press.

Heclo, H. (1978). Issue networks and the executive establishment, in A. King (ed.) *The New American Political System* (pp. 87-107, 115-124). Washington, DC: American Enterprise Institute.

Held, D. (1996). *Models of Democracy* (2nd edition). Stanford, CA: Stanford University Press.

Hemerijck, A. (2001). De institutionele beleidsanalyse: naar een intentionele verklaring, in T. Abma and R. in't Veld (eds) *Handboek beleidswetenschap* (pp. 83-95). Amsterdam: Boom.

Hemerijck, A. (2003). Vier beleidsvragen, in V. Bekkers and A. Ringeling (eds) *Vragen over beleid* (pp. 33-48). Utrecht: Lemma.

Hemerijck, A. (2013). *Changing welfare states.* Oxford: Oxford University Press.

Hendriks, F. (1996). *Beleid, cultuur en instituties: Het verhaal van twee steden.* Leiden: DSWO Press.

Hilgartner, S. and C.L. Bosk (1988). The rise and fall of social problems: a public arenas model. *American Journal of Sociology,* 94(1): 53-78.

Hill, M. (2005). *The Public Policy Process.* Harlow: Pearson Longman.

Hill, M. and P. Hupe (2002). *Implementing Public Policy: Governance in Theory and in Practice.* London: Sage.

Hogwood, B.W. and L.A. Gunn (1984). *Policy Analysis for the Real World.* Oxford: Oxford University Press.

Hogwood, B.W. and B.G. Peters (1983). *Policy Dynamics.* Brighton: Wheatsheaf Books.

Holmstrom, B. (1979). Moral hazard and observability. *Bell Journal of Economics,* pp. 74-91.

Homburg, V.M.F. (2000). Politics and property rights in information exchange. *Knowledge, Policy and Technology,* 1 (3): 13-22.

Hood, C. (1976). *The Limits of Administration.* Beverly Hills, CA: Sage.

Hood, C. (1983). *The Tools of Government.* London: Macmillan.

Hood, C. (1991). A public management for all seasons? *Public Administration,* 69 (1): 3-19.

Hood, C. (1995). Contemporary public management: a new global paradigm. *Public Policy and Administration,* 10(2): 104-117.

Hood, C. (2006). The tools of government in the information age, in R. Goodin, M. Rein and M. Moran (eds) *Handbook of Public Policy* (pp. 469-481). Oxford: Oxford University Press.

Hood, C., H. Rothstein and R. Baldwin (2001). *The Government of Risk: Understanding Risk Regulation Regimes.* Oxford: Oxford University Press.

Hood, C., O. James, C. Scott, G.W. Jones and T. Travers (1999). *Regulation Inside Government: Waste Watchers, Quality Police, and Sleaze-Busters.* Oxford: Oxford University Press.

Hoogerwerf, A. (1987). Beleid Berust op Veronderstellingen: de Beleidstheorie, in P. Lehning et al. (eds) *Handboek Beleidswetenschap* (pp. 23-40). Meppel/Amsterdam: Boom.

Hoogerwerf, A. (1989). Beleid, processen en effecten, in A. Hoogerwerf (ed.) *Overheidsbeleid* (pp. 17-34). Den Haag: Samsom.

Hoogerwerf, A. (2003). Beleidsvoorbereiding: het ontwerpen van beleid, in A. Hoogerwerf and M. Herweijer (eds) *Overheidsbeleid* (pp. 23-40). Alpen aan de Rijn: Kluwer.

Howlett, M. and M. Ramesh (1995). *Studying Public Policy: Policy Cycles and Policy Subsystems* (Vol. 3). Toronto: Oxford University Press.

Hoppe, R. (1999). Policy analysis, science and politics: from 'speaking truth to power' to 'making sense together'. *Science and public policy,* 26(3), 201–210.

Hoppe, R. (2005). Rethinking the science policy nexus. *Poiesis Prax*, 3: 199-215.

Hoppe, R. (2011). *The Governance of Problems: Puzzling, Powering and Participation*. London: Policy Press.

Howlett, M. (1991). Policy instruments, policy styles, and policy implementation: national approaches to theories of instrument choice. *Policy Studies Journal*, 19(2): 1–21.

Howlett, M., M. Ramesh and A. Perl (1995). *Studying Public Policy: Policy Cycles And Policy Subsystems* (Vol. 3). Toronto: Oxford University Press.

In't Veld, R.J., H.D. Bruijn and E.F. Ten Heuvelhof (1998). *Procesmanagement, over procesontwerp en besluitvorming*. Schoonhoven, the Netherlands: Academic Service.

Janis, I.L. (1982). *Groupthink: Psychological Studies of Policy Decisions and Fiascos*. Boston, MA: Houghton Mifflin.

Jasanoff, S. (1995). Procedural choices in regulatory science. *Technology in Society*, 17(3): 279-293.

Jasanoff, S. (1990). *The Fifth Branch: Science Advisers as Policymakers*. Cambridge, MA: Harvard University Press.

Jenkins-Smith, H. and P. Sabatier (1993). The dynamics of policy-oriented learning, in P. Sabatier and H. Jenkins-Smith (eds) *Policy Change and Learning* (pp. 41-56). Boulder, CO: Westview.

John, P., S. Cotterill, A. Moseley, L. Richardson, G. Smith, G. Stoker and C. Wales (2011). *Nudge, Nudge, Think, Think. Experimenting with Ways to Change Civic Behaviour*. London: Bloomsbury.

Johnson, J.J. and M. Waldman (2010). Leasing, lemons, and moral hazard. *Journal of Law and Economics*, 58: 307-328.

Jolly, R. (2003). *De lerende bureaucratie? Een onderzoek naar de betekenis van ICT voor leren in het openbaar bestuur*. Wageningen: Ponssen and Looijen.

Jones, B. D. and F.R. Baumgartner (2005). *The Politics of Attention: How Government Prioritizes Problems*. Chicago, IL: University of Chicago Press.

Jonghe, K. de and P. Bursens (2003). How to increase legitimacy in the European Union? The concept of multi-level governance legitimacy, PSW-paper 2003/4. Antwerp: University of Antwerp.

Keen, A. (2007). *The Cult of the Amateur*. New York: Doubleday.

Kersbergen, K. van and F. van Waarden (2004). "Governance" as a bridge between disciplines: cross-disciplinary inspiration regarding shifts in governance and problems of governability, accountability and legitimacy. *European Journal of Political Research*, 43: 143-171.

Kickert, W. and J. van Gigch (1979). A metasystem approach to organizational decision-making. *Management Science*, 25: 1217-1231.

Kickert, W.J.M., E.H. Klijn and J.F.M. Koppenjan (eds) (1997). *Managing Complex Networks: Strategies for the Public Sector*. London: Sage.

Kim, J. (1966). On the psycho-physical identity theory. *American Philosophical Quarterly*, 3(3), 227-235.

Kingdon, J.W. (1984). *Agendas, Alternatives and Public Policies*. New York: Harper.

Kingdon, J.W. (1995). *Agendas, Alternatives and Public Policies* (2nd edition). New York: Harper.

Kjaer, A.M. (2004). *Governance*. New Jersey: Wiley.

Klijn, E.H. and J.F.M. Koppenjan. (2004). *Managing Uncertainties in Networks*. Abingdon: Taylor & Francis.

Klijn, E.H. and J.F.M. Koppenjan (2006). Institutional design. Changing institutional features of networks, *Public Management Review*, 8(1): 141-160.

Klijn, E.H. and J.F.M. Koppenjan (2012). Governance network theory: past, present and future. *Policy and Politics*, 40(4): 187-206.

Klijn, E.H., J. Edelenbos and B. Steijn (2010). Trust in governance networks: its impact and outcomes. *Administration and Society*, 42(2): 193-221.

Klijn, E.H., B. Steijn and J. Edelenbos (2010). The impact of network management on outcomes in governance networks. *Public Administration,* 88(4): 1063-1082.

Koolhaas, E. and J.C.M. Olsthoorn. (1993). Milieurechtshandhaving, coördinatie en beleid. *Bestuurskunde,* 2: 78-86.

Koppenjan, J. and E.H., Klijn (2004). *Managing Uncertainties in Networks.* London/New York: Sage.

Korsten, A.F.A. and W.J.N. Ligthart (1986). Beleidsvrijheid, ambtelijk gedrag en beleidsuitvoering, in A.F.A. Korsten and W. Derksen (eds) *Uitvoering van overheidsbeleid. Gemeenten en ambtelijk gedrag belicht* (pp. 39-54). Leiden/Antwerpen: Stenfert Kroese.

Korteland, E. and V. Bekkers (2008). Diffusion and adoption of electronic service delivery innovations in Dutch e-policing. *Public Management Review,* 10(1): 71-88.

Kraemer and J. King (1986). Computing and public organization. *Public Administration Review,* 86: 488-496.

Lammers, C.J. (1978). The comparative sociology of organizations. *Annual Review of Sociology,* 4(1): 485-510.

Lasswell, H.D. (1936). *Politics: Who Gets What, When, How.* New York, Whittlesey House.

Lasswell, H.D. (1951). The policy orientation, in S. Braman (ed.) *Communication Researches and Policy Making* (pp. 85-105). Cambridge: MIT Press.

Lasswell, H.D. (1958). *Politics: Who Gets What, When How.* New York: Meridian Books.

Lester, J.P. and L.J. Wilds (1990). The utilization of public policy analysis: a conceptual framework. *Evaluation and Program Planning,* 13(3): 313-319.

Levi, M. (1997). A model, a method, and a map: rational choice in comparative and historical analysis, in M.I. Lichbach and A.S. Zuckerman (eds) *Comparative Politics: Rationality, Culture, and Structure* (pp. 19-41). Cambridge: Cambridge University Press.

Lievrouw, L. (2011). *Alternative and Activist New Media.* Cambridge: Polity Press.

Lievrouw, L. and S. Livingstone (2006). Introduction to the updated student edition, in L. Lievrouw and S. Livingstone (eds) *Handbook of New Media: Social shaping and social consequences of ICT's* (pp. 1-33). London: Sage.

Lindblom, C.E. (1959). The science of "muddling through". *Public Administration Review,* 19: 79-88.

Lindblom, C. (1965). *The Intelligence of Democracy. Decision-making through Mutual Adjustment.* New York: Free Press.

Lindblom, C. (1977). *Politics and Markets.* New York: Basic Books.

Lindblom, C.E. and E.J. Woodhouse (1993). *The Policy Making Process.* Englewood Cliffs, NJ: Prentice Hall.

Linder, S.H. and B.G. Peters (1989). Instruments of government: perceptions and contexts. *Journal of Public Policy,* 9(1): 35-58.

Ling, T. (2002). Delivering Joined-up Government in the UK: Dimensions, Issues and Problems. *Public Administration,* 80(4): 615–642.

Lipsky, M. (1980). *Street Level Bureaucrats.* New York: Russel Sage.

Louw, P.E. (2005). *The Media and Political Process.* London: Sage.

Low, N. (1991). *Planning, Politics and the State: Political Foundations of Planning Thought.* London: Unwin/Hyman.

Lowi, T.J. (1964). American business, public policy, case studies, and political theory. *World Politics,* 16: 677-715.

Lowi, T.J. (1972). Four systems of policy politics and choice. *Public Administration Review,* 32: 298-310.

Luhmann, N. (1969). *Legitimation durch Verfahren.* Frankfurt: Suhrkamp.

Luhmann, N. (1984a). *Soziale Systeme. Grundrisse einer allgemeinen Theorie.* Frankfurt: Suhrkamp.

Luhmann, N. (1984b). Staat und Politik, in U. Brehmbach (ed.) *Politische Theoriengeschichte (Sonderheft Politische Vierteljahresschrift)* (pp. 99-125). Opladen: Springer.

Lundvall, B. and A. Lam (1992). *National Systems of Innovation: Towards a Theory of Innovation and Interactive Learning.* London: Pinter.

Maarse, J.A.M. (1986). Uitvoering van beleid: enkele thema's, in A.F.A. Korsten and W. Derksen (eds) *Uitvoering van overheidsbeleid. Gemeenten en ambtelijk gedrag belicht* (pp. 23-38). Leiden/Antwerpen: Stenfert Kroese.

Maarse, J.A.M. (1993). De uitvoering van beleid, in A. Hoogerwerf (ed.) *Overheidsbeleid. Een inleiding tot de beleidswetenschap* (pp. 144-160). Alphen aan den Rijn: Kluwer.

Mahoney, J. (2000). Path dependence in historical sociology. *Theory and Society*, 29(4): 507-548.

Majone, G. (1997). From the positive to the regulatory state. *Journal of Public Policy*, 17: 139-167.

Mannheim, K. (1935). *Man and Society in the Age of Reconstruction.* London: Routledge.

March, J.G. and J.P. Olsen (1986). Garbage can models of decision making in organizations. *Ambiguity and Command*, 10: 11-35.

March, J.G. and J.P. Olsen (1989a). *Rediscovering Institutions.* New York: The Free Press.

March, J. and J.P. Olsen (1989b). The logic of appropriateness, Oslo: Arena/Center for European Studies University of Oslo (Working Paper 04/09).

March, J.G. and J.P. Olsen (2004). The logic of appropriateness, ARENA Working Papers WP 04/09.

March, J.G. and H.A. Simon (1993). *Organizations* (2nd edition). Oxford: Blackwell.

Margetts, H. (1998). Computerising the tools of government, in I. Snellen and W. van de Donk (eds) *Public Administration in an Information Age* (pp. 441-460). Amsterdam/Berlin/Oxford/Tokyo/Washington DC: IOS Press.

Marsh, D. and R.A. Rhodes (1992). *Policy Networks in British Government.* Oxford: Clarendon Press.

Maynard-Moody, S. and M. Musheno (2000). State Agent or Citizen Agent: Two Narratives of Discretion. *Journal of Public Administration Research & Theory.* 10(2): 329–358.

Maynard-Moody, S. and M. Musheno (2003). *Cops, Teachers, Counselors: Stories from the Front Lines of Public Service.* University of Michigan: University of Michigan Press.

Mayntz, R. (1980), Die Implementation politischer Programme: Theoretische Überlegungen zu einem neuen Forschungsgebiet, in R. Mayntz (ed.) *Implementation politischer Programme: Empirische Forschungsberichte* (pp. 237-250). Königstein: Anton Hain.

Mayntz, R. (1987). Politische Steuerung und gesellschaftliche Steuerungsprobleme – Anmerkungen zu einem theoretischen Paradigma. *Jahrbuch zur Staats- und Verwaltungswissenschaft*, 1: 89-110.

Meijer, A. and M. Bovens (2005). Public accountability in the information age, in V. Bekkers and V. Homburg (eds) *The Information Ecology Of E-government* (pp. 171-182). Amsterdam/Berlin/Oxford/Tokyo/Washington DC: IOS Press.

Meyer, J. and B. Rowan (1977). Institutionalized organizations: formal structure as myth and ceremony. *American Journal of Sociology*, 83(2): 340-363.

Meyer, J.W. and B. Rowan (1991). Institutionalized organizations: formal structure as myth and ceremony, in W. Powell and P.J. DiMaggio (eds) *The New Institutionalism in Organizational Analysis* (pp. 41-62). Chicago: Chicago University Press.

Mintrom, M. (1997). Policy entrepreneurs and the diffusion of innovation. *American Journal of Political Science*, 41(3): 738–770.

Mintzberg, H. (1979). *The structuring of organizations* (Vol. 203). Englewood Cliffs, NJ: Prentice Hall.

Mintzberg, H. (1994). *The Fall and Rise of Strategic Planning.* New York: Simon & Schuster.

Mol, N.P. and H.A.A. Verbon (1993). *Institutionele economie en openbaar bestuur. Perspectieven op de verzelfstandiging van overheidsdiensten.* Den Haag: VUGA.

Moore, M. (1995). *Creating Public Value: Strategic Management in Government*. Cambridge: Harvard University Press.

Moore, M. and J. Hartley (2008). Innovations in governance. *Public Management Review*, 10(1): 3-20.

Morgan, G.A. (1986). *Images of Organization*. London: Sage.

Morris, C.W. (1998). *An Essay on the Modern State*. Cambridge: Cambridge University Press.

Mudde, C. (2004). The populist zeitgeist. *Government and Opposition*, pp. 541-563.

Mulgan G. and D. Albury (2003). *Innovation in the Public Sector*. London: Strategy Unit Cabinet Office.

Mulgan. J. (2007). *Social Innovation: What It Is, Why It Matters and How It Can Be Accelerated*. Oxford: Oxford Said Business School.

Nagel, S.S. (1986). Efficiency, effectiveness and equity in public policy evaluation. *Policy Studies Review*, 6(1): 99-120.

National Clinical Taskforce on Organ and Tissue Donation, Final Report 2008: Think nationally, act locally, Department of Health and Ageing, Canberra, p. 34.

Negroponte, N. (1995). *Being Digital*. New York: Vintage Books.

Newman, J. (2001). *Modernizing Governments: New Labour Policy and Society*. London: Sage.

Nonaka, I (1994). A dynamic theory of organizational knowledge creation. *Organziation Science*, 5(1): 14-37.

NOS. (2015). *In beeld: vuurwerkramp Enschede van toen naar nu*. Retrieved on October 31, 2016 from http://nos.nl/artikel/2035474-in-beeld-vuurwerkramp-enschede-van-toen-naar-nu.html.

OECD (2007). Sickness and Disability Schemes in the Netherlands. Paris: OECD.

OECD DAC (2002): OECD DAC Glossary of Key Terms in Evaluation and Results-Based Management. Paris: OECD Development Assistance Committee.

Oh, C.H. and R.F. Rich (1996). Explaining use of information in public policymaking. *Knowledge, Technology & Policy*, 9(1): 3-35.

Orren, K. and S. Skowronek (1994). Beyond the iconography of order: notes for a new institutionalism, in L. Dodd and C. Jillson (eds) *The Dynamics of American Politics* (pp. 311-330). New York: Westview Press.

Osborne, D. and T. Gaebler (1992). *Reinventing Government: How the Entrepreneurial Spirit is Transforming Government*. Reading, MA: Adison Wesley.

Osborne, S. and K. Brown (2005). *Managing Change and Innovation in Public Service Organizations*. London: Routledge.

Osborne, S. (2006). New Public Governance. *Public Management Review*, 8(3): 377–388.

Osborne, S. and L. Brown (2011). Innovation, public policy and public services delivery in the UK. The word that would be king. *Public Administration*, 89(4): 1335–1350.

Ostrom, E., R. Gardner and J. Walker (1994). *Rules, Games, and Common-Pool Resources*. Ann Arbor, MI: University of Michigan Press.

Papadopoulos, Y. (2003). Cooperative forms of governance. Problems of democratic accountability in complex environments. *European Journal of Political Research*, 42: 473-501.

Parsons, W. (1995). *Public Policy*. Aldershot, UK and Brookfield, VT, USA: Edward Elgar Publishing.

Patton, M. Q. (1994). Developmental evaluation. *Evaluation practice*, 15(3), 311–319.

Patton, M.Q. (1997). *Utilisation-focused Evaluation: The New Century Text*. London: Sage.

Pawson, R. (2006). *Evidence Based Policy*. London/Thousand Oaks: Sage.

Perri 6, D. Leat, K. Seltzer and G. Stoker (2002). *Towards Holistic Governance*, Houndsmills: Palgrave

Pfeffer, J. and G. Salancik (1978). *The External Control of Organizations*. New York: Harper.

Pierre, B.G. and J. Peters (2000). Citizens versus the new public manager: the problem of mutual empowerment. *Administration and Society*, 32(1): 9-28.

Pierson, P. (1994). *Dismantling the Welfare State?: Reagan, Thatcher and the Politics of Retrenchment*. Cambridge: Cambridge University Press.

Pierson, P. (2000). Increasing returns, path dependency and the study of politics. *American Political Science*, 94(2): 251-267.

Pine, P.J. and J.H. Gilmore (1999). *The Experience Economy: Work is Theatre & Every Business a Stage*. Boston, MA: Harvard Business School Press.

Pollitt, C. (2003). *The Essential Public Manager*. Maidenhead: Open University Press.

Pollitt, C. and G. Bouckaert (2004). *Public Management Reform: Governing with the Past* (2nd edition). Oxford: Oxford University Press.

Pollitt, C. and P. Hupe (2011). Talking about government: the role of magic concepts. *Public Management Review*, 13(5): 641-658.

Porter, R. (1997). Trust in numbers. The pursuit of objectivity in science and public life. *The English Historical Review*, 112(447): 822-823.

Posner, R.A. (2007). *Economic Analysis of Law* (7th edition). Austin: Wolters Kluwer.

Pralle, S.B. (2003). Venue shopping, political strategy, and policy change: The internationalization of Canadian forest advocacy. *Journal of Public Policy*, 23(3): 233-260.

Pressman, J.L. and A. Wildavsky (1973/1984). *Implementation*. Berkeley, CA: University of California Press.

Provan, K.G. and P. Kenis (2008). Modes of network governance: structure, management, and effectiveness. *Journal of Public Administration Research and Theory*, 18(2): 229-252.

Putnam, R. (1995). Bowling alone: America's declining social capital. *Journal of Democracy*, 6(1): 65-78.

Radin, B.A. (2000). *Beyond Machiavelli: Policy Analysis Comes of Age*. Washington, DC: Georgetown University Press.

Rashman, L. and J. Hartley (2002). Leading and learning? Knowledge transfer in the Beacon Council Scheme. *Public Administration*, 80(3): 523-542.

Rein, M. and D.A. Schön (1994). *Frame Reflection: Toward the Resolution of Intractable Policy Controversies*. New York: Basic Books.

Rhodes, R.A.W. (1985). Power dependence, policy communities and intergovernmental networks. *Public Administration Bulletin*, 49: 4-31.

Rhodes, R.A.W. (1997). *Understanding Governance*. Maidenhead: Open University Press.

Rich (1997). Measuring knowledge utilization: processes and outcomes. *Knowledge and Policy*, 10(3): 11-24.

Richardson, J. (ed.) (1982). *Policy Styles in Western Europe*. London: Allen & Unwin.

Ringeling, A.B. (1978). *Beleidsvrijheid van ambtenaren: Het spijtoptantenprobleem als illustratie van de activiteiten van ambtenaren bij de uitvoering van beleid*. Alphen aan den Rijn: Samsom.

Ringeling, A. (1993). *Het imago van de overheid*. Den Haag: VUGA.

Rittel, H.W. and M.W. Webber (1973). Dilemmas in a general theory of planning. *Policy Sciences*, 4: 155-169.

Roe, E. (1994). *Narrative Policy Analysis: Theory and Practice*. Durham, NC: Duke University Press.

Rogers, E. (2003). *Diffusion of Innovations*. New York: Free Press.

Rose, R. (1993). *Lesson-drawing in Public Policy: A Guide to Learning Across Time and Space* (Vol. 91). Chatham, NJ: Chatham House Publishers.

Sabatier, P.A. (1987). Knowledge, policy-oriented learning and policy change. *Knowledge*, 8: 649-692.

Sabatier, P. (1988). An advocacy coalition framework of policy change and the role of policy-oriented learning therein. *Policy Sciences*, 21: 129-168.

Sabatier, P.A. (1993). Policy change over a decade or more, in P.A. Sabatier and H. Jenkins-Smith (eds) *Policy Change and Learning: An Advocacy Coalition Approach* (pp. 13-39), Boulder, CO: Westview Press.

Sabatier, P. (1998). The advocacy coalition framework: revisions and relevance for Europe. *Journal of European Public Policy*, 5(1): 98-130.

Sabatier, P.A. (2007). The need for better theories, in P.A. Sabatier (ed.), *Theories of the Policy Process* (pp. 3-17). Boulder, CO: Westview Press.

Sabatier, P.A. and H. Jenkins-Smith (1988). Symposium editors' introduction. *Policy Sciences*, 21(2): 123-127.

Sabatier, P. and H. Jenkins-Smith (eds) (1993). *Policy Change and Learning: An Advocacy Coalition Approach*. Boulder, CO: Westview Press.

Sabatier, P. and C.M. Weible (2007). The advocacy coalition framework: innovations and clarifications, in P.A. Sabatier (ed.), *Theories of the Policy Process* (pp. 1-4). Boulder, CO: Westview Press.

Salge, T. and A. Vera (2012). Benefiting from public sector innovation: the moderating role of customer and learning orientation. *Public Administration Review*, 72(4): 550-560.

Sanderson, I. (2002). Evaluation, policy learning and evidence-based policy making. *Public Administration*, 80(1): 1-22.

Sapru, R. (2010). *Public Policy-Making: Art and Craft of Policy Making*. New Delhi: Phi Learning.

Saward, M. (2001). *Making Democratic Connections: Political Equality, Deliberations and Direct Democracy*. Oxford: Oxford University Press.

Scharpf, F. (1997a), Introduction: the problem solving capacity in multi-level governance. *Journal of European Public Policy*, 4(4): 520-538.

Scharpf, F.W. (1988). The joint decision making trap: lessons from German federalism and European integration. *Public Administration*, 66: 239-278.

Scharpf, F.W. (1994). Games real actors could play: positive and negative coordination in embedded negotiations. *Journal of Theoretical Politics*, 6(1): 27-53.

Scharpf, F.W. (1997b). *Games Real Actors Play: Actor Centered Institutionalism in Policy Research*. Oxford: Westview Press.

Scharpf, F.W. (1998). *Governing in Europe: Effective and Democratic*. Oxford: Oxford University Press.

Scharpf, F.W., B. Reissert and F. Schnabel (1976). *Politikverflechtung. Theorie und Empirie des kooperativen Föderalismus in der Bundesrepublik*. Kronberg: Scriptor.

Schattschneider, E.E (1960). *The Semisovereign People*. New York: Holt.

Schillemans, T. (2013). Moving beyond the clash of interests: on stewardship theory and the relationships between central government departments and public agencies. *Public Management Review*, 15(4): 514-562.

Schmitter, P.C. and G. Lehmbruch (1979). *Trends Towards Corporatist Intermediation*. Beverly Hills: Sage.

Schneider, A. and H. Ingram (1990). Behavioural assumptions of policy tools. *Journal of Politics*, 52(2): 510-529.

Schneider, A. and H. Ingram (1997). *Policy Design for Democracy*. Lawrence, KS: University Press of Kansas.

Schneider, A. and H. Ingram (1993). The social construction of target populations: implications for politics. *American Political Science Review*, 87(2): 334-347.

Scholten, P. (2011). *Framing immigrant Integration: Dutch Research-Policy Dialogues In Comparative Perspective* (p. 320). Amsterdam: Amsterdam University Press.

Scholten, P. (2017). Can learning contribute to fundamental policy change? A constructivist perspective on expertise and change in Dutch migrant integration policies. In: *Policy & Society*, published online first

Schön, D. (1971). *Beyond the Stable State*. Harmondsworth: Penguin.

Schön, D. (1983). *The Reflective Practitioner: How Professionals Think in Action*. New York: Basic Books.

Schön, D.A. and M. Rein (1994). *Frame Reflection: Toward the Resolution of Intractable Policy Controversies*. New York: Basic Books.

Schuller, T., S. Baron and J. Field (2000). Social capital: a review and critique in Baron et al. (eds) *Social Capital: Critical Perspectives* (pp. 1-38). Oxford: Oxford University Press.

Schumpeter, J. (1934). *Theory of Economic Development: An Inquiry into Profits, Capital, Interest, and the Business Cycle*. Cambridge: Harvard University Press;

Schulz, M. (2014). Logic of Consequences and Logic of Appropriateness. Retrieved on April 10, 2017 from http://www.martinshub.org/Download/LoC_LoA_PrePub.pdf.

Scott, J.C. (1998). *Seeing Like a State*. New Haven: Yale University Press.

Scott, R.W. (1995). *Institutions and Organizations*. Thousand Oaks: Sage.

Scott, R.W. (2014). *Institutions and Organizations: Ideas, Interests & Identities*. Thousand Oaks: Sage.

Sewell, W. (1992). A theory of structure: duality, agency, and transformation. *American Journal of Sociology*, 98(1): 1-29.

Shulba, L.M. and J.B. Cousins (1997). Evaluation use: theory, research and practice since 1986. *Evaluation Practice*, 18(3): 195-208.

Silverman, D. (1971). *The Theory of Organization*. New York: Basic Books.

Simon, H. (1961). *Administrative Behaviour* (2nd edition). New York: Macmillan.

Simon, H.A. (1982). *Models of Bounded Rationality: Empirically Grounded Economic Reason* (Vol. 3). Cambridge, MA: MIT Press.

Simonis, J.B.D. (1983). *Uitvoering van beleid als probleem*. Amsterdam: Kobra.

Snellen, I.T.M. (1987). *Boeiend en geboeid*. Alphen aan den Rijn: Samsom H.D. Tjeenk Willink.

Snow, D.A. and R.D. Benford (1988). Ideology, frame resonance, and participant mobilization. *International Social Movement Research*, 1(1): 197-217.

Sørensen, E. (2006). Metagovernance: the changing role of politicians in processes of democratic governance. *The American Review of Public Administration*, 36(1): 98-114.

Sørensen, E. and J. Torfing (2011). Enhancing collaborative innovation in the public sector. *Administration and Society*, 43(8): 842-868.

Sparrow, M.K. (2011). *The Regulatory Craft: Controlling Risks, Solving Problems, and Managing Compliance*. New York: Brookings Institution Press.

Stone, D. (1988). *Policy Paradox and Political Reason*. New York: Addison-Wesley Longman.

Stone, D. (1989). Causal stories and the formation of policy agenda. *Political Science Quarterly*, 104(2): 281-300.

Stone, D. (2003). *Policy Paradox. The Art of Political Decision Making* (2nd edition). New York: Norton.

Streeck, W. and P.C. Schmitter (1985). Community, market, state-and associations? The prospective contribution of interest governance to social order. *European Sociological Review*, 1(2): 119-138.

Sunstein, C.R. (2016). The Council of Psychological Advisers. *Annual Review of Psychology*, 67: 713-737.

Surowiecki, J. (2004). *The Wisdom of Crowds. Why the Many Are Smarter Than the Few*. New York: Anchor Books.

Svara, J. (1998). The politics–administration dichotomy model as aberration. *Public Administration Review*, 58(1): 51–58.

Teisman, G. (2000). Models for research into decision-making processes: on phases, streams and decision-making rounds. *Public Administration*, 78(4): 937–956.

Termeer, K. (1993). Een methode voor het managen van veranderingsprocessen in netwerken, in J. Koppenjan, J. de Bruijn and W. Kickert (eds) *Netwerkmanagement in het openbaar bestuur* (pp. 105–121). Den Haag: VUGA.

Thaler, R.H. and C.R. Sunstein (2008). *Nudge: Improving Decisions About Health, Wealth, and Happiness*. New Haven: Yale University Press.

Thelen, K. (1999). Historical institutionalism in comparative politics. *Annual Review of Political Science*, 2: 369-404.

Thelen, K. (2003). How institutions evolve. Insights form comparative historical analysis, in J. Mahoney and D. Rueschemeyer (eds) *Comparative Historical Analysis in Social Sciences* (pp. 208-233). Cambridge: Cambridge University Press.

Thomas, M. and K. Klapdor (2008). The future of organ donation in Australia: moving beyond the "gift of life". Research Paper no. 11 2008–09. Parliament of Australia. Retrieved on August 9, 2016 from http://www.aph.gov.au/About_Parliament/Parliamentary_Departments/Parliamentary_Library/pubs/rp/rp0809/09rp11.

Thompson, J.D. (1967). *Organizations in action: Social science bases of administrative theory*. Piscataway, NJ: Transaction Publishing.

Tindall, D.B. (2004). Social movement participation over time: an ego-network approach to micro-mobilization. *Sociological Focus*, 37(2): 163-184.

Titmuss, R. (1970). *The Gift Relationship: From Human Blood to Social Policy*. Harmondsworth: Penguin Books.

Torfing, J. (2016). *Collaborative Innovation in the Public Sector*. Georgetown: Georgetown University Press.

Travis, R. and N. Zahariadis (2002). A multiple streams model of U.S. foreign aid policy. *Policy Studies Journal*, 30(4): 495–514.

True, J.L., F.R. Baumgartner and B.D. Jones (1999). Punctuated-equilibrium theory: explaining stability and change in American policymaking. *Theories of the Policy Process*, 97-115.

Tummers, L., V. Bekkers and A. Steijn (2009). Policy alienation of public professionals: Application in a new public management context. *Public Management Review*, 11(5): 685-706.

Turner, J. (1997). *The Institutional Order*. New York: Longman.

Van Engen, L. Tummers, V. Bekkers and B. Steijn (2016). Bringing history in. Policy accumulation and general policy alienation. *Public Management Review*, 18(7): 1085–1106.

Van de Graaf and Hoppe (1989). *Beleid en Politiek. Een Inleiding tot de Beleidswetenschap en de Beleidskunde*. Muiderberg: Coutinho.

Van Meter, D. and C. Van Horn (1975). The policy implementation process, a conceptual framework, *Administration & Society*, 6(4): 445–488.

Van de Ven, A., D. Polley, S. Venkataraman and R. Garud (2008). *The Innovation Journey*. Oxford; Oxford University Press.

Vedung, E. (1998). Policy instruments: typologies and theories, in L. Bemelmans-Videc, R. Rist and E. Vedung (eds) *Carrots, Sticks And Sermons: Policy Instruments And Their Evaluation* (pp. 21-58). Piscataway, NJ: Transaction Publishing.

Von Hippel, E. (1976). The dominant role of users in the scientific instrument innovation process. *Research Policy*, 5: 212–239.

Von Hippel, E. (2005). *Democratizing Innovation*. Cambridge, MA: MIT Press.

Von Hippel, E. (2007). Horizontal innovation networks – by and for users. *Industrial and Corporate Change*, 16(2): 1-23.

Voorberg, W., V. Bekkers and L. Tummers (2015). A systematic review of co-creation and co-production: embarking on the social innovation journey. *Public Management Review*, 17(9): 1333-1357.

Vries, H. de, V. Bekkers and L. Tummers (2016). Innovation in the public sector. A systematic review future research agenda. *Public Administration*, 94(1): 146–166.

Walker, R. (2007). An empirical evaluation of innovation types and organizational and environmental characteristics: towards a configuration framework. *Journal of Public Administration Research and Theory*, 18(4): 591-615.

Waterman, R.W. and B.D. Wood (1993). Policy monitoring and policy analysis. *Journal of Policy Analysis and Management*, 12(4): 685-699.

Webber, D. J. (1991). The distribution and use of policy knowledge in the policy process. *Knowledge, Technology & Policy*, 4(4): 6-35.

Weber, M. (1922/1928). *Wirtschaft und Gesellschaft*. Tübingen: Mohr.

Weick, K. (1969). *The Social Psychology of Organizing*. Reading: Addison-Wesley.

Weick, K. (1995). *Sensemaking in Organisations*. London: Sage.

Weiss, C.H. (1980). Knowledge creep and decision accretion. *Knowledge*, 1(3): 381-404.

Wildavsky, A. (1979). *Speaking Truth to Power: The Art and Craft of Policy Analysis*. Boston, MA: Little Brown.

Wildavsky, A.B. (1989). *Speaking Truth to Power*. Piscataway, NJ: Transaction Publishers.

Wilensky, H. (1967). *Organizational Intelligence: Knowledge and Policy in Government and Industry*. New York/London: Basic Books.

Willke, H. (1991). Systemtheorie (3rd edition). Stuttgart/New York: Fisher.

Wilson, W. (1887). The study of administration. *Political Science Quarterly*, 2: 197-222.

WRR, Scientific Council for Government Policy (2004). *Bewijzen van goede dienstverlening*. Amsterdam: Amsterdam University Press.

WRR, Scientific Council for Government Policy (2013). *Supervising Public Interests. Towards a Broader Perspective On Governmental Supervision*. The Hague: Scientific Council for Government Policy.

Zahariadis, N.(2007). The multiple stream framework: structure, limitations, prospects, in P. Sabatier (ed.) *Theories of the policy process* (pp. 65–92). Boulder: Westview Press.

Zain Al-Mahmoud, S. (2013). Safety groups agree on standards for Bangladesh garment factories. *The Wall Street Journal*, November 20. Retrieved November 1, 2016.

Zeef, P.H.H. (1994). *Tussen toezien en toezicht. Veranderingen in bestuurlijke toezichtsverhoudingen door informatisering*. Phaedrus: Den Haag.

Zincke, R.C (1990). Administration: the image of the administrator as an information processor, in H.O. Kass and B.L. Catron (eds) *Images And Identities Of Public Administration* (pp. 183-201). Newbury Park: Sage.

Zouridis, S. (2000). *Digitale disciplinering: over ICT, organisatie, wetgeving en het automatiseren van beschikkingen*. Delft: Eburon.

Zuboff, S. (1988). *In The Age of The Smart Machine: The Future of Work and Power*. New York: Basic Books.

Zuurmond, A. (1994). *De infocratie: een theoretische en empirische heroriëntatie op Weber's ideaaltype in het informatietijdperk*. The Hague: Phaedrus.

Index